LabNet: Toward a Community of Practice

TECHNOLOGY IN EDUCATION SERIES

Edited by
Raymond S. Nickerson

LabNet: Toward a Community of Practice

RICHARD RUOPP
SHAHAF GAL
BRIAN DRAYTON
MEGHAN PFISTER
TERC, Inc.

LEA LAWRENCE ERLBAUM ASSOCIATES, PUBLISHERS
1993 Hillsdale, New Jersey   Hove and London

Lawrence Erlbaum Associates, Inc., Publishers
365 Broadway
Hillsdale, New Jersey 07642

Funding for the LabNet project was provided by the National Science
Foundation, grant # TPE-8850465. Any opinions, findings, conclusions, or
recommendations expressed in this material are those of the authors and do
not necessarily reflect the views of the National Science Foundattion.

Library of Congress Cataloging-in-Publication Data

LabNet— toward a community of practice / [edited by] Richard Ruopp,
    . . . [et al.].
        p. cm. — (Technology in education series)
        Includes bibliographical references and index.
        ISBN 0-8058-1263-6 (c)   ISBN 0-8058-1294-6 (p)
        1. Science—Study and teaching (Higher)—United States—Data
        processing.   2. LabNet (Project).   3. Computer networks—United
        States.   4. Telecommunication—United States.   5. Science
        teachers—United States.   I. Ruopp, Richard.   II. Series.
    Q183.3.A1L33   1993
    507'.1273—dc20
                                                          92-20531
                                                          CIP

Printed in the United States of America
10 9 8 7 6 5 4 3 2 1

TABLE OF CONTENTS

Acknowledgments

This book is dedicated to the LabNet high school physics teachers whose names appear below (see also Appendix A); to the 393 new LabNet teachers who joined the project via the Big Idea Grants in 1991-92; and finally to the LabNet staff, both regulars and summer workshop, whose efforts kept the enterprise growing. This was the LabNet Community:

TEACHERS

ALABAMA Elizabeth Holsenbeck Mike MacMahon **ALASKA** Jack Cadigan **ARIZONA** Earl Barrett Robert Capen Thomas Vining **CALIFORNIA** Millicent Anderson Jerry Bodily Andria Erzberger William Leader Greg Lockett Steven Matusow John Mirabella Wilfred Oswald Gary Sokolis Lorenz Steinbrecher Richard Warner **COLORADO** Curt Bixel Eugene Kowalski Roger Larson Curtis Miller David Pinkerton Dave Reid Albert Thompson Robert Wilber **CONNECTICUT** David Gewanter **DELAWARE** Robert Adams Thomas Odden Pete Parlett **FLORIDA** Quinton Cole Catharine Colwell T Gayle Hodges Michael Weiss **GEORGIA** Sandra Rhoades **HAWAII** Carey Inouye **ILLINOIS** Bruce Keyzer Margaret Park **INDIANA** Cherie Ann Behn Guy Konkle Daniel Replogle Robert Seal Dave Willig **IOWA** Norman Anderson Ted Cizadlo William Cox Paul Jones Danielle Spaete Therese Tremmel **KENTUCKY** Bruce Jones Martin O'Toole Sr Mary Ethel Parrott Virginia Taylor John Wheaton **LOUISIANA** Ira Nirenberg **MASSACHUSETTS** Hilda Bachrach Daniel Buckley John Clarke Robert Cutter Judy Dadah Gita Hakerem Albert Palumbo Bill Satterthwaite **MAINE** John Despres **MARYLAND** Peter Burkholder Robert Lehman **MICHIGAN** Robert Blakely John Blythe Robert Dean Merrill Falk Merlin Fritzen Paul Serri Sheron Snyder **MINNESOTA** Steve Ethen Thomas Wolters **MISSISSIPPI** Helen Perry **MISSOURI** James Harpel **MONTANA** Michael Jablin John Potts **NEBRASKA** Joanne Langabee James McGahan **NEVADA** Andree Reed **NEW JERSEY** Harold Lefcourt Namie Smith **NEW MEXICO** J Timothy Black Roland Lackey Kelly Wedding **NEW YORK** Kenneth Appel Carole Escobar John Laffan Franceline Leary Nancy Moreau Thomas Mulholland Mary Nickles Sr Marion Rappl Charles Rasweiler Anthony Soldano David Sonday Br William Wright **NORTH CAROLINA** Nina Morley **NORTH DAKOTA** Robert Stefonowicz **OHIO** Jeffrey Applegate Gene Easter Curtis Hendricks Edward McDonnell Emmett Riordan Louis Turner **OKLAHOMA** Jane Rich **OREGON** Harry Burridge John Garrett George Gittens Lowell Herr Richard Sorensen Douglas Squire Tom Thompson Bob Tinnell Geriann Walker **PENNSYLVANIA** Gregory Cauller Elizabeth Chesick David Drummer Adam Edmondson Linda Frederick Edward Henke Ross Partington Nevin Ranck Maxine Willis **TENNESSEE** Derek Brown **TEXAS** Veanna Carpenter Betsy Culbreth Ronald Esman William Lash Robert Roe Pete Test Rajee Thyagarajan Ernest Young **VERMONT** Tom Warnock **VIRGINIA** J David Button Jean Condrey Marek Plucinski Patricia Rourke **WASHINGTON** Loren Lund Richard Lyon David Trapp **WASHINGTON DC** Diane Friedel **WEST VIRGINIA** S Thomas Bond **WISCONSIN** David Braunschweig Gerald Buck Robert Shaner James Weidner Jay Zimmerman **AMERICAN SAMOA** John Thomas **PUERTO RICO** Gregory Bush Luis Santana **CANADA** Steven Thomas

STAFF

TERC Brian Drayton John Foster Shahaf Gal Greg Geboski Sarah Haavind John King Suzanne Marcus Paula Marshall Meghan Pfister Dick Ruopp Bruce Seiger William Spitzer Bob Tinker Jeff Travers Alan Winter **DICKINSON COLLEGE** Tom Bross Patrick Cooney Priscilla Laws Desmond Penny Stephen Skinner **UNIVERSITY OF MICHIGAN** Carl Berger Joseph Krajcik Jean Krisch Mary Starr **NWREL** Don Holznagel Lowell Herr Dave Vernier John Abele **TUFTS UNIVERSITY** Dan Allard Ronald Thornton Bob Teese David Sokoloff Elena Sassi

PREFACE

Connected by a computer telecommunication network, ninth-graders from eight high schools scattered thousands of miles across Alaska work together, building a robot submarine to gather samples from the floor of Prince William Sound.

In Colorado, a near-failing student, formerly more interested in her suntan than in science, comes up with an ingenious physics project that combines the two: She studies ultraviolet radiation emitted by various types of tanning lamps.

In Virginia, two students, one scientifically inclined and one artistic, together explore the mathematical and aesthetic properties of certain striking computer graphics. Their topic: "Mandelbrot sets"—mathematical constructs that are central to science's new understanding of complex, chaotic systems, from weather to the stock market.

In Arizona, suburban high schoolers design and build model cars to meet strict performance specifications. They use computers to design prototypes, collect and store data, and write reports. To assess the performance of their vehicles, they generate detailed graphs of velocity versus time using a sonic measurement device connected to the computer.

This is high school science as some teachers and educational reformers today envision it—centered on student projects that encourage learning by doing... supported by modern technology... enriched by collaboration among students and teachers, both face to face and far apart. It does not sound like high school science as most of us remember it.

These examples are drawn from LabNet, a 3-year, $2.6 million effort funded by the National Science Foundation (NSF). The project was conducted by TERC (Technical Education Research Centers), a nonprofit educational organization in Cambridge, Massachusetts, dedicated to improving mathematics and science education.

Aimed primarily at high school physics teachers, LabNet had three interrelated goals:

- encouraging the use of student projects to enhance science learning;
- building a professional community of practice among high school science teachers; and
- exploiting the potential of today's new technologies—connecting teachers via telecommunication, and equipping students with powerful research tools in the form of sensors connected to microcomputers.

LabNet challenged teachers to create learning environments in which students could taste the experience and excitement of the working scientist. It challenged students to formulate their own questions, design their own research, and build their own experimental apparatus, guided by their teachers as mentors.

LabNet did not hand teachers a fixed curriculum made by "experts." Instead the project worked with teachers who wanted to grow in their craft, providing them with support and resources in the form of paid summer workshops, their own telecommunication network, hardware and software for collecting physical data via microcomputer, and ongoing technical advice.

But the most important form of support came from other teachers, members of the community of practice. Believing that educational reform works only when teachers play an active role—thinking about their work, setting the direction, helping each other change—LabNet relied on the community to provide not only support but also leadership. Although the project drew on top-level scientific expertise—two physicists were co-principal investigators—teachers were partners at every stage, from planning to implementation to evaluation and dissemination. In its last year the project gave 20 participating teachers grants totaling almost $350,000, to share their ideas and experience with others in their school districts or states.

Eventually reaching 562 teachers in 37 states, Puerto Rico and American Samoa, LabNet had a direct impact on their classroom practice. In a follow-up evaluation, the majority of teachers said they had assigned their students more projects and had used LabNet's telecommunication network to exchange project ideas with other teachers. Most said their students were using computers more, as well as collaborating with one another more frequently and asking more questions that reached beyond standard course content.

Participants also felt more connected to their colleagues and energized in their teaching. Said one:

> The greatest benefit of LabNet to me has been the feeling of confidence and a feeling of belonging to the physics teaching community.

And another:

> The last 2 years have been the fullest years of my teaching career, in part due to the inclusion of projects in the curriculum. I recommend this invigorating experience for everyone.

From many students, the response was equally enthusiastic:

> Projects have helped me understand science better. In a way, I am figuring out the answers for myself, which gives me a feeling of accomplishment.

> Projects are a fun and interesting way to learn. Projects also make you think a whole lot more than if you were to just read words from a book.

This enthusiasm was reflected in a wide array of student projects. High schoolers studied the effects of dimples on the trajectory of a golf ball, and of basketball shoes on jumping ability. They studied the physics of dance and skiing. They used physical principles to construct sculptural mobiles and thermally efficient solar houses. The list goes on.

Of course, because projects—as opposed to traditional labs—are inherently open-ended and uncertain, some "failed," like the ambitious attempt of an Iowa teenager to produce holographic images of objects under a microscope, using a laser, with optical fibers as the transmission medium. But this kind of failure can be dramatic success in learning. (The young Iowan went on to study science in college, and by his sophomore year had won a grant from NASA to work on another original project.)

The student response is impressive, especially in light of the fact that LabNet did not target the scientific elite. Its teachers touched young men and women at every level of academic achievement, from a kaleidoscope of ethnic groups, from urban, suburban, and rural communities, from poor families as well as the wealthy and middle class.

This is not to say that LabNet was an unqualified success. Some teachers were unable to mount many projects or to participate in the telecommunication network because they lacked necessary equipment. Others were smothered with demands on their time. Even among those who succeeded, many had to convince reluctant administrators, scrounge for space and equipment, and struggle to find time in already overfull schedules.

And because LabNet worked against the grain of established science education, it confronted ideological as well as technical and administrative difficulties. Some teachers rejected the project approach outright. Said one: "I teach objective, high-level, college-prep physics. I don't want my students to get lost in social interactions or 'activities' that do not prepare for college." Not many teachers seem to have fully embraced the philosophy behind the project approach. This is not surprising, considering that it is a radically different way to teach science. Rather, many seem to have integrated elements of the approach while still sticking to the traditional textbooks, lectures, and teaching of established facts and concepts.

The future of efforts like LabNet is uncertain. As several proponents acknowledge in this book, projects are messy and demanding—often at odds with existing ways of thinking, bureaucratic requirements, and current evaluation methods. And to date we lack the longitudinal data to establish the long-run effectiveness of projects in raising the level of scientific interest and competence of the country's youth. Whether projects will ultimately transform science teaching or become another footnote in the history of educational reforms remains to be seen.

The transformation of science teaching espoused by LabNet is very much a work in progress. Teachers who are newcomers to the project approach—and most of the current LabNet teachers—still struggle with how to incorporate projects into their science teaching. The integration of key players—teachers, scientists, educational researchers, reformers—as collaborators in an educational community of practice, with the goal of improving science education, is a process still in its infancy.

So there is much to be done. This book, then, is the story of LabNet's struggles, successes, and failures, the lessons that were learned, the issues that remain open, and a possible agenda to be followed for change. The authors hope that it speaks to everyone who cares about science education—not just the academic community but policymakers from the national to the school-district level, administrators, parents, and most of all to teachers, who put policies and philosophies into action and shape the lives and futures of our children.

THE BOOK AND ITS AUTHORS

This work is itself the result of a unique collaboration. It was conceived in the summer of 1991 by the core LabNet staff of four: Dick Ruopp, project director; Shahaf Gal, project evaluator; Brian Drayton, LabNetwork manager; and Meghan Pfister, project administrator. In a continuing discussion about the final report for NSF, a notion emerged that there needed to be a more widely available record of the project and its implications for future teacher-support projects. Under Dick Ruopp's leadership, we formed an editorial team: Together we shaped the core contents; together we reviewed and critiqued each other's work; together we decided to invite other voices from our community of science educators—LabNet teachers and colleagues at TERC—to join us and widen the discourse by adding to the book individual essays about projects.

As an editorial team we have reviewed every word written, made suggestions to each other that are interwoven in our individual pieces, and did the same with our contributing essayists. Making this book was a rich and rewarding professional and interpersonal experience. Disagreements were never left to fester. Solutions to problems were almost always a new synthesis rather than a compromise. The result is a tapestry meant to honor both the LabNet community and individual authors. We trust the results show.

The book is divided into 14 sections: this preface, a foreword, 8 chapters, a set of appendices, references, and author and subject indexes.

The preface is the work of Dick Ruopp with Jeff Travers, the book's internal editor. Dick Ruopp came to TERC in 1988, after 9 years as president of Bank Street College, steeped in the learning-centered developmental perspective. Under his leadership, Bank Street pioneered in the development and study of educational technologies, from microcomputers to videodiscs. Jeff Travers is a professional writer/editor who was once a physics undergraduate at MIT.

The foreword is by Greg Lockett, a LabNet participant and high school science teacher from Cottonwood, California. In it he describes his odyssey from a standard teaching approach to a project-enhanced modality. Greg Lockett is a former researcher at the Lawrence-Berkeley Laboratories.

Chapter 1, "An Introduction to LabNet," provides an initial framework for understanding the LabNet project and what it attempted to do. A glossary of terms that may be unfamiliar is included at the end. The chapter is written by Dick Ruopp and Meghan Pfister, who brought to LabNet a math background and experience as a database manager at Harvard.

Chapter 2, "From Current Practice to Projects," examines the background of the project from two perspectives: First, it provides a glimpse into today's high school physics classroom, together with a synopsis of the most commonly used high school physics text and a summary of what research tells us about today's physics teachers and students. Second, the chapter reviews a brief history of project science as an idea and in practice. Dick Ruopp is the author of the latter section. The author of the former is Sarah Haavind, who served as a consultant to LabNet. A high school teacher for 7 years, she now works as a curriculum writer, teacher-trainer, educational evaluator, and consultant specializing in science education.

Chapter 3, "Shifting the Approach to Science Teaching," presents evaluation results from LabNet. The chapter documents through questionnaire data and participant case studies the process of change in science teaching among LabNet teachers. The authors are Shahaf Gal with Greg Lockett and Sister Mary Ethel Parrott, another LabNet participant from Covington, Kentucky. Shahaf Gal brings to the project 7 years of experience in telecommunication and computer research in the United States and Israel. Mary Parrott is a veteran science teacher and a teacher-trainer in many science-education-improvement initiatives.

In chapter 4, "Support and Leadership in a Community of Practice," Shahaf Gal portrays LabNet teachers' involvement in their community of practice. He examines the contributions of a peer-support program and the LabNetwork. In addition, he presents examples of emerging teacher leadership in the community of practice through the Big Idea Grants program—a teacher-to-teacher workshop effort—using two case studies and participant evaluations of their workshop experiences.

Chapter 5, "Design for a Science Network," asks the question: "Given what we now know from the LabNet experience, how should a telecommunication network be designed to serve science teachers?" Brian Drayton tackles this question, considering not only the LabNetwork, but also the experience of other networks. To a degree, chapter 5 is meant to be a suggestive blueprint for future telecommunication efforts that could serve emerging communities of teaching practice. Brian Drayton brings to this effort a background in linguistics and botany, as well as 5 years at TERC working on microcomputer-based labs and the Star Schools project (see the glossary at the end of chapter 1).

Chapter 6, "Reflections on Project-Enhanced Science Learning—Teachers," is a collection of essays by seven LabNet teachers. These personal statements clearly reflect the rich diversity of experience and views about what projects are and how they should be implemented. Underlying that diversity is a common voice about the value of projects for student learning. The chapter concludes with a summary of student comments about project learning.

Chapter 7, "Reflections on Project-Enhanced Science Learning—TERC Staff," begins with an essay by Bob Tinker, co-principal investigator of the LabNet Project and TERC's Chief Scientist. A physicist by training, Bob Tinker is a long-time advocate of project-enhanced science education and a leader in development of tools like microcomputer-based laboratories and telecommunication software. His essay contrasts science that students see with the science of the scientist.

The chapter continues with five reflective pieces, three from staff of TERC's Science Center (Julyan, Kimball, and Muscella) and two from the Math Center (Hancock and Nemirovsky).

The concluding essay is by John King, LabNet's other co-principal investigator and teacher of undergraduate physics at MIT for many years. His essay is a detailed excursion into the world of doing physics projects.

Chapter 8, "Agenda for an Uncertain Future," by Dick Ruopp, ties together the three threads that weave through this book: the community of practice, telecommunication, and project-enhanced science. In recommendations directed primarily at teachers, scientists, and particularly the National Science Foundation, the chapter outlines steps that can be taken to strengthen the community and the teaching of science in both the secondary and elementary grades.

The appendices hold the following materials: Appendix A: The LabNet Teacher Community; Appendix B: Creating Permeable Boundaries for Reflective Expertise: Collaborative Evaluation on a Network; Appendix C: Spring 1991 Teacher Questionnaire with Data; and Appendix D: Big Idea Grants—Summaries.

Richard Ruopp
Jeffrey Travers

FOREWORD

When this essay by Greg Lockett arrived at TERC, the LabNet staff knew we had exactly the right piece to begin this book. As a high school physics teacher, holder of a degree in chemistry from the University of California, and a former researcher at the Lawrence-Berkeley Laboratories—and someone who almost failed calculus in high school—Greg is deeply aware of the ways in which we squander the scientific talents and natural curiosity of so many young men and women. In his insightful observations about his students, and reflections on his own personal experience, he shows us that there is a better way to teach, and a compelling reason for a project like LabNet.

Like my students, I am still learning. While my students learn about the physical world, I probe human nature. Like the recurring seasons, my thoughts periodically return to a central philosophical question: What is knowledge? This week, two poles in my internal dialogue came to life. For a brief, clear moment, two possibilities took the shape of Mark and Christy, students in my physical science class.[1]

I have strong bonds of affection with many of my students. I count both Mark and Christy as friends. Both are open, inquisitive, energetic individuals. However, they also display marked differences. Christy is college bound. She is articulate, adept with symbols, and an honor student. Mark is quiet. He often stumbles when he tries to speak, and he has earned average grades. He is always apologizing for his performance in my class. He explains that he "isn't good in science." This week, both students participated in a laser shoot. In this activity, students use a plane mirror to deflect a laser beam onto a target, which is moved around the room as the shoot progresses. Prior to the shoot, the class discussed the law of reflection. Christy gave a spontaneous textbook recitation on the subject. She used the correct vocabulary, "The law of reflection states that the angle of incidence equals the angle of reflection." She could draw a generalized diagram to illustrate this idea and could draw a diagram to illustrate the required placement of the mirror for a specific arrangement of laser and target. As is often the case, Mark listened attentively and respectfully. He said nothing during the discussion.

When we started the activity, a sudden reversal in roles occurred. Christy had a difficult time even touching the mirror. She could not place the mirror so that the deflected laser beam would hit the target. As the activity progressed, she became increasingly frustrated and finally stated that she was "never good in science." In contrast, Mark was an excellent

---

[1] Student names are fictitious.

shot. He didn't use the protractor or ruler that I provided. He looked at the laser, looked at the target, and positioned the mirror "by eye." He couldn't explain a method to other students who were curious about his success. He "just did it."

As I considered this dichotomy, I returned to the question: What is knowledge? Which student understood the law of reflection? Christy, who could express the relationship algebraically, geometrically, and in words, but could not apply the principle in a concrete situation, or Mark, who could not express the relationship in any symbolic fashion but could use a mirror to accurately reflect the laser beam? Once, I would have said Christy. Now, I find myself seeking classroom settings that foster the intuitive understanding displayed by Mark. As I considered this question, I realized that it also summarized my personal journey as a teacher.

Another thread, also from the general topic of light, illuminates my personal and professional transformation. Each year, I discuss sources of light. As a new teacher, I taught as I had been taught. I focused on the textbook. I used technical vocabulary like incandescence, fluorescence, and electric-discharge. I used movies and photographic reproductions in the textbook to illustrate these concepts. When my students could consistently give short, correct responses to written and verbal questions, I was satisfied with their "knowledge" on this topic and moved to the next topic. However, I soon became dissatisfied with this approach. My students were often bored and restless. This led to behavior problems. Worse than this, my students had difficulty recalling and applying their "textbook knowledge."

At the time, I thought that the use of surrogates (photographs and movies) for actual phenomena was the heart of the problem. I believed that students needed to have direct experience with a process before they could understand it. I adopted the maxim, "If I can't demonstrate it, I can't teach it." With this as a guide and goal, I started acquiring objects and equipment for my lecture on light sources. As time progressed, I obtained a Van de Graaff generator, a Jacob's ladder, a laser, spectrum tubes, a fluorescent-rock collection, various glow-in-the-dark objects and posters, a collection of incandescent bulbs with fabulous filaments, fireworks, and so on. As my collection grew, the emphasis in my classroom gradually shifted. I used the book less. I used less technical vocabulary. I asked for more predictions and explanations. Memorized responses became increasingly suspect. In every topic in every class, I centered on concrete examples. As my skill with demonstrations increased, problems with boredom and behavior decreased. My lecture on light sources became a dazzling tour de force of showmanship that was eagerly awaited each year. However, my students still had difficulty recalling and applying ideas. This was troubling.

Eventually, I realized that learning requires more than seeing. It requires doing. Students do not learn by passively absorbing knowledge. They learn about the physical world by exploring and manipulating their environment in a very concrete way. No matter how spectacular, instruction that focuses on the organized presentation of information to a passive audience is doomed to be quickly forgotten. Memories of the razzle-dazzle may persist for a lifetime, but the ideas embodied in the presentation will not be retained.

I now "teach" about light sources in a very different fashion. I still have all my props, but now I put them out at stations in a laboratory. I ask my students to consider this idea: A handful of fundamental physical processes produce all light. Although devices that utilize light can be quite different in appearance and function, most share common methods for producing light. I challenge my students to categorize the devices before them on the basis of the fundamental processes utilized by each to create light. After a discussion of safety issues, my students are free to "experiment" with the equipment. I say very little on the subject. By my doing less, my students learn more. I still have few problems with boredom and behavior, but now I find that students vividly recall their experiences. More importantly, they often make connections between old and new experiences and explanations. Years later when I encounter them outside of school, I am always met with a flood of memories about past experiences and experiments in my class.

As I considered Mark and Christy, I recalled this personal journey and professional transformation. I realized that they represented the origin and leading edge of this odyssey. So, what is the answer? What is knowledge? My best guess is that Mark and Christy each have half of the answer. Knowledge is both intuitive and symbolic in nature. However, I have come to attach more and more importance to Mark's intuitive understanding. I believe that such knowledge will eventually find a voice. I also believe that the symbolic representation of ideas is soon forgotten if the words are not given life in reality. So, I create more and more opportunities for my students to directly explore the physical world. I still try to bring them into direct contact with new and unusual phenomena. I frequently use projects to achieve these goals. I am less and less concerned with the symbolic representation of events. In a less distorted system of education, I believe that a more symbolic approach to science might be appropriate at the high school levels that I teach. However, after a decade of enforced passivity in a sterile "educational" environment, my students are like strangers lost in a desert without water and near death, who suddenly stumble upon an oasis. They can't get enough water.

Although I am very dissatisfied with our system of education, I am content with the progress of my students. The learning that I encourage can be easily recognized. It occurs when students become focused observers and active manipulators of their environment. I have a student named Paulette. She is physically attractive, a star athlete, brilliant, likable, and a little pretentious. Like many of my female students, she blends the contradictions faced by women in our society with the contradictions traditionally faced by all adolescents. By turns, she is playful and insightful, dreamy and fiercely competitive. During the laser shoot, Paulette was struck by a seemingly odd question. Could she create a ring of mirrors that could capture the laser beam in a circle so that the light would keep going around after the laser was turned off? She stared out the window for several minutes. She silenced males seeking her attention with a swift chop of her hand. Then she started collecting mirrors and trying different arrangements. In that moment, all of the teenage pretensions and posturing fell away and I glimpsed the child in each of us that reaches out to explore the wonders of the world.

We wonder why achievement in science seems to be declining. We wonder why students become less and less interested in science as they advance in school. We wonder why women don't pursue careers in science. It seems pretty obvious to me. As science teachers, we don't give the child in each student enough room to explore and learn and grow. Thwarted, our students seek other avenues for these natural and healthy inclinations.

I read proposals for the reform of science education that call for more: more structure (national standards), more accountability, more tests, more money, more teachers, more of all of the things that have failed to create a science-literate citizenry in our country. I believe that our students need less: less memorization, less pressure, less regimentation, less enforced captivity in lifeless rooms. Growth requires time and space for the child in each of us that marvels at the universe and reaches out to touch it. I try to provide that time and space in my classes. I try to create environments that encourage direct exploration and interaction with the physical world, because this is where students learn the most. As the teenage veneer slips away and the child emerges, I always marvel at the wondrous dance between humans and nature called science.

Greg Lockett
West Valley High School
Cottonwood, California

1 AN INTRODUCTION TO LABNET

Richard Ruopp and Meghan Pfister

Dick Ruopp and Meghan Pfister provide two frames of reference for understanding LabNet, one conceptual and one chronological. They first outline the aspirations and intellectual underpinnings of the effort, embodied in its three defining themes: the use of student projects to bring the excitement, motivation, and discipline of real scientific inquiry into the classroom; the vital role that a community of practice plays in supporting teachers and fostering educational change; and the potential of modern technology to support experimentation and exploration among students, as well as communication among teachers. The authors then show how these themes played out in the life of LabNet, tracing the history of its many activities from its inception in 1989 to the process of evaluation and reflection that led to the writing of this book. The chapter closes with a glossary of terms used throughout the book that may be unfamiliar to the reader.

THE BROAD VIEW

It is common currency that science education in the United States is not working well enough. The usual measure is a comparison of test scores with those of the past or those of other industrialized nations. But much more is at stake than test results—we are failing to excite the curiosity of young minds about the great questions of the physical universe. We therefore lose both a healthy supply of future scientists and the scientifically literate public that the times demand.

This book is intended to contribute to the important discourse on this fundamental issue. As sketched in the preface, it tells the story of LabNet— a prototype teacher-support project developed by TERC[1]—and the import of the project for science teaching in secondary (and by implication elementary) schools. To reiterate, LabNet began in January 1989 and ended in mid-1992. During that time, some 562 high school teachers of physics from 37 states, Puerto Rico, and American Samoa were involved in project activities.

---

[1] TERC (Technical Education Research Centers), located in Cambridge, Massachusetts, is a nonprofit educational organization dedicated to the improvement of mathematics and science education (for a fuller description see the glossary at the end of this chapter). The National Science Foundation (NSF) funded LabNet (Project #TPE-8850465). NSF's Teacher Enhancement Division invested $2.6 million in the effort. Of that amount, 70% went directly to support participants, 3% went to network activities, and the remaining 27% for operations and evaluation.

Three interconnected threads were woven through the fabric of LabNet. The first, and most vivid, was (and is) TERC's continuing advocacy of the use of projects to enhance students' science learning. "A physics project is an undertaking in which the student *does something*" (Vermillion, 1991, p. 7). A fuller definition by a LabNet teacher appears in chapter 2 at the beginning of the "Project Enhanced Science Learning" section. As is documented in chapter 3, many teachers responded positively to this thrust of LabNet, using projects for the first time or expanding the use of projects in their classrooms. The focus on projects arises from TERC's fundamental commitment to learning-centered education. We believe that students must be actively responsible for, and seriously engaged in, learning activities— that doing is the basis for knowing.

TERC's equally basic belief, that teachers are a critical and irreplaceable element in the learning equation, is reflected in LabNet's second thread—building a community of practice among LabNet teachers. Isolation is a fact of life for many teachers of physical science. They are often solo practitioners in their schools. Although contact with teachers of other sciences and trips to professional meetings may extend the benefits of affinity, they cannot substitute for daily intercourse with those practicing the same craft. Continuous interchange about common work is the hallmark of a community of practice.

Face-to-face contact is needed to build that community. To foster such encounters, LabNet held annual workshops in its first 2 years and a conference in the third. In the third year, responsibility for advocacy and community building shifted to participants. Competitive grants were awarded to 20 LabNet teachers to allow them to share both what they had learned and their own visions of science education with their local colleagues. Their efforts extended the project to 393 new teachers (included in the total number previously mentioned) and began the process of enlarging the community of practice.

The third thread woven into LabNet—promoting the use of new technologies in science teaching and learning—was intended to support both implementation of projects and development of a community of practice.

The microcomputer is having an increasingly powerful influence on the classroom. This is particularly true in science education, well beyond the simple use of computers for manipulating numbers and writing research reports. A compelling example is the microcomputer-based laboratory (MBL). An MBL is a microcomputer equipped with one of a number of "sensing probes" for collecting the data of various physical phenomena in real time, and special software for recording and displaying the results. (See the glossary at the end of this chapter for a fuller description.) The MBL puts a real-time science tool directly in the hands of the learner. Although it can be used for rote labs, it is better employed as a direct arm of real science investigations. It seamlessly ties collection of data and mathematical representations like graphs to the physical phenomena being studied. LabNet made significant use of MBLs to bring substance to the project idea.

But perhaps the most notable use of new technology in the LabNet project was telecommunication—computer-to-computer communication via telephone lines. (See the glossary at the end of this chapter for a fuller definition.) A dedicated network was created and made available to all participants. Most took advantage of this new medium to exchange project ideas, ask questions, and engage in common activities. As the first national network designed for high school teachers of physical science, the LabNetwork, through its public forum and private mail system, became a dynamic medium for building and sustaining a community of practice for physics teachers separated by many hundreds of miles.

This aspect of the project was particularly suggestive. Telecommunication is in its infancy. Both current hardware and software are crude instruments of communication. As the capacity of the medium increases to include easy exchange of graphics and sound as well as text, and ultimately pictures—both still and moving—it can become a formidable force to allow the teaching profession to become continually current and self-renewing. Unlike telephone communication, which is evanescent, or the mails, which lack immediacy, telecommunication is particularly suited to the schooling process. It is fast—but leaves the user choices of the timing of response. It is self-recording—so that the material can be reviewed and easily shared.

The implications of these three inextricably interwoven threads— project-enhanced science learning, a community of teaching practice, and the supporting role of new technology—are what this book seeks to explore. The subtext in all of this is teacher change, although not in the usual sense. The dominant mode of educational reform has been curricular. This has been true not only in science, but across the standard subject matters. Experts write new curriculum, teachers are trained or retrained to teach it. More recently, the widespread restructuring movement has paid attention to the role and power of the teacher in the educational enterprise. Unfortunately, the latter effort has been perhaps insufficiently concerned with what students should learn (the ends of education), and how they should learn it (the means).

LabNet attempted to integrate these two approaches—combining respect for the role of the teacher with concern for the substance and process of learning. Teacher-participants were made coadventurers in the process of thinking about, defining, and giving flesh to the project idea. Workshops and the LabNetwork provided arenas for support and mutual exploration. Thus, in telling LabNet's story, this book is also a case study of an unusual if not unique strategy for educational reform.

The book also identifies important barriers to reform. The shift from a teaching-centered to a learning-centered educational process is not easy, even though there is a long history of support for this developmental point of view. Without the willing engagement of teachers, and without a growing community infrastructure to maintain and spread the practice, reform does not work. Project science is harder to do than are textbook-lecture-labs. Teachers have to give up content authority, spend more time in dialogue and negotiation with their students, seek outside resources, and battle skeptics. That these barriers were overcome in many cases is testimony to the commitment of individual LabNet teachers and to the power of the project approach.

In summary, this book examines both the history of a single enterprise, and the implications of that endeavor for the improvement of science learning through the use of projects, through building a self-renewing community of science teaching practice, and through the use of a microcomputer-based communication system to support and promote change in present practices.

A Short History of LabNet

In 1989, TERC launched the LabNet project as a technology-supported teacher-enhancement program aimed at high school physics teachers. The proposal to the National Science Foundation (NSF) had been informed by TERC's experience in developing microcomputer-based labs (MBL), telecommunication networks for teachers and students, and curriculum units utilizing both MBL and telecommunication.[2]

LabNet aimed to support teachers in implementing project-enhanced learning in their classrooms and in disseminating these concepts to others. As originally conceived, LabNet was to consist of summer workshops for teachers; a telecommunication network designed specifically for them; and the development of "exportable lab" kits—MBL, support materials, and a videotape for use by teachers training other teachers. The workshops and the network, increasingly dedicated to the service of project science, became the dominant features of LabNet.

The First Year—1989

The Workshops

In July and August of 1989, LabNet held two workshops at each of two sites, Tufts University in Medford, Massachusetts, and Dickinson College

---

[2] TERC originally developed the "Red Box" interface as well as supporting curriculum; in addition, TERC is developing software and curriculum for IBM's Personal Science Laboratory. In telecommunications, TERC continues its 5-year partnership with the National Geographic Society developing curriculum for the NGS Kids Network (see the glossary at the end of the chapter).

in Carlisle, Pennsylvania. The workshops extended a collaboration among TERC, Tufts, and Dickinson to develop MBL tools appropriate for use in high school science education. Ninety-nine high school physics and physical science teachers from across the United States attended.

Participants worked with three prototype curriculum units, *Insolation*,[3] *Simple Sensors*, and *Radioactivity*, which aimed to help teachers integrate MBL and telecommunication activities into their science curricula. To support the MBL activities, TERC had begun developing a Low-Cost Interface (LCI) and several simple probes, and these were also introduced to teachers at the workshop. Participants were also introduced to several activities developed for the TERC Star Schools project (see glossary): *Connectany*,[4] *Triangle Chaos, Descent of a Ball*, and *Design of a Solar House*—units designed to integrate technology, telecommunication, and project-based teaching. Participants were then asked to develop their own projects, either building upon one of the three LabNet units or following their own interests. By the end of the summer, teachers had compiled over 200 pages of proceedings describing their own project work.

The Beginnings of a Network

At the workshop, teachers were also trained in the use of prototype telecommunication software, which was being developed at that time for the TERC Star Schools project. The new software provided protocols for handling the transfer of nontext files, such as spreadsheets and databases, between Apple II and IBM computers. The Star Schools electronic-mail network was organized into "clusters," user groups of 6 to 10 teachers each of whom shared a common interest in a given curriculum unit. Participating teachers could also communicate with others on the network outside of their cluster. User charges were fully subsidized by LabNet project funds.

Evaluating the First Year

The first set of summer workshops was evaluated via site staff reports and participant questionnaires. Teachers and site staff reported that the MBL hardware and software had to be refined much further in order to be

---

[3] *Insolation*: the amount of solar radiation arriving at the Earth (or at a point on it)—often measured in watts per square meter. At noon on a sunny day, the insolation is on the order of a kilowatt per square meter—decreasing as you approach the poles, increasing as you approach the equator.

[4] *Connectany*: a microworld in which students form patterns by drawing chords to connect dots on the circumference of a circle. The rule for which dots to connect is determined by defining number of jumps: how many dots to skip before landing at the other end-point of the chord. The play in the microworld is based on the idea of iteration, the repetition of a function or algorithm, and the game continues until a closed figure results from the pattern of jumps that the student has defined. The microworld lends itself to competitive and collaborative games. *Connectany* was published in 1991 by William K. Bradford, Inc.

useful to the majority of teachers. Also, most teachers anticipated that they would have considerable difficulty integrating the LabNet activities into their existing physics curricula.

The Second Year—1990

During the early fall of 1989, we learned from teachers that they were having difficulty gaining access to the hardware needed to run the telecommunication software we had provided. Even after obtaining the requisite hardware, they still often had problems using the software. Furthermore, the network's structure discouraged users who participated in clusters that were not very active.

Our first focus, then, as LabNet's second year began, was to make the network more effective as the main avenue of ongoing contact and support among teachers, and between TERC and the teachers. To achieve this objective, the project began a transition to a new network in the winter of 1989-1990. The new LabNetwork (see the glossary at the end of this chapter) offered several important additional features for users. It provided an on-line bulletin-board system; it gave us the capability to develop our own on-line databases; and it required no special access software or computer platform.

The new network was also easier to administer. Because it was located on a commercial network, it could be maintained independently of LabNet grant funding; in addition, a toll-free help line was available to its users, and a self-supporting administration and billing software was already in place. Finally, the cost was competitive with that of other commercial carriers.

The LabNetwork was introduced to a number of LabNet participants who attended the January 1990 American Association of Physics Teachers (AAPT; see the glossary at end of this chapter) conference. The Star Schools Network and the LabNetwork were operated in parallel for several months thereafter, and the project initially subsidized the entire cost of the LabNetwork for participant users (eventually costs were shared). Also, a small matching grant program was instituted to help participants acquire the hardware and software they needed in order to get on-line. Teachers could also use the funds to purchase MBL equipment or otherwise support their project work in the classroom.

In preparation for the 1990 summer program, we added two training sites to expand our regional coverage and increase our resources for training additional teachers. The University of Michigan at Ann Arbor and Northwest Regional Educational Laboratory (NWREL) in Portland, Oregon, joined Tufts and Dickinson as LabNet workshop sites.

Early in 1990, staff representatives from each site were convened at TERC to plan and design the content of the upcoming workshops. TERC and site physicists identified areas of mainstream physics that lent themselves to MBL work and at the same time were rich with opportunities for further student exploration. Site staff were then enlisted to help develop activities for the summer sessions. Development continued over the months preceding the first workshop, during which time TERC and site staff maintained ongoing communication with each other over the LabNetwork. We also used the network to solicit feedback from participants on workshop plans.

An experimental, interactive-videodisc prototype, intended to serve as a resource for teachers implementing project-based science teaching, was also developed for the workshop. The videodisc contained footage of several groups of students working on different projects; step-by-step instructions for setting up several types of MBL and telecommunication equipment; and a discussion among teachers about some of the issues involved in implementing a hands-on approach.

At this time, we also decided to develop a more intensive post-workshop follow-up program for participants. Eight teachers from the previous summer were recruited to serve as Teacher Liaison Consultants (TLCs) for the upcoming workshops. Two TLCs attended each of the four workshops to become acquainted with the participants there and to provide TERC staff with feedback on the progress of the workshop. Over the course of the year, TLCs remained in contact with the participants they had met and continued to provide them with support as requested. (See chapter 4 for an evaluation of the TLC program.)

The Workshops

Five LabNet workshops were held in the summer of 1990. The first took place in mid-July at Tufts University and was staffed by TERC and by site training directors. It provided LabNet staff and site trainers a chance to test and refine the workshop materials. TLCs also attended this workshop and received additional training to prepare them for their roles on site. The remaining workshops were held concurrently at all sites in August. One hundred and eighteen teachers, including TLCs, attended the five workshops. Over half of the participants (64) returned from the first year of the project; the remaining 54 were newly recruited.

The workshops wove together five different types of sessions over the course of 2 weeks. Ten "set experiments," or activity sessions, used MBL or other technology to cover basic physics concepts, including distance, velocity, acceleration, force, impulses, Newton's second law, and heat and temperature. Several of these experiments encouraged users to create their own simple MBL probes; others, designed for teachers who did not have access to MBL equipment, showed teachers how they might improvise instead, developing useful tools with inexpensive materials. Time was set aside for eight "philosophy" sessions in which participants convened in small groups to discuss such issues as the educational value of projects, classroom management issues, the pressure of curriculum requirements, and standardized testing. A number of sessions were spent brainstorming about possible projects, and teachers also worked either on their own or in small groups developing a project of their choice. Telecommunication training sessions rounded out the workshop.

Evaluating the Second Year

The summer sessions were evaluated via reports submitted by site staff and by TLCs at the end of the workshops. It was clear that site staff's investment in the materials, fostered through their involvement in the development process, had been an important factor contributing to the workshops' success. TLCs emphasized the importance of the informal discussions among participants during the workshop, in which teachers exchanged activity ideas, techniques, and success stories. The main criticism was that more time had been allocated for discussing projects than for *doing* projects. For reasons that are not entirely clear, the videodisc prototype went largely unused at all sites.

The formal evaluation of the project was launched in September 1990. LabNet staff visited the classrooms of several local LabNet participants, documenting teachers' thinking and practice in implementing the project-enhanced approach. A quantitative and qualitative analysis of the use of the LabNetwork began. In the fall of 1990, all teachers who had participated in either or both summer workshop sessions, as well as the few teachers who had joined the network as "affiliates"—without attending a workshop—received a questionnaire on their experience with the project thus far. From then on, participants were involved interactively in the project's evaluation. Everyone who had been sent a questionnaire also received a report of the findings and was encouraged to respond with feedback.

The Third Year—1991

Big Idea Grants

For the third year of the project, we were committed to implementing a "high-leverage" model of dissemination, in which participants from the first 2 years of the project had the opportunity to run their own workshop sessions locally. Project staff fleshed out a model in which LabNet teachers were invited to apply for grants to run local workshops for their peers. The idea was to develop a process by which teachers might disseminate the LabNet philosophy of project-enhanced science learning. An advisory committee consisting of several site staff from the 1990 workshops, TLCs, and outside consultants was convened in the fall of 1990 to review the model and our implementation plans. Upon the advice of this committee, we streamlined the grant application process, in which LabNet staff would aid relatively inexperienced applicants in developing their proposals. In order to encourage the greatest number of applicants, the process was designed to be unintimidating and to require as little of applicants' time as possible.

The November 1990 letter announcing the grant program asked participant applicants to describe their "Big Ideas" in just a paragraph or two. In conceiving their ideas, applicants were asked to consider such issues as effectiveness, enthusiasm, reality, outreach to disadvantaged populations, availability of local in-kind resources, and personal professional development. We ultimately received 32 responses to this initial announcement. In several grants a number of participants applied together. Applicants were then asked to submit a preliminary budget and a more detailed description of the project proposed. Again, guidelines were provided to help teachers plan realistically. Those applicants who were not yet on the LabNetwork received assistance in getting on-line. Applicants worked with project staff members who communicated with them regularly, largely via the network.

At this point, well-grounded proposals received preliminary approval, and development continued on the others. After most details had been ironed out, the proposal and budget were attached to a boiler-plate grant agreement provided by LabNet. This draft was reviewed and accepted by the teacher-applicant, and then a final version was drawn up and signed. In all, 20 grants, totaling just under $350,000, reached completion (see Table 1.1). In each case, the process took anywhere from 6 to 10 months of regular communication and development to complete.

TABLE 1.1

The 20 Big Idea Grants

Project Director	State	Focus	Participants	Amount*
Norman Anderson	IA	1-week HS Teacher Workshop: MBL, telecommunication, projects	19	$15,000
Jack Cadigan	AK	3-day HS Teacher Workshop: Large-group project coordinated via telecommunication	7	20,000
Robert Capen	AZ	1-week HS Teacher Workshop integrating physics and vocational curricula	16	11,000
Eugene Easter	OH	10 half-day HS Teacher collaboration sessions on MBL, projects	20	21,000
Ronald Esman	TX	Develop district-wide science-classroom network	7	5,000
Eugene Kowalski	CO	Teachers in one high school collaborate to develop integrated, multi-disciplinary curriculum	8	22,000
Franceline Leary	NY	1-week HS Teacher Workshop & follow-up: MBL, telecom, projects	14	17,000

(continued)

Harold Lefcourt	NJ	1-day HS Teacher Workshops: MBL, telecommunication, projects	24	9,000
Michael MacMahon	AL	1-day HS Teacher Workshops: MBL and project-based science	10	16,000
Nancy Moreau	NY	Telecommunication newsletter development	12	10,000
Tom Odden	PA	1-week HS Teacher Workshop & follow-up using PRISMS and PTTL	26	30,000
David Reid	CO	1-week HS Teacher Workshop & follow-up: MBL, telecom, projects	25	34,000
Sandra Rhoades	GA	1-week MS Teacher Workshop: Build-your-own technology	24	27,000
Robert Roe	TX	1-day HS Teacher Workshops to develop county network of teachers	25	6,000
Tony Soldano	NY	1-day MS Teacher Workshops: guided hands-on exploration of physical phenomena and student contests	48	16,000
Lorenz Steinbrecher	CA	1-week HS Teacher Workshop & follow-up: MBL, telecom, projects	10	7,000
Tom Thompson	OR	Develop District Network and MBL "lending library"	15	16,000
Geriann Walker	OR	Curriculum Development for student collaborations via telecom	2	4,000
Maxine Willis	PA	2-week HS Teacher Workshop & follow-up: MBL, telecom, projects	18	37,000
Jay Zimmerman	WI	1-day HS Teacher Workshops: MBL, telecommunication, projects	63	21,000
TOTALS	**14**	**20**	**393**	**$344,000**

* To nearest $1,000

The June Conference: "Communicating About Project Science"

In their communications with LabNet staff during the grant development process, teachers clearly had very different understandings of what constituted a project and of how to communicate the project-enhanced learning philosophy to other teachers. To encourage grant recipients to think about these kinds of issues as they launched their own dissemination efforts, LabNet planned a conference for early in June 1991, the theme of which was "Communicating About Project Science."

Prior to the conference, participants were asked to read two essays on student learning and the project approach. Participants were also asked to bring sample projects with them, including student projects and ideas that they would be using in their own workshops, to share with others and possibly to serve as the focus of group discussions.

In addition, a "draft" 50-minute videotape was created to serve as the focus for a discussion. The footage, largely taken of LabNet teachers and their students in the winter of 1990-1991, was split into three sections: five students doing or describing parts of their projects; the anatomy of a single project activity, which took place in a science class over several class periods; and two teachers discussing and answering questions about some of the issues they faced in implementing projects. This tape was completed in the fall and distributed, with a discussion guide, to all LabNet participants.

Of the 20 grants, 19 were represented at the conference by 29 participants. The conference itself was organized into a series of small group meetings, which came together periodically into a large group to distill the ideas raised in the smaller discussions. Each participant was also assigned to a group that was responsible for a short presentation during the workshop. Issues to be addressed in these presentations included five "dimensions" of the project-enhanced science learning process: the scientific quality of a project; experiencing and learning from projects; fitting projects into the realities of the classroom; reconciling the project approach and traditional science curriculum; and projects, politics, and the educational community (see chapter 8). Guest lecturers and conference staff led daily brown-bag discussions centered around these and related issues.

In the end, both staff and participants felt that the conference effectively helped participants to reflect on the meaning and nature of the project-enhanced approach to science teaching and learning. In communicating these ideas to others through their dissemination programs, these teachers have continued to refine and develop their thinking about such issues.

Evaluating LabNet—Fall 1991

Although formal evaluation began in the fall of 1990, it became the major focus in the fall of 1991, as project staff attempted to assimilate and communicate what we had learned from LabNet.

There were two basic assumptions that informed the design of the evaluation.

First, each teacher works in a unique setting, and every innovation takes on a local life of its own. A new educational practice, such as project science, is inevitably shaped by the teacher who applies it and by the context in which that teacher works. Evaluation must take into account the diverse ways in which innovations are introduced in different classrooms. For this reason, our approach to evaluation strikes a balance between questionnaire data—which generalize across the LabNet project as a whole—and narrative accounts of the experiences of individual teachers, which convey a sense of the rich diversity underlying the generalizations, and also contain concrete examples of teaching practice that readers who teach can adapt to their own local needs.

Second, change is about learning. In our view, change agents need to think of themselves as educators. Education is most effective when "students"—teachers, in this case—are active, responsible collaborators. For this reason, the evaluation process included opportunities for teachers to work closely with project staff at every step, helping to identify and shape what we learned from the LabNet experience. Teachers were involved in the design of most instruments; in most cases, data analysis was carried out together with teachers; and, finally, all of the reports were shared with the teachers and their feedback was sought and incorporated.

At the same time, we experimented with the use of the LabNetwork for evaluation. For example, the assessment of the TLC program was carried out primarily on the network. This enabled the TLCs to share their experiences on the network, to converse about it, and to write the evaluation report as a joint effort with the project's evaluator.

The evaluation drew primarily on the following sources of data:

- **TLC Reports**. An assessment of the TLC program was completed at the end of the 1990 academic year based on TLCs' reports of their experiences. As indicated previously, the evaluation made intensive use of LabNetwork to gather the data, to conduct a shared sense-making session regarding the data, and to write up the findings.

- **Spring 1991 Teacher Questionnaire**. To follow up the fall 1990 survey, a questionnaire was sent to all participants in the spring of 1991. Results were carefully analyzed by LabNet's evaluator in collaboration with two LabNet participants.

- **Student Questionnaire**. Students of selected participants responded to a questionnaire about their experiences, which was analyzed by the project evaluator and a LabNet participant.

- **Big Idea Grants Site Visits and Workshop Questionnaire**. Three Big Idea Grant sites were visited by the project evaluator in July and August of 1991 and Big Idea workshop participants completed a short questionnaire during the fall.

- **Case Studies**. In November 1990, LabNet's evaluator visited two participants in order to take a closer look at the influence of LabNet on their practice.

- **Network Analysis**. Collection of data on both the extent of use and the content of the LabNetwork continued during 1991.

The results of these various evaluation activities are reported in chapters 3, 4, and 5. Figure 1.1 shows a time line for LabNet, which may be of help as a reference. Following the figure is a glossary of terms unfamiliar to some readers, that are used in several places throughout the book. The next chapter, "From Current Practice to Projects," provides a backdrop against which the LabNet experience can be viewed more clearly.

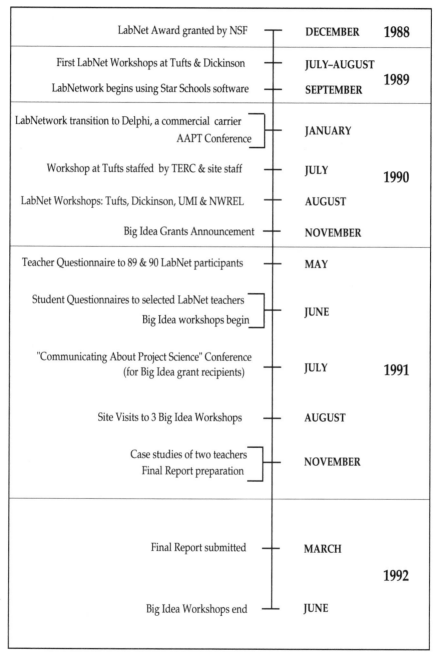

FIG. 1.1. LabNet time line.

GLOSSARY

AAPT—American Association of Physics Teachers. A professional association of physics and physical science teachers from the high school to the university level. The AAPT holds two conferences for its 10,000 members annually. (Approximately one third of its members are high school teachers.) In addition, regional associations often hold conferences and workshops of their own. The AAPT publishes *The Physics Teacher*, a magazine dedicated to "strengthening the teaching of introductory physics at all levels." It is 1 of 10 member organizations that comprise the American Institute of Physics. *See also: AIP.*

AIP—American Institute of Physics. The AIP is a nonprofit membership corporation chartered in 1931 for the purpose of promoting the advancement and diffusion of knowledge in physics and its application to human welfare. Its 10 member societies include the American Association of Physics Teachers, the American Physical Society, the American Astronomical Society, and the American Association of Physicists in Medicine. *See also: AAPT.*

Baud rate. The speed, in bytes per second (BPS), at which a modem transmits data over telephone lines in telecommunication—commonly 300, 1,200, 2,400 and 9,600 BPS. Speed of transmission is determined by the modems used to send and receive data. These days, most transmission takes place at 2,400 baud (bytes per second)—or, about a page of text (250 words) in 20 seconds. Thus, baud rate affects the time required to upload data to or download data from the network. All other factors being equal, a faster modem will reduce a user's total connect time; however, for technical reasons, a 9,600 baud modem is not four times as fast as a 2,400 baud modem. *See also: modem, telecommunication.*

Big Idea Grants (BIG). From the beginnings of LabNet, one of the project's aims was to develop a subset of LabNet-trained teachers to become trainers—disseminators of project-enhanced science learning (PESL)—in the third and final year of the project. In the fall of 1990, this idea took shape with the conception of the "Big Idea" grants. In a streamlined grant application process, designed to burden applicants as little as possible, LabNet participants were invited to apply for funding and support from LabNet to run their own dissemination efforts. The initial application consisted of only a paragraph or two in which the applicant described his or her "Big Idea." From these beginnings, applicants developed detailed proposals with the assistance and support of LabNet staff. Ultimately, 20 funded efforts ranged from full week-long, project-enhanced workshop sessions with follow-up meetings throughout the year, to single half-day intensive MBL sessions, to the development of county or district network services.

Delphi. Also Delphi/Boston. This is a commercial network owned and operated by General Videotex Corporation. Its host computers are located in Cambridge, Massachusetts, but national and international access is available through packet-switching carrier services. The LabNetwork was a private group on the Delphi network.

Descent of a ball project. One of the 10 six-week units that were developed for the TERC Star Schools project. The challenge is to design a structure using paper, staples, and cellophane tape (using the least amount of materials) that will retard a falling ball, such as a golf or ping-pong ball, so that it falls through a vertical distance of one meter in a one-meter cubic space as slowly as possible before coming to a halt. As originally conceived and implemented, students worked on the project in small groups to construct a prototype of their design, test it, modify it, and write up a report on the process. In addition, they communicated at regular intervals throughout the project, via the Star Schools network, with other groups of students working on the same unit during the same time period.

LabNet teachers later adapted the Descent of a Ball design unit. In the summer of 1990, a small group of teachers developed a common set of guidelines and, that fall, ran a national "Slow Descent" contest among their classes, communicating best times and mass/time ratios via the LabNetwork.

Eratosthenes project. Named for the Greek astronomer who accurately estimated the circumference of the Earth in the third century AD, this has been a popular network activity on both the Star Schools network and the LabNetwork. By measuring the length of an object's shadow and comparing this to the actual length of the object, students can determine the angle at which the sun's rays strike the Earth in their area at a given time of year. Data collected in places that are at least 10° latitude from one another may then be used to calculate the circumference of the Earth. As a hands-on classroom activity, it is popular among teachers on telecommunication networks because it can take advantage of—in fact, requires—a widely dispersed, national data-collection network. In order for the data to be useful, however, data collection must be coordinated and collection procedures, such as when and how the shadows are measured, must be agreed upon. See chapter 4 "Teaching Activities: The Eratosthenes Project" for more details about LabNet teachers' experiences with this activity.

Heating degree day project. A telecommunication-oriented project initiated on the LabNetwork by LabNet teachers. Students collected high and low temperatures in their area for 90 days. They then calculated the local heating degree day value from the mean daily temperature for the 3-month period of time. Small groups of students researched different types of heating fuel to determine which was the most efficient and cheapest in their area. The data were shared and compared over the LabNetwork with data collected by students in different regions of the country.

Internet. The Internet is a collection of some 5,000 networks in over 107 countries worldwide serving an estimated 5 million users, which interconnect using the same communication protocol (called Transmission Control Protocol/Internet Protocol—TCP/IP). Gateways provide message-packet forwarding among networks; basic services available to users include file transfer, electronic mail, and Telnet (the ability to log on to a computer remotely). The Internet began with ARPANET (Advanced Research Projects Agency Network) in 1969, developed to help university researchers share information. Since 1973 it has since grown to include such backbone networks as NSFNET and NEARNet. In addition, many networks, such as BITNET, are tied to Internet but are not an integral part of it. An individual user with an Internet account gains access to resources both on the Internet computer where the account is located and on any Internet computers that offer public information. The user also has electronic-mail access to all other Internet users, and to users on networks that are connected to Internet.

Kids Network, or NGS Kids Network. Begun in 1986, the National Geographic Society Kids Network was the first of TERC's telecommunication-based curricular projects. It consists of a series of science units for Grades 4–6, designed to be used by groups of students who share data, reports, and other information via a telecommunication network. During each unit, students examine a central topic through a series of hands-on activities. They conduct a core experiment, share their findings over a computer network, exchange letters with other students on the network, and examine the returned data with a number of software tools. Topics of study include rain, water quality, weather, trash, health, and energy. The work has been funded by the National Science Foundation, the National Geographic Society, and Apple Computer.

MBL—Microcomputer-based Laboratory. An MBL is a microcomputer equipped with one of a number of "sensing probes" for collecting the data of various physical phenomena in real time, and special software for recording and displaying the results. Most data are collected as time sequences (e.g., measure and record the temperature every 5 minutes), and the data are converted directly into XY graphs or, in some cases, two-variable data tables. MBL materials are available for students from Grade 4 through high school and beyond. These powerful tools for investigation are relatively recent, becoming available to students in the mid-1980s. TERC played, and continues to play, a seminal role in their development. Probes on the market currently include the following sensors: temperature, sound, light (photometric and radiometric), photogate, motion, atmospheric pressure, pH, physiology (EKG, EMG, heart rate, brain waves), and weather (humidity, wind speed, wind direction). Work is going on to develop, among other new sensors, a digital multimeter that can be used to measure voltage, current, resistance, capacitance, and so forth.

Modem. A modem is an electronic device used to convert the digital data output of a computer to audio tones that are transmitted across telephone lines. This output can be text, graphics, computer code, even sound. At the other end, a modem converts the audio signal back to a digital format so it can be read by the receiving computer. Because telephone lines are "dirty," modems send data in packets of bytes and wait for a "received OK" signal before transmitting the next packet. A modem's baud rating indicates the speed at which it can transmit data. *See also: baud rate, telecommunication.*

Paper tower project. This was originally developed by the TERC Star Schools Project as a warm-up activity for the "Descent of a Ball" design unit. The challenge is to construct the tallest possible structure using one sheet of paper and some cellophane tape. Intended as a one-period activity, it has been expanded by some LabNet teachers, into a 3-day unit in which students experience the process of brainstorming, developing a design, constructing a prototype, modifying their design, constructing a final structure, and reporting their results.

PESL—Project-Enhanced Science Learning. A term developed at TERC to describe the type of teaching method that LabNet aimed to help teachers use. Traditionally, learning has been seen as a process in which information is transmitted by an active teacher to a passive student. Recent research in cognitive psychology indicates that this is only a small part of what actually happens. Learners, in fact, approach new situations with prior knowledge, and "construct" new conceptual understandings by building on past experiences. (For example, the persistence of student misconceptions regarding a particular physical phenomenon appears to be due, at least in part, to a failure to address the prior experiences and knowledge of students which contribute to and that appear to support—to the student—the misconceptions.)

This view of the learning process generally constitutes a fundamental pedagogical shift for a teacher, and requires a corresponding change in teaching practice to a style which better reflects a constructivist view of the learner. Ideally, "constructivist" teachers,

> focus much less on their own actions, concentrating instead on their students' learning. They are able to monitor the progress of students' understanding and can fluently revise their lessons, putting in intermediate steps, extending applications in certain directions, or confronting misconceptions. In short, teachers...base their decision-making on what their students understand and as a result are much less concerned with what they, as 'constructivist teachers,' should or should not do. The

focus is on student learning in particular—not just on teaching behaviors which generate student-centered lessons. (Schifter & Simon, 1991, p. 14)

Project-enhanced science learning, or PESL, is a balance between the efficiency of traditional "transmission" teaching methods and the effectiveness of the "constructivist" approach through the implementation of student projects under teacher mentorship and guidance. *See also: projects.*

Projects. See chapter 2: "What is a Science Project?" for a definition by Greg Lockett, a LabNet teacher from Cottonwood, CA.

PSL—Personal Science Laboratory. A microcomputer-based laboratory developed and sold by IBM, for IBM and compatible computers, which allows a wide variety of sensors and probes to be interfaced with the computer via the modem port. TERC and IBM collaborated to develop software and curriculum units for the high school level which support the effective use of the PSL as a learning tool in the classroom. They continue to work on the development of software and curriculum appropriate for upper elementary level students.

PSSC—Physical Sciences Study Committee. Initiated by Jerrold Zacharias of MIT and funded in 1956 by the National Science Foundation, the PSSC developed into a broad collaboration among educators, physicists, researchers, and teachers to improve the physics curriculum and physics teaching at the high school level. Its innovations included numerous qualitative student laboratory activities; a wide variety of support materials, including laboratory kits, films, teacher manuals, and additional readings for students; and a massive teacher-training effort, which reached over 1,000 teachers in just 4 years. See chapter 2 "PSSC...and its Progeny" for more information.

PTRA—Physics Teacher Resource Agent. A project directed by the AAPT, funded by the National Science Foundation between 1985 and 1988. The program provided further education and support for just under 300 physics teachers nationwide. It was designed to improve their physics teaching skills and to prepare them to serve as "resource agents" to other high school physics teachers around the country. Each summer, 50 to 100 PTRAs attended an intensive, 4-week summer institute. Thereafter, each active PTRA received partial support to attend the twice yearly national meetings of the AAPT, at which special day-long PTRA sessions were held in addition to the regular meeting events. Over the 4-year course of the program, the NSF provided more than $1.35 million in funding. *See also: AAPT.*

Rube Goldberg project. LabNet teachers from many states challenge their students to Rube Goldberg projects, or contests, every year. Sometimes regional interscholastic competitions have been held at colleges and malls. According to one LabNet teacher, "a Rube Goldberg device is defined as 'a device or method to accomplish by extremely complex and roundabout means a job that actually could be done simply.'" A set of rules was posted on the LabNetwork by one teacher, but other teachers have developed their own. Possible Rube Goldberg devices include machines that will extinguish a candle, crush an ice cube, toss dice, pour a cup of coffee, turn pages, or flip coins. Students are required to use as many energy interchanges (e.g., mechanical to electrical; thermal to mechanical) as possible, excluding hazardous interchanges. Various limitations—such as a limit on the contraption's size—are included in the rules to keep the devices under control. A teacher suggests, "Make the scoring as clear-cut as possible. If you say the device must play a musical scale, who is going to determine if the sound is the musical note of the right pitch or simply a noise?"

Star Schools. The TERC Star Schools project was a $4.5 million grant from the U.S. Department of Education to provide math and science education in an environment that combined technology with engaging, hands-on experience. Using microcomputers and a telecommunication network, students in Grades 7-12 engaged in large-scale, cooperative investigations and shared findings with other students and professional scientists across the country.

Solar house project. One of the 10 six-week units that were developed for the TERC Star Schools Project. The challenge is to design a model of a house that can be efficiently heated by the sun. The "sun" used to test the houses is a 100 watt lamp, which is placed 25 cm from the "house." The main problem is to keep the temperature of the house, relative to the temperature of the room, as warm as possible. A suggested list of materials and evaluation criteria are provided in the curriculum. In this unit, students experience the process of brainstorming, developing a design, constructing a prototype, modifying their design, constructing a final structure, and finally reporting on and discussing their results. As originally implemented, students were also to communicate at regular intervals throughout the project, via the Star Schools network, with other groups of students working on the same unit during the same time period.

Telecommunication. Essentially, telecommunication is computer-to-computer communication via telephone lines—more recently termed *telecomputing*. A modem is used to convert the digital data output of a computer to audio signals that are transmitted across telephone lines. This output can be text, graphics, computer code, even sound. At the other end, a modem converts the audio back to digital so it can be read by the receiving computer. Speed of transmission is important. These days most transmission takes place at 2,400 baud (bytes per second). Because telephone lines are "dirty," modems send data in packets of

128 bytes and wait for a "received OK" signal before transmitting the next packet. Practically then, this translates to a page of text (250 words) in about 20 seconds, or 3 pages a minute. The price of faster modems running at 9,600 baud is coming down, although for technical reasons they are not four times as fast as a 2,400 baud modem. *See also: baud rate, modem.*

TERC—Technical Education Research Centers, Inc. Located in Cambridge, Massachusetts, TERC is a nonprofit organization committed to improving the quality and accessibility of education for students with diverse skills and backgrounds. TERC researches, develops, and disseminates innovative programs in science, mathematics, and technology for educators, schools, and other learning environments.

TERC was founded in 1965. Its original goal was to develop high quality, post secondary instructional materials for the training of specialized technicians. In the early 1970s, TERC's focus shifted toward secondary level hands-on science education and research and curriculum development for special-needs students. TERC pioneered the development of innovative microcomputer technologies for education, most notably microcomputer-based laboratories (MBL), in the late 1970s.

By the mid-1980s, TERC had begun its effort to develop mathematics curriculum modules that aimed to make mathematics more accessible to students. In 1986, TERC (with funding from NSF) and the National Geographic Society began their partnership to develop a nationwide, educational, telecommunication-network science program for Grades 4–6. Since then, TERC has developed several major educational network projects: the Star Schools network, funded by the U.S. Department of Education, and the LabNetwork and the Global Laboratory network, also funded by the NSF. *See also: Kids Network, Microcomputer-based Laboratories, Star Schools, Telecommunication.*

ULI—Universal Lab Interface. A microcomputer-based laboratory sold by Vernier Software of Portland, Oregon, the ULI can be used with any computer that accepts serial communication. It connects to Macintoshes, IBM computers, and IBM clones via the modem port, providing an interface with a wide variety of sensors and probes. Software for the ULI/Macintosh has been developed in conjunction with the Workshop Physics Project at Dickinson College (Carlisle, Pennsylvania) under the direction of Priscilla Laws, and as part of the Tools for Scientific Thinking Project at Tufts University (Medford, Massachusetts) under the direction of Ronald Thornton.

2 FROM CURRENT PRACTICE TO PROJECTS

Richard Ruopp and Sarah Haavind

LabNet's basic premise was that contemporary practices in science teaching cannot by themselves, however improved, reverse the current failure in science education. At the same time, in espousing project-enhanced science learning, LabNet built on a long tradition of thought and practice in education, which has found new support in modern cognitive psychology. In this chapter, Dick Ruopp and Sarah Haavind examine the background of the project from these two contrasting points of view.

Sarah Haavind reviews the state of physics teaching and learning in U.S. high schools, drawing on survey research conducted by the American Institute of Physics, among other sources. She sums up her findings by painting a composite portrait of a fictional physics teacher, "Jeff Anderson." This portrait, sympathetic but ultimately critical, will be instantly recognizable for anyone familiar with science teaching today.

LabNet was guided by a very different vision, which is articulated by Dick Ruopp. He explores the meaning, scope, and implications of project-enhanced science learning, illustrating with a fictional project on the physics of ballet—a counterpoint to the traditional classroom of "Jeff Anderson"—as well as numerous real cases. LabNet teachers contributed some of the thinking and most of the examples in his discussion.

Like most good ideas, the idea of project-enhanced learning—learning by doing—is not new. Its intellectual heritage can be traced back more than two centuries, and it has reappeared in many guises since then. On occasion it has influenced educational practice, although it has never become the dominant mode in our schools. In the final section of the chapter, Dick Ruopp traces some of this history up to the present, arguing that it is an idea whose time has come.

INTRODUCTION

I shall say very little about the value of good education, nor shall I stop to prove that the customary method of education is bad; this has been done again and again....I will merely state that, go back as far as you will, you will find a continual outcry against the established method...

We know nothing of childhood; and with our mistaken notions the further we advance the further we go astray. The wisest writers devote themselves to what a man ought to know, without asking what a child is capable of learning. They are always looking for the man in the child, without considering what he is before he becomes a man. (Rousseau, 1957, p. 1)

Jean Jacques Rousseau opened *Emilé* with these words some 230 years ago. Beyond questions of specific curriculum and method, the core issues of education were then, and are now, who the child is and how she or he learns. This is certainly the case for science education.

The traditional mode of teaching physics at the high school level—often called textbook-lecture-lab—and the project approach to physics learning, are not just two different methods. At base, they represent fundamentally different perceptions of the learner, the learning process, and the role of the teacher.

The primary and secondary education system of the United States, both public and private, was founded on the assumption that the adult society could specify with a high degree of accuracy what children needed to know and to be able to do as a result of their schooling. This was a reasonable premise in a time when general literacy meant basic mastery of the three "Rs": reading, writing, and 'rithmetic. It was also reasonable when the choice of a career was seen as a one-time decision, and the knowledge-and-practice elements of a trade or profession could be quite precisely identified. This narrow premise gave rise to the reigning educational world view for Grades K–12—a view based on simplicity rather than complexity, order rather than disorder, the authority of the teacher rather than the autonomy of the learner.

Like all human systems, schools have over the years built a set of behaviors that implement this accepted world view. Teachers attempt to become expert in their practice, and proficient in subject matter in their work with older children. School boards, superintendents, and principals try to select the materials that best serve the local understanding of what constitutes good education. State and local officials, aided by national testing authorities, select exams questions that, if answered correctly, establish the validity of the process. Curriculum designers seek to embody the latest knowledge and consistent pedagogical approaches. And students, for the most part, accept what they are given as the way their world works.

It is a truism that times have changed—radically. In this century, available information of every conceivable kind has increased by many orders of magnitude. Converting this information to knowledge is a difficult task that does indeed require the higher order thinking skills so much talked about. Curriculum designers now spice up their work with color pictures, a section on the latest developments in a field, even multimedia and software appendages. Local school officials are buffeted by conflicting views of what is important. Teachers, sensing clearly that their authority is in question—by parents, students, and certainly themselves—either hunker down, or seek new ways to do an increasingly difficult job. Many students don't do well on the tests they are given, don't do well in the classroom, and are restive—complaining that school is irrelevant to the life they foresee.

In our view, what has not changed rapidly enough to keep pace is the educational system itself. This is not surprising. Stability is a virtue in the most intensive institutionalized process in our society, but it is also the enemy of needed growth and development. Virtually nowhere within the system are the fundamental ends of primary and secondary education being debated in light of the changes that have occurred, are occurring, and will occur.

We believe that what is worth knowing must now be derived both from a careful look at the past and an informed guess about the future. And how students should learn must be discovered in the context of a different view of the learner and learning. The dominant paradigm has been one of learning from the outside in—children should learn what they are told to learn. The paradigm now must shift to an inside-out dynamic if we are to have skilled, lifelong learners. Students must become engaged, motivated, much more masters of their own educational destinies.

Nowhere is this more true than in science and mathematics education. The stakes are high, because proficiency in applied science, technology, and engineering are core national assets—and current teaching methods do not seem to ensure an adequate supply of scientists or scientifically literate citizens. This chapter makes the case for an alternative approach. Drawing on selected educational literature, both historical and philosophical, and on the experience of LabNet, we argue that enriching and enhancing science learning with projects is a particularly fruitful avenue leading from current to new and more successful practices. But first, let us take a closer look at high school physics teaching as it exists today.

PHYSICS IN THE HIGH SCHOOLS

Between 1986 and 1989, the American Institute of Physics (AIP, see the glossary at end of chapter 1) completed two nationwide studies: one was a survey of 2,485 secondary physics teachers and one focused on high school students who take science (Czujko & Bernstein, 1989; Neuschatz & Covalt, 1988). The reports provide a range of information about teachers, students, and life in science classrooms. According to the reports, one can conclude that the future does not bode well for science instruction.

The most common progression in science is a course in general science or biology for sophomores, chemistry for juniors, and physics for seniors. Slightly more than one third of secondary students take chemistry, and fewer than one fifth take physics. Many more students are at least receiving some introduction to science in secondary school than was the case in 1980. At that time, the majority of states (39) had few, if any, statewide graduation requirements in science. By 1985, nearly every state (42) required 2 or more years of science.

However, according to these reports, 60% of high school seniors have not taken chemistry or physics. Physics appears to be particularly avoided by women and minorities. Less than one third of the women who take chemistry also take physics, whereas more than half of the men do. The low proportion of females and minorities taking physics is partly attributed to the fact that such a small percentage of them take higher level mathematics courses. Yet even those women with exceptional achievement test scores in mathematics are significantly less likely than their male counterparts to take physics. Thus, there appear to be unique barriers steering women away from pre-college physics. For minorities, low reading achievement is correlated with avoiding physics. A 1980 study by the U.S. Department of Education (National Center for Educational Statistics) graphically makes the point (Fig. 2.1).

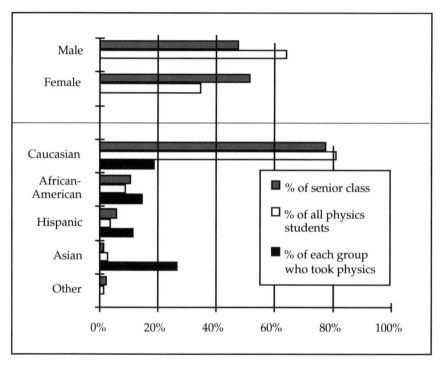

FIG. 2.1. Proportion of seniors who have taken
physics versus their proportion in the senior class.

For those students who do reach the perceived pinnacle of secondary science instruction, there is often less than a fully prepared and confident teacher to teach them. A shortage of qualified science teachers has been a critical issue in pre-college education for over a decade, and improvement is not in sight. Fewer undergraduates are choosing science (or mathematics) as a major, and the bright ones who do are more likely to take a job in research or industry than in secondary education. Only 6% of the 39% of physics undergraduates who go directly into employment choose to teach high school science. The AIP report conveys the stark reality by reporting that even after 20 years' experience and a master's degree, high school physics teachers' median earnings do not equal the median earnings level of master's recipients who are just out of school and beginning physics careers in private industry. In these hard economic times, many experienced teachers are leaving the classroom, even those who love the work.

Of those teachers still in the profession, the "average" physics teacher is a 41-year-old White male who has been teaching for 15 years. Physics has never been the main subject he teaches, because so few students take it. His schedule is filled with basic, average, and honors chemistry or math classes. He has been teaching physics for 10 years. He never earned a degree in physics. Instead, he took about five semester-length courses in the field when he was in college.

Only two of three teachers of physics are certified. Most have their degrees in either chemistry, math, or physical science. The AIP reports show that teachers with 10 or fewer years of experience lack the knowledge base and confidence of more experienced teachers, that there is an underrepresentation of women and minorities as teachers as well as students in the physics classroom, and that the methods and texts continue to focus on rote memorization rather than critical thinking and experience with real problem solving.

More than one third of newer teachers reported that they plan to leave teaching prior to retirement. Hints about what may discourage them can be found within the teacher survey. Nearly half of those polled expressed a desire for more contact with physics or science colleagues from other schools, universities, research, and industry. A common thread in the written comments was a feeling of isolation, especially from other physics teachers and physics professionals. Teachers have experienced a lack of collegial support and camaraderie, as well as few opportunities for substantive dialogue. They expressed a desire for more opportunities to hone their skills and to learn about new developments in the field. A number of teachers described mentor relationships with more experienced colleagues, which kept them teaching when, earlier in their careers, they were thinking of leaving.

The lack of diversity among students and teachers is not likely to change, given current trends. The percentage of physics teachers who are minorities remains fractional. Women, it is true, are entering the profession in greater numbers; they now account for about one quarter of all physics teachers. However, most women have entered the field only recently, and, compared to their more experienced male counterparts, a higher proportion report that they are likely to leave before retirement. Without a greater influx of women and minorities into the ranks of physics teachers, it is doubtful that the current composition of the classroom will change markedly in the near future.

A Window into Current Science Instruction

But probably the most striking finding of the surveys was the consistency of the textbook-lecture-lab approach to physics instruction across the country. "Jeff Anderson," the teacher described here, is a fictional character, but he and his class are a composite view of pre-college science classes today, as described in the AIP reports.

Jeff Anderson's classroom is at the end of the first floor corridor. Jeff tends to arrive early before school. Sitting at his desk with a thermos of coffee, he enters quiz marks in his grade book, reviews his notes, or writes college recommendations. The table beside his desk has a few items on it in preparation for the day's demonstrations. The board behind him is filled with solved equations left over from his last class. With the exception of a picture of Einstein next to the blackboard, the walls are bare. The center of the room has five neat rows of six desks each. Behind the seating arrangement are the lab tables—six of them. Each lab table is equipped with two sets of air jets and two pairs of reinforced holes drilled into the table for the metal rods that support the pulley structures created during some lab exercises.

Jeff Anderson started teaching 20 years ago—just as his district began implementing post-Sputnik pedagogy in science classes. At the time he taught chemistry. For the last 15 years he has been teaching the regular first-year physics course as well. He has a master's degree in chemistry and took some undergraduate courses in physics. He warmly recalls the exciting post-Sputnik days. His school adopted the PSSC physics curriculum for 4 years.[1] However, he and his colleagues were challenged at that time with the task of ensuring that students also covered the materials on the science achievement tests. By the time he began teaching physics, the entire school district had implemented a "back to basics" curriculum-restructuring plan and he started with a new edition of the textbook the school had been using since it opened in the 1950s—*Modern Physics*.[2]

Modern Physics is a conservative text in its typography and graphics, and in its presentation of material. The sequence it follows is pretty much the standard among physics texts. The book begins with mechanics and kinematics, and moves on to energy and heat. This is followed by waves, sound, and light. Then come electromagnetism and electricity, with chapters on electrical circuits

---

[1] For a description of PSSC see the glossary at the end of chapter 1.

[2] The *Modern Physics* program is published by Holt, Rinehart and Winston (Austin, New York, San Diego and Chicago). Since 1922, 18 editions have been published.

and applications. The final section of the book treats nuclear physics and other "modern" topics.

Jeff learned how to teach his first physics class by following that text. Much thought has been applied by the developers of *Modern Physics* to providing enough information for a teacher to teach an entire course without going beyond the prescribed curriculum program. It comes with teacher's editions of both the text and lab manual. The teacher's edition includes planning charts for every chapter, commentary, answers to questions, and solutions to problems. Suggestions are written to assist a teacher with teaching the course for basic, average, or advanced students. Recommended demonstrations are described in the commentary. Additional resources, such as videocassettes and computer software, are offered for each subject area. Also included with the program are a set of chapter tests that supply both multiple-choice questions and problems to solve, along with solutions. The student materials include a text and a lab workbook. Jeff has continued to rely on the text, although he has added some material of his own.

Despite his use of a structured and traditional curriculum, Jeff is a popular and well-respected teacher. His fondness for teaching, his commitment to students, and his humor and personality have won him the appreciation of his students and the respect of his colleagues.

The student make-up of Jeff's class is typical of most high school physics courses. The boys outnumber the girls by almost two to one. Everyone in Jeff's class is also taking trigonometry or calculus. The overall student body is about 40% Black, 50% White, and 10% other minorities (mostly Hispanic). But in Jeff's physics class, there are four Asians and one Black student. The rest of his students are White. The students know each other quite well; they have been in many of the same math and science classes throughout high school. They also spend time together after school as many work on the yearbook, serve as representatives in student government, or participate in other extracurricular activities. Many are applying to leading colleges. A number of these students would be in an honors physics class if the school could afford to offer one.

It is a Monday morning in November and Jeff stands behind his desk to introduce Newton's Laws of Motion to the class. He asks the students to open their text, and then, noticing the absence of some books, he says: "Where are your textbooks?"

The answers drift up front from various points in the room: "I didn't know we needed it." "I didn't bring it." "It's too heavy to lug around."

The 1984 edition of *Modern Physics* is a nearly 3-pound tome, containing 25 chapters and more than 700 pages. It is, however, the text of choice among physics teachers for both regular first-year and honors courses—used in all 50 states. There is actually too much material in this text to cover in a single-year course and, like most physics teachers, Jeff concentrates on some areas and barely covers others. The creators of the text intended this comprehensiveness to encourage flexibility, but for many like Jeff, it creates a pressure to cover as much of the material as possible. Like most other physics teachers, he spends a good deal of time with mechanics and a general introduction to waves and then moves quickly through heat, optics, electricity, magnetism, and, if there is time, issues in modern physics.

Modern Physics is not the most vivid of texts. It has only eight color plates and a 16-page glossy insert titled "How the Sciences Work Together." The rest is printed entirely with black and blue ink.[3] However, the particular strength of *Modern Physics* is its rigorous attention to the mathematical formulations of the laws of physics. As a result, it tends to be quite abstract.

After pointing out the appropriate section in chapter 3, Jeff launches into the two recommended demonstrations. The first demonstration illustrates the concept of inertia (Newton's First Law). After years of repeating this demonstration he no longer reviews the directions in the teacher's edition. Yet he proceeds with an almost uncanny replication of them, down to the suggested questions. The teacher's edition is precisely scripted:

INERTIA–1

Materials: balloon puck or cart on air track[4]

Procedure:

Explain to the class how the balloon puck or air track practically eliminates friction by creating a layer of air on which the puck or cart can move. Push the puck or the cart with a very slight force. Tell the class to note

---

[3] The chief competitor to *Modern Physics* is *Physics: Principles and Problems* (1992) by Paul W. Zitzewitz and Robert F. Neff, published by Glencoe-McMillan/ McGraw Hill Publishing Company, Westville, Ohio. There have been six editions of the program since the first was published in 1971. It has color photographs, drawings, and diagrams throughout, with important information highlighted in colorful inserts. The program includes student and teacher editions, a problems and solutions manual, lab manual (student and teacher editions), a teacher resource package, transparency package, lab software, a lesson-plan booklet, a study guide for students, an English/Spanish Glossary, and a computer test bank.

[4] In teaching Newton's laws and the conservation of momentum, physics classes usually consider primarily ideal conditions: concentrated masses, moving in a frictionless environment. How does a teacher like Jeff demonstrate that in the

how slight the force was and how far the puck or cart moved. Repeat the demonstration several more times. You should then think aloud about how captivating it is to watch this object because it seems to continue moving long after it "should have stopped." Point out to the students that our experiences have always reinforced the idea that an object in motion will eventually stop. However, we see that this conclusion is not as evident if friction is minimized. From this demonstration, we can extrapolate to the unattainable condition of motion without friction and support Newton's first law.

Then ask the class to explain, using Newton's first law, "What happens to you when you are in a car that stops suddenly?" What happens to you if you are in a car that suddenly accelerates from rest?"

Jeff's students generally enjoy his demonstrations. His enthusiasm for the specialized gadgetry and his dramatic style make watching him entertaining and, he hopes, instructive.

Jeff follows this first demonstration with another. Again, he performs the demonstration in front of the class as students take notes sporadically as the key points are revealed. Occasionally an observing student is called on to answer a question, often within certain parameters ("Describe, using Newton's First Law..."). Very little discussion takes place, and students ask few questions.

Jeff has often expressed frustration at his student's lack of thoughtful questioning. He knows they enjoy him, and therefore like coming to his class, but he wishes more of them would take an interest in the course material. Following the second demonstration, he asks if students have any questions. One young man raises his hand and when acknowledged, says, "Yeah, when's the test?" At first, Jeff is disappointed with the question, and laments in a jovial manner that the students are missing the excitement of Newton's genius. Then he responds, telling the class that they will have a quiz on Friday of this week, and the test on chapter 3 will take place on the next Friday. The discussion reminds him of some practice problem sets he created 4 years ago and has filed in a cabinet beside his desk. He offers the yellowed mimeograph pages—every student takes one.

---

real world? Because the ideas of kinematics and momentum are fundamental, physics teachers have shown a lot of ingenuity in producing apparatus to approximate the ideal conditions so easily described in textbooks.

In the 1960s, there was a breakthrough with the introduction of the air track. This apparatus consists of a metal or plastic track, attached at one end to an air pump, and perforated with many small holes. A little shuttle (they come in various shapes) rides on the cushion of air produced by the air escaping from the holes in the track. This allows students to watch "frictionless" motion in one dimension. This device is enormously popular in physics labs—it would be rare to find a school that offers physics without at least an air track.

They then make notes in their notebooks as Jeff turns to write the evening assignment on the board. The students must read Sections 3.8 and 3.9 in the text and bring in the answers to Questions 1-5 on page 63 to review in class the next day. The bell rings and as everyone leans over to retrieve various knapsacks of books, a few move to the teacher's desk to chat with Jeff before heading out the door.

At home, students will first read Section 3.8, titled "Law of Inertia." It begins with a brief historical account of Sir Isaac Newton and then moves on to explain the phenomenon of inertia in detail. Galileo's contribution is also acknowledged later in the section. Section 3.9, titled "Law of Acceleration," is more technical. The concept is more complex, and mathematical formulations for expressing this law are presented. However, although the students are asked to read Section 3.9, no mathematical calculations are assigned for homework yet. Questions 1 through 5 require students to copy answers about the laws from the text and to do some simple drawings. For example, in order to demonstrate comprehension of Newton's First Law the text asks students to, "Draw a sketch of your physics book lying at rest on the desk. Draw arrows representing all the forces acting on the book." Thus, they experience easy success the first night they are alone with the new concepts.

On the second class day, Jeff introduces Newton's Second Law of Motion. He again uses the recommended demonstrations and assigns the recommended homework, this time including six problems requiring mathematical calculations.

The class does not meet on Wednesday, but on Thursday, the students have a lab session. First, about 15 minutes is spent reviewing Questions 5 and 6 of the problem set because some students found them difficult. Jeff reviews the steps for problem solving:
"First, read the problem."
[He reads the problem aloud.]
"Then write down what is given and what is needed."
[He jots the appropriate scientific notations on the board.]
"Then always draw a diagram and fill in the quantities in order to visualize the problem."
[He draws.]
"What do I assume in this problem?"
[He asks.]
A student answers and Jeff asks another question, "What equation do you know that ties all of this together?" And so it goes until the board is filled with equations, and the students who were confused have the proper procedure documented on their homework papers. Everyone passes the work in and moves back to the lab area.

For the lab, students are instructed to turn to Experiment 4: "Acceleration," in their lab books, which includes the proper procedure, tables to fill in with the correct data, space for calculations, and three data analysis questions for each student to answer on his or her own. The purpose of the experiment is to create a situation where students can verify the relationship among force, mass, and acceleration, thus demonstrating Newton's Second Law to themselves. Using a cart, masses of varying weights, string, and a recording timer, students must construct a specified apparatus and then perform specified tests. The tests reveal the effect on the acceleration of the cart of adding varying weights to each end of the apparatus.

The class gets to work. The instructions are clear and exact. Students are shown with both description and an illustration how to set up the apparatus and then how to perform the procedure that will enable them to verify the relationship among force, mass, and acceleration.

A data and calculations table shows students what data to gather, and how many trials of the procedure to record. They are instructed to perform specific calculations and to plot a specific graph. In order to answer the three questions of analysis, students are guided to think about the implications of the procedure for motion and acceleration. Jeff circulates to monitor students' graphing procedure.

If a student can follow directions precisely, he or she will get the desired results and do well on the lab experiment when Jeff gives him or her a grade for the effort. The grade-conscious class works industriously to measure accurately.

By the following Friday, Jeff and his class will have completed the work in chapter 3 and students will be ready to take the test. The test for chapter 3 includes 30 multiple-choice questions, some of which are comprehension questions, some of which are computation questions, and an additional five are problems that students must solve, showing their work.

Jeff tells his class to answer all 30 multiple-choice questions and to choose three of the five problems to solve. He likes to give his students this choice of problems so that they can perform the calculations they know best.

The Limitations of Traditional Instruction

A teacher like Jeff teaches a solid course. His students do well on the physics achievement test and on district tests. When a student falters, he is there to provide extra help. He is well respected by his teaching colleagues and district administrators. When the American Institute of Physics surveyed secondary school teachers of physics during the 1986-1987 school year, the results showed that physics teachers and their classrooms generally resemble Jeff and his class. What then is the problem?

Simply that, despite the good intentions and hard work of Jeff and his students and many like them across the country, fundamental concepts of physics are not being learned. One indication: Research reveals some critical gaps in the understanding of students who take physics classes like Jeff's. Although they can apply rote calculating skills to solve mathematical problems, they have difficulty knowing when to apply a particular algorithm or using their physics knowledge to explain everyday events.

Halloun and Hestenes (1985), for example, found that students who had successfully completed a physics course in college could not apply such basic physics concepts as Newton's Laws of Motion to real situations. One question in their study asked: If you twirl a ball on the end of a string at high speed on a vertical plane in front of you, and then let go, what direction will the ball take from that point, (ignoring air resistance and any effect the string might have)? Most students thought—as most of the general population might also guess—that the ball would maintain its circular motion. In fact, as soon as the ball is released, there is no force keeping it on its former curved path; the only force acting on it is gravity. It initially moves at a tangent to the circle; its exact path from that point depends on its initial velocity and the angle of the tangent with respect to the downward force of gravity. For example, if released on the upswing, it angles out of the circular path, peaks, and arcs to the ground. Although the successful college student subjects in this study had undoubtedly applied complicated formulaic problem-solving techniques to pass the course, they had not learned to think about the real implications of Newton's discoveries, even in the most simple of situations.

Similar conclusions emerge from the study conducted by project STAR, an astronomy curriculum development project at the Harvard University Observatory. It looked at students' understanding of the causes of the seasons and the phases of the moon. Bob Tinker (1991) described the results in his article "Thinking About Science." Ninth-graders and Harvard seniors were asked the same questions, and majorities in both groups revealed a poor understanding of these familiar events. For instance, a common error was to explain that the summer season is a result of the earth moving closer to the sun. (One can assume that most of these same students know that in the Northern Hemisphere you can escape the winter cold by flying south to exotic resorts, even though they seem to forget that fact momentarily in the midst of their explanations.) The only difference the researchers found between the two groups was that the high schoolers spoke with less certainty. (For further information on common misconceptions and critical barriers to understanding science concepts, see Apelman, Hawkins, & Morrison, 1985, and Mestre, 1991.)

What accounts for the apparent lack of deep scientific understanding among students in this country, even those who have taken years of high school science? It is not possible, given current evidence, to answer this question unambiguously. However, it is our contention, based on psychological principles, our discussions with teachers, and common sense, that a large part of the problem rests with the textbook-lecture-lab approach to teaching.

In our view, textbook learning fails on many levels. Science texts are invariably heavy volumes that resemble dictionaries or encyclopedias, rather than interesting material that can motivate a student to read them cover to cover. And perhaps more importantly, their logical progression and simplified explanations spoon-feed information to students in neat parcels rather than encouraging the students' interest, creativity, ingenuity, and problem-solving abilities.

The equipment and materials used for demonstrations and labs are specially designed and are found in physics classrooms around the nation. They are not items one would be likely to find anywhere else—neither in commonplace environments nor in a physicist's laboratory. The carefully designed equipment and procedures can relieve students of the responsibility to think. Although students like Jeff's may be physically active in the laboratory, they may well be passive intellectually, just as they tend to be passive when listening to his lectures and observing his demonstrations.

Students are not encouraged to come with their own questions about physical phenomena, to design their own ways to search for explanations, or to think collaboratively with other students. Instead, Jeff has been the active person in the classroom, applying force to the cart or puck, asking questions, or calling on students to answer his questions. Yet even Jeff is not fully in an active mode as he follows the instructions presented in his teacher's text. The person who was the most inventive and creative in this situation was the curriculum writer who put the lesson together, gave it to reviewers to read and teachers to pilot, and then redrafted it into a final version for printing.

How different would the learning have been if the students were asked to perform the demonstration themselves in small groups? How different would it have been if the students were told Newton's first law and then asked to come up with demonstrations in small groups that they would then share with their teacher and classmates at the end of the session? How different would it have been if students were shown a real-life motion phenomenon and challenged to explain it? Even better, what if a student saw a phenomenon he or she could not explain and came into class asking about it? In other words, what if they had an opportunity to try being Newton and developing the First Law on their own? How different would the learning be if students were called on to think and act instead of go through rote procedures, in class, at home, and in the laboratory?

Questions like these are at the heart of some current efforts to reform science teaching, including LabNet. These efforts are aimed at enabling students to *construct* knowledge, starting with familiar tools and common know-how. In this constructivist mode, the teacher no longer simply transmits knowledge or serves as the central (only) authority in the classroom. Instead, he or she is one of a number of resources available for students to tap in constructing physics knowledge, often through scientific endeavors of their own design. (For a further discussion of reform efforts in physics, see Swartz, 1991.)

The constructivist approach goes far beyond reforms that merely reorder subject matter or update the textbook problems. In our view, such reforms do not fully address the current problems in science instruction. Students will continue to think they understand phenomena because they can apply algorithms and get the "right answers." As long as the basic textbook-lecture-lab approach continues to dominate science education, students are unlikely to learn to think scientifically or become scientifically literate.

In the next section, we turn to reforms that we believe offer more hope of moving the field—reforms that provide teachers with the tools to transform their classrooms into exciting places where students discover and learn to apply basic concepts, and where the teachers themselves become co-learners.

PROJECT-ENHANCED SCIENCE LEARNING

A little boy is walking a small yellow cur in front of his house. A big man with a large vicious dog comes along and says, "Little boy, if you don't get that small yellow cur out of my way, I'm going to have my large vicious dog eat it up." As the big man continues to speak, the small yellow cur runs around the little boy and bites the leg clean off the large vicious dog. At this point the big man says, "My God little boy, what kind of cur is that?" To which the boy replies, "Well, before I cut off his tail and painted him yellow, he was a crocodile!"

The point of the crocodile story is that things are often different than they seem. What looks innocuous on the surface may have a bigger bite than you expect. And that is true for project-centered science. At first glance, project-enhanced science learning looks pretty tame. One could even argue that projects are only a small variant on ordinary labs. But they are not. They are much more. In fact, projects are quite revolutionary.

This revolution is part of a broader, and yet not fully recognized, movement in U.S. public education. A movement that puts the learner and learning, not the teacher and teaching, at the center of the educational process—not student centered, but learning centered. This movement, with deep historical underpinnings but still in its infancy, is quite different from the current school reconstruction efforts. And the slow but sure adoption of project science learning is a central feature of the movement, because science projects lend themselves to real inquiry in a way that is difficult in other subjects. The seeds of this revolution have been sown for a long time. What is different is that practice is beginning to change, and important research findings support that change.

What Is a Science Project?

Greg Lockett, a LabNet teacher from Cottonwood, California, provided what can be called a "purist's" definition of what a project is:

> Children learn by doing. If you want students to learn physics, they must "do" physics. From this view, the goal of the teacher is to re-create the process and experience of working in a physics laboratory. As experimenting is central in physics, experimenting takes a central role in the project classroom. Several features are important in this approach. Students are free to choose a research problem. They do not know the solution to their problem at the outset of their project. While students must work within the constraints of time, resources, and their current knowledge, they are given considerable time and freedom to attack their problem as they see fit. Collaboration is acceptable and desirable. The end product of student work can vary widely (reports, papers, equipment, experiments, constructions, models, etc.). Student success is not easily measured by objective tests.
>
> In this process, the goal of the teacher is not the efficient transfer of large amounts of information and mathematical problem-solving skills. The goal is to give the student an immediate and compelling "inside" view of science (physics). The teacher functions primarily as a facilitator. In many respects, she or he is like a research director in a laboratory. She or he familiarizes new researchers with the laboratory, obtains needed resources or suggests alternatives, resolves disputes from equipment-scheduling to squabbling among the researchers, and in general attempts to maximize the creation of new ideas and technology within the laboratory. At all points, the teacher is guided by the current practice of physics and the goal of re-creating that practice within the classroom.
>
> The goals of the project paradigm are broader and deeper than those of the basal-text paradigm. At the highest level, they include first-hand knowledge of what science is, how it works, and its limits. Mathematical problem-solving skills are encompassed within a broader structure that includes research skills (using libraries), motor skills (building apparatus and operating it), cooperative social skills (collaborating on projects), communication skills (oral reports during informal lab meetings, writing scientific papers), and thinking skills (logic, induction, deduction, analysis, synthesis). Skills are learned as needed. Motivation is rarely a problem since the context makes the need for the skill obvious to the student.

The standard textbook-lecture-lab approach is founded on the notion that education is a *transmission* process. The teacher (or publisher) sends, and the student receives. John Locke's image of the student's mind as a *tabula rasa*, a blank tablet, is operative in this transmission definition. Facts are to be inscribed, knowledge moved from the mind of the authority to the mind of the uninitiated. Tests are to be employed to see if the transmission process is working. In this model, answers are more important than questions, solutions are more valued than clear understanding of the problem. Here, content is chosen to the exclusion of process.

Projects embody a different vision of both the world and the science-learning process. A project is a scientifically valid inquiry into the nature of some particular physical phenomena. It is to be entered into willingly, hopefully with enthusiasm, by a student—an inquiry that provokes conversations with peers and teacher. Conversations that include questions, conjectures, the request for additional information. Conversations that are, in fact, informative. Conversations that *transform*, rather than *transmit*. Two-way transformational communication, rather than one-way transmissions, as Roy Pea has argued (Pea & Gomez, in press).

An Example: The Physics of Ballet [5]

Consider this hypothetical example.

You are a physics teacher named Martin Kirksmith. You have been teaching physical sciences for 22 years. You have a master's degree in earth sciences and are self-taught in the field of physics. Your experience with LabNet has encouraged you to expand your use of projects to supplement your text, lectures, and labs.

In September, you tell your junior physics students that they are to begin a major project by early October, and complete it by the middle of December. The class is shown videotapes of two projects from previous years. In one, a student explains the physics of karate to the class. In the other, three students take a bathroom scale and ride a high-speed elevator up and down an office building, to see the effect of acceleration and deceleration on measured weight.[6]

You give the class criteria for selecting a project to think about. You explain what form their reports to the class are to take. You ask them to divide themselves, two students to a team. Small teams make more work for you, but your experience has been that they work better. You tell them they have 2 weeks to set up their teams and turn in a preliminary project proposal.

---

[5] This example was given in a keynote address at the June 1991 LabNet Conference. In July, this note came from Kenneth Laws, professor of physics at Dickinson College: "I was particularly struck by your description of a (hypothetical?) project involving the *grand jeté* in dance. You must either claim extra-sensory perception or you were aware of a project I supervised 3 years ago on—yes, the *grand jeté*. You missed, though; the student was a senior physics major, not a high school junior!" (See Laws, 1984; Laws & Lee 1989.)

[6] Project examples are from the North Cobb High School, Kenneshaw, Georgia.

One of the proposals that comes to your desk is from Margy and Emily, two of the four young women in the class. You don't know much about them. They do reasonably good work, but rarely speak out. Emily is a serious student of classical dance. They want to do a study of the physics of ballet. The proposal is somewhat vague and lacks specific implementation plans, although there is a certain note of enthusiasm. You write some questions on their page and give it back: "Where do you think the interesting physics questions are?" "What do you want to look at?" "How will you measure it?" And a transformational conversation has begun.

You meet with Emily and Margy for 15 minutes a week later. They have decided they want to study one of the great spectacles of the ballet, the *grand jeté*. The one boy in Emily's dance class, and another girl, have agreed to dance for them. With Emily, that will make three observation units. Margy's father has suggested using the family videotape camera to record the events. You ask one question, "How will you use the camera as a measuring device?"

They go away for a week and when they come back they have worked out some answers. Margy, who never used a video camera before, took several clips of Emily doing the *grand jeté*. They had set up a long strip of wrapping paper as a backdrop. For measuring, it had vertical lines every foot. But when they looked at it on the VCR, they could not stop the action in a way that would allow them to do any meaningful measurement. Emily's father has a technician friend at the local PBS television station. They have visited and found out that video cameras operate at 30 frames a second. The technician has offered to add a time code to their videotape, and let them use a sophisticated playback deck that will let them see their work frame by frame.

You ask them how they can determine whether or not their camera really operates at 30 frames a second. You also suggest they read a short piece on the work of Eadweard Muybridge. He used photographs to study animal locomotion in the 1870s. He is particularly famous for having proved that when a horse runs, it has, at one moment, all four feet in the air. They come back and say they are now going to make their measure a grid, as Muybridge had done. You talk about the scale of the grid, and together work out the math for balancing measurability with precision. A few days later they hand in a small report. It tells you that they took a 2-minute video clip of a digital stopwatch running in hundredths of a second, had it time coded, and then calibrated the speed of the family video camera at 29.26 frames per second. The transformation proceeds.

And so it continues. They take their video and discover that if a dancer is too far away from the grid, the lines are out of focus. They make a small excursion into focal length, f-stops, and the circle of confusion. Then they have their data, and Margy's mother, who is a financial analyst, teaches them how to use an Excel spreadsheet to make time-distance graphs. They come around and ask for help in calculating the force that the toe of the ballet shoe exerts when it lands at the end of the *jeté*. You have to sit and work it through because it is not immediately apparent to you. They finish all their calculations for acceleration and deceleration, height, distance, speed, the effect of gravity. They try to determine the difference among the three dancers as a function of weight and muscle strength, but can only come up with some speculations. They make their report to the class and it is well received, even by the boys, several of whom can be seen trying a *grand jeté* themselves after school.

What did Emily and Margy learn? As measured by standardized tests, probably less than they would have learned studying a physics text and preparing for an end-of-chapter exam. And during this whole process you, Mr. Kirksmith, never transmitted information. You asked questions, made suggestions, worked collaboratively, had rich learning conversations. If a different form of assessment were available, one that measured the ability to solve real problems, that measured working knowledge gained, then in all likelihood a great deal of significant learning would be confirmed.

Projects in LabNet

The project Emily and Margy undertook was chosen by them, as was their paired grouping. And they were almost ready to do the work—that is, they had enough science background and knowledge to undertake the effort, make use of sound advice and support, and reach a successful conclusion. Although there are many critical dimensions to projects (we identify and discuss five in chapter 8, "Critical Dimensions in PESL: A Framework for Dialogue"—scientific, pedagogical, practical, curricular, political), from a *developmental* learning-centered perspective at least three factors seem to us to be key: student readiness, student grouping, and student choice.

We know of no systematic effort yet to analyze projects according to their key developmental characteristics, and the attempt here is only to raise a few important issues. The judgments that follow are based on informal data from three sources: (a) personal conversations with LabNet teachers; (b) a review of the essays that came as a result of our call to LabNetters to participate in reflecting on projects (see chapter 6); and perhaps most importantly, (c) a reading of many project-specific messages on the LabNetwork over the 2 years. Of the three factors, we think the issue of choice is the most salient.

How important is student readiness? This seems to us a matter of delicate balance. Clearly if a student has insufficient background and resources, that is, conceptual and practical tools—some knowledge of laws, math, and procedures—then a project, however chosen, can lead to failure of the wrong kind—the kind that leaves the student feeling defeated and too intellectually overwhelmed to learn anything significant.

On the other hand, if a project does not stretch the student, does not lead her or him into new and unexpected byways, cause the right kind of failure—the kind where an adopted theory or model is shattered by reality, where the project team members are forced to rethink their assumptions—then it can well be an inconsequential experience.

Who is to determine student readiness? Hopefully students themselves will come to know what they know, to be good judges of their own ability to gauge the hurdles and challenges they will face taking on a new project. But clearly this is an area where the skill of the teacher is paramount. Asking the right questions, giving the right encouragement, arguing the project focus down to the manageable—all are critical. This is the domain where skills and perception of self-worth combine, sometimes collide. This is where developmental sensitivity to the individual student is a great asset to the teacher who believes in project-enhanced learning.

How are students to be grouped? From the teacher's point of view, decisions about this dimension have important classroom-management as well as pedagogical consequences. In a class of 24, groupings of 2 or 3 or 4 students into work teams means the difference of 12, 8, or 6 projects to monitor and reports to listen to or read—no small variation in a teacher's workload. From the standpoint of "doing science," collaborative teams reflect how most scientists work these days. Competition can be shifted from student versus student to team versus team, a healthy antidote to excessive individualism.

When students look at who they are paired with, quite different issues arise. Is he or she smarter than I am? Is this a friend, someone I don't know, or an enemy? How well can I work with this person? For young people, answers to these questions can be consequential. Looking at the LabNet experience it is clear that there are a variety of practices: Some teachers like groups of two, some three (although few larger); some assign students randomly, some ask students to pick their own partner or partners; at least one pairs the student with the highest academic record to the one with the lowest, the next highest with the next lowest, and so on. One teacher specifically pairs members of the opposite sex, "I make a point of pairing up a male and female as lab partners for a number of reasons: They tend to learn more from each other, it seems to limit the 'testosterone poisoning' which leads to dangerous experimentation, reduces the amount of silly giggling which sometimes occurs, and provides an opportunity for a better interaction between partners" (see Kelly Wedding's essay in chapter 6, "Learning to Think Through Project Science"). Clearly, grouping arrangements also provide teachers an opportunity for developmental sensitivity, although the optimal solution is far from clear.

Who chooses projects? We think that in many ways this is the toughest, most interesting developmental issue. As Greg Lockett indicated earlier, a purist vantage point puts a premium on student choice. Psychologically and scientifically this makes some sense. In the abstract, students, as do practicing scientists, should pursue the phenomena of most interest to them. Certainly the degree of perceived choice and motivation go hand in hand. And the evidence is clear that projects are highly motivating. So student-selected projects are one very important source of project initiatives—"I wonder if golf balls will travel a shorter distance if they are cold?"—but not the only one.

In the mid-range of choice is the "negotiated" project. The originating idea can be the student's or the teacher's, but it then gets shaped in the crucible of discussion and amendment. This is what happened between Martin Kirksmith and his two students. And this is what happens between many LabNet teachers and their students. A student gets a notion from a newspaper article about using weather data to explore chaos, but does not know how to get started without some help. A teacher gets excited at a conference about a new way to make hologram prints but doesn't have time to pursue it and finds a student who will take on the enterprise. This certainly is fertile ground for mentoring, for a teacher to display ignorance as a virtue, for a student to learn that in science questions are as important as answers.

Finally, and not surprisingly, there is the most common form of choice—by the teacher—the assigned project. The evidence from the LabNetwork is that major all-class projects are the most common: Descent of a Ball, Paper Tower, Rube Goldberg, The Solar House. (See the glossary at the end of the chapter 1 for descriptions of these projects.) On the other hand, many teachers have developed lists of projects for students to choose from, and this practice begins to move away from rigid prescription and may also be amenable to negotiation. Let's take a look at some specific examples of projects that have appeared on the LabNetwork.

An Array of Projects on the Network

Perhaps most notable in project list-making was a new enthusiastic LabNet convert, a biology teacher from Colorado. In the space of 3 weeks, she put more than 150 project ideas on the network, primarily directed at students, for biology and the environment. Here's a sampling of some of those projects:

```
HUMAN BIOLOGY MEDICAL SCIENCE PROJECTS
There are many projects you can do that demonstrate
homeostasis in living systems:
Design an experiment that shows feedback between pupil
size of a human's eye and differences in light
intensity.
```

Design an experiment that illustrates that the ratio of
surface area to volume helps animals control
temperature.

Using frogs and ice cubes, relate the nose movements to
reduction in water temperature.
_*_

STUDENTS WHO ARE INTERESTED IN ENVIRONMENTAL
PROJECTS!!!!

Here are some ideas to think about.

Design an experiment that demonstrates the effect of
fossil fuels on the carbon/oxygen cycle. Use an MBL ph
probe.

Do a survey of your family's trash. When you throw away
your trash where does it go? How much do you produce?
What kinds etc. How could you reduce this solid-waste
problem?

How does the use of fertilizer on your lawn affect the
carbon, nitrogen, and oxygen in the ecosystem? Design a
project to study the effect of fertilizer on algae in
the water supply.

Using the second law of thermodynamics, and statistics
you gather, write a paper explaining why people in the
poorer nations of the world must exist on primarily a
vegetative diet.

Read the ecological classical book *Silent Spring* by
Rachael Carson. Why is this work still a classic?
_*_

This shower of projects notwithstanding, the most common teacher-
initiated project ideas on the network had to do with physics. Here are a
few:

Rubber Bands

2053 17-NOV 21:32 Curriculum Issues
    RE: physical law (Re: Msg 2046)
    From: BKEYZER
    To: KUANTUN (NR)

We just finished a rubber band projectile lab. We fired
rubber bands horizontally from table tops and determined
initial velocity. Additionally we graphed the
relationship between stretch and initial velocity. We
will "revisit" this lab when we discuss Elastic
potential energy. Our graphs, theoretically linear,

have raised some questions about the behavior of rubber bands, which will be pursued by several students as independent projects. Reading your note gave me the idea to encourage this extra study.

Thanks,

Bruce Keyzer in Rockford, Illinois.

_*_

Paper Clips and Data Points

1889 23-SEP 20:04 Other
      From: DSONCORNY
      To: ALL

Last year I was surprised at how many groups and individual students arrived at conclusions to their projects with so little data. We looked at regression lines and the number of data points required for a good correlation, but nothing seemed to help. This year, before anyone got started with projects, I used the following activity to illustrate the idea of collecting enough data.

As students walked into class I greeted each of them with a paper clip. Every question about the clip received a response similar to "everyone needs a paper clip to take physics." After sitting through class for most of the class period wondering what the clip was all about I asked them to open the clip and break it by bending back and forth keeping track of the number of bends to break the clip. I recorded their data on the way out the door.

The next day I repeated the sequence but would not tell them why we were doing this activity. Their comments were great and soon other teachers began asking me what's with the paper clips. Each evening I plotted their data on a bar graph. Soon they just held out their hand as they came in the room then started breaking the clip. I told them they would find out what was going on as soon as my computer allowed me to.

The series of graphs showed a gradual shift toward the mean, which was not evident until several hundred clips were broken. Now, when anyone shows me insufficient data I can say, "Remember the paper clips?"

David Sonday

_*_

Heating Degree Day Project

1999 31-OCT 15:26 Student Projects
　heating degree day project data collection
　From: AEDMOPA
　To: ALL

To all heating degree days participants. Several people have asked about what type of data is to be collected. I will try to answer with the following format:

Step 1. The students are to collect the High and Low temperatures in degrees F on a daily basis.

Step 2. The students then record the average of the High and Low temperatures.

Step 3. The students then subtract their average temperature from the standard temperature value of 65 to arrive at the Heating Degree Days.

Step 4. The students are asked to calculate the total square feet of heated space in their homes. It may include heated basements or attics.

Step 5. The students are asked to determine the monthly cost for heating their home through monthly electrical, natural gas, coal or heating-oil bills.

Step 6. The students are asked to convert their amount of fuel usage to BTUs through conversion factors, which are listed as follows:

    1) Electricity: Number of kilowatt hours x 11,600 = BTUs consumed

    2) Natural Gas: Number of cu.ft. x 1,030 = BTUs consumed

    3) Fuel Oil: Number of gal. x 138,690 = BTU's consumed

    4) Coal: Number of tons x 24.5 million = BTUs consumed

Step 7. The students are asked to compile their data to answer the following questions:

    1. What is the monthly BTU consumed per square feet of heated space?

    2. What is the monthly energy cost per square feet of heated space?

    3. What is the monthly BTU per heating degree days value?

I have placed a copy of a student team project on the
common workspace for interested parties to download.
The name of the file is Heating. I hope the above
directions answer some of the questions pertaining to
the collection of data and the writing up of the report
for e-mail purposes. Adam aedmopa

_-*-_

A Floating Magnet

2007 31-OCT 19:19 LabNet News
     PHYSICS DEMO
     From: NMORENY
     To: ALL

Lenz's Law (The Falling Magnet)

When a magnet falls through a conducting pipe, the
currents induced in the pipe create a field that, in
accordance with Lenz's Law, opposes the fall of the
magnet. This may be demonstrated by dropping a small,
powerful magnet through about 2 m of copper aluminum
pipe. If the magnet is light and strong enough, it will
be slowed dramatically. Light, strong magnets, such as
those made of neodymium, work very well. "Cow magnets,"
obtainable from farm-supply stores, may also be used.
The diameter of the pipe should be close to the size of
the magnet. Of course, thicker-walled pipes allow a
larger current and a more dramatic slowing of the
magnet. If this demonstration is done before a
discussion of Lenz's Law, it will be an interesting
discrepant event and lend itself to be used as an
activity-based problem-solving activity. Students find
it interesting to look down the tube and watch the
magnet as it "floats" down the tube.

_-*-_

Not all exchanges on the network were about specific projects. Sometimes discussion went to underlying issues and at the same time displayed
a refreshing candor:

2149 5-JAN 14:52 Curriculum Issues
     philosophy
     From: BKEYZER
     To: ALL

Conceptual vs. traditional.

I would like to start a dialog regarding how to
best prepare students for further study of physics.

What is better, a course with emphasis on mathematical problem solving, or one that emphasizes lab skills and research projects, or one which emphasizes concept development, such as PRISMS or Hewitt's Conceptual Physics? Should we offer the Sears and Zemansky type of physics to the better math students and Hewitt for the kids who barely manage a C in algebra 1? Or is a conceptual approach better for ALL students as a first course and leave the mathematical treatment for a second course where the student will get, in Hewitt's words, "computation with understanding!" How do instructors at the college level feel? What about future employers? Is there any research relating to these questions?

I am embarrassed to admit that I have been teaching students about physics for nearly 15 years and although I feel that I am fairly good at motivating students to learn I am not sure of what approach will do the students the most good. I am sure many of you on the network have had experience with both approaches. I value and respect your views.

Bruce Keyzer (BKEYZER)

_*_

2155 13-JAN 21:37 Curriculum Issues
   RE: philosophy (Re: Msg 2152)
   From: WEDDING
   To: HLEFCOURT

I was pleased to see the question Bruce brought up because I am grappling with it myself. I teach four huge sections of trig-based physics and one AP (B) course. The AP course just gives me the hebee jeebees because they don't understand anything but can number crunch until the world looks level! I get really frustrated with them because they don't seem to care about the concepts anyway. There is hardly any time for labs with the APs and they are such grade junkies that I can sometimes feel my hair turning gray as I stand in front of the class. Their projects were pathetic.

In my trig-based classes, however, I am doing a lot of project-based teaching, lots of thought labs where there is very little given information and they are having a great time and seem to be learning a lot. They understand the concepts much better and their mathematical abilities are only a bit behind the AP

```
students. Until the past 4 weeks, the classes were neck
and neck, but I had to assign heat and gas laws for AP
over the holidays in order to get through the materials.
```

```
Egad, I've gone on and on....The point I am making is as
follows: My trig students have a better time, do a lot
more labs, think a bit better and do just about as well
as the APs. The APs plow through and can calculate
anything but understand almost nothing....I believe in
lots of gloriously off-the-wall labs where they have to
THINK, problems in class and as much in the way of
concepts as I can get into them through discussion and
labs....
```

```
Kelly
_*_
```

THE PROJECT METHOD: A BRIEF LOOK AT HISTORY

Project-enhanced learning is not an invention of the last decade. The kind of questions raised in this last exchange have a long and distinguished history going back to debates about the ends and means of education in ancient Greece. The current impetus begins a quarter-century ago. We take up the story once again with Rousseau:

> Teach your scholar to observe the phenomena; you will soon rouse his curiosity, but if you would have it grow, do not be in too great a hurry to satisfy this curiosity. Put the problems before him and let him solve them himself. Let him know nothing because you have told him, but because he has learned it for himself. Let him not be taught science, let him discover it. If ever you substitute authority for reason he will cease to reason; he will be a mere plaything of other people's thoughts. (Rousseau 1957, p. 131)

Like general debates about the ends and means of education, projects are not new. It can be fairly said that Rousseau was an early and ardent advocate of the project "method." He rebelled against the sweeping notion of the child as born in original sin. Rather, man was naturally good. Evil was an invention of society. The corollary of this is that education should proceed from the inside of the child out, not from the outside in. What the child *does* is all important to the educational process. "Teach by doing whenever you can, and only fall back on words when doing is out of the question" (Rousseau 1957, p. 144).

In Book III, when Emilé is a young adolescent of 15, Rousseau recounts this story. A stick half in water seems broken to a child, an error in judgment caused not by observation, but by induction. But do not be quick to take the stick out of the water, because, "...you may undeceive him, but what have you taught him? Nothing more than he would have soon learnt for himself. That is not the right thing to do. You have not got to teach him truths so much as to show him how to set about discovering them for himself. To teach him better you must not be in such a hurry to correct his mistakes" (Rousseau 1957, p. 168).

As Rousseau's pupil, Emilé is not an ordinary child by now—he is well along the road to reasoning (now called higher order cognitive skills). He knows how to be cautious before answering a question. And he, along with his tutor, knows how to demur: "There is no phrase so...often on our lips, as, 'I do not know;' neither of us are ashamed to use it." So, said Rousseau, "Let us examine it":

> The stick immersed half way in the water is fixed in an upright position. To know if it is broken, how many things must be done before we take it out of the water or even touch it.
>
> 1. First we walk round it, and we see that the broken part follows us. So it is only our eye that changes it; looks do not make things move.
> 2. We look straight down on the end of the stick which is above the water, the stick is no longer bent, the end near our eye exactly hides the other end. Has our eye set the stick straight?
> 3. We stir the surface of the water; we see the stick break into several pieces, it moves in zigzags and follows the ripples of the water. Can the motion we gave the water suffice to break, soften, or melt the stick like that?
> 4. We draw the water off, and little by little we see the stick straightening itself as the water sinks. Is this not more than enough to clear up the business and to discover refraction? So it is not true that our eyes deceive us, for nothing more has been required to correct the mistakes attributed to it....
>
> Emilé will never know dioptrics unless he learns with this stick. (Rousseau 1957, pp. 168-169)

There are several other narratives of a similar vein in Book III—provocative reading for those interested in one philosophical and psychological root of the project approach. The banner for the point of view that supports children doing-to-learn was carried in the eighteenth and early nineteenth centuries by the Swiss Johann Heinrich Pestalozzi (1746-1827), and his student from Germany, Fredrich Froebel (1782-1852), who was father of the kindergarten movement. In this country Horace Mann (1796-1859), founder of Antioch College, and most importantly John Dewey (1859-1952), laid the foundation for learning by doing.

Projects in Early 20th-Century America

H. B. Alberty (1927) in his *A Study of the Project Method in Education* traced the first educational use of the term *project* to the year 1908. It was then that a program of part-time project-based agricultural work was instituted at Smith's Agricultural School in Northampton, Massachusetts. It was successful and was installed in all the vocational-agricultural high schools (and associated students' homes) in the state. The issue being addressed by this experiment, according to the U.S. Commissioner of Education several years later, was:

> Possibly the greatest difficulty in teaching this subject (Agriculture) is that of making it sufficiently concrete and practical. Too often the teaching begins and ends with the assignment and recitation of lessons from the pages of a textbook. To make the teaching effective, each lesson must follow the necessary pedagogical order from concrete experience through interpretation and generalization back to concrete practical application. The pupil must become an intelligent worker and director of his own work, and must learn not merely by looking on and listening, but by intelligent participation. (Alberty, 1927, p. 18)

The "home" projects, scheduled for the summer, were focused on improvements—planting shade trees, building walks, increasing the yield of potatoes from a selected plot. They were carefully supervised, tied to school work, and had the following sequential elements:

(1) A carefully drawn plan, covering a considerable period of time, with a definite aim, including some problems new to the pupil, and outlining with sufficient detail the methods to be employed. This plan should be written and should be an exhibit in connection with the summer's activities.

(2) An agreement between parent, pupil, and teacher, based upon the plan already prepared so as to eliminate later disagreements. The boy's financial privileges should be clearly stated.

(3) Instruction in the school, both in regular course and in special individual study to the end that the project work may be done intelligently and that the home may furnish the kind of laboratory practice best adapted to the school work.

(4) Detailed records of method, time, cost, income and other important factors which shall finally be summarized in,

(5) A report, including both a story and a complete accounting for the entire project period.

(6) Supervision by a competent instructor of such a nature as to help the student to succeed in his project, to encourage him at times when difficulties arise, and to hold him to his agreement, and incidentally to impart instruction supplementing that of the classroom. (Alberty, 1927, p. 19)

Here are all the elements that could translate well to a contemporary science project: planning, an intelligent social contract among the affected parties, tailored educational instruction, data collection and record-keeping, narrative and analytic reporting, individualized professional support—with parent involvement and financial incentives to boot.

Not only was the project program successful in Massachusetts, but it also spread nationally, and was embodied in the Smith-Hughes Act of 1917, which even had a provision for home projects that was described by one commentator at the time as, "...an agricultural enterprise with a definite aim...intended to throw the boy on his own resources and develop his power of initiative, as well as give increased knowledge in farming methods" (Alberty, 1927, p. 20). Elements of this initiative have survived in the 4-H clubs (head, heart, hand, health). Alberty said that in addition to agriculture, the project method "was adopted by teachers of science and the practical arts, except that the work was carried on at the school" (p. 30).

The debate in the second decade of this century (as it is now in some quarters), had to do with the organizing principle behind the curriculum. Should it be logical or psychological?[7] Should it proceed from what adults know, or what the child can learn? Scholars have spent vast amounts of time sifting, organizing, naming, quantifying, ordering, and classifying information into the various divisions of knowledge—science, literature, history, and so on, with subdivisions ad infinitum. Why not have knowledgeable adults make curriculum for naive children?

The psychological or developmental argument proceeds from a different basis. It says that children need to be fully engaged in order to stretch their learning capacity to its fullest. Motivation is an important part of the learning equation. The task must seem real and important—the stuff of the adult world, not child's play. As another early scholar in this field put it: "A project is a definite and clearly purposeful task, and one that we can set before a pupil as seeming to him vitally worthwhile, because it approximates a genuine activity such as men are engaged in real life" (Stormzand, 1924, p. 148).

Adults learn this way all the time. I have a problem to solve: What do I need to know to solve it? I am meeting a new client next week from the X Corporation, I'd better read their last annual report; and, say, didn't Smith formerly work for X? I'd better talk to him. My company is sending me to France for two years; I'd better learn something about the country, maybe take some language lessons; and what was that about 1992 being a big deal in Europe? I've been assigned to teach physics next year, and I only had three college courses in the subject; better call Jane M., she's been teaching it for years; maybe there's a summer course at the local university; better review the textbook. In each case, the learning is incidental to the presenting task.

Making factual knowledge and various kinds of skills the indirect consequence of carrying out an interesting, even challenging task makes sense.

---

7 *Psychological* was the term used then. Alberty talks about psychologizing subject matter: "To psychologize means to translate systematically organized race experience [read "cultural heritage"] into vital and personal individual experiences" (p. 10). We prefer the term *developmental* and *developmentally appropriate* when talking about trying to get the interaction between content and the learner to work.

Learning is pressed into service for doing. Alberty selected this kind of "indirect" learning as being at the heart of the project approach, correctly defined:

> The project method in education is that teaching procedure which aims at securing learning (i.e., the acquisition of knowledge, habits, skill, ideals, etc.) *indirectly* by means of activities which have the following characteristics: 1. The goal which is supposed to dominate the pupil and to lure him on to the accomplishment of the end, is not the *learning sought* by the teacher, but is some concrete result or accomplishment. 2. The learning essential to the satisfactory completion of the activity is always *instrumental* to the goal. That is, whatever learning is achieved is a by-product of the activity, and is not directly aimed at by the pupil. (Alberty, 1927, p. 82)

Here is an example Alberty cited using an important page from the history of science—the invention of the barometer. Early in the 17th century, the Duke of Tuscany could not get water from a deep well using a lift pump. Surprised, he consulted Galileo, who set up an experiment that showed that atmospheric pressure was equal to a column of water 32 feet high (at sea level). Galileo died before completing the experiment and Torricelli, his pupil, substituted mercury for water and concluded with certainty that the liquid rose in an exhausted tube because of the weight of air and not because of the vacuum. Pascal carried the work further, literally, and found that the mercury sank in Toricelli's apparatus when it was carried to the top of a tall tower—and it sank a full 8 cm when taken 1,000 feet up a mountainside.

All of this led to the barometer, invented by Otto von Guericke of Magdeburg in 1750. He, in a flight of fancy, used a column of water that peeked from the roof of his house. A small wooden carving floated on the water, and in fair weather it would survey the surrounding scene and in foul would disappear inside. He was accused by his neighbors of being "in league with Satan!" (Alberty, 1927, pp. 4-5).

All this could be taught by the book. And in someone's lexicon, knowing these facts would be a test of cultural literacy. But what about a project that could lead by indirection to the same knowledge and more? Weather can be of great importance to kids. It determines baseball games, outings, adults' good and bad tempers, and for the farm lad (or lass) with which we started this section, it is directly relevant to crops. Nowadays, weather prediction gets one into satellites, and MBLs, and chaos theory. Still, building a barometer is a good project, fraught with possibilities for science, and history, and literature—the great sagas of the sea and sailing. Figure 2.2 shows a diagram Alberty set forth to make the point—a problem and a solution, with possible learnings on the way.

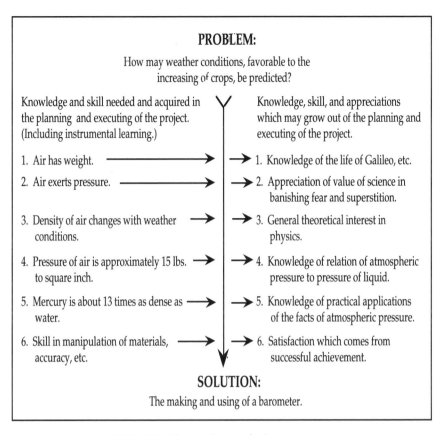

FIG. 2.2. The making of a barometer.

More Recent "Precursor" Efforts

[P]rogressive education began as part of a vast humanitarian effort to apply the promise of American life—the ideal of government by, of, and for the people—to the puzzling new urban-industrial civilization that came into being during the latter half of the nineteenth century....In effect progressive education...[was] a many-sided effort to use the schools to improve the lives of individuals....this meant several things.

First, it meant broadening the program and function of the school....

Second, it meant applying in the classroom the pedagogical principles derived from new scientific research in psychology and the social sciences.

Third, it meant tailoring instruction more and more to the different kinds and classes of children who were being brought within the purview of the school.

Finally, Progressivism implied the radical faith that culture could be democratized without being vulgarized.... (Cremin, 1961, pp. viii-ix)

The project method was but one of many innovations that was rooted in the soil of the "progressive" movement in education. The five essential hallmarks of this long (1876-1957) and influential force that reshape both public and private education were as follows:

- to see the child at the center of the educational process, with full opportunity for self-expression and the exercise of initiative;

- to emphasize learning by doing, including diverse contacts with the real world;

- to make the curriculum relevant and meaningful to the learner, with rich materials available for free use;

- to make the teacher more of a guide than a "task-master," able to act with self-authority born of solid preparation and professional autonomy;

- to make the school a reflection of the contemporary world, and also the home, through close cooperation with parents.

In short, the progressive view of education was radically different from the narrow prevailing perceptions about school and schooling at the end of the Civil War. To give flesh to these progressive notions, it is instructive to read John and Evelyn Dewey's (1962) description of various educational experiments circa 1915 in *Schools of Tomorrow*. It is clear in reading Cremin (1961), that directly or indirectly John Dewey, although not the founder of the movement (he nominated Francis W. Parker for that position), was the intellectual architect of its most trenchant ideas. It is worthwhile when thinking about project-enhanced science to re-read Dewey (1916, 1929, 1933, 1938, 1939, 1956, 1964).

And over time these views made a difference to what happened in this country's schoolrooms.

> [B]y the end of World War II progressivism had come to be...conventional wisdom. Discussions of educational policy were liberally spiced with phrases like "recognizing individual differences," "personality development," "the whole child," "social and emotional growth," "creative self-expression," "the needs of learners," "intrinsic motivation..." "teaching children not subjects," "adjusting the school to the child..." Such phrases were a cant, to be sure, the peculiar jargon of the pedagogues. But they were more than that, for they signified that Dewey's forecast of a day when *progressive* education would eventually be accepted as *good* education had now finally come to pass. (Cremin 1961, p. 328)

All of this is to say that the progressive movement was the seedbed for project-enhanced science learning, and yet it itself did not survive. The attacks on the progressive movement began in the 1940s and grew to a crescendo in the early 1950s. The central argument was that the intellectual content of schools had been lost, the schools had taken on too many functions, teachers were ill prepared in the arts and sciences. The term *progressive education* was discredited and the Progressive Education Association collapsed. The aftermath of the war saw a movement toward conservative politics that affected education as everything else. Cremin (pp. 348-351) cited seven reasons for the death of the movement: internal factionalism, inherent negativism, inordinate demands on teachers, a victim of its own success, the post-war swing to the right, excessive professionalism, and, finally, failure to keep pace with a changing society.

The rise of Sputnik in the fall of 1957 was a *coup de grâce*, a certain sign to many that the U.S. educational system was failing. Yet no comparable force for broad educational reform has arisen in the decades since. Most efforts have been episodic and driven by student test score declines. Many of them have been curricular. One such initiative to improve high school physics education was begun more than a year before the Sputnik satellite went into orbit.

The Physical Science Study Committee (PSSC) and its Progeny

The committee chose to plan a course dealing with physics as an explanatory system, a system that extends from the domain inside the atom to the distant galaxies. The course tells a unified story—one in which the successive topics are chosen and developed to lead to an atomic picture of matter, its motions and interrelations. The aim was to present a view of physics that would bring a student close to the nature of modern physics and to the nature of physical inquiry. Finally, the committee sought to transmit the human character of the story of physics, not just the codifications of the findings. The student should see physics as an unfinished and continuing activity. He should experience something of the satisfaction and challenge felt by the scientist when he reaches vantage points where he can contemplate both charted and uncharted vistas. (Finlay, 1966, pp. 67-68)

This was the vision of the Physical Science Study Committee's focus as interpreted by Gilbert C. Finlay, an original member of the committee, and a professor of education at the University of Illinois. The PSSC curriculum, an introduction to physics slated for the junior or senior year of high school, for both pre-scientists and "lay" students, was an ambitious undertaking. It was begun in 1956 at MIT under the aegis of Jerrold R. Zacharias, a molecular physicist who worked on radar during the second world war. It was a collaboration of scientists of the likes of Bruno Rossi, Philip Morrison, Ned Frank, and Edward Purcell (Swartz, 1991, p. 27) and high school physics teachers. Institutional partners included Cal Tech, Cornell, Bell Labs, and the University of Illinois.

Together, over a 4-year period, they developed textbooks, laboratory apparatus, lab guidebooks for students, movies of physical phenomena narrated by scientists, and 10 achievement tests. For additional support there was a four-volume teacher's guide, and a series of paperback books written by scientists for students, which dealt with technical, historical, or biographical material. The project ramped up quickly. By the end of the 1959-1960 school year, more than 1,000 teachers had been trained in summer institutes, and an estimated 34,000 students had taken the course (Finlay, 1966, p. 75). Swartz (1991) speculated that over PSSC's first 20 years, 2 million students "were directly affected...for less than $3 per student" (p. 25). Funding came from the newly established NSF with additional support from the Alfred P. Sloan and Ford Foundations.

Was PSSC project-enhanced physics? Certainly not in a definition where students select and develop their own projects. On the other hand, its thrust was toward students thinking about physics differently and becoming engaged with the experimental work of the scientist. According to Finlay (1966), "In this course, experiments—whether they are performed by the student, analyzed in the textbook, or shown on film—are not used simply to confirm an earlier assertion. The laboratory experiments are designed to provide firm rooting for the growth of ideas by providing direct, non-verbal contact with relevant data....The student is responsible for thinking out the nature and meaning of what he is to do" (p. 69). And Dow (1991) said that "The new materials and approaches generated enormous enthusiasm among students, who were learning to do science by creating their own apparatus from simple materials and by getting directly involved in solving problems of their own design" (p. 3).

LabNet teachers who have used the PSSC material uniformly reported that it was a step beyond standard texts, and that it was exciting to teach. Its influence was far reaching. The PSSC initiative directly or indirectly influenced or fostered a number of other curricular efforts (Swartz, 1991): Harvard Project Physics, which was meant to appeal to a wider audience of students; Introductory Physical Science (IPS) for junior high; the Princeton Project for eighth-graders; the Intermediate Science Curriculum Study (ISCS) for seventh through ninth grades; and, for elementary school, the Science Curriculum Improvement Study (SCIS) and the Elementary Science Study (ESS). Perhaps one of the most famous related efforts was *Man: A Course of Study* (MACOS), which became the victim of a major political assault in the 1970s that had a profound impact on NSF's role in elementary and secondary education (Dow, 1991).

The point of this list litany is that almost none of these curricular projects have survived. Only PSSC is available commercially in close to its original form—a seventh edition has just been published. Curricular projects in other areas—social studies, language arts—have also come and gone. The evidence is quite decisively against any durable educational reform through curriculum improvement.

A Contemporary View of Learning and Teaching

Although projects have not yet been proven to be the best alternative for increasing the supply of would-be scientists or science-literate citizens, there is strong indirect support for the project approach from recent work in the cognitive and learning sciences.

Roy Pea (Pea & Gomez, in press) wrote that the learning sciences now have a vision that derives from four basic shifts in perspective.[8] The first shift is in the nature of learning and the learner. The second is that learning must be seen as located in communities of practice. The third shift is in the nature of the materials needed for learning. And the fourth is the shift in the role of teaching itself.

One: there is a new view on the nature of learning and the learner. The old view was founded on the belief that the task of education was to transmit subject matter through well-crafted lectures, demonstrations, and other presentational formats. The current research-based view, which arises from the work of Dewey and Piaget and Bruner and others, to quote Pea and Gomez (in press), "...sees the development of intelligence generally, and of subject matter understanding in education in particular, as actively constructed by the individual. New knowledge is acquired in relation to previous knowledge, building on intuitive, informal experiences." In other words, students must do the work to acquire the facts, the skills, the principle, the theories, not for their own sake, but as tools of the mind for reasoning and problem solving. This view certainly supports a move to increased independent project work.

Two: learning is located in communities of practice. Here the notion of lifelong learning comes to the fore. We seek to become members of a specialized community, and we work to sustain that membership. The high school physics teacher may sometimes be both a teacher and a scientist. She or he perhaps has multiple memberships in associations of scientists, or of physicists, or of teachers of physics, or perhaps all three. The language the teacher uses, the expertise he or she has, is conditioned by the communities she or he belongs to, and in which he or she practices.

Pea and Gomez (in press) said, "...in science, such a practice consists of ways of talking and acting (which includes many shared goals, concepts, procedures), belief systems about what is interesting about problems. It includes shared views about when it is appropriate to use particular tools, and evolving kinds of sense-making activities that seek to develop scientific concepts of the world (e.g., modeling, theory building, simulations)." In a community of practice, learning becomes collaborative. Meaning is

---

[8] I am deeply indebted to Roy Pea, a colleague who was at Bank Street with me, and who has recently moved from the Xerox-funded Institute for Research in Learning in Palo Alto to become the John Evans Professor of Education and the Learning Sciences at Northwestern University's School of Education and Social Policy. Over the years, we have had many conversations on this subject, and he has kept me apprised, in a cogent manner, of what cognitive science knows about the learning process.

arrived at through conversation in the social sphere. And real meaning is always derived from immersion in, and conversations about, authentic tasks. An authentic task is one that is perceived by those involved as real, important, and for students, partaking of the adult world. Communities of practice are especially useful for supporting innovations like project-enhanced learning where the craft is relatively new.

Three: there is a new understanding of what are the appropriate materials for learning. There is a chain, a causal sequence that leads from the student to subject matter mastery. For decades now, the attention of reformers has been on the subject end of that chain, the curriculum. Examples include the 1960s and 1970s work of the Physical Science Study Committee, the Biological Science Study Committee, Project Physics, the Chemical Bond Approach, the School Mathematics Study Group. Currently, two such efforts are under way, the NSTA Scope and Sequence Content Project and the AAAS Project 2061.

All such efforts at sequencing subject matter more intelligently, and presenting content more lucidly, are necessary and worthwhile. But they are only half the story. The other half is the student. We test students for factual knowledge of science and mathematics, and when they fall short, we bemoan our loss of competitive position in the global economy. Then we go on to blame students. If they only worked harder, this situation could be alleviated. So let's add more hours to the school day, more days to the school year. If our analysis of the root problem is correct, this is like saying add more time to prison terms and the likelihood of rehabilitating the criminal will increase.

The reality, we contend, is that most textbook-based curricula are unrelated to student's prior school experience or their understanding of the real world beyond the school's boundaries. They are, in a word, decontextualized. Bob Tinker (1991), in his "Thinking About Science," cited the relevant research findings for science—the work of Halloun and Hestenes and Marcia Linn, among others. But there is also a growing body of evidence that supports the same conclusion for all other major subjects. Students need, and want to learn, subject knowledge and skills, not as ends in themselves, but as means to engaging with authentic tasks and solving real problems. Projects meet this requirement.

And finally: there is an emerging view of a new role for the teacher. In this view the teacher is no longer the sole and central authority. Rather, the teacher provides leadership in building a short-term community of learning. The teacher's role-based power is used to promote meaningful conversation, to provoke, to inspire, instead of transmitting and controlling. For teachers to establish a learning community several things must happen. They must work on real problems, which may be new to them, are interesting to them, and also to their students. They must think out loud about the problems, and argue the steps in the reasoning process. Then they must invite students to contribute and collaborate in the problem-defining, problem-solving process. Finally, they have to promote discussions that reflect on what they have been through and what they have learned. Projects provide the perfect opportunity for a teacher to explore this new role.

What are we to conclude about this evolution? Slowly, but surely, there is a shift, first in thinking then in practice, from one-way transmission of information to a two-way construction of meaning that is transformational (Pea & Gomez, in press). If we want students who are knowledgeable, skilled, and interested in science, whether they intend to become scientists or simply science- and technology-literate citizens, then we are right to focus on the student as learner. We are right to educate ourselves in effective learning processes. Knowledge and skills are most meaningful in the context of communities of practice; accepting that will provide us with invaluable clues for structuring learning experiences that both we and our students will see as authentic tasks. The material we teach, and the technology we employ, should be viewed not as ends but as means for the student to construct an ever-widening set of understandings. This will release us to consider new materials and new methods.

It is clear that projects meet all the tests of these new understandings derived from research in the learning sciences. At best they are initiated by the learner and subject to redesign in disputatious conversation with peers and a teacher, the students' immediate community of practice. Projects certainly lend themselves to a view that materials should be means as well as ends. And they provide an unparalleled occasion for teachers to test their new and more dynamic role.

The next two chapters chronicle the experience of LabNet community members with projects, with support projects like the LabNetwork and the Teacher Liaison Consultant program (see chapter 4), with participants taking leadership roles, and some of the central learnings from those experiences.

3 SHIFTING THE APPROACH TO SCIENCE TEACHING

Shahaf Gal with Greg Lockett and Sister Mary Ethel Parrott

In a methodological prologue to this chapter and the next, Shahaf Gal, Greg Lockett, and Mary Parrott argue that significant, lasting educational change takes place through incremental "shifts" in prevailing practice and in the perspectives of individual teachers—a process nourished by constant reflection and interchange within the community of practice. Shifting, especially in the early stage represented by LabNet, is marked by a patchwork of diverse, small-scale experiments, as teachers selectively adapt new ideas to local conditions.

Given this view of change, it would have been misleading to evaluate LabNet by conventional methods, based on standardized testing of students or comparison of teachers' practices to an "expert" model; instead the authors have tried to reach a qualitative understanding of how, and to what degree, LabNet shifted teacher attitudes and classroom practice (the subject of this chapter), and established a community climate supportive of change (the subject of chapter 4).

To achieve such understanding requires a "teacher's-eye view" of the project. For this reason, Shahaf Gal, LabNet's Director of Evaluation, not only based the evaluation primarily on teachers' questionnaire responses, but also enlisted two teachers—Greg Lockett and Sister Mary Ethel Parrott—as collaborators in analyzing the data and communicating the results.

This chapter presents their findings on teachers' use of projects, microcomputer-based laboratories (MBL), and the LabNetwork. The picture that emerges is promising, although not entirely conclusive. At the outset, LabNet teachers on the whole used the traditional textbook-lecture-lab approach; as a result of their participation, the teachers dramatically increased the use of projects in their classes. MBL to a great extent, and to a lesser degree telecommunication technology, were accepted from the start; teachers incorporated MBL activities into their classes and over time made increasing use of the LabNetwork's electronic Mail and Forum (bulletin board) features, often to share project ideas and information. However, it is not clear how many LabNet teachers altered their fundamental philosophies; at the end of the project many had begun to experiment with project-enhanced science learning, but for most, it clearly will take more time for the philosophical seeds planted by LabNet to germinate.

For most, but not all. For a few teachers, LabNet was a catalyst for profound change in philosophy and practice. The chapter concludes with detailed case studies of two of these teachers—an experienced teacher from a large suburban high school in Arizona, and a new teacher from a small rural school in Oregon, different in many ways but alike in their determination to find better ways to teach.

INTRODUCTION:
A FRAMEWORK FOR EVALUATING LABNET

This chapter and the one that follows examine the extent to which LabNet achieved its goals—fostering the use of project-enhanced science learning (PESL); helping to build a community of practice among teachers; and motivating and equipping teachers to use microcomputer technology both in their teaching and in communicating with one another. This chapter focuses primarily on changes in teaching practice; chapter 4 focuses on the changed role of teachers within their professional communities. Teachers' use of technology crosscuts the concerns of the two chapters and is discussed in both.

These two chapters are about "evaluation," but not in the usual sense of the word. There is no elaborate statistical analysis, no scorecard of the project's results. For reasons detailed here, traditional measures and methods are, we argue, wholly inadequate to capture the nature of the change LabNet sought to evoke. What we have tried to do instead—"we" being LabNet's director of evaluation and two LabNet teachers—is to describe both in quantitative and qualitative terms the evolution of the changes that took place among teachers over the course of the project, mainly as seen through teachers' eyes, and to analyze how these changes relate to the project's goals. We begin, in the next section, by explaining why we have chosen this way to tell LabNet's story.

As chapter 2 makes clear, project-enhanced science learning is more than a mere technique, more than another arrow in the quiver of the traditional science teacher. It represents a fundamental departure from the philosophy governing the current practice of "Jeff Anderson" and most physics teachers in this country—the basal textbook-lecture-lab approach. Let us briefly recap the key points of difference and then trace their implications for evaluating LabNet.

The Reigning Approach: Textbook-Lecture-Lab

The espoused goal of standard high school physical science courses is preparation for college physics. Because college physics is dominated by mathematical problem solving, this aspect of physics has come to dominate high school courses. The standard course is organized around a basal text and various materials designed to accompany and supplement the text. The texts tend to follow the historical development of physics itself, treating sequentially mechanics, heat, waves, sound, light, electromagnetism, and "modern" physics. These texts are encyclopedic; few topics are treated in depth. Generally, the goal of the text is to introduce and elucidate key equations used in the various branches of physics. Although there are usually both conceptual and mathematical questions at the end of each chapter, mathematical questions dominate in number and degree of difficulty.

Lectures by the teacher are the prevailing in-class form of interaction. Labs and problem-solving sessions are also used. The labs tend to be "cookbook" in nature: Students follow a precise set of instructions and are graded on how closely their results match expected outcomes. In problem-solving sessions, students ask specific questions about problems that have been assigned. Typically, the teacher responds by demonstrating a "correct" solution. Students are generally evaluated on the basis of "objective" tests that rely heavily on mathematical problem solving.

Although not all high school physics teachers or classes in the United States may match this description exactly, we believe it captures the style and philosophy that has dominated much of physics education for the latter half of this century. This approach has been under repeated attack, especially since the early 1980s; various alternatives have been suggested, developed, and attempted. However, this form of instruction has been extraordinarily resistant to change.

The Challenge of PESL

The project approach, echoing a theme in educational philosophy that goes back at least to Rousseau, starts with a very different basic assumption: Children and adults alike learn by doing. To learn physics, a student must "do" physics. Because experimenting is central in physics, experimenting must take a central role in the classroom.

Several features are important in this approach. Students are free to choose a research problem. They do not know the solution to their problem at the outset of their project. Although students must work within the constraints of time, resources, and their current knowledge, they are given considerable time and freedom to attack their problem as they see fit. Collaboration is acceptable and desirable. The end product of student work can vary widely (reports, papers, equipment, experiments, constructions, models, etc.). Student success is not easily measured by objective tests.

In this process, the goal of the teacher is not efficient transfer of large amounts of information and mathematical problem-solving skills. The goal is to give students an immediate and compelling "inside" view of science (physics)—firsthand knowledge of what science is, how it works, and what its limits are. The teacher functions primarily as a facilitator. In many respects, he or she is like a research director in a laboratory. He or she familiarizes new researchers with the laboratory, obtains needed resources or suggests alternatives, resolves disputes, and in general attempts to nurture the development of new ideas, discoveries and/or inventions within the laboratory. At all points, the teacher is guided by the current practice of physics and the goal of re-creating that practice within the classroom.

In PESL, mathematical problem-solving skills are encompassed within a broader structure that includes research skills (using libraries), motor skills (building apparatus and operating it), cooperative social skills (collaborating on projects), communication skills (oral reports during informal lab meetings, writing scientific papers), and thinking skills (logic, induction, deduction, analysis, synthesis). Ideally, skills are learned as needed. Motivation is rarely a problem because the context makes the need for the skill obvious to the student.

Thus, PESL and the prevailing basal-text approach are not just different methods of teaching. The two approaches start from opposing psychological and epistemological premises and arrive at vastly different visions of the goals of education and the role of the teacher. To summarize the differences in the language of chapter 2: In the prevailing approach, the teacher's job is to feed knowledge to the learner from the "outside in." In PESL, it is to provide experiences, materials, and support to help the learner construct knowledge from the "inside out."

The Failure of Top-Down Reform

Just as learning in the basal-text approach takes place from the "outside in," most previous efforts to reform science education on a national scale have taken place from the "top down." In top-down reform, an ideal curriculum and teaching method is crafted by experts. Teachers are gathered at central locations and the new material or method is inculcated. Teachers return to their classrooms and implement the new material or method. Success is measured by: (a) the match between teacher practice and the expert model; and (b) improved student performance on standardized objective tests. Interestingly, after various national efforts to reform science education, science test scores still suffer in comparative international studies, and the supply of potential scientists continues to decrease.

These failures, we argue, can be attributed to both tactical and strategic errors. Tactically, top-down reform fails to recognize that the world of the teacher is shaped predominantly by local forces. Teachers practice within a complex web of legal, social, and economic relationships that vary widely across different regions of the country. To be successful, new programs must "fit" within the local web. Strategically, top-down reform has failed because it has focused on curriculum content and teaching methods, narrowly conceived. It has not attacked the root of the problem, namely the basal textbook-lecture-lab approach itself, which leaves students, including the "best" students, ignorant of the real process of science and untouched by its excitement.

How Real Change Can Happen

Evolution is the process by which the impossible becomes possible through small, accumulating shifts. Concentrate on the direction, not the size of the change. Begin with actions that seem tinier than necessary but which are small enough to be maintained. The rate of change is slow at first but do not prematurely judge your efforts. Change happens through spirals; the work grows upon itself. As little changes accumulate, they will reinforce one another and make larger changes possible. Gradually balances will shift. (Krapfel 1989, p. 176)

These are the words of a natural scientist writing about the process of shifting perspectives on personal and natural phenomena. In the same manner we believe that fundamental educational change on a national scale, such as movement from the textbook-lecture-lab approach to PESL, can happen—but not by top-down implementation of an ideal science curriculum. Fundamental change is more likely to occur by a process of *shifting*. Shifting implies a series of small, sustainable steps rather than a rapid conversion to a new order. Each shift acknowledges the local context and sets the foundation for the next shift. Each shift interacts with and modifies the prevailing web of forces in a way that permits the next shift to occur. Over an extended period of time, this accumulation of shifts translates into profound educational transformation. Every teacher experiences shifting in a unique way as he or she attempts to adapt a new model to the local context. The image is one of a river with a thousand channels, each channel seeking the same goal by its own path.

LabNet may be construed as an attempt to stimulate a fundamental shift at a very early stage in this process. The project "hooked up" with teachers who saw a need and had the desire to transform their ways of teaching. It provided them with teaching models, collaborative learning opportunities, equipment, and support. But it was up to the teachers to seize these opportunities and decide how they would be used. To the extent that LabNet succeeded, it could be expected to produce a wide variety of results as teachers adapted PESL to the realities of their schools and local communities.

The "constructivist" view of cognitive development that we sketched in chapter 2 applies to teachers as well as students. Just as students actively construct their knowledge of the physical world, so teachers construct their knowledge of their craft. Teachers are not passive creatures whom educational reformers either change or fail to change. They are active, thinking beings who can change themselves, using opportunities they create or that are generated for them.

Change in the Community of Practice and the Use of Technology

To this point our discussion has focused on evaluation in relation to one goal of LabNet—promoting project-enhanced science learning. What of the other two goals, helping to build a community of practice and fostering the use of technology? It is important to realize that the three goals are not separate but intimately connected. The framework for evaluation that we have laid out is therefore relevant to all three.

We believe that, in order for teachers to grow and change in the ways we have discussed, a supportive community of practice is essential. Ongoing dialogue with fellow professionals helps teachers reflect on their experience, understand it, and change it. Dialogue also allows new ideas and new understandings to spread. When an intervention like LabNet ends, the community can sustain the process of change and help teachers continue to learn on their own. Thus, dialogue within a community of practice is critical for the gradual, long-term shifting that we believe characterizes change in both individual perspectives and nationwide educational practices. In chapter 4, we assess the degree to which LabNet succeeded in establishing this kind of dialogue.

As for technology, LabNet's goal was not the increased use of modern hardware and software per se, but their use in support of project-enhanced learning and the building of a community of practice. Microcomputer-based laboratories (MBLs) open up a wide range of project possibilities because they make measurement and data collection easy for many physical phenomena. A telecommunication network makes possible a type of interaction over long distances that can potentially support both the development of a community and the dissemination of project ideas, findings, questions, etc. As we evaluate the use of MBLs and the network in this chapter (and, in the case of the network, in chapter 4 as well), our concern is to discover whether the technology served these intended purposes.

Dilemmas of Evaluation

Our view of educational change implies that many traditional tools and standards of educational evaluation cannot be used to gauge LabNet's success or failure. New ways of looking at educational practice and teacher development require new ways to evaluate change. In particular, LabNet would not be expected to meet the criteria for "success" associated with top-down reform. To the degree that the project succeeded in its own terms, teacher practice would not correspond to an expert model. (For a discussion of fundamental educational change and its evaluation, see for example Bamberger, Duckworth, Gray, & Lampert 1982; Bamberger, Duckworth, & Lampert, 1981; Bruce & Rubin, 1992; Cohen & Garet, 1983; Erickson, 1986; Guba, 1985; and Skrtic, 1985.)

Just as LabNet collides head on with traditional program-evaluation approaches, it also collides with a bulwark of the basal-text approach—standardized objective tests as these now exist. For example, student performance as measured by "objective" tests of mathematical problem-solving skills would be largely irrelevant for measuring the kind of individual change that LabNet aspired to produce. The knowledge and skills measured by these instruments correspond closely to the emphases of most textbooks, although they are only a small subset of the broader galaxy of skills required by working scientists. Defining success in terms of test scores in effect allows a particular technique of evaluation to dictate the goals of science education and stifles any attempt at fundamental change. But if we reject standardized tests, and top-down standardization of teacher training, how else can we measure the success or failure of LabNet? And how can we communicate our judgment in a manner that will convince an appropriately skeptical reader?

The success of any attempt to change science education in the United States will be measured by the emergence of more and better scientists and by the spread of scientific literacy in the general population. But such outcomes are unlikely to be traceable to any one project. We need ways of evaluating reform in the near future that tell us whether we are moving in the direction sketched in chapter 2.

LabNet sought to change the way a particular group of teachers went about doing science with their students (or, more precisely, to create opportunities for these teachers to change their own practice). But we did not expect them all to change in the same way—there was no one "expert" model. In using PESL, by definition, teachers must adapt to the specific needs, interests, and abilities of their students. Further, we recognized that each teacher would find his or her own way to make use of the resources and experiences that LabNet provided, and that these uses would reflect the individual's past experience, expertise, and working environment (including equipment, parental, and administrative expectations, local culture, etc.). One dilemma then was how to design an evaluation that would both capture the many individual experiences and account for their local importance. Our work here relies on the insightful perspective developed in the anthropological studies of cultural change of Geertz (1973, 1983), Clifford (1988), and Bourdieu (1990, 1991).

Another dilemma is embedded in this context of professional growth—how to account for the multiple and particular adaptations and also construct a picture of change in a community of practice. We recognize that part of the change occurs in and in relation to community activities. There is a constant interactive and open-ended exchange of thought, experience, and input from students and other teachers. We wanted to preserve both kinds of experiences.

A number of researchers have adopted the notion of the artistry, "the conversations" with materials and people, involved in producing change. For example, Bamberger and Schon (1977, 1983) and Bamberger (1991) described students learning to construct musical notations. Schon (1987) showed how professionals shape their work environment and attempt to share their expertise with apprentices. Lave (1986, 1988) spoke of this process in the context of everyday mathematics and apprenticeship. (For a range of views that relate professional change to cognition in social context, see Resnick, Levine, & Teasley, 1991.)

Further, because shifting occurs over time, longer than the length of a 3-year project's life, how does one identify the project's contribution to teachers' growth? We did not expect LabNet to result in abrupt "conversion experiences" for most participants. Just as we believe that large-scale educational change takes place through an incremental shifting process, we believe that change in individual teachers takes place through a gradual process of shifting perspective.

Teachers who keep growing continually question their practice and its effectiveness in stimulating students to learn. Out of this questioning come changes in perspective and practice that lead to new questioning and more changes. Evaluation practice needs to tell us about this process of incremental growth, and also make note of the project's unique contributions to it.

To respond to these dilemmas, the evaluation had to be deeply ingrained in LabNet activities. We formulated an evaluation plan that was carefully tuned to LabNet and could critically examine its outcomes.

To "construct" the experiences of participating teachers, we used surveys, questionnaires, interviews, and site visits. We supplemented these data with resources of the historian, journalist, even the novelist: namely our personal experience and observation of the life of the project and the personal testimony of participants. Our presentation weaves together quantitative information, qualitative analyses of teacher statements, and individual case narratives—each of which, we hope, contributes to the understanding of LabNet in a different way. In this sense, we took an ecological perspective to create a composite and integrated picture of teachers' experiences. (For an excellent example of this approach, see Lightfoot, 1983. The theoretical perspective can be found in Barker, 1968, and Bronfenbrenner, 1979.)

All the data we collected were critically examined by teachers to ensure that they were grounded in the reality of working in the educational system. A method we used to expand this reality test was to stake out a position, make it public to all participants, and seek their comments and criticism. In this sense, we attempted to make the work of the evaluation integral to the wider process of learning in the community. The approach to evaluation here follows that of participatory action research, as initiated by Lewin (1946, 1947a, 1947b) and developed by Argyris and colleagues (Argyris & Schon, 1974, and Argyris, Putnam, & McLain, 1985). In this approach, participants and researchers formulate a problem, jointly study and share results, and in so doing inform their future steps. Action research informs the participants and staff about the nature of the problem and then seeks ways to design an effective intervention. It can be said to be educational process (Lewin, 1948).

Evaluation as Collaboration and Dialogue

There is a final aspect of the evaluation that deserves comment. Just as LabNet was a collaborative effort—in which project staff and teachers learned from each other constantly, jointly redefining the project—the evaluation was also a collaboration, drawing on the different expertise of teachers and researchers. In this sense, although the findings represent what can be considered the "official" voice of the project, it is also a gathered voice of the community of science teachers and staff who were project members. For example, analysis of the teacher questionnaire was part of the dialogue between LabNet staff and teachers that continually reshaped the project.

The participation of teachers in evaluating LabNet was essential. Just as anthropologists entering an unfamiliar culture need interpreters who are experienced and immersed in the local setting, researchers need teachers to help make sense of the myriad local and individual adaptations that occur when a reform or innovation moves into the real world of schools.

This chapter's discussion of change in teaching practices, for example, and some of the next chapter's discussion as well, are based on a questionnaire that was sent to all participating teachers in the spring of 1991 (see Appendix C). Not only did teachers provide the data, but two LabNet teachers also collaborated with the LabNet's director of evaluation in analyzing the questionnaire and writing earlier reports on which it draws. Unless other sources are specifically cited, questionnaire findings reported here are from Gal, Lockett, and Parrott (1991).

The three authors operated both individually and as a team, in a process that balanced individual opinions and personal understandings with the need for a common framework. Their joint work also was an experiment in the use of telecommunication, linking Covington, Kentucky; Cottonwood, California; and Cambridge, Massachusetts. (In Appendix B, the three reflect on their experience and on the use of telecommunication as the medium for collaborative long-distance writing.)

In addition, the individual case studies that appear in this chapter and the next are joint works of the program evaluator and the teacher-subjects, who not only were observed and interviewed but also commented on and contributed to the write-ups as they were developed.

Organization of the Chapter

The chapter has two major sections: The first, "Gauging the Shift," describes changes in the classroom practices of LabNet teachers as a group over the course of the project. Drawing primarily on teachers' questionnaire responses, the section begins by characterizing LabNet's starting point—the backgrounds of teachers and students, teachers' initial philosophies and methods, and their perceptions of the types of change needed to improve science education. It goes on to describe changes along three dimensions—use of projects, use of microcomputer-based labs, and use of the LabNetwork. The chapter's second major section, "Seizing Learning Opportunities," depicts the process of change through the stories of two individual teachers.

GAUGING THE SHIFT

At the end of the second year of LabNet (May 1991), all participants received a questionnaire covering three main areas: (a) demographic, personal, and classroom information; (b) science teaching activities; and (c) support received to carry out LabNet's activities. The questionnaire consisted mainly of structured items, but also asked for open-ended comments, which teachers provided abundantly. We sent out 163 questionnaires and received 102 responses, a 63% response rate. Most of the responses (82) and the highest response rate (69%) came from 1990 teachers (a majority had also attended the 1989 workshop as well). Unless otherwise indicated, all findings in this section are based on analysis of the questionnaire data provided by the 78 teachers of these 82 teachers who returned questionnaires by July 15, 1991. (For complete information on responses of the 78 respondents other groups, see Appendix C.)

Background: Teachers and Classrooms

The 78 teachers were from 33 states. One in four were women. Half taught in suburban schools, one third in urban schools, and the rest in rural areas. On average, they had taught science for 20 years; 16 of those years were in physics teaching. Most taught more physics courses than other science courses, such as biology or chemistry. Except for this last factor, these findings parallel those of the national survey of physics teachers discussed in chapter 2 (Neuschatz & Covalt, 1988).

Teachers reported that enrollment in their physics courses included 55% male and 45% female students. Most of the students were White (76%). Minorities made up the remaining 24%. Latinos were the largest minority group (10%), followed by Asians (7%), African-Americans (5%), Native Americans (1%), and other minorities (1%). As a whole, the representation of minorities in classes of LabNet teachers is higher than in the classes surveyed by the U.S. Department of Education (National Center for

Educational Statistics, 1980). Still, the composition of the LabNet student population clearly mirrors the underrepresentation of minority students in science classes nationwide (see Fig. 2.1 in chapter 2).

Philosophy and Classroom Practice

The philosophical perspectives and previous teaching practices of participants were not addressed in the teacher questionnaire. However, conversations with the teachers strongly suggest that most started at a point not far from Jeff Anderson, the imaginary teacher of the last chapter. Most taught (some more, some less) using the textbook-lecture-lab approach.

In making this assertion, it is not our intent to stereotype or criticize the LabNet teachers. We recognize their many differences in style and personality. However, in quiet counterpoint to these differences, there was an undeniable philosophical homogeneity. We believe that teachers would not have found this conclusion particularly controversial; when they joined LabNet, most would have affirmed the constellation of ideas associated with the basal-text approach.

At the same time, LabNet participants were acutely aware of the criticism that has been leveled at physics education during the last decade. In response to this criticism, many had made substantial investments of personal time and energy in exploring and implementing various improvements in their classroom practice (such as their participation in LabNet). The two most common improvements were: (a) increased use of demonstrations to elucidate basic concepts; and (b) increased use of sophisticated equipment in laboratories, especially MBLs. In many cases, participants were also leaders in other state and national programs to improve science education. In a very few cases, teachers had made more radical breaks with traditional practice.

Sensing a Need for Change [1]

In an effort to learn more about LabNet teachers' initial perceptions of the need for change in science education, we turned to the applications of teachers who joined in the second year of the project. On the second year application, teachers were asked what they saw as the major problem or need with respect to their current practice. Their answers are summarized in Table 3.1.

---

[1] This section is based on Gal (1990a).

TABLE 3.1
Primary Need/Problem in Science
Education as Identified by Teachers*

Problem or Need	Percent of Teachers Citing
Need to learn about new computer applications and need for access to telecommunication network	26
Work environment: budget, facilities, etc.	26
Need to motivate students, especially underrepresented students	20
Need to encourage project-enhanced learning	20
Other (include personal growth)	8
	100%

* Based on a qualitative analysis of the responses of 54 teachers who joined LabNet in 1990.

Project-enhanced learning. Some 20% of teachers, a sizeable minority, said that encouraging project-based learning was their number one need. But what is more significant is the fact that 80% put other concerns first. This finding reinforces the impression that most LabNet teachers were not out to challenge the basal-text approach.

Work environments. One of the top two types of concerns, mentioned by 26% of the teachers, had to do with the need for appropriate work environments for science teaching. Many teachers felt that school and classroom in fact limit their ability to teach, let alone introduce change. The old story of overcrowding, inadequate budgets, and overwork with administrative activities was cited by many. These problems, one teacher believed, "will go on forever."

At times the descriptions seemed to imply that science teaching occurs in an abyss—in an environment oppressively limited in its capacity to maintain learning at all, be it in science or any other subject matter. Some responses expressed a sense of acute urgency and frustration. One teacher from an urban school wrote:

> There are several areas in teaching secondary physical science in our high school which have created problems for me during the past years. Our space is extremely limited, and our facility is antiquated. Many rooms are utilized eight periods a day by several teachers. We have problems with heating, lighting, and providing a safe environment for science education. There is no place to do lab set-up and preparation. We also have a problem because of shortage of lab and instructional materials as well as a shortage of secure storage.

Technology. A large number of teachers (26%) cited the need to learn about new technologies, including computers (18%) and telecommunication (8%). Teachers saw learning about new educational technology as a professional responsibility without which their teaching would become outmoded. As one teacher wrote, "Rapid advances in technology are changing things in this country so fast that I fear that the content of what I teach may be outdated in just a few years."

Teachers were worried that students' current exposure to the capabilities of computers is limited and incomplete. Physics classes, some believed, can expand students' knowledge of the use of computers far beyond the currently popular but limited use of the computer for computer-aided instruction (CAI), especially in math and science. Students can learn that computers are powerful and effective tools for data collection and analysis.

There were also teachers who perceived the new technology, particularly telecommunication, as a way to overcome professional isolation. Feelings of isolation are probably more common among teachers in geographically remote places or those in small schools where they are "the whole science department," but teachers in large high schools can experience these feelings too. One teacher said,

> One of the major problems which I have encountered in my twenty plus years in the public schools science classroom has been the isolation imposed by the process of teaching. I am the only physics teacher at my high school. It is frustrating and discouraging to be unable at the end of the day to share concerns and "bounce" ideas off of colleagues with common interests.

Student motivation. Quite a few of the teachers were concerned with the skewed composition of their science classes and with the related, widespread perception that science is esoteric. Comments usually connected limited motivation and underrepresentation of a wider audience. One teacher commented, "Unless the student is a White male with above-average math ability, science has no place in their life." This perception is reinforced in minority students and girls when they avoid science classes from the start. They shy away, believing that their likelihood of failure is high. Said another teacher: "Physics is still perceived as a too-difficult science, to be studied only by the elite. In my school that not only discourages kids, it discourages the minority population disproportionately."

Teachers also believed that *students* share the blame for the state of science education. One wrote, "Large numbers of students enter their [class]rooms with an anti-science attitude." Another observed that students develop an "academic inferiority complex," perceiving scientific ideas as "a collection of abstract concepts that have been divined through some 'magical' scientific process unachievable by average persons." Teachers wanted to show students the relevance of science to their lives, and to make them into active participants in the scientific inquiry—which they felt students attempt to avoid. Students, some felt, are passive and reluctant to take charge of their own learning:

> I find that students have trouble with my chemistry and physics courses when I try to get them to learn concepts rather than plug in information. It takes me several years to get some of my students to think for themselves, and question and research ideas presented in class. I find fewer and fewer students wishing to take the time to do investigations and experiment. They would rather be entertained, and this disappoints me.

These perceptions show how deep and how diverse the problem of change in science education is felt to be by the teachers we questioned. Teachers were certainly aware that science education is in trouble. They less often connected this with a need to fundamentally change their way of teaching. What is important is that the LabNet teachers saw themselves as responsible for and committed to making a difference. They were willing to invest themselves *personally* in trying to make that difference.

Teachers' Use of Projects

LabNet's impact on project use. Responses to the teacher questionnaire show that LabNet was extraordinarily successful in shifting teachers toward the use of projects in their classes. In 1991, after 2 years with LabNet, 70% of the teachers reported that they did more projects as a result of their participation. Qualitative and quantitative questions both confirmed this result. Of the teachers, 10% described themselves as extensive users of projects, and 80% described themselves as moderate users (Table 3.2). The students of LabNet teachers completed an average of four projects during the school year, with an average project length of just over 14 days.

TABLE 3.2
Use of Projects in Science Teaching

To What Extent are Projects Used in Your Science Teaching?	
Extensively	10%
Moderately	80%
Not at all	10%

The statistics shown in Table 3.2 are impressive. It was clear from conversations with participants and from 1990 teachers' applications, discussed earlier, that many individuals joined LabNet because of an interest in MBLs or telecommunication rather than projects. In fact, many participants were very skeptical about the use of projects. LabNet was successful in convincing participants that projects are a valuable tool, and in motivating these individuals to explore the use of projects in their classes.

Shift or retrenchment? The increased use of projects by LabNet teachers bore the mark of a "shifting" model of educational reform in its early stages, rather than a "top–down" model. The self-reported descriptions of project implementation reflect a wide variety of approaches. This is to be expected as teachers take a common idea and adapt it to local conditions. However, there is also strong evidence that these explorations were being conducted by teachers who still accepted the basal-text paradigm (Table 3.3).

TABLE 3.3
LabNet's Influence on Work Assigned to
Students, as Perceived by Their Teachers

	% Increase	% No Change	% Decrease
Student use of computers	79	21	0
Student execution of projects	70	30	0
Student collaboration on class activities	60	40	0
Student questions about science concepts or issues not included in regular curriculum	55	45	0
Student use of textbooks	4	72	24
Student preparation for standardized tests	3	80	17

Of the teachers, 72% reported no change in their use of textbooks. And 80% reported no change in their preparation of students for standardized tests. Resistance to change in these areas is understandable since a textbook and standardized tests are two hallmarks of the basal-text paradigm, and the durability of the basal-text paradigm, supported by local school expectations, has already been noted.

Extensive changes in practice usually accompany profound changes in educational philosophy. However, changes in practice can also be used to sustain belief in an old paradigm that is being challenged. In essence, the change is viewed as an adequate response to criticism and the old educational paradigm is left intact. It is too early to say which path will be taken by LabNet participants, fundamental shift in perspective or retrenchment. To assure a continued shift toward the PESL approach, teachers need to learn from and build on their initial success.

Projects, cooperative learning, and questioning strategies. Data from the teacher questionnaire (see Table 3.3) suggest a linkage between projects and two other topics that are currently generating interest, research, and adherents in the educational community: cooperative learning and questioning strategies. Sixty percent of the teachers reported that their students collaborated more as a result of their participation in LabNet. Fifty-five percent reported changes in the types of questions students asked. We suspect that both of these results were caused by the increased use of projects. Linking projects with cooperative learning techniques and questioning strategies seems to be a natural step. Such a marriage might have

the potential to accelerate the use of projects in science classrooms significantly.

Evaluating projects. The teacher questionnaire also asked a series of
questions about evaluation of projects (Table 3.4). Teachers were given the
following selection of evaluation factors: student presentations, written
final reports, group skills, observation of students practices, student notebooks, quizzes and tests, and other. They were then asked to identify the
specific techniques that they used to evaluate projects.

TABLE 3.4
Methods Used to Assess Students' Projects

Percent of teachers who evaluate projects		93%
Average % of student's final grade which projects constitute		17%
Participants Evaluate Projects on the Basis of:*	**% Yes**	**% No**
Student presentations	72	28
Student written final reports	69	31
Group skills	52	48
Observation of students	49	51
Student notebooks	31	69
Quizzes/tests	12	88
Other	40	60

* Based on the responses of 60 teachers who reported that they evaluate students'
projects

Most teachers (93%) evaluated their students' projects. On the average projects constituted 17% of students' grades. That shows that projects
have become an accepted method for evaluating students' work. Of course,
we would want to see project evaluation become a larger part of student
assessment. An indication that LabNet teachers may be taking this approach is suggested by the limited use teachers made of traditional methods to evaluate students projects. Ninety-five percent of the teachers
reported using more than one means of evaluation. Only 12% (seven teachers) reported using quizzes and tests. This would seem to be a healthy
development, given that physics education has been sharply criticized for
over-reliance on objective tests. Projects seem to call for a wider range of
evaluation tools. Promoting this linkage may help accelerate the use of
projects among teachers who are concerned about the testing issue.

On a deeper level, these findings reflect the fundamental tension between the project approach and the basal-text approach. The use of objective tests is one of the principal hallmarks of the latter. Teachers who use
projects, even on a limited basis, find themselves seeking and using other
forms of evaluation. As suggested earlier, one shift in practice leads to

another, and relatively small shifts taken together can add up to a fundamental transformation in educational philosophy.

Teachers' Use of Microcomputer-Based Laboratories (MBLs)

In today's world, teaching science without computers is like teaching horseback riding without horses. It can be discussed in theory, but the development of practical skills is considerably hindered. As a consequence, there is a general consensus among science teachers that computers merit an important place in science classes. LabNet teachers noted their need to become better acquainted with computers. There is also broad recognition that the computer is a powerful instructional tool. Regardless of its role in science, it can be used to teach certain important scientific concepts efficiently and effectively.

The most notable example is the use of sonic rangers to teach graphing and kinematics. TERC has played a significant role in developing hardware and software for use with MBLs and in training teachers, including LabNet participants, to use this technology. Unlike project-enhanced learning, MBLs have been widely accepted by science teachers, and their introduction into science classrooms has not been slowed by teacher resistance. It has been integrated with the accepted basal-text and lab traditional course materials.

LabNet's impact on MBL use. Of the reporting teachers, 85% identified themselves as users of MBLs, mostly moderate (60%) and some more extensively (25%) (Table 3.5). Fifteen percent of the participants reported making no use of MBLs.

TABLE 3.5
Participants' Use of MBLs in Their Classrooms

Use	Percentage
Extensive use	25%
Moderate use	60%
No use	15%

This finding indicates quite an extensive diffusion of MBL technology into LabNet classrooms. The participants were trained to use the MBLs in the summer workshops. But the questionnaire did not ask teachers to report the extent to which their use of MBLs is due to LabNet. However, personal communications with various participants and public communications on the forum indicate that many participants shared an active and continuing interest in MBLs and that LabNet at least reinforced and supported this interest.

As one might expect, the use of MBLs is related to the number of computers available to a teacher. On average, eight computers were available to each teacher. Of the 71 teachers who responded to this question, 63%

had access to one to six computers. Among this group only 9% (four teach-ers) used MBLs extensively. Of the 27% teachers with more than six com-puters, 50% used MBLs extensively. The association between number of computers and frequency of use, obvious as it is, may imply that more attention needs to be paid to MBLs in classrooms that have only one com-puter. In the absence of the requisite hardware, projects like LabNet may need to be coupled with mechanisms for providing equipment to partici-pants if workshop training is to be efficiently transformed into classroom change.

From MBL activities to PESL projects. LabNet advocated the use of both projects and MBLs. Thus, the intersection of the two, the MBL project, is of particular interest. Teachers were asked to describe a project one or more of their students had done. Thirty-seven teachers responded (Table 3.6). Probably much of the MBL usage cited by participants as "projects" would have been better characterized as MBL *activities* prescribed by teach-ers. The distribution of MBL activities reported as projects performed by students of LabNet teachers closely follows the topics traditionally stud-ied in high school physics.

TABLE 3.6
The Distribution of MBL Projects Performed
by Students of LabNet Teachers

Project Type	Number of Projects
Mechanics	15
Temperature	7
Light	6
Sound	4
Radiation	1
Electricity	0
Other	4

Although science teachers working within the basal-textbook paradigm would probably approve, we must question whether such a distribution would have arisen if students had been free to select their own projects. Without choice and its consequent responsibility, an important element of the PESL approach is missing. On the other hand, to the extent that MBLs by their nature encourage students to improvise and experiment, teacher-selected MBL activities may have the potential to evolve into true, student-initiated projects.

Teachers' Use of the LabNetwork

Frequency of usage. Fifty-eight teachers (74% of the 78 respondents) used the network. Of these, 34 (59%) used the network once, twice, or more each week. Twenty-four teachers (41%) used the network less than once, once, or twice a month (Table 3.7). The median was once or twice a week. Some teachers indicated that their usage declined as spring approached.

TABLE 3.7
Frequency of Use of the LabNetwork

Frequency	N	%*
Less than once a month	6	10
Once or twice a month	18	31
Once or twice a week	29	50
More than twice a week	5	9
	58	100%

* Based on responses of 58 users.

Twenty persons (26%) indicated that they did not use the network at all. Overwhelmingly, nonusing teachers cited technical problems or lack of equipment (Table 3.8). It should be noted that several of the respondents qualified their response to indicate that "did not use at all" actually meant used sparingly (not one of the preformulated options), or that they had discontinued use.

TABLE 3.8
Primary Reasons for not Using the LabNetwork

Primary Reason	N	%*
Lack of equipment	11	55
Technical problems	8	40
Lack of experience	1	5
Have no use for the network	0	0
	20	100%

* Based on responses of 20 nonusers.

The futility of a telecommunication network for those without telecommunication equipment is obvious. For whatever the reason, these were teachers who were prevented from full participation in the project.

Usage of network features. The LabNetwork menu contained eight features: Mail (standard electronic mail); Forum (a bulletin board where public messages were posted, even if designated for a specific person); Databases and a Workspace (file area from which information and programs could be downloaded or to which they could be uploaded); and several organizational and helpful features (Using LabNet, Entry Log, Member Directory, and Help). Table 3.9 shows the percentage of use by respondents of each feature.

TABLE 3.9
Features of the LabNetwork

Network Features Used at Least Once:*	
Mail	98%
Forum	98
Help	66
Member directory	65
Using LabNet	63
Entry log	32
Workspace	20
Databases	15
* Respondents checked as many as were applicable	

By far the most utilized features were Mail and the Forum, which virtually all members used. The least used features were the Workspace and the Databases. The Mail and Forum features were used, among other reasons, for getting assistance from other teachers and TERC staff. It would be interesting to know why the Workspace and Databases were rarely used. Was it because these features were not as practical? Was the initial exposure to telecommunication insufficient for participants to feel comfortable with these features? Our observation at one of the workshops was that although participants were encouraged to use all features, a concerted effort was made to ensure that all could use Mail and the Forum. Staff demonstrations and comments implied that the Workspace and Databases required more expertise and were somewhat cumbersome. We return to this issue in chapter 5.

The popularity of the Mail feature was especially obvious. On average, participants estimated that they had sent over 30 messages during the 1990-1991 school term. However, the distribution of messages sent was skewed toward the lower end. The mode was one to nine messages. Although 24 teachers estimated that they had sent 30 or more messages, 38 sent fewer than 30. The three teachers who served as Teacher Liaison Consultants (see chapter 4 "The Teacher Liaison Consultant...Program") sent in excess of 100 messages; their frequent use of the network is an indication of their effort to fulfill their roles as supportive contacts.

Benefits of the network. The most highly rated benefits of network participation were exchanging ideas about projects, and requesting and giving technical support (Table 3.10). Social exchanges (also popular in Star Schools; Weir, Krensky, & Gal, 1990) were useful to 90% of the respondents. Discussing general teaching approaches was regarded as definitely beneficial, but not nearly to the extent of the three previously mentioned items. Only about 50% of the teachers found exchanging and analyzing student-collected data beneficial, with a mere 9% rating it "very benefi-cial." It should be noted that this feature was entirely optional, and started quite late in the project. Several respondents wrote that the network was useful for developing their "Big Idea Grant" proposals. A few mentioned the usefulness of communicating with TERC staff or TLCs.

TABLE 3.10

Benefits of the LabNetwork

	Very Beneficial	Moderately Beneficial	Not At All Beneficial
Exchanging ideas about specific projects with students and teachers	45%	45%	10%
Requesting/giving technical support	45	45	10
Conversing with network colleagues (social exchanges)	34	61	5
Discussing general teaching approaches	20	57	23
Exchanging and analyzing student-collected data	8	41	51
Other	67	33	0

Teachers were also asked to give a specific example of how the net-work had proved useful for their science teaching. Sixty-two teachers re-sponded. The most frequently cited example was the use of the network to generate or develop project ideas (18 teachers, 29%). For example, one teacher noted: "I was able to get project ideas from those who have used projects for several years." For another teacher, Forum messages "pro-vided ideas and inspiration to start projects," and another specifically sought Geriann Walker's list of projects. She wrote, "I found out about G. Walker's list of ideas for projects which I requested and got, and used quite a lot." One teacher mentioned how he used the network for planning and carry-ing out an energy-conservation project with other classes. He wrote: "The planning and implementation of the energy-conservation project previously mentioned was a collaborative effort of four LabNet participants. This com-bined effort made it possible to develop a truly comprehensive unit on energy conservation which could be utilized in a variety of settings."

Interestingly, although exchanging and analyzing student-collected data was low in the previous rating, it was the second most mentioned example (17 times, 27%). Most often, these were positive experiences. Teachers wrote that their students enjoyed the network and found it useful to their work. "Students get excited when they know they can put their abstracts onto the Forum and publish them," noted one teacher. Another teacher wrote, "[Students] participated in a paper airplane contest with a school in another state. Had one student get technical information for her chemistry project." Teachers often assisted students with their work: "When students were having technical difficulties, teachers on the network provided information and support. One student received the necessary type of chromatography paper and lots of good ideas."

Several teachers mentioned that the sharing of student data "should" or could have been more beneficial. This perception of students' use is consistent with the relatively low "benefit" rating this item received.

Requesting and giving technical support was also a common example mentioned by teachers (10 teachers, 16%). Support ranged from small to large technical needs, and for various purposes: from deciding on what computer to purchase to learning how to use MBL-interfacing equipment. One teacher learned from other teachers' messages to use a stopwatch-photogate system. Another wrote, "[I] found out about a neat evaluation of the Macintosh LC computer. Boulder has now ordered 48 of these systems." And one teacher learned specific functions of Microsoft Works software. The examples provided show once again that keeping up with educational technology is important for successful teaching. Having resourceful people who could help was crucial.

Discussing general teaching approaches and sharing of ideas about teaching and demonstrations was also noted (9 times, 15%). At times the examples cited reflected the mode of collegial support. As one teacher expressed it, "Another teacher would send me a message, 'Jim, how did you do this demo?' It felt very good to answer and to help other teachers when I was still in the middle of Wisconsin. Other teachers were very helpful in answering my questions." And another said, "A colleague needed information about using the computer to measure light intensity. I posted a message for him on the forum and was able to relay useful information to him."

Consistent with the high ratings given to the benefits of receiving support and of social exchanges with other teachers, eight teachers (13%) mentioned that the network reduced their sense of isolation or provided other unspecified social support. One teacher found the network to be "[A] great way to keep in touch with LabNet workshop colleagues." And another claimed that, "I am no longer isolated to the degree I once was." Breaking the sense of isolation was mentioned by others: "The greatest benefit of LabNet to me has been the feeling of confidence and a feeling of belonging to the physics teaching community...." "Kept me in touch with outside people. In rural Iowa I am the only science teacher in our school." "[Telecommunication] removes the isolation the physics teacher often has. I can communicate directly with other teachers." Only one teacher replied that most experiences were negative, in that the system was too slow and contained too many messages. The uses and benefits of the network clearly relate to its role in supporting a community of practice, a subject which we discuss in more detail in chapter 4.

SEIZING LEARNING OPPORTUNITIES

The case studies that follow tell the stories of two science teachers who have quite different backgrounds and work in different educational environments, tracing their transition from traditional science teaching to a project-enhanced approach. The cases serve as windows on shifts in educational practices. They also provide a broader perspective on what took place in the LabNet community.

The cases highlight critical features of the shifting process, mentioned earlier: First, it is personal and individual; teachers adapt any educational innovation to fit the local context, as well as their own needs and the needs of their students. Second, shifting takes place in small steps. Teachers are willing to accept and act on a given innovation only if their prior experience and knowledge have brought them to a point of readiness that enables them to understand the opportunities the new approach presents. Finally, not all of the process is planned, either by teachers or by would-be innovators. In fact, the cases suggest that many of LabNet's individual successes were achieved because LabNet staff and teachers were alert to unexpected opportunities for learning and were quick to seize them. Effective integration of innovation may well have more to do with creating appealing and accessible learning opportunities than with prescriptive, predefined dissemination programs.

Two Teachers

Bob Capen teaches in Canyon Del Oro, a suburban high school in Tucson, Arizona. He has been teaching physics for 23 years. Geriann Walker is in her fourth year of teaching science. She teaches in Elmira High School in rural Oregon. Over 2,300 students attend Canyon Del Oro: At Elmira High School there are only 300. Bob teaches five sections of physics, some with more than 30 students. Geriann alternates yearly between physics and chemistry, and teaches physical science every year. Her classes are never larger than 24 students—which is the size of her classroom. Bob has acquired much of the high-tech hardware for physics teaching: Geriann still struggles to gather equipment. Bob has been exposed to many training workshops and teacher conventions, and has been a teacher-trainer. He served as a Physics Teaching Resource Agent (PTRA; see the glossary at the end of chapter 1 for more detail) for 3 years prior to joining LabNet. For Geriann, LabNet was only her second workshop, and her first intensive exposure to project science, to other science teachers, and to experience in training teachers.

What Bob and Geriann share is a commitment to improving their science teaching—plus the willingness to collaborate with other teachers. They have both become leaders in their local community of practice. By sharing their personal stories of learning and growth in these case studies, they hope to help other teachers reflect on and improve their own work.

Bob and Geriann agreed to let their names be known to readers. Anonymity artificially disengages the practice of teaching from its natural context: a specific teacher who works and learns in a unique environment. Also, making one's identity known to others is a way of taking on the responsibility and the risks involved in membership in a community of practice. Being a community member is about *personal sharing* of experiences—successes and failures.

Like Bob and Geriann, we also see the cases as a way to make vital data available to teachers for discussion. Discourse about real experience is an important component of any community of practice.

THE MAKING OF A PHYSICS TEACHER
— Bob Capen, Canyon del Oro High School, Tucson, Arizona —

Students

It is 8 in the morning—still cool. Through the back gate of the school, students drive into the parking lot. On the metal steps that lead to Bob's class, a group of boys and girls sit. They are busy discussing the latest problem Bob gave them to finish at home. Some are stuck. None of them knows whether he or she did it right. They have come early hoping Bob will take a few moments to help them out.

Yesterday Bob gave the students the problem to work on. He told them, "Hang off a horizontal bar, once with your arms vertical and once with your arms as far apart as you can make them. Then calculate the force for both situations." There is no textbook to show them the right answer. They must rely on what they have heard from Bob, on their network of friends, parents, other adults, on what they have read, and on their own thinking. The door to Bob's class opens. The students climb the stairs and stand around Bob's table:

"I can't do it!"

"You can't ask us to do this."

"Mr. Capen, this is what I did. What do you think, is it right?"

A few minutes past 8, and the students are already shooting questions at him. He enjoys it. He knows they are frustrated by the problem—he expected that.

Bob is not about to resolve their frustration. Instead he encourages them. "Well, did you ask Chris? She seems to know, why don't you ask her? You got a good start, what would you do next? Now, that's a very interesting approach, where did you get it: from reading, or a friend?" One student shares his solution. He read through the chapter on vectors in the textbook and noticed that he could turn the physics problem into a geometric problem of equilateral triangles (see Fig. 3.1).

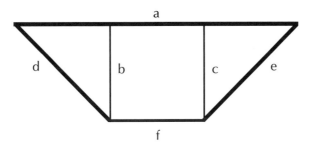

FIG. 3.1. A student's solution: To represent the
problem in geometric form.

Bob thinks this one through. The problem will stay with him—
he will ask Brian, the math teacher, about this oddball solution.

It is 10 past 8, time to start the first class. Bob acknowledges the
students' frustration and their attempts to solve the problem. He
encourages them to continue what he sees as a good effort, and
extends the time for them to work on the problem. They now have
the weekend to work. Not bad, he believes. Later that day, he
receives the first reaction from a worried mother, whose daughter
sat blankly staring at the problem for 2 hours with no success. What
should she do? "Is it all right for her not to do the problem?" she asks.

This is a moment in Bob's physics class. For this kind of problem to become such an engaging experience for the students and
Bob, it took much work. It is a road Bob started on 23 years ago as
a young science teacher who relied heavily on textbooks, and who
over the years sought ways to improve learning opportunities for his
students and himself. *Students learn when teachers learn.* This motto
has driven him, slowly, at times by trial and error and sometimes
through training, to try project-enhanced science learning. His route
also shows a transition toward a growing involvement in the community of practice of science teachers.

Learning Physics

Canyon Del Oro school lies on the edge of the city. Above the
school is the lower range of the Catalinas. Bob loves to hike in the
mountains. The lower range, overlooking Tucson, is arid—you walk
through fields of cacti. In the mid-range pine trees and the first brush
appear, becoming dense as you go up. But only at the peak of Mount
Lemon, looking at the panoramic view below, can the climb, the
bare rocks, the heat and the cacti be fully appreciated. There, huge
pine and spruce trees grow in a dense and mildewed forest.

Bob was certified as an earth science teacher in 1968. Then, as
now, earth science was the course where students labeled "short
attention span," "lower achievers" or "disciplinary problems" were

sent. Earth science, Bob felt, did not use his best science teaching ability. He aspired to become a physics teacher.

In those days, 22 years ago, his school was almost new and small—about 750 students—and the school attempted to be innovative. For example, the school experimented with modular scheduling. In the science curriculum, as an alternative to the standard textbook approach, the school adapted the recently developed Physical Science Study Committee (PSSC) physics curriculum (see the glossary at the end of chapter 1 for more detail). The PSSC curriculum introduced more laboratory experiments and the use of new laboratory equipment. For example, the demonstration of accelerated motion, usually done by a teacher pushing a car model down a slope at his desk, now changed. In PSSC, students personally pushed a small toy car and measured its velocity using a device that printed dots on a roll of paper, which can then be graphed.

When after 2 years of teaching earth science, Bob was asked to teach physics, he wholeheartedly agreed. It was the opportunity he had been waiting for, even though he had to make up much work. He knew that he was unprepared. In college, he had had only 8 hours of physics. Bob sought ways to manage the classroom that compensated for his lack of physics expertise. He also looked for every opportunity to learn more physics.

Especially in his first years of physics teaching he selected individualized instruction as his way of handling the professional uncertainties of teaching the class. Bob recalls:

> I can remember my first year of teaching. I had a kid who knew more physics than I did, and it scared the living daylights out of me. He went on to California Institute of Technology. I'd be up there struggling to share what I thought was my expertise in physics, and this kid would sit there with his eyes closed. If I ever made an error, he immediately opened his eyes and said, "That's not right," and challenged me.

> So I was forced into learning an awful lot of physics from that. And I was forced into becoming very uncomfortable. I'll have to admit that going to individualized instruction was a way of getting me off the hook. I probably used it as a way of getting away from having to stand there and have kids picking on me for doing something wrong in front of the class. So I have to apologize to those kids. I made a lot of mistakes. But it was part of my professional growth. It forced me into something else which, in the end, I think, was very beneficial.

> It was a very negative experience. But if I had not had a guy who was that sharp who challenged me, probably I might still be standing up there today, sharing my wisdom with all these kids and telling them, "This is the way you solve problems."

Learning from negative experiences is an attribute Bob utilized to his advantage. His students, he thought, need to experience difficulty as well, in order to become comfortable working with scientific problems like the horizontal-bar problem.

Professionally Bob sought ways to improve and extend his physics knowledge. Because PSSC emerged as the latest physics curriculum, which focused on small group or individualized instruction, Bob chose to use it in his class. He spent much time learning how to use PSSC and learning physics. Today, on the shelf in his room sit all the editions of PSSC, starting with the second edition (which came out at the same time Bob started teaching physics). Harvard Project Physics followed, but Bob stayed with PSSC. His frustration with PSSC was that the materials were beyond the reading ability of most of his students, and that the lesson plans and sample problems, which lacked clear structure, discouraged teachers from using it.

In his fifth year of teaching, with the collaboration of two university professors, Bob prepared a study guide that divided the PSSC curriculum into 35 "manageable" units. These units were organized to help teachers cope with the loose structure of PSSC. Each unit was to last a week. Students were to work by themselves. At the end of each week, they were tested before they could advance to the next unit. A very individualized approach to learning, indeed.

Through this approach, Bob learned to appreciate the many ways students can reach an answer. The more he worked with students in an individualized manner, the more he saw their diverse ways of thinking. Over time, he noted how they each progressed at a different pace and by a unique route. He also found that one-on-one instruction enabled him to respond to each student's particular difficulties. Bob recalled:

> This individualized instruction was something I had never tried before. And it was something that made me realize that it's important to sit down with a kid and let him struggle to solve a problem so that you can learn to ask him questions without giving him a direct answer, but ask him leading questions that will lead him to an answer. And hopefully, when you structure things that way, the kid will learn to look at problems from perhaps his own perspective, where he generates the idea of one or more solutions. And you have enough knowledge that you can ask him questions so that he leads himself to his own solution or her own solution.

Within a few years this kind of individual instruction became impossible. Classes grew in size and Bob had more sections to teach. It became harder to pay attention to each student. But now, about 10 years into teaching, Bob favored individualized learning for the challenges it brought to him and his students, and no longer because he was afraid of being caught not knowing physics. He sought ways to maintain the individualized attention within the new constraints.

Extending His Reach

The year 1985 was a turning point in Bob's teaching career. He joined the American Association of Physics Teachers' (AAPT) outreach program, Physics Teaching Resource Agent (PTRA), which had experienced physics teachers train their peers. Bob became a trainer of teacher-trainers. It turned out to be an opportunity for him to see that while dealing with basic concepts, physics can also be fun for both teachers and students. He gained teaching expertise, taking the responsibility to share his skills with other physics teachers. He joined the Tucson Area Physics Teachers, a group of local physics high school teachers and professors from the University of Arizona, which since then meets once a month to discuss physics and the teaching of physics.

Again, his learning had an impact in his classroom. Other physics teachers demonstrated to him that he could "let his hair down": to gain students' motivation and enthusiasm for physics, it is all right to be an energetic crusader. He learned to integrate serious work with the fun and joy of learning. He realized that he was becoming the science leader in his school, the champion of physics, and that it was legitimate to use that role to draw students to his class. His physics class grew to five sections. Then he actively helped to change the order of the science curriculum in his school. Now, physics was offered before chemistry and biology. This move had to withstand resistance, especially from parents who felt that it degraded the course and made it less appealing to colleges. Bob also became aware that few girls were drawn to his classes. Intrigued by the phenomenon, he sought ways to make physics more inviting to them. And, he realized that the "low-achieving" students were also left out. These were the kinds of students he first taught, and now he wanted to engage them in better science learning. He began to look for ways to involve these underrepresented groups in doing more science. Bob was also concerned that his science teaching was becoming outdated by the lack of newer technology. He sought ways to introduce computers and MBL interfacing devices to his teaching.

Bob continued to seek ways to expand his use of science projects, which he saw as incorporating his individualized learning perspective, and also a way to stay in touch with other physics teachers. Two opportunities converged that allowed him to continue to pursue his learning and also to respond to the new emerging needs. Duane, the industrial arts teacher in his school brought to his attention a grant that they could receive if they taught a new curriculum,

Principles of Technology (PoT), that was being pushed by the State Board of Education. Under this grant, they could receive state-of-the-art technology, better enabling Bob to teach the "lower end" students who take industrial arts. Bob decided to apply for the grant, but he disliked the curriculum. He felt that it was excessively structured and did not fit his emerging teaching style. He sought ways to modify it, to bring it closer to his way of teaching.

LabNet was another opportunity. It emphasized projects, collaborative work with other teachers, and use of computers and telecommunication. At this point Bob placed LabNet's conception of science projects in his framework of individualized learning. This would change.

Bob's LabNet Experience

A physics teacher friend, who participated in LabNet's first year workshop, told Bob that it was fun and had good things to offer. Bob decided to try it, and he joined the project in its second year, 1990.

In the 1990 workshop, teachers were encouraged to build projects for their classes. Bob crafted a car with a small motor, which pulled itself up an inclined plane, and then he measured the input and output of energy. He thought of it as a project that could help students learn about the conservation of energy.

The project was small. However, it prompted Bob to reflect about the learning environment he wanted physics students to experience. The project was a culminating moment of learning, which resulted in a new way of thinking. The thought of doing a project in phased segments as a way of teaching came into sharp focus:

> It was funny. Once I started thinking about teaching a year-long science course, then it was easy to come up with other phases that fit around that one idea that I got. So now we have essentially six phases. And it carries us through the whole year in terms of the projects that these kids do.

The car project became the heart of the work he planned for the students of PoT. Over the 1990-1991 academic year, he and Duane prepared the six-phase project. In the first phase, the students design and build a car that rolls with a constant velocity down an inclined plane. To do this, they use a computer-aided design program on the Macintosh. In the second phase, they build an accelerometer to put onto their car. Then, in the third phase, their task is to put an electric motor on the car so that it will move at a velocity between 5 and 15 centimeters per second. This requires the students to work with gears or pulleys. In the fourth phase, they measure the efficiency of the electric motor attached to the car. In the fifth phase, they modify the car to carry various loads at a constant speed, using additional sets of wheels that vary the friction. Finally, in the last phase students design a way to put energy into the car. Each person has to put into the car a specific number of joules of energy from an electrical or mechanical source. Then the cars are tested to see whose car will travel the farthest on that given quantity of energy.

Things fell into place, and Bob shifted from focusing on individualized learning to doing science projects—a new "road," one that he recognized has limits, but a road he firmly believed could enhance science learning. In the case of the PoT curriculum, he scrapped the textbook.

Along with becoming acquainted with LabNet's approach to projects, Bob was intrigued by LabNet's explicit advocacy of linking teachers across the curriculum—which was what he and Duane were trying to do. Telecommunication had been used in his district by the State Board of Education to communicate with teachers, but few responded. It was, some teachers believed, an attempt by the board to use the network to exert more control over their work. In another telecommunication project, initiated by a professor of education at the University of Arizona, a chemistry teacher from Bob's school became part of an international network, linked with classes in Israel that discussed ecological problems.

Bob's experience with telecommunication in the summer workshop made him aware of its potential to connect students, and led him to think about ways to integrate it into his teaching. With funding from the Principles of Technology grant, Bob and Duane purchased Appletalk and network equipment. Together they designed an interdisciplinary course that combined their science and industrial arts courses and used the local area network to do a project. In the physics classroom, students were given a problem that required them to design a piece of equipment in order to solve it. They then sent their specifications to the industrial arts classroom, where they created a mock-up of equipment using a computer-aided design program, and then built it. The students then tested the prototypes in the science class.

Reaching Out to Other Teachers

Bob's second year with LabNet was another transition, in which he changed his mode of providing teachers with learning opportunities. As a PTRA Bob had trained teachers to do what he knew best. He provided them with demonstrations they were expected to replicate in their classes. However, if projects are what students should do, teachers need to be prepared for that kind of work. His own participation as a learner in LabNet's summer workshop showed him that the experience of doing projects had a big impact on teachers. He therefore wanted the participants to experience doing projects themselves: To come up with a design; to build; to feel the uncertainty and inadequacy that often emerge when one gets stuck while doing a project; to come up with questions; to construct their own ways of teaching the materials; to collaborate. In the process, he wanted them to become aware of interdisciplinary opportunities in their schools—and the difficulties in doing interdisciplinary work.

Teachers change, Bob felt, when they are exposed to alternative ways of teaching. But there is a thin line that must be walked between merely doing more of the same and suggesting too radical an alternative. Workshops that fit too closely with what teachers already do will only reinforce their current mode of work. A far-out alternative will lead to resistance and probably rejection. Bob wanted his workshop to present a viable alternative to the current curriculum and way of teaching, but one that would make sense to teachers.

Through the Big Idea Grants that LabNet offered, Bob ran a very well-received workshop for 16 of his colleagues in Arizona. In it he introduced collaborative and interdisciplinary work among industrial arts and physics teachers. The workshop also served to test possible links between the mathematics curriculum and the car-building project in his school. (This workshop is described in greater detail in chapter 4.)

For Bob, the Big Idea Grants program was an opportunity to reinforce and affirm his personal change by leading teachers in his school and state in a similar direction. It also helped him to consolidate his emerging, project-based teaching approach. The successful workshop turned Bob and his school into a magnet force in Arizona, attracting other teachers toward interdisciplinary, project-based efforts in their own arenas. Needless to say, whether workshop participants actualize what they learned remains in their own hands. But now they have really *experienced* an effective alternative to the traditional curriculum and teaching.

The changes in Bob's teaching are only a step along the way. He is now applying for an NSF grant to continue to disseminate his workshop to more science teachers in Arizona. His school district administrators have become aware of his work and are actively supporting his efforts. And, as shown in the beginning of the case, his physics teaching now regularly incorporates more collaborative student-inquiry oriented activities.

A TEACHING FAST START

— Geriann Walker, Elmira High School, Elmira, Oregon —

Geriann Walker is a young science teacher in her fourth year of science teaching. In the constant pursuit of improving science education for her students and herself, she has been able to generate new alternatives for science teaching and professional growth, not known before in her school or district.

Students

The bell has just sounded—five students are already working. John[2] discusses his project with his teacher, Geriann. A senior, John is a bright student who is a self-taught computer user and loves programming. At home he spends most of his time programming and tinkering with robotic toys. In the beginning of his senior year he thought about dropping out, feeling that school simply was not relevant. His difficulty with school structure was apparent in Geriann's research class. John wanted to build a small robot programmed to "learn" to avoid obstacles as it goes through an obstacle course. But in the beginning John found it extremely difficult to break down the project into daily tasks, manage his time, and achieve results on schedule. A series of discussions with Geriann followed, which resulted in a structured, doable project. John now works on his project by himself in the library, where the computers are located. He is also working on a program that will do the data analysis for Melanie's project.

Melanie is a senior. Melanie sits by the computer; she is responsible for downloading and filing LabNetwork messages directed to Geriann. But now, she waits intently to see if she has received any responses to her inquiry. A week ago, she posted a note on the LabNetwork Forum. In it she asked for schools to volunteer to be part of her national sample of a survey of students' attitudes toward their school sports programs. She has already received two positive responses from LabNet participants, from the southern and eastern parts of the United States. Now, she hopes that schools from the west and north will join her study. This way she will be able to sample about 200 students.

This year, school funds in Elmira hit rock bottom. As a result, students have had to pay for all intramural sports activities. Melanie's favorite sport, field hockey, was suspended because the students could not afford the coach's salary. Her dance team was about to suffer a

---

[2] All students' names are fictitious.

similar fate, but the participating girls came up with the needed funds. This led Melanie to wonder if sports were being treated the same way at all schools. Her research project seeks an answer to this question. Geriann referred her to other teachers in the school. With help from a team of teachers—sports, math, and social studies—she developed a survey questionnaire and research design.

Sitting by Melanie's side at the computer is Jim. He too is waiting to see if there are responses to an inquiry he made. Jim loves cars. He wants to test the drag on various car models and suggest ways to improve them, but does not know the formula used to calculate drag, nor the procedure to test it. Geriann wants to learn more as well. She has encouraged Jim to post a message in LabNetwork Forum, asking other physics teachers to provide him with more information. Jim will have Ray as a partner in his experiments. Ray is interested in the impact of air patterns on airplane wings. Together Jim and Ray will build a wind tunnel to test air flow over model cars and aircraft. Ray sits at his desk. He reads through a book that describes various wing designs.

Tim walks over to Geriann's desk to ask for help. He is not making progress in his music project and he is concerned. "He is not pushing himself," she says to herself. A large measure of how the students get evaluated is the extent of their personal effort in relation to their capabilities.

These six students are taking part in a research class Geriann started last year. Next year, 10 students (5 girls) have already "booked" a place. Still in its infancy, the idea for the course came out of Geriann's first year with LabNet. It is her attempt to give additional opportunity to students in her school to pursue their own scientific interests through involvement in projects. Although many teachers might envy her small classes, Geriann has been able to create for herself and her students learning environments that are more suitable than the typical science classroom. The course symbolizes Geriann's position in her school and the professional growth she has achieved as a young teacher.

The Love of Science Teaching

Elmira High School is located in a small community outside of Eugene, Oregon. Elmira is in transition. Until lately, the town lived off the timber industry. But now, with the decline of logging, its citizens find themselves seeking other jobs in Eugene. At the same time Eugenians have been making Elmira their "bedroom."

To get to Elmira, one drives through cleared, flat farming land. At the road intersection leading to the school, cows chew grass at their casual pace—the image of a rural school. But this image does not hold for the pace of school culture and for Geriann's classes. Student involvement is high. Students and teachers are busy maintaining their school's social and administrative life. This is the home of the Falcons, strong contender for the state's football title. At the front office, students have taken over many of the secretarial duties, trying to limit the diversion of school funds to such tasks.

For Geriann, teaching at Elmira is keeping the beauty of a life she appreciates, at the same time maintaining a high level of learning for students and professional growth for herself. It matters to Geriann that students in rural communities get opportunities to expand their scientific knowledge and become more informed about their surroundings, particularly about environmental issues. Science education could also be a ticket for them to go beyond their community, by continuing on to higher education.

Geriann's roots are in Eugene, where she grew up and studied. As a teenager, Geriann already knew that she wanted to teach. But at the time her interests were in English and history, which she studied when she first enrolled at Reed College. Then she attended chemistry courses taught by a bold and enthusiastic female professor and was captivated. She decided to major in chemistry. She became a teaching assistant at the university, and had opportunities to continue as an academician. Here she drew the line. Geriann wanted to work with others, to teach, not to do research. At the university she felt professors were too busy doing research to devote themselves to teaching. Teaching high school students seemed to her a better choice—a choice that would enable her to share her knowledge with others. She applied to the one place where she wanted to teach and got the job. She sees herself now as part of the local school and community, with no desire to wander any further.

Professional Fusion

In her first year, Geriann taught physical science and physics. Now, being the only science teacher who teaches both physics and chemistry, she alternates the courses each year. This has turned out well: It gives her more time to incorporate the training and experience she gains from various workshops.

There was little in her university training that prepared her for the daily realities of teaching; there was much attention on the breakdown of pedagogical tasks—which teachers rarely have time to do. In her only course on educational media, she learned how to work the 16mm projector and a slide projector.

She started teaching physics using what she knew. Physics involved the use of a textbook, crunching one chapter after another, with students doing labs constrained to yield the "right" results. In physical science she again followed the prescribed textbook. But for Geriann the orderly class with its anticipated results and orderly students was a red flag. It signaled to her that unless she took the initiative to shape her classes and her own professional growth according to her principles, she would be in a rut for the rest of her career. She noticed that one of the reasons for teachers' stagnation is their isolation and limited initiative in seeking opportunities for professional growth. They tend to "putz around," she commented, so careful of their time and determined to minimize their involvement. She decided not to stall, but push ahead. Thus, her first year of teaching became a point of personal commitment to become an expert both in science and in pedagogy.

Coincidentally, early that year she received an invitation from the University of Oregon to join an MBL workshop. At first, frightened by the prospect of meeting other teachers and exposing her "green" state of teaching knowledge, and feeling overwhelmed by the demands of her first year of teaching, she was about to pass on the invitation, but a good friend convinced her to go. The workshop, which displayed various MBL interfaces, excited her. It showed her the possibilities for using computers to display and manipulate real data. And it showed her ways to teach physical concepts in a more inquiry-oriented way. At the workshop she also met other teachers who came to share their know-how and to learn new ways of teaching. She returned to Elmira recharged, with new equipment for teaching, and with a list of teachers who became part of her professional network.

Geriann became aware of the need to "toot her own horn" about the things she does, so that people would be aware of her work. Following her workshop she wrote an article for the local newspaper describing the equipment she received for improving science teaching, and the kinds of new activities in which she planned to involve students. The article led to inquiries from the school board about her work. In contrast to the reaction of most teachers, who see school officials as a threat, Geriann invited the superintendent and the board of education to come to her class to see her work with the new tools. They came, and they liked what they saw. The superintendent found himself joining students in experimenting with the MBL equipment. He got hooked. And he was impressed by how Geriann implemented what she learned at the workshop.

Gathering Professional Momentum

A University of Oregon staff member told Geriann about the LabNet project. She came to the first summer workshop. Again, she loved the connections with dedicated and experienced physics teachers. These men and women, mainly from another generation of teachers, became fond of the young teacher who was eager to learn. But they had a hard time hiding their skepticism about how long she could sustain her enthusiasm, before being burned out by routine demands of the educational system.

Geriann came away with the lists of projects that LabNet staff gathered from teachers and distributed to participants. Back in Elmira, that book became a useful project-idea resource. She also liked the idea of linking classrooms by use of telecommunication, especially to get students into dialogues with other students. Students, she felt, need more channels of communication with their peers, without adult intervention. They need forums to explore their knowledge, something networks can provide. In her comments on the fall 1990 Survey of LabNet participants (described in chapter 1) she called on LabNet to stress more than it does the development of projects that utilize the network for sharing data and data analysis. Science reports, she argued, are "dead" products of "assembly-line teaching." Students need, she said, to interact with a "peer audience," to write and discuss their ideas. She asked for a phone line for her classroom to be dedicated to telecommunication. The school district agreed— certain that she would make good use of it.

To fund the research class and projects in other classes, Geriann formed an afternoon science club. Following the suggestion of a fellow LabNetter, she solicited contributions from local businesses. They became the main source of funds for the club and project support. The club also funds its activities by collecting recyclable paper and by cleaning the stands after football games. These activities provide the club and Geriann with visibility in the community.

Reflecting on her experience back home, Geriann felt that the LabNet workshop didn't fully discuss the inherent tensions between projects and the standard curriculum, which had been clear to her from her first year of teaching. But also apparent to her was that working in teams in an exploratory mode could generate enthusiasm among students. And she liked LabNet's curricular focus on real-world, socially relevant topics, such as radon seepage and radioactivity, which she felt would excite the interest of her students.

The second LabNet summer workshop focused much more on the critical barriers to doing projects in science teaching. Geriann liked the "philosophy" sessions, because they raised the problems that arise in attempting to integrate projects within the current curriculum. Listening to experienced teachers and the issues they faced prepared her for the obstacles and objections she might confront if she eventually goes in this direction.

For the time being, Geriann decided on a different solution, however. She separated projects from the regular science classes. Because she had established her credibility as a science teacher, her school principal was ready to let her start a new science research projects class. The principal too saw the potential that Geriann envisioned, for such a course to become a magnet for students interested in science beyond the standard subject matter. The class was launched in Geriann's second year of teaching.

When LabNet offered the Big Idea Grants, Geriann seized the opportunity. Her Big Idea was to develop an interdisciplinary, project-based curriculum that would involve the other two science teachers at Elmira in using the network. Gary and Ron are veteran science teachers. Geriann continuously nudged them to explore new ways of teaching. At first it was not easy for the two teachers to accept Geriann as a leader. But when they saw that her interest was not in encroaching on their turf but in sharing the wealth, they became more open to her suggestions. Her idea also included a trial of the new materials she developed. She connected with Tom, a LabNet participant who also teaches in rural Oregon. His Big Idea Grants focused on training rural teachers to use telecommunication, specifically, the LabNetwork. These teachers would serve as a field test of Geriann's new curriculum, while they learned to use the network.

The LabNet conference on "Communicating About Project Science" (see chapter 1) was useful to Geriann in another way. She again saw the importance of focusing on teaching approaches, instead of technology or teaching procedures. She appreciated the direction taken in the conference, of treating the teachers as experts in assisting each other. And, she liked the time provided for teachers to share ideas and demonstrate what each one was doing.

After the conference, Geriann worked for 2 weeks with Gary and Ron. Together they designed a unit that fit with Gary's biology and Ron's earth science curricula. They chose to take an interdisciplinary perspective on ecology and biome studies. At the same time Geriann developed a unit on acid rain for her chemistry class. The unit was to involve students in "classroom and fieldwork investigations [which] are designed to be used in conjunction with a telecommunication network," they wrote in the introduction. Their aim, they added, "is to encourage collaborative student-designed projects as a regular feature of the chemistry and biology curriculum in senior high schools." They also envisioned, as a result of the integrative study, more collaboration among the three of them.

By the beginning of the 1991 academic year, the materials were ready to field test. It was left to Ron and Gary to begin to use what they prepared. They are now beginning to use the network, seeking partners to work with, and trying out the unit. Will they follow through? Geriann is not fully certain. There are enough incentives *not* to do projects: the increased time commitment, the messiness of the classroom, the diversity of student response, and the continual surprises.

Students' Experiences of Science

Now in her fourth year of teaching, Geriann feels that she is "light years ahead" of many of her peers. Science teaching, she has become convinced, is not only what is written in textbooks or demonstrated in labs. It is also responding to the kinds of questions students ask and attempt to answer about their physical environment. With her research class doubling in size, she now feels ready to focus her attention on improving her regular classes.

Projects are more difficult to introduce in her chemistry classes. The risks of having students experiment freely with chemical elements and with equipment are real. Yet Geriann has adapted chemistry labs to be more project-oriented, and she will introduce an acid-rain unit she developed this year. She has also introduced changes in the 9th- and 10th-grade physical science curriculum: When the students study motion, she has integrated mini-projects, such as launching a water-bottle rocket. The students also use MBL-interfacing equipment, like motion detectors, to study concepts of acceleration, velocity, and force, as well as misconceptions about motion. Geriann stresses the use of the computer because it helps the students learn to do graphical analysis of data. And, more important, they learn to interpret graphs and connect what they see in the data with the movement of actual objects.

Once the students have a good grasp of the concepts, they work on the Descent of a Ball project, which captured her attention during the first LabNet workshop. She liked the idea of projects that ask students to design and build. As part of this exercise, students construct a meter-high structure using paper, tape, and paper clips, to slow the descent of a golf ball. The students receive a list of concepts they need to incorporate in their designs. Then they practice creating triangular supports. Following these preparations, the teams are given time to come up with their plans. When they do, they send the plans via the LabNetwork to Tom's class, which is part of the competition. His teams of juniors then relay back their suggestions for improvements and also tell Geriann's students about their own designs. At that stage, the students are given three to four periods to construct their structures. Often, the sense of frustration and anxiety reaches its highest pitch at the first stage of implementation—that is where the abstract ideas are put to the test. This is a moment when the teacher's skill in helping students learn from experience is also tested.

In the second period of construction, Geriann has to miss a class—a price she hates to pay. Although she is aware that many teachers enjoy being away from class Geriann believes that outside involvements are at the students' expense. Nevertheless, her participation in school and district education activities occasionally demands her absence, especially because many of these activities are scheduled during school hours. This time, she has been asked by the county's director of curriculum to present the idea of projects and the use of telecommunication to other teachers.

After being absent for a class period, Geriann reviews her students' work on the Descent of the Ball task, and lets them know she is disappointed because she does not think they have used their time well. She then asks them to continue and walks to her desk. The class is like a beehive humming with activities. Students cut and paste pieces of paper, measure the various components, and roll the ball in trials.

One team is divided about the tasks and can't reach agreement about how to proceed. Geriann intervenes. She listens to them all, and then suggests a way that incorporates approaches proposed by two of the students.

At the end of the period, pleased by the students' progress, she lets them know that she appreciates their work. The students are evaluated on their teamwork, their attention to the structure, their incorporation of physics concepts they have learned, on the basic design idea, and on their suggestions for improving the project as they go along. The grade will be about 50% of the unit total.

One night, a school parents' conference is held. In preparation for it, Geriann has called 10 parents she especially wanted to come meet with her. This is part of her outreach. She believes that parents have much to do with their childrens' success or failure. Not all the invited parents show up. But at the meeting she meets with 40 parents representing about half of the students she teaches. She is pleased.

For Geriann, success is measured by the depth of students' involvement in learning science. This is the goal of all the workshops she attends, her efforts to involve parents, the time she spends with students in school. Geriann believes these activities on the part of teachers can improve learning when teachers perceive their careers as engaging projects—to be nurtured as long as they teach.

This is the kind of path she is trying to carve for herself.

SHAPING NEW PATTERNS OF SCIENCE TEACHING:
CONCLUSIONS

The full impact of LabNet has not yet been felt. It is clear that many teachers introduced projects into their classrooms as a result of the LabNet experience. This may well have been done on a trial basis, in the same way that other innovations might be tested. There was almost certainly no large-scale movement toward initiation of project-based courses.

At the same time, as seen most clearly in the cases of Bob Capen and Geriann Walker, there *are* teachers who go through a progression from conventional, textbook-lecture-lab teaching, through limited innovation involving increased use of demonstrations and hands-on learning, to adoption of a true, project-centered approach in at least some of their classes. How many others will eventually follow the same path remains to be seen.

Change, as we argued earlier, takes place slowly. There may be doubt or discomfort. Even when convinced that change is necessary and desirable, people often need to proceed by small steps. Many LabNet participants had been involved in innovation, but probably not of a radical kind. Even if convinced of the way to go, most recognized that it took time to prepare—or in some cases to get the needed equipment and assistance.

For now, we believe that the data presented in this chapter substantiate the following conclusions:

LabNet helped teachers to enrich their science teaching. LabNet enabled participants to learn new technological applications including telecommunication and microcomputer-based laboratories (MBLs). It helped many teachers to feel more comfortable with the use of both types of tools in their classrooms. To a lesser extent, but still with a considerable degree of success, the project disseminated its project-enhanced science-learning approach. A small but significant number of teachers went through a conceptual change in their teaching and took the difficult road of attempting to fully integrate projects into their science teaching.

The local work environment shaped the use that each teacher made of LabNet's innovations. For teachers, the work environment consists of their school, their classroom, and the constituents of the local educational system. These affected, in a mostly restraining way, what teachers were able to implement. For example, there were teachers whose administrations were not willing to provide a dedicated telephone line for telecommunication. Others lacked funds to buy equipment. And yet most teachers found ways to implement parts of LabNet. Many began to do projects in their classrooms. Some of the projects were organized activities where the entire class carried out the same activities (e.g., descent of a ball, or construction of a solar house or a paper tower). Other projects were taken up by individual students or teams of students. These ranged along the spectrum of the physics curricula.

Most of the teachers found ways to integrate the knowledge they acquired into their current ways of teaching. Many LabNet participants learned and used the LabNet materials. They improvised with these to fit their current ways of teaching. That is, they found meaningful ways to incorporate MBLs, telecommunication, and projects into their teaching routines. Most often, where changes in teaching were found, they need to be understood within the current practice of the teachers.

There were also a few teachers who saw their priorities as different from LabNet's and, therefore, chose not to engage their students in such learning.

The conclusions raise the issue of what kind of teacher preparation is needed to help teachers shift from the basal-text approach to PESL. One necessary condition for effective change is the supportive role a community of practice can undertake. Therefore, in the next chapter, we return to this issue following our discussion of the role of the community of practice in this project.

4 SUPPORT AND LEADERSHIP IN A COMMUNITY OF PRACTICE

Shahaf Gal

To what extent did LabNet succeed in building among its teachers a community of practice capable of sustaining the momentum of change? This is the question Shahaf Gal addresses here.

He first examines the opportunities that LabNet offered participants to give and receive peer support, focusing on two mechanisms specifically designed for that purpose—the Teacher Liaison Consultant (TLC) program and the LabNetwork itself. Although the TLCs suffered from some confusion about their roles, they provided technical and moral support for many participants and, for TERC, an invaluable link to the "front lines." The LabNetwork was used continuously by the majority of LabNet teachers, later joined by others who were brought in by the Big Idea workshops. E-mail gave them a conduit for conversations on a wide variety of topics—technical support, project ideas, thoughts about teaching, and social exchanges. The Forum served as a "public piazza" where groups of teachers could share shoptalk and converse about classroom activities of general interest. It also allowed teachers and students around the country to collaborate on multi site projects, one of which, the Eratosthenes project, is depicted in detail. The network has taken on a life of its own; as of this writing, it is still active.

Perhaps the most innovative and successful feature of LabNet was the Big Idea Grants program (BIG), which funded workshops that were initiated and run by LabNet teachers. The chapter includes case histories of two of them—one that brought together teachers of physics and industrial arts to collaborate in a design and construction project and one that brought hands-on project-enhanced learning to middle school teachers in rural Georgia.

The workshops reached hundreds of new teachers, most of whom had had few prior opportunities for in-service training and who were hungry for new ideas. Virtually all participants found the workshops valuable, and most intended to put what they had learned into practice. Clearly, LabNet teachers' understanding of the practical needs of colleagues in their local areas enabled them to strike a responsive chord. The BIG program proved to be not only a cost-effective means of dissemination but a source of genuine empowerment for LabNet teachers, enabling them to take leadership roles in their community of practice.

Introduction

The fabric of a community of practice is woven from the actions and interactions of individuals. In a community of teaching participants employ similar work practices, develop a similar teaching approach, use similar tools for that purpose, and communicate with people who share their interests. Relevant studies that use the term have been done by Lave and Wenger (1991), Wenger (1990), Star (1991), Star and Griesemer (1989), Latour (1987), Latour and Woolgar (1979), and Knorr-Cetina (1981). Riel (1987, 1990) and Levin, Riel, Miyake, and Cohen (1987) discussed the idea of electronic apprenticeship as part of a community of practice, and Bruce and Rubin (1992) discussed teacher collaborative work in Project Quill. For a developmental perspective on apprenticeship and cognitive development in a community of practice, see Lave (1988), Rogoff (1990), and Resnick, Levine, and Teasley (1991).

LabNet offered teachers new forms of community participation in an effort to nurture and invigorate the community, as well as to support individuals in changing their teaching practices. For example, the network gave teachers a way to share experiences, concerns, successes, and failures as they shifted toward project-enhanced teaching. Similarly, LabNet's summer workshops provided a forum for discussing projects, asking or providing assistance, and learning to use tools like MBLs and the network itself.

This chapter focuses on two kinds of community participation: giving and receiving peer support, and taking leadership roles. Most of the discussion is organized around three features of LabNet that were designed to facilitate such participation:

- **The Teacher Liaison Consultants (TLCs)**, eight experienced LabNet teachers who each provided ongoing teacher-to-teacher assistance to 12–15 peers.

- **The LabNetwork**, which functioned for many teachers as a central "city piazza," a meeting place for the whole community, where professional knowledge was exchanged.

- **The "Big Idea" Grants**, which provided financial support for teachers to take leadership roles in the community by sharing their knowledge with others, most of whom were new to the LabNet approach.

Community-Wide Support

We view teachers as professionals who are, or should be, continually trying to improve their practice. But to implement any educational innovation, teachers need support from other professionals who work in similar situations and whose collective experience can provide insight and helpful suggestions.

A rich body of literature describes the process of supporting the introduction of change in schools (Berman, Greenwood, McLaughlin, & Pincus, 1975; Hall & Hord, 1987; Hord, 1987). That schools have not changed has to do with the kinds of attempts to introduce change and with the criteria used to judge change (Popkewitz, 1984, 1987, 1991; Sarason, 1982, 1990). This important discussion is beyond the scope of this book. However, the reader is invited to critically examine and evaluate our findings against his or her own perceptions of change. To carry out such a discourse is an imperative for any community of practice.

The need for support among LabNet teachers was confirmed by the May 1991 teacher questionnaire. Teachers were asked how much support they needed in order to implement the program (Gal, Lockett, & Parrott, 1991; see also Appendix C). Fifteen percent reported that they needed extensive support, 63% reported a moderate need, and only 22% saw no need at all.

Anticipating this need, the project had incorporated a three-pronged support system, consisting of the workshops, TLCs, and the network. As Table 4.1 shows, teachers drew on these and other sources of support. The majority of participants (59%) reported turning to other teachers on the network. Some (44%) turned to TERC staff, and 26% turned to TLCs. Other sources of support included administrators and teachers within their own schools. There was also some indication of the use of other support organizations or networks (AAPT, PTRA, Woodrow Wilson Fellows)—an outcome that speaks well for the positive impact of other programs seeking to enhance physics education.

TABLE 4.1
Support for Implementing LabNet

When You Needed Support, to Whom did You Turn?*	
Teachers on the network	59%
TERC staff	44
Other teachers in my school	34
School administrators	30
Teacher Liaison Consultants	26
Other	15
* Respondents checked as many sources as were applicable.	

Let us now examine more closely the two of these sources that were specifically established by LabNet as mechanisms to provide ongoing support to teachers in their school environments—TLCs and the network.

THE TEACHER LIAISON CONSULTANT (TLC) PROGRAM[1]

The TLC program was a modest innovation, created by LabNet staff in response to a perceived need. It was designed to support working teachers from widely diverse geographical areas. Eight experienced teachers were each linked with 12 to 15 of their LabNet peers, using the telecommunication network.

By encouraging collegial partnerships among physics teachers and by focusing on "support" rather than "instruction," LabNet intended the TLC program to promote and enhance professional growth among participants. In addition, although the program was itself small, it was designed to serve LabNet's larger goals:

> *Advancing project-enhanced learning,* by providing a way for teachers to share information and address such critical questions as: What problems are encountered while initiating projects in the classroom? What solutions are explored? What works? What doesn't work?

> *Fostering a community of practice,* through communication between teachers and TLCs, thus helping to reduce teachers' sense of isolation.

> *Encouraging the use of telecommunication technology,* as teachers became accustomed to using the network to communicate with TLCs.

As in any new program, it was necessary to stretch and pull the original concept to accommodate the realities of implementation. Particularly intense feelings were generated around the question of how to carve the TLCs' role in a way that fit with both expectations and reality. Teacher Liaison Consultants experienced moments of frustration and anxiety, and at other times moments of inspiration, satisfaction, and accomplishment. Their experience has broader implications for the design and effective functioning of peer-support programs, which we explore below.

Selection and Training

In March 1990, eight teachers were selected from among the 1989 LabNet participants to become Teacher Liaison Consultants for the 1990-1991 academic year. Selection was based on the teachers' first year of participation in LabNet and took into account their eagerness to share information as well as their teaching approach. Many of the eight chosen teachers had incorporated projects into their curricula and were adept at using technology as well. Most had previous experience training other teachers.

---

[1] This section is based on two internal evaluation reports, one prepared by Shahaf Gal and the other by Paula Marshall (TERC, 1991).

Each TLC signed an agreement with TERC accepting the roles and responsibilities, which were: (a) to assist participants during the summer workshops; (b) to establish a collegial relationship with 12–15 teachers they had met at one of the four workshops; (c) to develop and write a 1-year plan with each participating teacher; (d) to follow up on each teacher's progress, offering assistance as needed during the year to help teachers carry out their plans; and (e) to submit reports to LabNet staff on their teachers' progress on a regular basis. Each TLC received $3,000 for the year as a honorarium for his or her participation.

In June 1990, the first of five summer workshops was held at Tufts University. During the 9 days of that workshop, the TLCs, along with the other LabNet members, received hands-on experience with various project activities and materials, telecommunication equipment, computer interfaces, and MBLs. One half-day of discussion was set aside for TLC training. This was the first and only time that all of the TLCs were able to meet as a group to discuss and elaborate the goals of the program.

The remaining four workshops were held in July and August at several sites around the country: Dickinson College, Northwest Regional Educational Laboratory, Tufts University, and the University of Michigan. Two TLCs were assigned to each workshop. It was during these workshops that the TLCs began their 1-year association with the teachers in their group.

The summer workshops were the launching pad for the year's activities. During the workshops, the TLCs were expected to meet informally with their group of teachers, to talk about individual classroom and teacher's needs, and then to develop an individualized plan, which would be followed up throughout the year.

Working With Teachers

In the 1990 fall survey (Gal, 1990c), 65% of the respondents anticipated that the TLCs would have a moderate or large impact on their participation. In contrast, about a fourth (26%) of the LabNet respondents indicated on the teacher questionnaire in the spring of 1991 that they had actually sought the assistance of their TLCs. That the TLCs were used less than anticipated may be due to the newness of the concept, to the way the process of providing assistance was designed and carried out by the TLCs, or to teachers' reluctance to accept the TLC role.

To learn about the TLC program, five TLCs and the program director were interviewed midway, in January 1991. TLCs were asked about their work helping other teachers. In the spring of 1991, the program was jointly evaluated by the project evaluator and the TLCs. The unique evaluation design used the LabNetwork to create a final report on the program, based on both the TLCs' individual and shared experiences and comments.

Becoming One of the Chosen Few

The teachers chosen to become TLCs felt honored, but many were not sure why they had been selected. Some were insecure about their skills and were somewhat intimidated by the competent group of physics teachers they were expected to "lead." Some were concerned about the teacher responses to the role of the TLC because power and position also come with being chosen, something not all the TLCs felt comfortable with. "When anyone is set apart in a group of this talent, the outcome is usually the same. It's Newton's Fourth Principle of Human Nature—WHY THEM?"

Others were acutely aware of their own feelings, and some began to seek a strategy to construct their roles effectively.

> My first thoughts of being associated with the TLC Program were riddled with insecurities. However, during the summer workshop it became apparent that no one was an expert on all three components [MBL, telecommunication, projects]. Also, it was very apparent that everyone present was quite comfortable with at least one of the three. Therefore, my rationale and strategy began to form. Help the strong become stronger and nibble at the rest with encouragement.

Role Confusion

Many TLCs wrote in their final reports that they were confused in the beginning about the actual goals of the program and their role in reaching those goals: Were they supposed to get teachers on-line, or to encourage teachers to do projects in the classroom, or to support the use of MBL when doing projects? How should they proceed if a teacher did not want to or could not do any of the three? Consider these three responses:

> When we began this summer, we (or at least I) were under the impression that the goal was to get people on-line, to promote LabNet, and get people involved in the forum. By the time we had finished the summer sessions, the emphasis had shifted to project-based physics and how to implement some form of it in the classroom.

> When [the Coordinator] recruited me, he indicated that I was going to fulfill a role analogous to the role that he had filled the previous summer. I saw this as a kind of ombudsman–troubleshooter for TERC. I believe the project leadership lost a sharp focus on the project goals prior to the summer. I saw LabNet as largely a telecommunication project with an interest in advocating greater use of MBL and projects. I did not see the bottom line as fostering the use of projects in science classrooms and supporting this goal with telecommunication and MBL. I believe I would have proceeded differently if this had been clear to me.

> The focus seemed to shift as time went by. As I said in my initial reaction, it seemed that we had three foci instead of one focus. Optics tells us that it gets fuzzy without one focus.

TLCs' confusion about the goals and priorities of the program was understandable, since these had evolved over time. The TLCs were LabNet members during the first year of the project, when the goal had been to increase the use of the telecommunication network among teachers, and many TLCs responded to that call. But during the 1990 summer workshops, LabNet's goals crystallized into a more cohesive format focused on project-enhanced science learning. The TLCs' mission was not adequately redefined in response to the new task.

The plan for a year-long collaboration between the TLCs and their teams of teachers did not materialize. As a result, the TLCs defined their roles differently than first imagined, and began to set their own criteria.

Carving Out the TLC Role

How best should the TLCs assist teachers? The TLCs had to confront this question on their own. The original plans had faltered and no alternative plans were offered by TERC; the TLCs were working with limited directions as to how to perform their roles; and there was little communication among the TLCs themselves. Yet, above all, most of them remained dedicated to trying to assist their fellow teachers.

Most often, teacher support is provided within a predefined context that includes: (a) an assumed awareness of what the teachers do; and (b) a hierarchically structured relationship that stresses the knowledge and authority of the trainer over the trainee. This is the model common among the helping professions, and is similar to the model of manager–subordinate. In both models there is a clear understanding of who is the client (or the boss), who is in charge, and how assistance is to be offered. For example, a psychologist is recognized as a person who provides professional help to people who have emotional problems. This "objectification" creates the great divide between the "helper" and the "patient."

For an example of these issues in psychology and education, see Rogers (1951, 1969). The constraints of such helping relationships are also demonstrated in the works of Argyris and Schon (1974), Schon (1983, 1987), and Putnam (1991). These authors demonstrate that helping relationships constructed around power and expertise alone often create conditions that exacerbate the situation they attempt to resolve, and therefore limit professional learning.

In a community of practice, where professionals bring multiple kinds of expertise, it is likely that any one person will master some aspects of the profession but need help in other areas. Therefore, the traditional model of assistance is not conducive to a supportive role in a community of professionals, in which everyone is at the same time a helper and a learner.

The TLCs sought a collaborative helping mode that fit the situation they faced: working with geographically distant peers. Some spent time on outreach, trying to make first contact with their assigned teachers. Others were predominantly troubleshooters, helping teachers only when there was a problem with equipment, and so forth. And many focused on helping teachers to get on-line, or even more fundamentally, to get the equipment they needed in order to get on-line.

The kind of help offered by TLCs varied as they responded to the needs their teachers presented. Some TLCs worked with very experienced teachers and shaped their role to be mainly facilitative, focusing on shared experiences. For example, one TLC wrote:

> Many of the participants were more talented, experienced (with both computers and projects). [What] was I supposed to establish with these individuals? My approach was to try and build friendships built on mutuality rather than some notion of superior (me) to inferior (the participant). Within this circle, my role as a TLC is of secondary importance. We interact as equals with a common interest, science and science teaching. I imagine that this would have happened whether or not I was a TLC. For me, it reaffirmed the value of telecommunication in breaking down teacher isolation and establishing a community of science educators.

Others worked with less experienced teachers and had to help them with technical and logistical issues. For example, one TLC helped a teacher to figure out an alternative to the Control-Z "send message" function so he could send messages on his Mac Plus, which doesn't have a Control key. This sounds like a small technical matter, but it was of critical importance for his use of the network. Another TLC helped a teacher who was new to telecommunication to use the Talk Is Cheap software. Some TLCs helped teachers prepare their Big Idea Grants.

At times the TLCs were called to assist teachers in dealing with their administration. This was where the TLCs often met "The Wall" of resistance in a school system. These tended to be frustrating experiences. One TLC described his encounter:

> An example that was a little more frustrating was the case of Ed. I called and found out there was no movement on the part of his Principal. I wrote what I thought was a very good letter to the Principal but it didn't change her mind. I didn't get the impression that this was a case of we can't do it, just a case of we won't do it. Although it was a failure in terms of getting Ed on-line, I feel successful in doing what I could and was supposed to do. I also know that Ed is carrying through with the concepts of projects, and that is good.

> Jeanne had difficulty with her central office administration concerning the obtaining of hardware and telephone lines. It seems that the central office staff did not feel that it was necessary for her to get on-line with the rest of the TERC staff. A letter to the higher-ups may have helped to generate some movement, although not exactly in the preferred direction. She still ran into a stone wall with respect to TERC. The communication did not last long once it was determined that the central office was not going to budge.

A serious challenge for TLCs arose when teachers chose *not* to ask for help, or when the attempts to communicate and to provide assistance were rejected. One TLC recalled, "I was surprised that some of my people seemed to resent (or at least were embarrassed) when I contacted them in January." At the same time, there were teachers who needed and wanted support but did not know how to ask for it. These reactions may have been due partly to the way in which help was offered, but probably the main cause was that asking for support—acknowledging the need, being willing to have another teacher know the need, having another teacher provide help—is not part of the standard repertoire of teaching. The sense of vulnerability, perhaps even shame often associated with seeking help needs to be overcome, a tough but worthwhile undertaking.

The difficulties of assisting teachers who did not want support frustrated some of the TLCs. "We seem to have all validated the old maxim," wrote one, "that you can lead a horse to water, but you can't make him drink."

The TLCs found that they had to navigate their work very delicately with their teachers. It was at that point that the TLCs needed to rely on their "people" skills to encourage the participants to communicate the needs and frustrations they were experiencing. This was a difficult role for some TLCs.

Proactive and Reactive Support Roles

As they worked, the TLCs shaped their roles using their past and current experience and personal "reading" of the situation. The TLCs defined their role as "helpers," "providers," or "on-call resource people." They developed different strategies. Some of the TLCs responded to their "helper" role proactively and others reactively. Each of the strategies had its advantages and pitfalls. The TLCs who chose a proactive stance attempted to *reach out* to the teachers.

> I provide encouragement and a sounding board for their ideas, problems, and efforts in the classroom, in school and on the forum. I communicate on the network with those who are currently on-line and send a note to all of them approximately once a month. For those who are not on-line, I make a phone call on a regular basis every 6–8 weeks. In my group, I have several teachers who are not responsive to these methods and are basically either not interested in being involved or have still not received equipment in order to get on-line. This last group responds positively to telephone conversations. I have come to realize how difficult it is to get someone on-line...they may need equipment that was promised, budget cuts...they are too busy with science fairs, Olympiad, recycling, and just plain good teaching to go on-line or they don't want to take part. The last group was the most difficult.

Proactive TLCs expected that their efforts would be appreciated and teachers would respond favorably to their efforts. The basic driving force for them was the desire to help those who needed help. The frustrations of TLCs who worked in this mode arose particularly when these efforts met resistance, when teachers "did not want to drink from the well." But most painful and frustrating were the situations when no response at all was received. "It is a waste of time," concluded one TLC, "to try to communicate with individuals who do not desire it." Another wrote: "What surprised me? The number of times I had to call to get in touch with some participants (and never actually reached a few by telephone), [and] the total lack of participation by others. I came to realize how difficult it is to get someone on-line."

As a result of his frustrating experiences in trying to assist teachers, one TLC shifted from a proactive to a reactive supportive role:

> People who do not want to be communicated with do not communicate. I sent out mailing (USPS) complete with self-addressed post cards—I got two back. I sent out mass mailings (e-mail)—I got no response. Several times I attempted to call but got no answer. I determined that the best way to get through to people was to wait until they needed, or at least perceived that they needed my help, and then I would respond to their needs...this seemed to work best.

Some TLCs chose a reactive stance to begin with, and waited to be called for help. One TLC wrote:

> An analogy would be like a waiter, there when you need him or her but not standing directly behind you at the table. [It] seems to me like being a TLC is sort of like being a member/sponsors of MADD or SADD or being a fireman or policeman. Success is measured in what doesn't happen, not what does happen. If you aren't needed, then that's better than if you are needed.

And another said,

> I was very pleased to help those who asked for assistance. I did lend a sympathetic ear to my charges who were not on-line much when I called them on the telephone.

Of course, a dilemma for those who chose a reactive role was how to judge their success, not knowing how much need there was for their services. An additional problem for this group was the constant waiting to be called. At times skills in detecting a need for support had to be used:

> One very successful interaction I have had as a TLC has been with Mike...in Alabama. Mike is a wonderful teacher with a terrific attitude. I became concerned about Mike not being on-line very often and contacted him by phone. I discovered that he was still trying to get equipment.

Teacher-to-Teacher Supportive Roles in a Community of Practice

Taking on a supportive role in a community of practice like LabNet is demanding because it is a nonroutinized task and because the work is with teachers who are at most times independent and capable. Teacher-to-teacher support, however, is essential in the making of a community of practice. A few lessons can be drawn from the TLC program about how such support can be effective.

First, a teacher-to-teacher support effort can work only when both sides are committed to change. The first weeks of classes during the school year are demanding for all teachers. Time and effort are cherished commodities, especially when a teacher is trying to learn new routines, adopt new teaching approaches. For both TLCs and LabNet teachers, balancing the ideals one is striving for with the realities of time constraints and fiscal limitations inherently creates struggles and demands compromise. Commitment to change can be the spark needed to overcome the discomfort of too much to do, not enough funds, or inadequate support from administration. Without commitment to change in classroom practices, a TLC program could never hope to accomplish its goals.

Second, a teacher needs not only peer support, but administrative support if he or she intends to design a new learning environment and to get through the difficult times. As the examples of the TLCs' interactions with school administration indicate, having more clout with administrators could have helped them function more effectively in their supporting role as well.

Third, teachers are not accustomed to being in a "learner" role, and for some, becoming a "learner" again is a source of resistance to seeking support. Perhaps a critical barrier is unwillingness to admit confusions, misconceptions, and difficulties. Teachers are often invested in being "right" and in control. In general, the classroom experience demands this of them, or so they have been trained. Allowing themselves to ask questions and admit their misconceptions requires practice in an environment where sharing the experience of being "wrong" is an important part of the formula for learning.

Such learning environments, where failure is part of the learning, are not easy to create. Generally, professionals tend to keep work-related problems private. To show them is considered a sign of weakness and perhaps even incompetency. Also, professionals usually lack forums to communicate and explore problematic issues—how can one share what is considered nonexistent (Argyris, Putnam, & McLain, 1985; Argyris & Schon, 1974, 1978)?

Fourth, a related difficulty is the fact that teachers are also not accustomed to the "helper" role; often professionals lack skills for assisting others (Schon, 1983, 1987). LabNet assumed that the TLCs' interpersonal skills would be ancillary to their experience and expertise in the realm of physics teaching. However, experience indicated that LabNet needed to focus more on crucial "people skills," the how-tos of being a provider of services. How does one build or encourage confidence in a colleague? How does one encourage participation when there is resistance? How does one provide assistance in a way that effectively responds to those in need of support?

I don't think anyone is really prepared for a job like being a TLC. I had all the communication and people skills, teaching experience, and general computer skills. However, these were not the only skills needed by a TLC. I found that I also needed patience, creativity in thinking, and more patience. I discovered that I developed skills as I worked with my people. I learned how to encourage those with little time and money, how to manage hostility due to lack of both of the above, and how to ask questions so that they provoked progress on the other end, not promote frustration.

Fifth, those in a supporting role need to have ways of interacting with and supporting each other. Most TLCs felt that group members needed to share their experiences with each other on a routine basis. Because the TLCs did not speak with one another regularly about their role, they did not know what other TLCs were experiencing. The TLCs often felt isolated, an ironic twist because the purpose of the program was specifically to reduce that feeling among teachers. Although they always had the LabNetwork's Managers Forum to use, most did not. Their desire to build solidarity and a vision of purpose, to have a place to discuss their strategies and a place to go for support was stated over and over in their final reports.

I think Nevin [Ranck] hit the nail on the head. If we, the TLCs had had time to work together to formulate a plan, set goals, etc., between Tufts and wherever, I think we would have been more focused.

If I were to continue as a TLC, I would want to share my experiences and ideas with the other TLCs, [and] then jointly develop a handbook of goals, timelines, procedures, strategies, resources, etc. I would like to [solve] typical problems, learn how to stimulate more dialogue on the network, and how to contact teachers who don't seem to want to hear from you.

The potential of such interchange emerged clearly during the evaluation effort. It was then that most TLCs saw for the first time their partners' experiences. Al Thompson wrote:

I see a lot of similarity in our responses. Mainly in the frustration of not being able to get more of our charges on-line or active in LabNet related activities. Now that I am aware that the other TLCs had similar experiences to mine, I feel better about what I was able to accomplish and less dissatisfied with my own performance as a TLC.

In retrospect, it seems that clearer structure for the TLCs' activities was needed and that someone had to orchestrate the group's activities. For example, when the evaluation of the program was conducted, all responded with much interest. More TLC solidarity would clearly not have been a panacea for all of their difficulties, but it would have given the TLCs a stronger support base, an on-going dialogue for suggestions, and a sounding board during their difficult and frustrating moments.

I believe that if we had had some time at Tufts last summer to work on a "handbook" of TLCing, then we could have been a more unified group...the nuts and bolts were not as clear as I would like them to have been.

In hindsight we probably should have had an evening or two as TLCs to develop forms, etc., to generate our reports so that they weren't so open-ended.

Finally, and more generally, almost any effort at educational innovation or reform can benefit by incorporating teacher-to-teacher programs in a community of practice. TLCs could achieve what project staff can rarely do—become attuned to the changes in the community and be very close to the situation. The effectiveness of a project like LabNet can only be enhanced by having "eyes and ears" grounded in teachers' reality.

We TLCs were to, among other things, find out what kind of influence the three-part LabNet program had on the participants. The relatively small group of TERC folks in Boston could never have done this.

The commitment and effort made by TLCs fanned an interest in project-based science. It introduced and, in some corners, encouraged and reinforced the use of a telecommunication network. Equally important, the TLC program gave participants experience and feelings of being active collaborators in shaping the implementation of LabNet.

For me it reaffirmed the value of telecommunication in breaking down teacher isolation and establishing a community of science educators.

The friendships, acquaintances, networkings, etc. have helped me in my classroom operation.

It's always a great feeling when you think you've been helpful to someone.

A NETWORK FOR PROFESSIONAL EXCHANGE

This section details teachers' use of the LabNetwork as a medium to support their professional activities. To examine teachers' participation on the network, three quantitative and qualitative longitudinal studies were performed from September 1990 to February 1992, covering a period of a 1 1/2 years. The first network study was from September to late December 1990. The second study covered January 1991, and the third was from October 1991 to February 1992. The complete findings from the first and second studies appear in Gal (1991, May).

Two basic analyses were performed: The first focused on patterns of network "logins." Login data (user name, date, time of day, time on-line) were automatically gathered and sent each day by Delphi, Inc., the network host. These daily reports were entered in a specially designed program that performed statistical analysis of the data (e.g., to generate the average time on-line per user during a certain period).

Second, qualitative studies of all network messages sent to the Forum were carried out during September 1–December 26, 1990 (311 messages or 81 per month) and December 27, 1990–January 31, 1991 (98 messages or 87 per month). Forum messages were downloaded and saved on a specially programmed Hypercard stack. The messages were coded by categories, such as content of message, sender and receiver, time period, and links with other messages (threads).

Participation on the Network

Every network relies on continuous use. Users need to stay up to date and frequently check on network activities, and most important, contribute messages. LabNetwork use increased dramatically during the period of the study, from 71 to 123 teachers. Fifty-two new teachers joined as a result of the Big Idea workshops in the summer of 1991. To an extent, two groups of network users formed—LabNet veterans and newcomers. Their patterns of use were different and reflect important trends of network growth.

Throughout the 18 months (September 1990–February 1992), most LabNet veterans (70%) persistently kept up with the network. Veterans who got on-line in 1990 continued to use the network during the whole period, on average once to twice a week. Among them, there was a small group of more intensive LabNetwork users, some of whom logged on to the network almost daily.

The newcomers joined the network mainly in the beginning of the 1991-1992 school year. During the 4-month study covering the time of their network activities, they averaged one to two calls a month—about half the rate of the veterans' group. The newcomers, it must be realized, joined on their own behalf without any direct assistance from TERC. Being aware of the difficulties in setting up and starting network communication, reported in the prior chapter and further elaborated in the next chapter, it can be considered an achievement to have them on-line.

The Forum: LabNetwork's "Piazza"

LabNetwork was designed for teachers to contribute to the network in any way in which they felt comfortable. There was no one "right" approach. For example, a user could simply login to read personal and public messages. Another could limit his or her use to private mail to send and receive messages. A third could both contribute to the public Forum and send/receive personal messages. These options reflect various levels of interest, needs or perhaps willingness for public involvement (and exposure).

Of the multiple ways to use the network, public network dialogues via the Forum are most important because they served as a basis for establishing a broad-based community of science teachers. The Forum was the *public domain* of the network. Metaphorically it served as the network's city "piazza" (a place where people gather to talk to each other) where teachers from 37 states could "meet." This is where LabNet teachers with diverse interests could post messages, read and respond to the messages of others, ask questions, receive answers, and provide assistance to fellow teachers.

In January 1991, 25 veteran teachers, representing close to one third of the veteran group of users, contributed at least one message to the Forum. In the final study about 1 year later, the number of teachers contributing messages to the Forum grew to 32. The additional members, perhaps, show a growing sense of the utility of the network.

Newcomers added very few messages to the Forum. Only five of them posted messages on the Forum. The slow growth of participation raises the issue of what could help make teachers feel more comfortable in contributing their expertise sooner. This issue is discussed in chapter 5.

Professional Discourse on the Network

Messages on the Forum reflected the professional interests of teachers at work. During the first period of the qualitative content study, 120 "threads" initiated by LabNet participants over the Forum were analyzed. A thread consists of all the connected messages on a given topic displayed on the Forum. Threads are started when at least one message is posted, with the intention of eliciting responses from other network members. Taken in sum, threads create the texture of the community of practice's professional discourse.

Teachers' professional discourse can be roughly divided between teaching activities and "shoptalk." Network dialogues in the teaching activities category are those directly related to classroom work—for example, a conversation between two teachers whose classes are collaborating on a project. Teachers also spend much time "talking shop"—gathering information about science activities and teaching aids, improving technological expertise, and seeking additional financial and technological resources. Such shoptalk is similar to that of auto mechanics, who ask each other about new places to buy reliable and reasonably priced tools, call another mechanic to discuss engine problems they cannot diagnose, and so on. Examples of shoptalk are common in the sociology-of-knowledge literature. Shoptalk among scientists and the theoretical perspective related to this approach can be found in Latour and Woolgar (1979) and Traweek (1988).

Professional discourse is a unique and very important kind of community support. This support is not organized and planned in advance. Rather, it is shared everyday knowledge and expertise offered on call. This kind of support rarely culminates in a big "Aha!" but rather in know-how that is immediately relevant to the business of the day.

Networks are particularly helpful in facilitating shoptalk discussions: The medium lends itself to short, concise, and informative discourse in response to a specific request. The Forum offers a place where quick suggestions and opinions can be gotten to a posted question.

Here we present examples of one teaching activity and a few shoptalk messages. The network messages are left as they were posted. The attempt is to preserve the pragmatic, rough—sometimes messy—yet very much to the point, everyday language used in professional network discourse. Their purpose is to get the job done. The shoptalk examples show the date and time messages were sent. These serve as place markers. They also help provide a sense of the pace of network activities and show when teachers find time to work—usually late at night or early in the morning.

Most schools are currently not organized to support such activities throughout the day. Nor do they recognize the importance of such network activities to the professional growth of a teacher. To understand the potential benefits, one should ask while reading these examples: Where can I receive such information at my workplace? What ways do I currently have to assist me in knowing about resources, and for testing new ideas?

Teaching Activities: The Eratosthenes Project

Eratosthenes was a Greek mathematician and astronomer who lived in the third century AD, who accurately estimated the circumference of the earth. His method was to determine at exactly the same time the angle the sun's rays make with the vertical in two locations different in latitude (north to south; see the glossary at the end of chapter 1). For students, such a project is intriguing. Several LabNet teachers provided their students with an experience of this method and its implications, using the network to coordinate the process of data collection and to share their findings.

On August 31, 1990, Mary Nickles, a science teacher from Mercy High School in Rochester, New York, posted a message on LabNetwork's Forum inquiring about another school "within a 10 degree latitude band, to exchange data for calculating earth's circumference using Eratosthenes method." Mary received no replies through the Forum. But, a month and a half later, on November 14, Bruce Keyzer, a physics teacher from Guilford High School, Rockford, Illinois, again posted a message seeking school partners to perform the Eratosthenes experiment:

Eratosthenes Anyone?

I have two students who as part of a project wish to determine the circumference of the earth. They would like to find a student or group of students in a location having a latitude much different from Rockford, Illinois.

The cooperating students need only determine the angle the sun's rays make with the vertical at local noon and the time of local noon. We will need the latitude and longitude of your location. Anyone interested please respond via e-mail to BKeyzer.

_*_

Three days later, Tom Bross from Moravian Academy, Bethlehem, Pennsylvania, expressed an interest in the experiment. He suggested setting a day to do the experiment and added an idea, "Maybe several locations can agree to do the experiment on the same day?"

There was a problem, however, in having Tom as a partner. Tom's school is located at a latitude too close to create a measurable difference in the sun's angle. Five days following his original message, Bruce responded to Tom's message through the Forum:

```
19-NOV 22:39 Student Projects
    RE: Eratosthenes (Re: Msg 1244)
    From: BKEYZER
    To: TBROSS

Tom would be glad to try Eratosthenes. I have two
students whose objective as part of a larger project is
to determine the circumference of the earth. I was
hoping to find someone from a much different latitude
and use the angle difference at local noon to determine
C [circumference]. Our [Bruce and Tom] latitudes are
nearly alike as we found experimentally last year.
Maybe we could use our local noon time difference to get
the circumference. I suspect this may be more
difficult. Dave Button wants in too. Lets all set a
day after T-day [Thanksgiving Day] to give it a try. We
can collect data [and] see what can be made of it. I
have some students who would enjoy the challenge.

_*_
```

Bruce refers in his message to Dave Button, a physics teacher from Osbourn Park High School, Manassas, Virginia, who responded to his earlier message, that he was "game too." On the same morning Harold Lefcourt, from Morris Knolls High School, Rockaway, New Jersey, also joined the project. Soon after, Mary Ethel Parrott, Milton Academy, Covington, Kentucky, joined as well.

Now there were five teachers whose activities Bruce Keyzer had to coordinate. In his next message, 2 weeks after initiating the joint experiment, Bruce sent a message to coordinate the activities of the participating teachers, setting a date and time for observation, and suggesting that the communication channel be through the private Mail, "[to] avoid cluttering the Forum." He also inquired whether more teachers would like to join. He wrote:

```
Eratosthenes Project Update

Harold Lefcourt, Dave Button, Tom Bross, and Bruce
Keyzer have indicated an interest in the project. I am
suggesting we try to take data on Tuesday Dec. 4, 1990.
If the weather does not cooperate on that day try for
```

```
the nearest sunny day. We could send results via MAIL
to one participant and carbon copy to the others. Using
MAIL will avoid cluttering the FORUM. Please let me
know if you plan to measure on Dec. 4. Anyone else
interested? Join us! Just determine the angle the sun's
rays make with the vertical at local noon and the time
of local noon (when shadows are shortest).
_*_
```

Between this message and the actual experiment, four additional teachers joined the project: Curtis Miller, Lakewood, Colorado; Sandra Rhoades, Marietta, Georgia; Jack Cadigan, Juneau, Alaska; and Bruce Seiger, Wellesley, Massachusetts. They communicated their interest to Bruce Keyzer through the private mail. The Eratosthenes activity now involved nine teachers.

Bruce Seiger asked for an important clarification, "How will you be determining angle of sun's rays (from the shadow)..." The same night (22:45), about 30 minutes after Bruce Seiger posted his message, Bruce Keyzer posted a message on the Forum explaining his method for making sure when it is high noon (shortest shadow). He suggested that students measure the shadow made by a vertical object set in a school window every 5 minutes from about a half hour before noon time. When the shadow is the shortest students should measure the angle—shadow length divided by object height.

On December 4, 1990, as planned, the students performed the experiment. Early the next morning (6:18 a.m.) a disappointed Bruce Seiger posted a message on the Forum:

```
NO SUN for us!!! Rain rain and more rain with a chance
of snow!! We would like to try again next Tuesday due
to our rotating schedule!! Bruce A. Seiger for the WHS
students PS nice data - hope more folk got data then we
might be able to work with other data than our own!!

Anyone else had success???!!! Bruce
_*_
```

However, other teachers were successful. That night, Curt Miller, Tom Bross, and Bruce Keyzer posted their students' data on the Forum. They included the latitude and longitude, the angle of the sun, and Tom added the data showing the shadows' length as measured every 5 minutes. A week later, Dave Button added his students' findings. By now, however, most of the discussions took place on the private Mail. The promised report of Bruce Keyzer's students was posted on the Forum, making it available to those that were following the experiment. This project demonstrates how the network can facilitate science learning through the design of a project, the coordination of data collection, and the sharing of results.

Shoptalk Examples:

Seeking Information About New Curriculum Activities

```
6-DEC 22:19  Curriculum Issues
    Subject: PRISMS
    From: GLOCKETT
    To: ALL
```

Our district would like to adopt an activity based
science curriculum. We have material about the FAST
program and are exploring it. I know that there is
another program out there called PRISMS. We can't seem
to find an address or phone number for a representative
of this program. Anyone have that magic information
near at hand? I'd love to hear from you. I'd also love
to hear from any of you who have experience with these
programs or another activity based program. I'm a
hopelessly free-style artist, but the district and some
of the other faculty members feel the need for a little
more structure. I applaud the fact that they have let
go of the idea of a basal text centered course and would
like to help them as much as I can. Thanks—Greg
_*_

```
1296 6-DEC 22:41  Curriculum Issues
    RE: PRISMS (Re: Msg 1295)
    From: BKEYZER
    To: GLOCKETT
```

Greg;

A good place to get info re PRISMS is: Roy Unruh
University of Northern Iowa, Cedar Falls, IA 50614. I
attended four 1 day workshops on PRISMS. I have the
materials that accompany the program and have dabbled
with some of the activities. The program uses a learning
cycle approach similar to Hewitt. I tend to agree with
the philosophy but find some of the activities a bit too
"corny" the program did originate in IA after all! If I
can be of any more help let me know. Bruce
_*_

```
1320 10-DEC 23:16 Curriculum Issues
    RE: PRISMS (Re: Msg 1295)
    From: RELYON
    To: GLOCKETT
```

There is something called the National Diffusion
Network. My guess is that each state has a facilitator.

The NDN is offering a summer institute for PRISMS at Willamette University in Salem, OR- all expenses paid. This is for folks in the 15 western states. I don't know the dates.

The Washington State office is at the Highline Educational Resources and Administrative Center at 15675 Ambaum Blvd. S.W. Seattle, WA 98166. The phone is 206 433-2453. They also are having an institute in the Mechanical Universe. Hope this is of value.

Dick Lyon, Nooksack, Washington (RELYON)

-*-

Software Assistance and Offers

1322 10-DEC 23:30 Hardware/Software
    RE: LCI (Re: Msg 1280)
    From: ERNESTYOUNG
    To: DBUTTONOPHS (NR)

Dave, can you send me a copy of the info on importing into a spreadsheet from the LCI (RE MESSAGE 1275 AND 1280)? That's one of those things that I didn't master quite as well as I would have liked last summer. Send to Ernest D. Young....

Remember that I have those dreaded IBM's (clones, not the real things) if that makes any difference.

Thanks, Ernest

-*-

1316 10-DEC 20:25 Other
    Microsoft Works
    From: DSONCORNY
    To: ALL

Microsoft has a great offer for Works users. For $2.50 they will send a training package containing a workbook and disk on putting a computer to use in the classroom. It normally sells for $20. The offer is good until Dec 31, 1990. Send a check to Microsoft Works Booklet Offer, 21919 20th Avenue SE, Box 3011, Bothell, WA 98041-3011. Indicate you want a 3.5" disk for the MAC or a 5.25" or 3.5" disk for a PC. It is fairly basic but is great for anyone getting started plus it does have some good pointers. For more info call 1-800-227-4679.

-*-

A Calculus Problem

1388 26-DEC 08:51 Curriculum Issues
    PROBLEM IN THOMAS
    From: SERRI
    To: ALL

The calculus teacher who operates from a theoretical
framework rather than the experimental framework that I
use asked me the solution to the following problem that
appeared in her AP Text (she is using Thomas):

"A vertical cylindrical tank 30 ft high and 20 ft in
diameter is filled to a depth of 20 ft with kerosene
weighing 51.2 lb/ft^3. How much work is done in pumping
the kerosene to the level of the top of the tank?"

This is the entire problem. Students who have had
physics argued with her about the answer in the answer
book. Please Indicate your solution and Why. PS.
Harold I have an AP Physics course And we meet for 50
minutes 5 days a week. We do the AP C version.

Also an interesting solution to your dilemma might be to
re-do the physics but from an angular framework. I am
currently doing our AP course from that framework
although with a calculus base but it seems to be working
also appears that that methodology can be adapted to a
non-calculus based course.

_*_

1391 27-DEC 20:02 Curriculum Issues
    RE: PROBLEM IN THOMAS (Re: Msg 1388)
    From: HLEFCOURT
    To: SERRI

PAUL: Good to hear from you. The question from Thomas
is interesting since my calculus teacher, who found that
she had to cover work this year for the AP was quite
unhappy, but to me it had the advantage of another
approach to work when the students were more comfortable
with the integral.

With specific regards to your question, on first look,
one would seem to have to integrate Fdx, where F would
be the weight of the liquid (assuming no gain in KE),
but mg would be a variable (but the real question is
what distance each part of the liquid is raised). Am I
over-examining the situation?

The approach to AP sounds interesting. Have do you
cover the translational physics. My problem (I think)
is trying to do too much. I have been using Workshop
Physics and other activities to make the course "hands-
on" and conceptually strong, but am still trying to fit
in problem solving- Most of my AP students are not
sufficiently motivated to do problem solving without
prodding. I am trying to adjust my strategy for E&M
(where some of the concepts are extremely abstract).

By the way we are also doing the C level

_*_

1394 27-DEC 20:56 Curriculum Issues
    RE: PROBLEM IN THOMAS (Re: Msg 1388)
    From: TBROSS
    To: SERRI

Paul, my first thought is to equate the change in
potential energy to the work done.

Assume the kerosene is all at the ground level at the be
ginning. The center of gravity of the filled tank is
halfway up, which is the h in mgh, the final potential
energy. All you must do is calculate m.

If I'm missing something, let me know.

Tom TBROSS

_*_

1395 28-DEC 16:43 Curriculum Issues
    RE: PROBLEM IN THOMAS (Re: Msg 1391)
    From: SERRI
    To: HLEFCOURT

Harold I did the Fdx as a standard physics problem using
work is equal to force times distance. I used the
location of the center of mass to determine the work.
If I'm not mistaken my answer comes out double the
correct answer.

For the C version I do mechanics first but follow a
traditional outline that you find in any physics text.
I begin with kinematics. . . I assume the students
remember most of the first year course so I introduce
the rotational motion and spend time on it all along the
way. For example If we talk about the kinematic formula
d=1/2at^2 + vt, I try it using the angular formulation.

```
I look at the labs I did with the linear form and try to
adopt an angular form to that.  I use a device called a
spinning which I used when I was teaching a 7th grade
science course called ISCS.
```

```
The device can now be ordered from Redco Science 1-800-
248-0491.  11 Robinson Lane, Oxford, Connecticut 06483.
```

```
I've written some labs but they are still in a rough
stage.  The electromagnetism section I am still trying
to complete.  I've been able to get through two thirds
of the course and use many of the old PSSC Physics labs.
I'm still not real comfortable with the material and am
constantly writing and changing things.
```

```
PS.  We're using Halliday and Resnick 2nd Edition.
```

```
_*_
```

```
1396 28-DEC 16:46 Curriculum Issues
    RE: PROBLEM IN THOMAS (Re: Msg 1394)
    From: SERRI
    To: TBROSS
```

```
I did it that way using the center of mass and the
change it undergoes.
```

```
My answer comes out either double or half of the answer
that Thomas gives.
```

```
I think somewhere there [the] answer is just wrong?
```

```
_*_
```

Patterns of Network Discourse

Network discourse often took the form of "threads" (strings of messages dealing with the same topic). In the first qualitative study of Forum messages (September 1–December 26, 1990), there were 108 threads (about 26 per month). Teachers, not surprisingly, initiated most of the threads (86, or 80%). Project staff initiated 7 (6%), and students, who joined the network in the last month of the analysis (December 1990), initiated 15 (14%).

To begin a thread is to want to share an issue with a wider audience. Nearly half (46%) of the teachers who used the network started at least one thread. However, as might be expected, only a small number of teachers showed a high level of activity in the public domain.

The content of the threads represents the teachers' interests and needs across the school year. Table 4.2 summarizes the threads shared over the network during the first 3 months of the study, which coincided with the beginning of the school year.

TABLE 4.2
Kinds of Threads Initiated on the
Network Forum 9/1–12/26/90

Kind of Thread	N	%
Teaching activities	34	32
Teaching resources	27	25
Planning curriculum and teaching	21	19
Technical assistance	14	13
LabNet administration	12	11
Personal	0	–
Totals	108	100%

During this period, the focus of interest seems to have tilted toward shoptalk. Although almost one third of the threads dealt with teaching activities (such as individual student projects and classroom activities like the Eratosthenes project), more than half (57%) of the threads dealt with teaching resources, planning curriculum and teaching activities, and technical assistance—shoptalk related to teaching activities.

Teachers wanted to know about resources available for teaching (25%), to learn about MBL computer interfaces, and about places to acquire lab equipment. They also sought information about various teaching methods and related curriculum (19%). For example, teachers communicated about kinds of physics textbooks, the design of new physics courses, ways to demonstrate new physics concepts, and detailed information about ongoing student projects. Teachers were also concerned with effective implementation of the new electronic tools in their classroom (13%). They wanted to know about ways to access additional state and nationwide educational networks, how to download messages more efficiently, and about appropriate setup of MBL sensors. LabNet administrative messages were 11% of the threads—most often project notices about available grants or "free" network time.

The second study of the Forum (December 27, 1990–January 31, 1991) revealed 26 threads (9 continuing threads and 17 new threads). It showed a similar ratio between teaching activities and shoptalk. This is not surprising. Teaching requires teachers to prepare, to learn about new ideas, and to improve their technical expertise. The network effectively fostered shoptalk—a distinct virtue in the support of the teaching craft.

Many of the threads were one message long—reminiscent of a bulletin board format, and also consistent with shoptalk. For example, when a teacher encountered a technical problem, wanted help, and decided to post a query on the network's Forum, another teacher might post a response on the Forum (or might answer directly through the network Mail). But when one teacher had responded publicly, others tended not to join in unless they had additional or different information. Responses tended to be quick and concise.

The average number of participants in a thread was two, and the average number of messages three. The most common pattern was one initiator and one or two respondents (Table 4.3). Half of the threads lasted 1 day (Table 4.4). In fact, there were threads that ended within minutes. For example, in Message 1296 (from the shoptalk messages in the previous section), BKEYZER responds with information about project PRISMS 22 minutes after GLOCKETT posted his message inquiring about it.

TABLE 4.3
Number of Participants in a Thread, and
the Number of Messages in a Thread

# Participants in Thread	%	# Messages in Thread	%
1	46	1	48
2	30	2	24
3	8	3-5	19
4	8	6-10	7
5 or more	5	11-15	2
16 or more	3		
	100%		100%

TABLE 4.4
Time Period of Thread

Days	%
1	51
2	9
2-10	19
10-30	9
30-60	6
60 or more	6
	100%

The time period was longer, and the number of participants and of messages were higher, in threads dealing with teaching activities. For example, in the Eratosthenes project, the participating teachers exchanged 14 messages over a 28-day period.

A similar pattern took place during the Descent of a Ball National Contest, which was initiated over the network. In the contest, teams of students had to design a paper-and-tape structure that slowed the descent of a ping-pong or golf ball. There were three cycles to the competition. In the first month, five teachers joined the competition, carried it out, and shared their results. They then started a second round of competition involving an additional six teachers. And, 2 weeks later, a third cycle of competition was carried out by another group of three teachers, who used the first-round teachers as experts to provide them with the necessary guidelines for the project. Other projects, such as moon-watching and meteor-shower observations (see chapter 5), exhibited the same kind of cycle.

LEADERSHIP FOR LEARNING: THE BIG IDEA GRANTS

There is a tendency for teachers to rely on others to provide not only support, but also the leadership for learning. Often, teachers react to opportunities presented to them, rather than initiating change themselves. This behavior is part of the dynamics of the standard "delivery" model of educational change—the recipient is passive, simply following procedures. The deliverer is active, making sure that things work according to plan. Too rarely are opportunities provided for teachers to design learning activities for other teachers.

As the LabNet project progressed, one of the most important shifts in emphasis was toward collaborating with teachers and providing ways for them to take initiatives. Collaborating in educational change often means including teachers in the process of thinking about the issues involved, but leaving the authority and the decision making in the hands of the project staff. LabNet instead *shared* the leadership role with teachers by having them think, design, and implement their ideas for introducing changes in teaching and learning.

The most important example of this approach was the Big Idea Grant program (BIG) of 1991-1992. The program enabled teachers to apply for funds from LabNet, primarily to design and lead workshops for other teachers closer to home. For many teachers the Big Idea Grants were a step forward in their level of involvement. Assisting other teachers is a commitment to professional growth.

Our discussion of the Big Idea Grants has two sections: The first describes two grants in action. One was a workshop led by Bob Capen, who was introduced in chapter 3. Bob's workshop reached industrial arts and physics teachers in Arizona, in an attempt to engage them in doing joint projects. The second grant workshop was carried out by Sandra Rhoades in rural Georgia. In her workshop, Sandra exposed middle school teachers to new ideas of teaching science by using hands-on projects. The two workshops highlight more general issues—the transition toward educational leadership on the part of BIG grantees, the responsiveness of the projects to local needs, and the expansion of learning opportunities for participating teachers.

The second section sets forth a composite picture of the Big Idea Grants—the process by which they were developed, their scope and diversity of content, their outreach into the larger community of science teachers. Twenty workshops were carried out in 14 states, staffed by 27 LabNet teachers, at times in collaboration with university faculty or other teachers. The number of LabNet teachers involved, the effort they were willing to make, and the success of their endeavors all highlight the important fact that given the opportunity, local teacher-leaders can effectively design workshops for their peers.

Each of the workshop leaders designed a different approach to introduce project-enhanced science learning to participants. This variety is a reflection of their "local knowledge" (Geertz, 1983) and underscores the fact that they are more familiar with indigenous conditions and values than are outside educational agencies. The 20 workshops also reached quite diverse audiences. Finally, in almost every grant, support was also provided by the local schools or by the school district, or a neighboring college or university. The involvement of administrators, both with financial assistance, and at times also in the routine aspects of the workshop, proved the potential for collaborative work.

AN INTERDISCIPLINARY TEACHING AND LEARNING PROJECT
— Bob Capen, Canyon del Oro High School, Tucson, Arizona —

Bob Capen applied for a Big Idea Grant to run a regional workshop for his colleagues in Arizona. In it, he wanted to show teachers how to integrate projects into the state-provided Principles of Technology (PoT) curriculum. This curriculum introduces students to four energy systems: heat, light, electricity, and motion. Bob felt that the existing curriculum did not fit with students' learning-by-doing projects. The workshop was also designed to introduce collaborative interdisciplinary work among industrial arts, mathematics, and physics teachers. Bob believed that although physics teachers know theoretical concepts, they lack the expertise to build things. And, although industrial arts teachers are experts in building things, they lack the conceptual framework of physics necessary to introduce broad principles in conjunction with the product. Finally, the workshop served to test possible links at Bob's school among the three subject areas. He matched the $11,000 grant from LabNet with close to $10,000 more in in-kind contributions from his school.

Bob joined forces with Duane, the industrial arts teacher, and Brian, a math teacher, to run a workshop structured around designing and building a car—the idea he began to work on during his first year with LabNet. To achieve that goal, teachers were supplied with materials and worked in three main areas: They were taught how to use a semi-CAD program for the Macintosh; they used the industrial arts shop to build what they had designed; and they tested their cars in the physics lab using computer-interfaced motion detectors.

Forty teachers applied to the workshop, although there was little publicity. The demand for the workshop surprised Bob; he expected not many more than 16 teachers to apply for the 16 places he had available. The extent of the demand gave him a clear sense that he had struck a real need. Many teachers are isolated and compartmentalized in their schools and are looking for ways to become part of a broader community of practice. The participants came from 10 different schools in Arizona. There were teachers from a school for the deaf and blind; others came from small communities surrounding Phoenix; one participant was a teacher of science education at a community college in northern Arizona, who oversees science programs at Indian reservations and rural communities. For 9 of the teachers, some of them teaching over 20 years, this was their first professional workshop, and for another 4 it was their second.

From the start, it became apparent that the workshop leaders and the teachers had different agendas. The teachers came expecting to be told what to do "as usual," and then go home and apply it. Dave,[2] a participant whose experience is described later, said,

> I thought I was going to get the core books, tear through those, you know—look through those and say, boy I got this figured out, I'm going to do this, right? And I can see now, that's just going to have to be my guide supplement, my handbook, and I need—there are other things I need to do.

Bob Capen and his staff had a different approach in mind. They wanted the participants to design teaching activities that would serve each participant's specific classroom needs. They believed that the way to accomplish that was by putting participants in a situation identical to what their students would experience. Discussing the conflict of expectations, they said:

> *Bob*: My concern was, is, that they wanted to know how to teach this Principles of Technology course. And that's not the purpose of this institute. The purpose is to get math, science, and industrial

---

[2] All participant names are fictitious.

arts teachers communicating with each other, through the vehicle of a project....

Brian: They're just like the students, though, "Tell us what we need to know."

Duane: They want to pick your brain and go home and do what you did. And we're saying, we want you to take from us what you like and incorporate in your program, instead of taking our program home with you. But they were used to, and they wanted to, and the easiest way out is to take yours and go home and do it. But we know that if you don't have your own personal time and personality involved in your own program, you're not going to be any good at it.

Doing projects was the vehicle of change Bob and his staff wanted the participants to experience. As they said, they wanted to move the participants out of their "comfort zone," to feel like students, to think like students, and to experience the process of problem solving and its often related frustrations. They believed that teachers need to concentrate on providing students with situations where they are forced to think, come up with their answers, try them out, experience what happens when things *don't* work, and then come up with improved approaches.

Incorporated into their thinking was their belief that if projects are the better way to teach, then the role of the teacher changes. In this new situation a teacher is another learner. A teacher is also the person who is capable of directing students to resources, and helping them construct their learning environments. Knowledge shared by students and teachers also changes. Students and teachers now exchange know-how relevant to solving a scientific or technical problem. In this case, much more interdisciplinary and collaborative work has to take place among teachers. Students need to be able to rely on teachers from various departments, and what students learn has to be coordinated across departments. Their workshop was an attempt to exemplify the possibilities of such an approach.

Experiencing Like Students

In this section, we follow an industrial arts teacher, Dave, from Phoenix, working with a physics teacher, Carol, from Tucson. Dave, who was previously quoted, came to the workshop thinking that he was going to be shown how to teach the PoT program. He has been teaching woodworking and automotive repair for more than 20 years. Having to think of a project was difficult for him, especially when he found out that he needed to learn a new computer application. He became even more concerned because of the physics involved. That is an area he appreciates and teaches to some degree, but he has never worked with a physics teachers who knows physics. Carol has been teaching physics for 5 years. She has never worked with industrial arts tools. When she teaches physics she uses a car to demonstrate the laws of motion, but she has never built one, and cannot explain the mechanisms involved in making a car move.

After a frustrating first 2 days, especially for Dave with the computer, they started to work on their idea for a car. They first tried to come up with a plan they could both agree on—beginning with the function they wanted the car to perform. All the teachers designed their cars around things they wanted their cars to do. For one teacher, it was showing energy output. Therefore, he built a car with a motor that functions as a dynamo. Another pair wanted to demonstrate the role of traction. They designed a car whose axles could be placed in various positions, enabling them to test the effect of alterations in position on traction.

Dave and Carol decided to design a car that would roll at a constant speed on a plane inclined at between 5 and 15 degrees. They thought that a heavy car would react best to changes in elevation. With DREAMS, a Macintosh CAD program, they designed a car that would be heavy. Their car was to be built from many pieces of plastic board aligned along the length of the car. They then moved to the industrial shop area. There, reading off the computer printout of their design, they cut the plastic boards and drilled holes for the axle. In the process, Dave taught Carol how to use the machinery for construction.

After assembling the car, they tested it. Carol taught Dave how to use the photogate sensor connected to a computer to time the car's movement and how to read the data it provided. However, because the car was quite heavy and the board quite short, the car's rate of acceleration did not measurably change across the range of inclinations.

In their final presentation to the group, they shared their learning about that aspect of the car's performance. Dave described how the car "doesn't stick to the board." Carol described the same problem using physics concepts: The car was "friction free." They both learned to appreciate one another's professional contributions.

The challenges Dave and Carol faced are similar to what their students will face given a similar situation. These are the kinds of questions teachers and students could find themselves asking when working on a real problem together—questions about the mechanics, the physics, the design of the car.

Back at his school Dave shared his thoughts with two fellow teachers, Bill, a physics teacher, and John, an industrial arts teacher. Asked whether the workshop leaders followed what they preached,

Dave recollected his work with Carol. He recalled his frustration at seeing that there were so many possible ways to build the car, and all were "correct." He remembered the difficulty of coming up with a good design and the desire to have a second chance to improve their car and to learn more.

The experience led him to reflect on his teaching. The workshop, he said, helped him "...get back on track," to recall why 22 years ago he decided to become an industrial arts teacher, to help students learn to think, to develop their own original ways of making sense of things. His current way of teaching "does not really take that much original thinking on their part." They are usually "spoon fed," he added. He wondered whether his students will experience similar feelings.

Most teachers, like Dave and Carol, at first experienced frustration, only to become, in the words of Bob, "eager beavers." Every team of teachers constructed a car or a structure for testing cars. They all developed their own ideas about how to teach PoT in their own school setting. The physics teacher who built a car that tested energy relationships will have his students build cars and have them come up with the energy concepts in electricity through measuring the electrical output of the electrical motors of their cars. Another teacher, concerned with racial balance in his class, believed that building cars will attract more minority students, who may then be encouraged to study physics. For a biology teacher, the car-design project illuminated the limits of his biology teaching. Biology, the way it is taught, he said, "is a trivial pursuit of classifications." Doing a project, he added, shifts the students' attention to making things and thinking about the science embedded in them.

Many teachers saw the workshop as a model for the kinds of collaborative work they could do with teachers from other areas. One physics teacher's car project spurred thoughts of a joint effort he could undertake with his English department. Students would do the experimentation in his class, and would write up their reports as part of their English requirements. A science teacher from Arizona School for the Deaf and Blind commented on the challenge that lies ahead for him, in trying to integrate the work of the industrial arts and science teachers in his school:

> I think a tremendous amount of groundwork would need to be done to break down the old thinking of "this is my area and I don't want anyone in another area to come in and tell me what to do." All the old sayings such as, "Can't teach an old dog new tricks," "There is only one way to do things," and so on need to be overcome. This would not be an easy task...

The enthusiasm of the participants was reflected in their evaluation of Bob's workshop. All felt that the workshop responded "a great deal" to their needs. Half of the participants felt that the workshop was beneficial to their science teaching because they learned new teaching approaches. To another third, learning about the computer applications was most beneficial, and the rest mentioned collaborative work or a mix mentioned earlier. Not surprisingly, 14 of the 16 teachers wrote that they would "definitely" integrate the components they found useful in their classrooms. They wrote:

> I received many ideas on how to use computers in my class and Paul got really excited about the prospects of teaching the course at our school.

> I have developed a good working relationship with the technology teacher. I am motivated and have many good ideas to put to use.

> I appreciated how well I was able to cooperate with my industrial arts partner.

> [The workshop] gave me an insight to project-based instruction.

> The industrial arts teacher from my school and I developed extensive plans to work together in several units.

> I am going to try to utilize the design aspect of doing projects more in my classes.

When asked whether they would suggest the workshop to other teachers all of the teachers confirmed that they would. One of the teachers responded to this question, "I already have! I would also like to get a math teacher involved in the next workshop. An outstanding experience!" And another teacher wrote, in suggesting other teachers to join such a workshop, that "It [the workshop] opens up your mind to new ideas and provides a spark for teaching."

RURAL MIDDLE SCHOOL TEACHERS: GET PHYSICAL!
— Sandra Rhoades, North Cobb High School, Kenneshaw, Georgia —

Sandra Rhoades is an experienced physics teacher from a suburb of Atlanta, Georgia. In her classroom, Sandra has integrated projects to provide students with opportunities to learn physics by doing. Last year, some of her students' projects included the physics behind karate moves, measuring the force of acceleration in motion of elevators, and building paper towers.

Over the years, Sandra became aware of the disparity that exists in her state in science-teacher training. Sandra enjoys the relative wealth of knowledge and materials of a suburban school, which also benefits from constant training and professional development opportunities. All these advantages are part of being close to the center of things. Yet, she knows that other teachers in her state do not fare as well. The situation of science teachers in middle schools is especially alarming. If some resources are available for science teaching, high school science teachers are the first to receive, whereas middle school science teachers scrape for any leftovers.

Students, Sandra noted, are turned off of science by the time they reach high school. In fact, Georgia is among the states with the highest dropout rates. With middle school teachers across the country having little or no background in physical science, and lacking the pedagogical skills to interest students in learning it, the situation is a recipe for failure—especially in the rural areas of the South, and specifically in Georgia.

Sandra found in a 1986 study that 48% of Georgia's middle school teachers had fewer than 20 quarter-hours of science preparation, and that 41% had no science study within the last 7 years. In her application for the Big Idea Grant, Sandra expressed her concern. She wrote, "We must make science exciting! It must be taught in a meaningful manner, stressing student involvement and cooperative learning through project-based problem solving. We must work to attract women and minorities into science at an early age."

No one would disagree with her message. But very few rural teachers are reached. Many of the more remote districts lack a science coordinator and certainly do not have the resources to bring into the classroom high-tech hardware and applications.

Sandra decided to run her workshop in the southwest region of Georgia. There, surrounding the city of Brunswick, a well-to-do and quite famous resort area, are some of the state's poorest counties, with the highest percentages of minority residents (65% to 80% Black Americans) and the most heavily rural populations. Women constitute about 90% of the middle school teachers in this area.

Sandra's aim was to excite the teachers about science. She wanted to boost their motivation to work with students. At the same time, she wanted to expand the teachers' knowledge of science, and to provide them with simple and inexpensive ideas that they could use with their students. She believed that if she could build a cadre of teachers that are excited and ready, chances are that they would carry their learning and enthusiasm into the classroom.

She convinced the McIntosh County district to serve as the site for her workshop. It borders on Brunswick and is considered Brunswick's poor and neglected cousin. The local educational administration gladly provided all the needed resources to ensure that the workshop would take place. At the same time, Sandra informed the department of education in Georgia of her workshop and left it to them to select two teachers from each of the nearby school districts. She insisted on a pair of teachers from each district, knowing how hard it is to introduce change when working alone.

The response was overwhelming and the places for the workshop were quickly filled. Twenty-four participants from 12 surrounding districts attended. Some of them, not having enough money to stay at Dorian, the site of the workshop, commuted 80 miles each way to attend. For 9 teachers, this was their first workshop, and for another 7, it was their second. The majority of the participants were women— which is the opposite of the often male-dominated science departments in high schools. Five were Black Americans.

Sandra and her partners had the participants build water bottle rockets made of empty soft-drink bottles, and launchers constructed from foot-long pieces of wood. Air is pumped into the bottles, which are partially filled with water. The rockets are then released. Sandra had the group take the rockets to the local beach area and fire them. The participants were startled by the change of venue. Most would not have considered such a move prior to this workshop, because they did not perceive science to be *located* outside of the classroom setting, outside of the textbook. To many, the idea of taking their students outside was intriguing. To some it seemed risky. The staff then had the participants build a simple motion computer sensor. The probe was not handed to the teachers—they had to learn how to build it. Each of them received a packet of materials and they were assisted in the building task. If there was one experience most teachers remember—for its frustration—it was the process of soldering the transistors and wires. But what many recalled as the moment of exhilaration was when their interface worked.

Next the staff showed the participants how they could demonstrate lasers to their students and have them make holographic slides. Then each of the participants had 2 days to work on a project to take back to their classroom. For many of the participants this was the first time they had built something from start to finish. Wanting them to experience the whole process, Sandra and her staff had the teachers buy the materials at a local hardware store. That way, they felt, the teachers would learn to mess around with hardware and feel comfortable acquiring such stuff.

Joe, who returned to teaching after retiring from the Air Force, decided to build a water-rocket launcher to show his students. Excitedly he envisioned how he would take his students to the schoolyard and how they would compete amongst themselves. He could already see his school principal walking out, beaming at Joe's work with the students. Mark was concerned with the safety of the water-rocket device. He built one with a wider stand. He also drilled a hole in the board to allow for the rocket stand to change inclination. That way, he could involve his students in comparing the distance and height the rocket would travel as the angle of the trajectory varied.

At the same time, Norma struggled to solder another motion probe. She wanted her students to use the interface to learn more about motion.

A new teacher of only 6 months built a motion probe to help his students understand the speed of a camera's shutter. He wanted to teach them photography. Many students in his school do not know about photography because their parents are too poor to afford a camera. Another teacher, while building a rocket launcher, explained the importance of having more hands-on activities in his classroom. "Students," he said, "tell you that they understand. They say they do, but they don't." Hands-on activities would help him know whether his students integrated concepts well enough to use them. Sadly, he added, the laser equipment is beyond his school's budget. He has access to one computer, when other teachers are not using it.

In their evaluations, 19 of the 24 participants felt that the workshop met their needs "a great deal," and 5 said that it "somewhat" met their needs. For most (67%), the reason the workshop met their needs was that they learned about new teaching approaches. Twenty-two participants felt that they would "definitely" integrate ideas from the workshop into their classrooms. Over half mentioned teaching approaches as the component they would integrate, and four teachers mentioned computer applications. Most importantly, participants left with enthusiasm to integrate their learning and to continue to seek opportunities to pursue their professional development:

> I became more knowledgeable as to how computer interfacing devices can be used for scientific purposes. I can also use these devices with my students. This workshop was very helpful to me in my quest to keep abreast of new developments in technology. I feel better able to prepare my students for today's world.

> The activities were motivating and inspiring. They were presented in a way that could apply to all grade levels. The leaders brought in very helpful ideas of how to integrate science with math, social studies, language, arts, etc. Great ideas! I can't wait to use them.

For Sandra and her staff, the workshop proved to be a test case for meeting the needs of middle school teachers, especially in rural areas. The local school district asked her to come again. They want more teachers to learn new ways to teach science. That sense of urgency was shared by many of the participants. One teacher wrote:

> Most middle school teachers do not have enough training in science courses ...we *must* keep students asking questions about things they use and see every day. We must be able to answer these questions for them and create interest in the field of science. We need *more!*

And another said,

> We need MORE! Please help. There have been no hands-on work-
> shops in our area. Any area of science information is greatly needed
> in our district!

To Sandra, that meant preparing her show for the road, looking
for additional interested sites, or perhaps returning to McIntosh County
and strengthening the new starts for these science teachers.

THE OUTREACH OF THE BIG IDEAS

Bob and Sandra's Big Idea Grants were part of the larger BIG program
described in chapter 1 (see also Appendix D). The BIG workshops were
extremely diverse. For example, Sandra's workshop targeted middle school
science teachers who had little exposure to teacher training. At the other
extreme, four LabNet teachers in Colorado joined together to lead a workshop aimed at highly experienced high school teachers. The leaders also
set different goals for their workshops. In any composite picture of the
workshops, the "feel" for this kind of local variation tends to get lost. Still,
a broad picture of the Big Idea Grants helps focus on the participants' gains
from the effort. It also suggests issues the community of practice needs to
address for the workshop participants to become active members. Both
themes are interwoven in the following discussion.

Skepticism—Then Success

It is instructive to review some of responses to the program when it was
first proposed. The idea of funding teachers to carry out local and regional
workshops of their own design was introduced at a LabNet national advisory meeting. Some of the reactions were quite skeptical. They ranged
from opinions that the idea just would not work, to claims that the program could be considered a success if even five LabNet teachers applied.

These skeptical views were at least in part due to a common perception that teachers tend to lay back, do not have the time to take the initiative, and are reticent about the process of grant writing. The BIG program
prepared for that situation.

It was decided from the start that the process of grant writing should
be collaborative—that the purpose was not to solicit polished grants. Instead each LabNet staff member worked with a small group of applicants
to prepare grants that combined the teachers' experience and knowledge
of the local setting with our desire to see teachers do more science projects
in their classrooms (and in the process pick up more know-how in grant
writing). The title, "Big Ideas," reflected that purpose. Teachers were asked
to focus on the core idea of a workshop, or curriculum, or telecommunication project they wanted to do. It was not expected that they would know
at the outset exactly how to implement their ideas and how much money
they would need.

Expecting a very limited response, the LabNet staff was pleasantly surprised when, within a month of the announcement, 32 ideas for workshops and projects accumulated—about *one of four* teachers contacted sent in an initial grant proposal. So it became clear to us that teachers do have ideas about helping other teachers. As we worked with the applicants, one of the important tasks was to let them know that they were not expected to duplicate the scope and thrust of the summer workshops TERC had presented. We wanted them to think about what was best for their local audience—to work according to their needs.

Over the next 6 months, staff and teachers worked on the proposals mainly by communicating over the network, sending drafts back and forth, and critiquing plans and budgets. Over time, it became clear that most applicants needed assistance in preparing their budgets and in designing workshops that did not attempt too large a bite. Teachers wanted to achieve a lot in too little time. It was also important not to lose sight of the local applicability of the workshops. Workshops could easily be designed to a standard format where one size seems to fit all. We did not want teachers to fall into this mode. This is where, we felt, many training efforts fall short—in not adapting sufficiently to local needs.

It was also felt that tangible local recognition of the effort was important. The staff insisted on teachers coming up with in-kind support from the hosts of the workshops, be it their school or a university. Teachers' resourcefulness, again, proved itself. All grantees were able to come up with in-kind support. At times, the in-kind was greater than the grant amount. Overall, in-kind support reached an estimated $125,000—a ratio of almost 3:1—for every $3 they received from TERC, teachers came up with $1 in matching support.

During the period when grants were being drafted, the staff rejected two ideas for workshops. In addition, 10 teachers chose not to pursue their Big Ideas, in most cases for lack of time or personal reasons. Twenty teachers continued developing their grant proposals and received funding for a total of some $344,000, or an average of just over $17,000 per grant. The assessment process for the workshops was collaboratively decided with the grant project directors. Instruments were designed and revised by a small team of staff and workshop leaders. All participants filled out a form in which they were asked to evaluate and comment on their experience. Receipt of their stipends was dependent on returning the form, so the response was 100%. Additionally, workshop leaders completed a final report in which they described the workshop and raised issues they felt need to be addressed in similar future efforts.

The participant evaluation forms were returned directly to TERC to protect their anonymity in the event that they might feel uncomfortable responding directly to their workshop leader. For this purpose, stamped envelopes addressed to LabNet were distributed by each workshop leader along with the assessment forms. Once the forms arrived at TERC, participants' evaluations and comments were summarized and the evaluation results were sent back to each workshop leader.

Response

The acceptance of the workshops was exceptionally high. The Big Idea Grants (Table 1.1, chapter 1) ultimately reached 393 teachers. The information presented here is based on questionnaire data from 266 teachers located in 250 schools across 16 states (participants who responded to evaluation questionnaires by November 15, 1991).

The majority of the workshop participants (85%) were high school teachers. Nearly half (46%) taught physics in addition to other science courses. Almost one quarter (23%) taught physics only. These numbers are consistent with the findings of the American Institute of Physics survey, which show that physics is most often taught by nonspecialized science teachers (Neuschatz & Covalt, 1988). One third (31%) of the participants taught either some science or other courses but no physics. An example of the latter are the middle school teachers in Sandra Rhoade's workshop and the industrial arts teachers in Bob Capen's workshop.

This distribution has implications for the scope of the community of practice, as well as the level and content of future learning materials and discourse. LabNet specifically focused on physics teachers—participants were selected based on their physics background. The LabNet workshop training materials and the selection of technology, such as the MBL, were designed around the physics curriculum. Should the community expand its membership, a broader base for training and community dialogue will have to be sought.

The fact that many participants taught more than one science course also points to a great deal of potential for enriching the community through increased opportunities for interdisciplinary work. This potential is exemplified by Geriann Walker, introduced in chapter 3, who teaches physics and chemistry. With her partners in the science department, she developed an interdisciplinary curriculum around acid rain, in which each of the science fields is utilized. A telecommunication network could also become a vehicle for such collaborations.

The Big Idea Grants typically reached experienced teachers (Table 4.5). Most of the participants (72%) had over 5 years of teaching experience. As a group, they had been teaching for an average of 13 years. Over a third (38%) had been teaching for more than 15 years, while almost one of every ten teachers (9%) had been teaching for more than 26 years.

TABLE 4.5
Number of Years of Science Teaching

Number of Years Teaching	Number of Participants	%
1 - 5	74	28
6 - 10	40	15
11 - 15	49	19
16 - 25	76	29
26 - 30	24	9
Total	263 *	100%
Average	13 years	

* Three respondents who were not high school teachers were excluded.

The Big Idea workshops reached many teachers who often do not participate in workshops or training. Although many of the participants can be considered veteran educators, they reported having relatively limited participation in teacher-training events. Almost one fifth of the teachers (19%) had not participated in any workshops prior to their Big Idea workshop experience. An additional 51% had participated in only one or two workshops. The final 30% had been to three or more workshops.

When the participants' teaching experience is linked with the number of workshops attended, these numbers are telling. The average participation in workshops was over one but less than two workshops. Thus, with the average years of teaching being 13, on average, teachers had participated in a workshop only *once in more than 6 years*.

The findings add validity to the Big Idea Grants program. The workshops reached teachers who are not active in professional-advancement activities, or who have not had the opportunities. Sandra Rhoades's workshop is a case in point. In her state, most districts do not have a science coordinator, and very few workshops are available for middle school teachers. At the same time, few of these teachers were active in organizations that could offer them opportunities for professional growth. Many teachers who participate in professional workshops and gatherings have the feeling that they usually see the same faces every time—but not most of the faces of the teachers that the BIG workshops served.

This picture of limited exposure to teacher training adds to the challenge of teacher preparation. Toward this end, there are advantages in a community of practice that has the resources that LabNet had. For example, having access to telecommunication can link teachers in an ongoing way. Instead of occasional workshop participation every few years, teachers could engage in a continuing discourse about their work on a day-to-day basis. The experience of veteran teachers can also be utilized by the community members, especially by beginning teachers, as it was in Geriann Walker's case.

Making a Difference

The Big Idea Grants seem to have connected with teachers hungry for learning. The majority of participants (78%) felt that the workshop met their needs "a great deal." One fifth (21%) reported the workshops "somewhat" met their needs. Only two teachers (1%) reported that the workshops they attended did not meet their needs very much. When asked about the likelihood that they would integrate the workshop experience into their classroom practice, 87% reported that they would "definitely" do so. Another 12% reported that "perhaps" they would integrate what they learned into their classes. Three teachers (1%) reported that they would probably not integrate anything from the workshop.

Computer applications were the workshop component cited by the most teachers (45%) as one they would use in their classrooms (Table 4.6). These applications included ready-made ULI and MBL interfaces (see the glossary at the end of chapter 1), and ones that they built. Doing projects interested one third (33%) of the teachers. The kind of projects ranged from hands-on demonstrations, like building rocket launchers, to in-depth student-initiated work. Only 4% of the teachers wanted to add telecommunication (most workshops did not introduce the LabNetwork). And, in the context of daily needs, telecommunication seems an extra, because it also requires an initial investment that teachers tend to avoid: getting a modem, a telephone line, learning to use telecommunication software, and so on.

TABLE 4.6
Components of Workshop That Teachers Expect to Integrate in Class

Components of Workshop	Number of Participants	%
Computer applications	101	45
Teaching approaches	74	33
Telecommunication	10	4
Interaction with teachers	4	2
Other	35	16
Total	224*	100%

* Six teachers did not respond to this question.

Virtually all participants (98%) said that they would recommend a similar workshop to other teachers.

The likelihood that participants will implement what they learned depends also on the support of their administration. Participants were asked whether they received any kind of support from their school administrators (Fig. 4.2). Of the teachers, 26% reported that they received no support, formal or informal. Many times the responses were that the administration did not know about their participation, and in some cases the teachers believed that they do not care. Seventy-four percent reported that they received some kind of support from their administration.

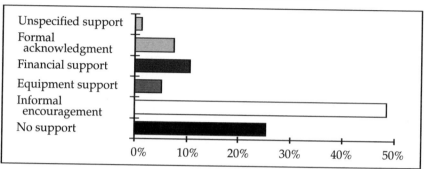

FIG. 4.2. Administrative support received by Big Idea participants

As can be seen from Fig. 4.2, in most cases (49%) the participants received informal encouragement from administrators. These ranged from "a pat on the back" to commending teachers for seeking professional development. Only a few received financial support (11%) or formal acknowledgment (8%). Financial support included the costs of participation in workshop, or salary benefits. Administrators at times provided formal acknowledgment by counting the workshop toward certification or sending a formal letter of appreciation. Five percent of the teachers were provided equipment for their participation in the workshop including modems and interfacing equipment.

In many ways, then, the Big Idea Grants served as a catalyst for teachers to take leadership roles. At the same time, they provided the community with opportunities for growth among its current and new members.

PATTERNS OF COMMUNITY PARTICIPATION: CONCLUSIONS [3]

LabNet proved useful in connecting teachers to one another as a community of practitioners. It provided ways for teachers to support one another as they experimented with new ways of teaching, and it provided pathways for some teachers to emerge as leaders, disseminating new educational ideas to others. More specifically:

---

[3] This section is based on Gal et al. (1991).

LabNet's support system strengthened connections among teachers and the project's staff in the community of practice. Through the use of tele-communication, the summer workshops, and the assistance of the TLCs, most participants became active members, to varying degrees, of a community of practice of science teachers. This community was able to provide teachers with diverse kinds of support, from solving technical problems to information about curricular issues and scientific content. It also enabled teachers to make use of a wide range of learning opportunities.

Most of the teachers utilized the LabNetwork to support their teaching. The LabNetwork served as an effective carrier of teaching activities, shoptalk about teaching, and collaborative research. Ways in which networks need to improve their technical capabilities to serve this function more effectively are discussed in the next chapter.

The community of practice, with TERC staff serving as catalyst, created opportunities for teachers to take leadership roles. TERC staff designed programs and provided support and leadership. Teachers took active roles in the community of practice in multiple ways—some through involvement on the network, others in creating changes in their classes, and still others through assistance to other teachers. There were teachers who engaged in more formal leadership roles, serving other teachers in the community as TLCs, or in reaching out to new teachers as Big Idea workshop leaders. In most cases, the leadership role was experienced as personal growth and produced a greater commitment to the community of practice.

Teachers' leadership roles in the community of practice tended to respond well to local needs. Teachers demonstrated the critically important abilities to construct their BIG workshops and projects to fit local needs and to reach out to peers who otherwise had not been involved in ongoing learning in their teaching careers. This kind of grass-roots activism is one successful outcome of the community of practice.

The Community of Practice and the Transformation of Teaching

In chapter 3 we observed that, although most LabNet teachers began to use projects on an experimental basis, few abandoned the basal-text approach in favor of project-enhanced learning. Projects were, at least provisionally, treated as a methodological adjunct or procedural adjustment to the reigning approach. We ended the chapter by asking how teachers can be helped to make the difficult transition from an approach that is familiar, comfortable, and entrenched in the educational system to one that, for most, is less comfortable and more demanding, but that in our view can advance science education dramatically. This chapter and chapter 3, we believe, offer some useful suggestions for accomplishing such an improvement.

Perhaps the most general and important suggestion is to adopt a collaborative approach in which teachers function as change agents and equals—as opposed to a top–down approach in which teachers are passive recipients of other people's ideas. The success of the BIG workshops shows that teachers are willing and able to take the lead in spreading educational innovations. Their inherent credibility as fellow practitioners, coupled with their ability to identify local needs and to structure programs adapted to the local situation, made them highly effective at recruiting, training, and motivating other teachers.

The TLC program was perhaps less successful because of flaws in its design and management. Nevertheless, TLCs were able to help many otherwise isolated teachers, whose experimentation with projects might have been nipped in the bud without their support. Similarly, the LabNetwork was used effectively by TLCs and many other teachers to give and receive technical advice, encouragement, and project ideas. Suitably modified, all three mechanisms—teacher-initiated workshops, designated "peer-support persons," and electronic telecommunication—should play a valuable role in future reform efforts. What is more, for many workshop leaders, TLCs, and network users, the process of reflecting on their own practice in order to help other teachers seems to have crystallized their thinking and increased their commitment to project-enhanced science learning—a "bootstrap effect" of profound importance for educational change. Perhaps the most compelling testimony of this process is to be found in the essays that teachers contributed to this book (chapter 6).

The aforementioned elements were built into LabNet because of one fundamental assumption: That a supportive community of practice can help to sustain the slow, stepwise process of "shifting" that eventually leads to a fundamental transformation in teaching philosophy and practice. We believe that the findings of this chapter and chapter 3, although far from conclusive, tend to confirm our basic assumption and offer hopeful signs that a genuine transformation is under way among a small but growing group of LabNet teachers.

5 DESIGN FOR A SCIENCE NETWORK

Brian Drayton

Many teachers who have tried to use a new piece of hardware or software will wince in recognition at Brian Drayton's portrait of "Erica," a fictional teacher struggling to learn telecommunication technology. There are thousands of Ericas among the nation's science teachers—intelligent, eager to acquire new skills and tools to aid their teaching, but short on time and long on responsibilities. Responsiveness to the needs of the "Ericas" is the key to building a telecommunication network capable of supporting a national community of practice.

Brian Drayton keeps "Erica" firmly in mind as he reviews what has been learned from the LabNetwork. He puts the function of the system from the user's point of view first, and its technical form second. For each of the system elements (e-mail, forum, databases, and so forth) he asks: What worked for teachers, and why? What did not work, and why? How could the system be made more accessible, practical, flexible? He also places design concerns in the context of broader issues, such as the make-up of the community served by the system, and the role of researchers and educational innovators in universities and organizations like TERC.

INTRODUCTION

LabNet was committed to supporting and stimulating a community of teachers who agreed that science teaching needed to change, and that the change would depend in very large part on shifts in their classroom practice. This transformation could not happen easily, and earlier chapters have argued that teacher change requires a kind of reflective conversation that extends over a long period of time and has many threads in it. In order to overcome the limitations that time and distance set for this conversation, LabNet used an electronic communication network—essentially computer-to-computer communication via telephone lines—the means by which the community of practice could collaborate in transformational exchanges.

This chapter discusses the functional design of a network for a science teaching community, basing the discussion on the LabNet experience. A telecommunication network can uniquely serve to support a community committed to enhancing teacher practice, although the extent of a network's usefulness will vary somewhat with the functions available on a particular network (as detailed later in the chapter). The attractive possibilities, however, often remain possibilities only, because of logistical or administrative constraints, or because of limitations of current hardware and software.

145

After a consideration of these difficulties, the chapter outlines the design elements necessary for an effective, flexible network to support a national community of teaching practice.

Networks for Teachers

Telecommunication for teacher enhancement, such as that explored in the LabNet project, is unique among so-called "new educational technologies," in that it affects what happens in the classroom indirectly. That is, unlike various audio-visual aids that have been added to the classroom, and unlike MBL tools for the science class or language laboratories for the study of foreign languages, this particular kind of telecommunication is for the teachers first and foremost. In this sense, it is comparable to membership in a professional society, rather than to some piece of educational equipment.

This characteristic, the focus first on the teacher as the agent of change in the classroom, dictates many of our ideas about the shape and functionality of a telecommunication network for a community of discourse about science learning. As will become clear later, we believe that, in fact, this community includes other members beyond science teachers themselves; but if the technology does not serve the teachers, its value is lost.

Until now, networks for educational use have fallen into three general categories. Each of them has points of value, but none yet fully satisfies the need for a medium to support the creation of an electronically communicating community of practice—a community that is in the business of real change in the classroom.

The first category is the administrative network, which ranges in size from a local area network of connected computers within a school building, to a county- or statewide network. See for example the description by Bull, Harris, and Cothern (1992) of the Virginia PEN network, which discusses a system with a wider range of intended application than usually envisioned for other systems, such as the commercial packages of CNS, Inc., currently used by hundred of systems for classroom and curriculum management.

A network is a very efficient tool for administration, and a whole industry has grown up to supply software and other resources for networks whose principal aim is educational management. Although LabNet and similar networks have found telecommunication a natural medium for logistics, we will not discuss this particular use further.

The second category is exemplified by networks like FrEdMail, K-12Net, the Kids Network, PSINet, and many others. These networks are multipurpose, and by design, mix teachers and students. This mixture has stimulated much interesting and enjoyable discussion on the networks and in the literature, although each model has its drawbacks (see Riel & Levin, 1990; Weir, 1992).

The third type of network, focused primarily on teaching and established for the benefit of teachers, to which LabNet belongs, is rarer and has existed as part of experimental projects. The ETC experimental network, Common Ground, is an example of an important precursor to LabNet. Many of the elements that we find valuable to our purposes are found there. The most important is the explicit commitment to an examination of practice, as one basic focus of discussion, and one part of the teachers' "shop-talk." For an analysis of the network and its implications for communications among teachers, see West and McSwiney (1989) and West, Inghilleri, McSwiney, Sayers, and Stroud (1989).

Another fascinating experiment was the development of the Quill network in Alaska, created as a teacher-communication network to support a project on "writing as problem solving." A thorough study of this experiment touches on many aspects of technology and educational innovation, including a careful consideration of the factors affecting teachers' use of a network, and its role in building a community of practice (Bruce & Rubin, 1992).

Organization of This Chapter

This chapter traces a widening spiral. It begins at the center with a look at the daunting practical difficulties that face a teacher who is trying to get started using telecommunication. The focus then widens to a description of the LabNetwork, one particular solution to "the teacher's dilemma." In the next section, entitled "The Medium," the focus widens again, to the features and functions of various network tools (electronic mail, bulletin board, databases, etc.), examined in light of LabNet's experience and that of other projects. Next, in a section entitled "Who Is the Community?" the chapter places design issues in a larger context, asking who the network should serve, and how different choices about the community of users affect network design. Finally, the chapter concludes by outlining the design elements that we believe are necessary to support a community of science teaching practice on a national scale.

THE TEACHER'S DILEMMA

With the good press that telecommunication gets, with the cheerful reports in the educational literature about the availability and value of technology in the schools, one might think that technical issues are melting away. In fact, however, our experience with large-scale telecommunication projects gives us a very different view of things. For a teacher new to telecommunication, every step has its own pitfalls.

Here is a portrait of a teacher's progress that is not at all uncommon or obsolete. This composite portrait is closely modeled on actual cases, involving good and intelligent teachers trying to hit a moving target.

The teacher, Erica, reads about LabNet in *The Physics Teacher* in April, and decides to sign up for the next year. To get off on the right foot, she attends the summer workshop, and spends some time learning about telecommunication, but most of her attention is focused on other skills that she sees will be really valuable for her classes—learning some new productivity software, some computer-interfacing stuff, some new Science Olympiad ideas; the interchange with colleagues is invigorating, and Erica looks forward to continuing over the network.

Now Erica goes to her administrator, and asks permission to install a phone line that can be used for telecommunication. This seems to be a practical necessity, because all other phones in the building are fully deployed for voice communications. After a little discussion, Erica makes the case that having a line with a modem on it, which she would only be using a very few hours per week, might be of value to the librarian and to other teachers. The administrator can see that this is the wave of the future, and wants to go along, but all appropriations for this kind of thing have been made months ago.

With much ingenuity, the administrator finds the installation money, and touts the addition to the school's repertory, but admonishes the teacher that she must be frugal, that the thing must pay off soon, and that she must seek supplementary funding.

Meanwhile, Erica has been getting equipment together. She has an Apple IIe. What modem will work with it? The librarian, who is looking forward to access to several on-line services, has a PC clone—how about a modem for that? Could they share? How about cabling? And where will the modem live?

Erica then seeks advice (in her workshop manual and from friends who know about such things) about software. In order to make sense of that, she has to figure out details about baud rates, parities, file-transfer protocols, stop bits, carrier services, and more. It has now been 3 months since the summer workshop where Erica learned to use one public-domain "telecom" package. The telephone company has put on a burst of speed and gotten the line in, and Erica finally seizes half an hour to get on-line, and let people know that she is still alive and interested. After three attempts, the software claims that she has connected, but all she sees is hieroglyphics. She consults the manual, which has no index entry either for hieroglyphics or "What to do if...." Her half-hour is up. She calls the LabNet number, and asks for help. The network person interrogates her, makes a guess at the problem, and tentatively suggests a fix. Erica tries it the next day.

It seems to work—she gets to log on at last! But now what? The system tells her that she has 14 mail messages, and that the forum contains 875 items; the number of the message she last read is 1. All Erica has to do now is (a) learn how to get into Mail, (b) learn how to use Mail, (c) learn how to get out of Mail, and (d) learn how to do the same things with the Forum, so that she can sort through the 800+ messages she has missed. After an hour of work, a conservative estimate is that doing all this will take her another 5 hours at a minimum, and then she might want to learn how to up- and download files—ASCII text? Graphics? Compressed or not?

When will this begin to pay off?

The LabNet project aimed at transforming the physics classroom, and was committed to the use of telecommunication as a primary means to that end. While keeping the ultimate goal in view, however, we were quite aware of the teacher's painful situation nowadays, as she or he meets successive waves of demands for change and improvement.

The teacher who is supposed to learn a complex piece of software is also, in the current climate of educational ferment, supposed to be learning the uses of other technologies, integrating them with the computer, restructuring the curriculum in concert with the rest of the faculty, and (as we advocate) changing his or her style of instruction to incorporate a more observant, learning-centered, constructivist epistemology—and all this on a shrinking budget.

It must be stressed that this is not just a new, nightmarish visitation upon the teacher. In every decade, some societal crisis has focused attention on the schools, most often on secondary school, after the "output" from the system has been examined by various shiny, analytical instruments. The curriculum in most subjects has gone through many "revolutions" in this century, each reaching a high-water mark, only to recede, leaving a line of wrack behind. As technological developments have taken a directive role in the quotidian (as opposed to the industrial or scientific) world, schools have been expected to incorporate the latest information transfer and management systems (Cuban 1986; Sarason 1990).

The teacher's working conditions rarely include adequate time for the acquisition of new technological or other knowledge. In-service training is not well designed for learning and integrating such skills into the teacher's routine—not just classroom preparation, but the teacher's practice overall.

Further, as discussed elsewhere in this book, science teachers tend to be isolated from teacher colleagues on the one hand, and from colleagues in their science on the other. Therefore, the community activities that support and stimulate change in practice—shoptalk, advice, and example—are little available.

With these very real and pervasive obstacles as a backdrop, the next section describes the LabNetwork from the user's point of view.

THE LABNETWORK

Most LabNet participants connected to the network using the Tymnet carrier service, which has local access numbers in many locations across the country. For those who had no such local number near them, Delphi (see the glossary at the end of chapter 1) provided access through a toll-free number (the cost of whose installation was borne by the LabNet project). Each member had a username (built on the person's name and state of residence), and a password.

When users log on for the first time, they move through a programmed series of menus that allow them to choose a new password and to set certain characteristics of the interface, such as the number of characters per line, the number of lines on the screen, and so forth. Users can recall this initial program at any time if they wish to change the settings they have made. Otherwise, this initial program effectively vanishes, and as far as we could tell, these initial choices, once made, were rarely altered, unless a user began using a new computer.

Once logged on, the user sees "banners," messages that the network manager can create in order to make announcements to the whole network. (These can be permanently visible, or they can be flagged so that a user only sees them once.) Banners are no more than a few lines long, and there can be no more than eight. A sample set follows:

```
Username: TERCBD
Password: ••••••

Hello TERCBD

Welcome to LabNet!

Copyright (c) General Videotex Corporation.
Technical Education Resource Centers.

Logon at   : 26-FEB-1992 14:15:40
Last Logon : 25-FEB-1992 13:34:04

** See FORUM 1145 for a revised description of the FORUM
TOPICS **

─────── ANNOUNCEMENTS ───────
*** See USING LABNET for articles on using FORUM, MAIL,
and for Hardware/Software documentation. ***
.................................................................
Send questions and suggestions about the network to
TERCBD (Brian Drayton)
```

After the banners, the user is at the system prompt:

```
LabNet>What do you want to do?
```

This is the entry point to all the other system services. The user can (by typing a command) connect to the Forum, to Mail, to the Workspace, or to Databases. (If you have mail waiting to be read, you will see a notice about it before the banners go by.) The system allows you to type an abbreviated version of any command (usually one or two letters are enough).

Each subsystem has a characteristic prompt, which helps users orient themselves. At each prompt there are several possible commands, and the user can ask for reminders or help from the system at each decision point. In general, you must return to the top-level LabNet> prompt in order to enter a new subsystem. The most important exceptions are that you can call up Mail from within the Forum, and that you can put files into the Workspace and recall files from it while in either Mail or Forum.

Mail and Forum allow the user to read a message and reply to it, and also to post a new message that has no antecedents. In both cases, you can either type the message while connected to the network, or use a prepared message file, written on your personal computer, transmitted to and stored in the Workspace. You can also take any message or group of messages on the Forum or in Mail and have them filed as a text file in the Workspace, from which you can have them sent to your personal computer. Once stored there, the message can be called into the user's word-processing program as with any other text file.

The Forum, Mail, and Database look like this upon entry:

Forum

```
LabNet>What do you want to do? forum

LabNet's Forum is the focus for on-line discussion.
Some of the more popular commands include:

ADD New Message (Thread)  DIRECTORY of Messages
REPLY To Current Message  FORWARD Message by Mail
READ Message(s)           DELETE Message
FOLLOW Thread             FILE Message to Workspace
BACK to Previous Message  HELP
EXIT

To see a complete list of commands available in Forum,
type question mark "?" at the Forum> prompt.

Type read 1145 at the FORUM> prompt for a description
of topics.

Welcome to the LabNet Message Forum.

Forum contains messages 800 to 2257.
Highest message you've read is 2206.

Press RETURN to READ NEW Messages.
FORUM>Reply, Add, Read, "?" or Exit> read 2207
```

```
2207 3-FEB 21:37  Other
   genetics/biotechnology labs
   From: TTHOMOR
   To: ALL
```

A teacher on another network is requesting information
on successful genetics or biotechnology type labs. Does
anyone out there have something you want to share? Let
me know. I can forward names, addresses or activities.

Tom Thompson
_*_

Mail

LabNet>What do you want to do? mail

MAIL> dir

# From	Date	Subject
1 BOS1A::GWALKER	23-AUG-1991	acid rain curriculum
2 BOS1C::WEDDING	26-AUG-1991	RE: 1-800
3 BOS2A::RUSTY	27-AUG-1991	800 line is back up
4 BOS2A::NMRANCK	27-AUG-1991	binary up/downloads
5 BOS2A::RUSTY	27-AUG-1991	RE: Picked up?

_*_

Databases

LabNet>What do you want to do? databases

TOPIC>Which topic? ?

Databases Available Menu:

Other	Hardware/Software
Alternative Energy	Meteors
LabNet News	Student Projects
Astronomy	Managers Only
Design	PREVIEW Area
Curriculum Issues	ZZFORMS Area
Ways and Means	

TOPIC>Which topic?

It is possible to get on the network, file, and download everything new on the Forum since you last used it, and download your mail, in about 5 minutes, once you understand how the various parts of the system relate and you are practiced in its use. Some telecommunication software allows you to write scripts—sequences of commands that effectively automate routine procedures, such as logging in and picking up new messages.

This approach minimizes the time on-line, and therefore the cost. It is not possible to work with this efficiency until you have learned the system, typically spending 1 to 3 hours (depending on previous experience) to explore the system structure and to learn how your telecommunication software and the network interact.

Further, when you try something new on the system, the time on-line is lengthened beyond the routine. As you gain familiarity with the system, you learn to "think like the system" and can therefore anticipate and learn system features more quickly. Some systems provide simulations which can cut the time needed to learn the system's conventions before getting on line, though "live" experience inevitably raises unanticipated questions.

The time on-line relates directly to the costs. Originally, we had recommended that teachers budget $50 per month, because we were not sure how they would use the network, and the teachers varied widely in their familiarity with the medium. This budget amount turned out to be pessimistic. There were occasionally people who spent that much or more per month, but the average was far less. Over the period from September 1991 through January 1992, for example, the average monthly cost was $11.95, which represents slightly less than 1 hour's on-line time. The rate that most LabNet members paid was 21¢ per minute, or $12.60 per hour. This was a special rate worked out with Delphi for the LabNet group. Most network systems have cheaper "off-peak" rates, as well as the "peak rates" for daytime access.

On-line costs available to telecommunication consumers continue to drop little by little. Commercial off-peak rates less than $10 per hour are not hard to find and even lower rates are sometimes available. The costs of efficient use are now in roughly the same range as a subscription to a professional journal. Nevertheless, these costs can be problematic for teachers, as schools do not habitually provide for this new category of expense.

THE MEDIUM

[O]n-line resources must include more than just information. The network conversation as demonstrated in the LabNet forum is one such resource. This kind of conversation is potent because it is interactive and asynchronous. Time delays, and the fact that the medium encourages multiple threads of content, encourage the cycle of reflection, experimentation, and reporting that adds to the depth of the conversation.[1]

Electronic networks offer a variety of services, each of which can make a particular contribution to the functioning of the system. In this section, we discuss the tools provided by the LabNetwork; our purpose is to outline the general design issues surrounding each type of tool, and show how LabNet results have shaped our thinking on these issues. Throughout our

---

[1] The quotation is from a TERC proposal to NSF. For a discussion of some relevant issues see Black, Levin, Mehan, and Quinn (1983).

discussion, the specification of each tool is important, but even more critical are the kinds of interactions each tool can support. Before turning to specific tools, we place them in a broader context, examining the potential of telecommunication as a medium, and the practical impediments to its use.

The Promise of the Medium

A cautious observer of the history of educational technology might predict that telecommunication will turn out to be another of those innovations that can never deliver what its advance publicity would suggest. The following is a typical promissory example: "It could be argued that CMC [computer-mediated communication] is the ideal vehicle for breaking up the educational 'package' and facilitating the processes of internal reflection and reorganization through dialogue, argument, and debate" (Mason & Kaye, 1990, p. 17).

Yet, despite formidable disincentives, enough teachers and students have used networks (as have enough workers in other environments) that the advantages of telecommunication are not a matter of guesswork. Chief among them are the following.

It is Flexible in Content

A notable feature of this medium, in contrast to other high technologies for the classroom, is that it carries no content of its own; it does not seize control of the stage—it is a conduit of great power and flexibility, but only for the purpose of overcoming the disadvantages of distance and time. It cannot supplant any player in the school setting, but can enlarge the universe of discourse.

Although the medium itself is content-free, any particular network may be restricted or dedicated to a particular content area or type of discourse. Early in the LabNet project we faced a decision about how much content to provide for discussions on the network. At first we assumed that the most important function the network could play was as a means to share practical materials—specific activities for the physics classroom, for example. This assumption grew out of our own and others' experiences with networks whose success seemed to be due in large measure to the provision of structure and content. However, as we began the LabNet experiment and observed early responses, we concluded that the LabNetwork should not be so focused, because its goals were not like those of other networks, including TERC's other network projects. We left it to teachers to define the content of network communications.

It Breaks Geographic Isolation

This has been an important point in the LabNet experience. Many schools have only one teacher (if that) for each science specialty—one physics teacher, one chemistry teacher, and so forth. Shoptalk of the sort that integrates specialty knowledge with pedagogy and logistical considerations is hard to come by in these situations. Professional organizations, such as the American Association of Physics Teachers (AAPT) and the National Association of Biology Teachers (NABT), supply some of what is missing, by occasional large meetings and by publications, but such media are not adequate, because of their infrequency and removal from teachers' daily practice—they do not provide interactive partnership. The LabNetwork helped teachers connect with each other quickly and often:

> The network has provided me access to other physics teachers. I have gained valuable help from them already this year.

> Communicating with other physics teachers and starting on projects that will extend to the future is WONDERFUL! (quotes from Gal, 1990b, p. 5)

It Increases the Number of Voices in a Conversation

A corollary of the previous point is that a conversation can be many-sided on a network that has bulletin board facilities. Where use is frequent, the network provides a real forum, a round-table discussion with many voices. This is a prime setting for peer influence, for collaboration, and for reflection in the context of practice.

It is Asynchronous

Many methods of communication are recommended to us because of speed and instantaneous feedback—that, for example, is the attraction of fax technology. Network communications can be very quick, and several of the excerpts from the LabNet Forum show how one can sometimes get responses within minutes (although there is more often a time lag of a day or more; see chapter 4 for an example of quick turnaround). In fact, however, asynchronous communication has several advantages, especially for people like teachers with little freedom during working hours (i.e., during the school day) to use and respond to the network.

- It allows the user to control the time of communication. This means that the teacher can fit network participation into his or her day. The task of finding time remains, but the network does not impose any particular schedule itself.

- This ability to control the tempo of participation means that one can participate in depth. The conversations can include the fruits of reference to various sources of information, the reports of experimentation and classroom experiences, so that the exchanges of information are intricately bound up with the learning and teaching activities that provide much of the subject matter for discussion.

- Because network bulletin boards typically maintain a large percentage of the messages sent in some kind of archive or other holding area on the network, earlier conversations can be scanned and revived or used for reference. One of the functions of a moderator on a network can be to review earlier material for relevance to current concerns. The usefulness of the historical record is greatly enhanced if the material is also searchable by topic or keyword.

- An asynchronous bulletin board can carry a wide range of conversations (Beals, 1991, pp. 74-77).

When a network can carry more than text messages, it enables the participants to communicate in many modes. Because these discussions are open, and not ephemeral, unlike private e-mail exchanges, the public, multiparty discussions can further change relationships between students and teachers, make relating to a community of peers more realistic, and therefore help alter power relationships between teachers and other members of the educational system. This kind of change is consonant with the approach to education that we advocate, in which teachers (and students) are seen as creative members of the educational community, taking part in conceptual and policy developments rather than being the recipients of other authorities' output.

Impediments to Adoption

There are two factors that place real and powerful constraints on teachers' use of telecommunication: time, and the variety of hardware and software available for any particular application. Educational innovators tend to see these difficulties as logistical and not matters of principle; they look forward to an era when all these problems will have been solved. In the long run, however, they might have more durable results if they include the teaching and learning community in the design of the next steps, regarding the current troubles of implementation as the state of the art, the incubator for the next stage of development. In the end, such participation would result in more widespread and lasting adoption of new technology.

Time Constraints

Time is important for teachers on two counts, as reported in almost every study ever done of educational telecomputing (Riel & Levin, 1990; Weir, 1992). First, time is scarce for learning new technologies. Even a teacher who has used computer applications like word processors or MBL systems might easily require 3 to 5 hours to get used to the features of a new system, and this might cost as much as $60 in on-line charges.

Software designers are too rarely sensitive to the time demands on teacher-users and the profound effect of learning time on the acceptance of a given system. For example, one study of electronic-mail systems found that different interfaces required as few as 2 or as many as 12 hours of training before users achieved the same levels of proficiency. Ease of learning was directly related to the acceptance and use of the different systems by teachers in public schools.[2]

The fact that there is a "meter running" is sometimes inhibiting to teachers who need to get on and explore the new system—doubly so if it includes large reservoirs of on-line text (database entries, bulletin-board discussions, etc.). A crucial skill to learn is efficient use of the software, but shortcuts are hard to get across until someone understands how the system works—thus workshop sessions full of "shortcut tips" are of limited use for the new user. The sense of economic restriction is heightened by the fact that telecommunication does not yet fall into the usual categories of expenditure for school systems.

The time needed to learn a system is greatly extended by sporadic use. A teacher who gets on-line once a month will very likely have forgotten many of the facts he or she had gleaned in the last on-line session, which are a necessary part of the "at-your-fingertips" feeling that helps a user get around quickly and efficiently. Thus, each infrequent session is likely to feel like a cold start, until the teacher realizes that more frequent use is an important element of efficiency and of profitable network interaction.

The second way in which time constrains new users of telecomputing is the difficulty of incorporating the technology into the already packed daily routine:

> One of my biggest problems was time. Six classes in a seven-period day. Training a new physics teacher....

> LabNet is a great idea. The biggest problem is: We get too busy to plan and implement new ideas. I get swamped and fall back on the "old ways."

> How much new do I want to bring in, and what am I going to have to get rid of to make room?

As noted in chapter 3, when respondents to the Spring 1991 Teacher Questionnaire who had not used the LabNetwork were asked why, the most common reason given was time (Gal, Lockett, & Parrott, 1991, p. 24). It takes time to understand how the material (information, discussion, and other resources) from a network can fit into the rhythm of preparation and conducting of classes. Should the students be active on the network? Should I use the network as part of class time? If not, when and how will I get access? How will it cut into my use of other resources—and will that be a net loss or gain for me in my work? The saving grace of the LabNet experience for most of those who found it useful was that they were talking to their peers, to other practitioners of the craft and art of physics teaching;

---

[2] Bull et al. (1992, p. 2) presented a very helpful case study of network design. See also Bruce and Rubin (1992). West et al. (1989, p. 30) provided a thoughtful consideration based on the Common Ground experience, with a somewhat different emphasis from LabNet's.

this kind of interchange is very often of value, providing both "resources" in the usual sense—ideas for activities, answers to science questions, and so on—and the resource of perspective that comes from shoptalk.

The Variety of Hardware and Software

The second impediment to the use of telecommunication is the variety of equipment and software that exists in the educational world. Among the machines currently used by teachers are the Apple II series, IBM and IBM-compatibles, Commodore and Amiga systems, Macintoshes of all types, as well as older machines. This variety creates serious compatibility problems, which are exacerbated by the many proprietary software packages on the market. Even when compatibility problems can be solved, they add significantly to startup time. As one struggling LabNet teacher remarked:

> I have a Zil modem and a Mac at home that I'm comfortable with, but I've got a different system, an Apple IIe and Prometheus modem at school, and I haven't found a way to upload files yet...so it's a matter of getting to the manual and finding the right sequence. (quote from a 1990 interview with a LabNet teacher)

Network Tools

E-mail

The core service on a network is electronic mail (e-mail). This allows private exchanges, or exchanges within a group specified ad hoc (with such devices as mailing or distribution lists, carbon copies, and the like). E-mail confines the conversation to the addressees, and even if a new member is added to the distribution list, the history of the group is mostly not available. Such media do not allow auditors and browsers, and therefore play a different role from other services, such as bulletin boards, in the community of practice that we envision.

In tandem with bulletin-board services, e-mail allows a partitioning of the types of messages that are composed. In our experience, teachers have welcomed this flexibility. It adds to the usefulness of the system, because purely small-scale exchanges do not clutter the public forums, and the interlocutors do not have to worry about whether their conversation is of general interest. As noted in chapter 3, the mail feature of LabNet was very popular. On average, participants estimated that they had sent over 30 messages during the 1990-1991 school term (Gal et al., 1991, p. 26).

E-mail carried all kinds of messages: personal notes, follow-ups on Forum messages, data or program files, large documents, technical support, and project management. E-mail was a common way to respond to student queries posted first on the Forum, since many of these dealt with areas of inquiry not of general interest.

A major problem caused by the heavy use of e-mail is that sometimes material that is very much of general interest is hidden from view. This can actually lead to morale problems at the stage of a network's development when public messages are few—people get on and see little public activity, so they are discouraged from participating. In fact at such times there may be lively private correspondence. The mail systems used by TERC have been protective of privacy, but when we have tracked mail volumes, or asked for information about people's usage habits, we have invariably found a higher than predicted amount of private exchange.

TERC staff have sometimes wondered if this is only a problem to the staff, who want to have a clear overall picture of what is happening—a desire not felt with the same urgency by the ordinary user, who is using each of the network tools as appropriate for his or her needs. In at least one case, however, a major initiative (investigating the lifetimes of incandescent light bulbs under various conditions) began on the network, and then moved to e-mail, so that despite frequent appeals for updates, most of us never heard the results from this interesting comparative experiment.

The "core" nature of e-mail comes in part from the fact that it is often the easiest to learn of the various on-line features, and its use has the best nontelecommunication analogy—written mail of various kinds. The intuitive accessibility helps teachers learn the basic functions quickly, so that on an active network the rewards of telecommunication are visible from the early stages of use. Further, the e-mail system is, despite possible modifications and extensions, a one-on-one exchange, and this allows users to build their electronic network use on their personal network—other users whom they know personally, whether through project-related workshops or other professional contacts. This communication fits preexisting patterns. Not surprisingly, those who are comfortable with telephone or memo communication make rapid progress in the use of e-mail.

On the other hand, there is one analog with postal mail or personal conversation that is not so accessible on an electronic network—nontext data. When I send a letter to you, I can enclose a photograph, news clipping, or even a computer disk. When I send you an e-mail message, how shall I enclose things with my note? This barrier is not an intrinsic one at all: Most e-mail systems, including the Delphi system, have facilities for all types of file exchange. The implementation of this capability, however, has been a source of frequent frustration for LabNet users, and few have overcome the barriers to its use. The two most important impediments are the task of learning the transfer protocols necessary to send and receive files in non-ASCII format, and the problem of software compatibility between sender and receiver. Although both matters are straightforward enough as stated, the great number of software options that exist render them daunting for many users, who do not know much about how the software works, or what its precise functions are. In this case, the individual operating systems on personal computers have far outstripped the developments in telecommunication software and protocols.

On most personal computers, operating systems are increasingly hidden from the uninterested user—you can point at icons and move them with a mouse, and the right things happen: The focus is on the function, not the process. In telecommunication settings, however, one is often faced with choices that require some new knowledge of the chooser: Do I need to compress this data? Hadn't I better have a modem with error-checking? Why does the program keep telling me about retries and errors in transmission? Will the receiver be able to get this, if his version of *Works* is different from mine?

To the technophile, these questions have direct answers; to the teacher hard-pressed for time, the contrast with one's well-known desktop system is forbidding. The upshot in many cases is silence, or a sheepish recourse to the U.S. Postal Service. New developments in telecommunication software promise hope for the near future, but with the great variety of equipment now in use in the educational market, the effects of innovation will necessarily be slow.

Bulletin Boards

In the following discussion, we use *bulletin board* or *forum* to describe a network facility for public, asynchronous, message exchange. Some systems, such as EcoNet/PeaceNet, call such facilities *conferences*, but this term is widely understood to mean real-time network discussions that are more like telephone *conference calls*.

The next most common network service, often built as an extension on the e-mail system, is some kind of forum or bulletin board. Forums allow the development of a conversation that is effortlessly public; that is, everyone with access to the network can "listen in" and participate as they wish. Such community discussions can include a mix of all kinds of messages—practical information, personal information, requests for advice, and gossip and its superset, metacognition.

LabNet's Forum was, in the language of chapter 3, like a city piazza, a central "meeting place" for many-party, transformational discussions, which are a necessary foundation for a widespread change in practice. Evaluative discourse is a stimulator of change, as well as a reinforcer of community values. In our experience, the network can be a welcoming environment for such explorations, but only in the context of practical discussion and some personal knowledge.

It was in large part because the TERC Star Schools system, based primarily on e-mail, lacked a facility for this kind of bulletin board that LabNet transferred to the Delphi system, which had a bulletin board as part of its service (there were other considerations of software design and maintenance, which are addressed later). This bulletin board, the Forum, is mostly maintained by the user group in question (e.g., LabNet), with aid from Delphi on request. The interface is customizable to a certain degree, in collaboration with Delphi: The user group managers can supply their own system-level messages to the group, can alter help messages, and can alter members' network privileges. Any group member can read messages from the Forum, and can add new messages or reply to old ones. Messages stay on the network, accessible to all, until removed, either by the system manager or by the person who posted the message originally. There is no system for self-archiving of the Forum messages (this feature is discussed more in the final section of this chapter).

The Forum and Mail are closely connected: You can call up Mail from within the Forum to respond privately to a public message. Each user has an area of memory on Delphi called the Workspace, in which he or she can store files downloaded from Mail and also files created from Forum messages. The Workspace serves as a kind of transfer station between Delphi and the user's computer. When uploading messages for the Forum, or files to send as Mail, you upload to the Workspace. Files created on Delphi, either from Mail or the Forum, are moved into the Workspace, from which the user can then download them to his or her own computer for storage and use. In this way, you can create a large file from the Forum and transfer it to your personal computer for later use and processing. The connection between Mail and Forum encouraged LabNet members to use both. It also created the question of when to use which medium. Although some messages, clearly personal, were not for the Forum, and some were clearly of general interest, many seemed to fall in between, and early on there was frequent conversation about what was appropriate.

An important consideration is the network's ability to structure the entries in the bulletin board/forum. A first requisite is the ability to see and search through a directory of the contents. Most services allow one to search through various fields associated with each message, such as sender, receiver, date, or subject. More is necessary, however, in a conversation that includes more than a few participants, or that lasts more than a short time, as messages accumulate and topics of conversation multiply. There must be some way of tracking messages that are interrelated by subject matter, but also that are part of a historical sequence.

On the Delphi system, this typical problem is solved by the mechanisms of threads and topics (see chapter 4). Topics set general areas of discussion: examples from LabNet include "Curriculum issues," "LabNet news," "Hardware/Software," and project-focused items like "Astronomy," "Eratosthenes," and "Meteors." Every message belongs to one of the topics. The topic names are chosen by the network manager, and set up by Delphi. This arrangement created an inflexibility in the system that was detrimental from the point of view of the LabNet experiment, as is discussed in more detail later.

Besides belonging to a topic, each message is identified according to another criterion: Is it the beginning of a conversation, or is it a response to a conversation already begun? Messages that reply to a previous message, together with the first message in the conversation, are linked together as a thread. A thread is a data structure, which the system can manipulate to some degree—the user can see a directory of all messages that are part of a thread, can go to the head of the thread, and can move backward and forward along it.

These structural characteristics make it possible to explore the contents of the forum, but there are certain difficulties. In the first place, the topic structure is constrained by the system software, so that a forum can have no more than (currently) 16 topics. Further, if the conversation proceeds to the point that a whole new topic makes sense, it is very difficult to reorganize, subdivide, or otherwise rearrange the materials to reflect a new conception of the group's interests.

For example, several LabNet teachers decided to collaborate on a meteor watch: Students from classes in widely separated locations would all watch the same meteor shower (see later for excerpts from the network exchange). This would involve some logistical discussions, and the sharing of some background information about watching meteor showers, about the historically recorded behavior of this particular shower, and so forth. LabNet set up a new topic, "Meteors," to organize this discussion, and the analysis and reporting that would follow. After this shower had passed (and various classes had had various degrees of success in their observations), teachers suggested other possible network projects in astronomy. We decided (in part because of teacher requests) to rename the topic, and use the meteor discussion and its sequels to start things off in the new topic, Astronomy. The system bookkeeping made that practically difficult, so that messages either were deleted, or downloaded to the manager's disk, deleted from the Forum, and uploaded from the manager's disk as though they were new items.

This kind of inflexibility is counterproductive, and is another example of the way that software systems, like operating systems, make demands that are arbitrary from the user's point of view, and have no particular compensating value. The Common Ground network had similar problems with the categorization of discussion topics on their forum (see Katz, McSwiney, & Stroud, 1987, pp. 10ff; West et al., 1989, p. 28).

This issue contributed to the decision by some teachers, as mentioned earlier, to communicate about their "light bulb" experiment using e-mail, rather than the public Forum. This project, based on ideas discussed in some LabNet workshop sessions, provided an interesting opportunity for whole class projects, as each class studied the lifetime of several bulbs of standard wattage under various current conditions. This instructive project would introduce students to many fundamental aspects of experimental design, data collection and analysis, and the communication of results and progress.

The organizing teachers used the Forum to find others who were interested in collaborating in the project—helping to decide on basic experimental design issues, and sharing data and reports frequently. While the teachers were organizing, they asked TERC to set up a Forum topic for the project. At the time, the network manager recommended that the project use an existing "omnibus" topic, until it was clear what the volume of communication about the project would be. The organizers decided that the lack of separation for the discussion would be detrimental to the success of the project, and consequently the collaborators agreed to use e-mail instead of the public Forum.

A related facility that is desirable but not often found is the ability to build hierarchical structures, such as subdirectories (subtopics). The ability to subcategorize allows the network conversation to branch naturally, but take advantage of the data management facilities to keep a clear structure within the growing number of messages. A very common situation in which this can further the development of a network conversation is in the growth of a new topic, when, early on, the amount of interest in some nuance of the subject is not known. When a certain momentum has developed, then it is helpful to be able easily to separate the new circle into its own area.

The LabNetwork's method of file organization may have been something of a deterrent to LabNet users. A common query to the network manager at workshops was what current "Topic" to use for a particular discussion that a LabNet participant wanted to start. From the point of view of user comfort, especially under the time pressures that teachers feel, it is important to realize that technophiles—people for whom telecommunication is an accepted part of their repertoire—have learned to live with a common software dilemma. The designer of a system, no matter how widely he or she may consult others, will in the end make design decisions that will not feel right and natural to all users. Experienced software users recognize this (at least implicitly) as unavoidable, and are accustomed to working around or otherwise reaching an accommodation with the designer's ideas. The new user, on the other hand, especially if occasional, will often feel disinclined to put up with someone else's choices.

Unwillingness to work within an externally imposed framework may be especially pronounced and widespread in settings like LabNet, in which the network is in the service of a developing community whose conversation includes both "subject matter," such as the science and pedagogy of optics or lasers, and the structure and dynamics of the community itself. Such a group of users will want to have a notable role in the way the information on the network is structured. It will then have to face the challenge of maintaining the structure as it has developed.

Perhaps for reasons such as these, perhaps for reasons intrinsic to the types of discussions that people wished to have, few threads on the LabNetwork included more than three replies (though there have been some notable substantive exceptions). The meteor watch was one such exchange, which required the coordination of several parties and a decision about the protocol for the observation. Even here, there was little back and forth; the leader suggested the time and asked if anyone else was interested. Several teachers responded. The leader defined the time (dictated by the behavior of the meteor shower, of course), and then suggested a procedure. There were a couple of questions of fact, and then reports from all parties (mostly that weather had prevented them from taking data), but although the thread had multiple entries, there was little development of content, and no interpretation of the results, nor reports about classroom follow-ups.

From: JCPOTTS
To: ALL

I am proposing that a large number of LabNet sites should collaborate on gathering information of the type described above.

This project would provide an opportunity to integrate a number of diverse topics such as astronomy, time signals, wave phenomena, optics etc. The information generated would be unique and of some very real value. The data could be submitted to appropriate astronomical groups and thus provide our students with an opportunity to contribute to the advancement of science.
_*_

From: TERCBS
To: JCPOTTS

Count me in John!!! I can commit at least 100 eyes in Wellesley MA
_*_

From: CRINGER
To: JCPOTTS

JC, I would like more information on the meteor watch... Although the atmosphere around here is not the most transparent, and we suffer from 50% overcast weather, we might get lucky. If you like, upload your proposed method and time lines. Sounds like a perfect application of the Lab Net concept.

Emmett Riordan (Cringer)
_*_

From: TERCAW
To: JCPOTTS

Two things about the meteors project.

1. I've just realized that April 22nd is Earth Day.
Maybe we can somehow link the meteor watch to that?

2. I'd like to interest some regular meteor watchers in
our project. I've been given one contact: American
Meteor Society....

How did you choose the April 22nd meteor shower in
preference to one of the better known ones? (For example
the Perseids in August or the Leonids in November).
—*—

From: JCPOTTS
To: TERCAW

I selected this shower because it is the only good one
between now and when school gets out for the summer If
there is quite a lot of interest I would like to get
such observations set up as a regular type of activity.

I am hoping this will generate some real interest in
LabNet. I feel that LabNet can be a powerful teaching
tool if we can just get people involved.
—*—

From: TERCAW
To: JCPOTTS

...I'm just sorry that LabNet is not in contact with
similar organizations in other countries so we could
really cover the entire duration of the meteor shower.

There's also lots of basic physics that could be tied to
the meteor observations (kinetic/ thermal energy,
momentum, orbits, statistical reliability of counting
experiments) and different observation techniques
(photography, having observers thirty miles apart
observe the same meteor to get an idea of height and
speed)...
—*—

From: JCPOTTS
To: ALL

For all of you who will be participating in the
meteor count I hope you have clear skies and good
weather. I want to caution you to tell your students to

be sure to dress very warmly. Even if the weather is
nice dress as if it were winter. Particularly be sure
to wear insulated boots or overshoes and a couple of
pairs of very warm socks. Students tend to forget that
they will not be moving around much and they will get
cold.

The Audio-visual person and I found an interesting
way to prepare star maps. We used a scanner to
digitalize a star map from Sky and Telescope into a Mac
and then reversed the image and printed it on the laser
printer/ We then made a transparency on the xerox. I am
using a back lighted (red bulb) viewer and the kids will
mark the meteor trails on a sheet of tracing paper Best
of luck.

We are hoping for clear skies here but the weather
forecast is not overly optimistic (that is all right
because it is usually wrong anyway).

_-*-_

From: JCPOTTS
To: TERCBS

Bruce — I plan to have my students observe on the
morning of the 22nd. The available references indicate
that the Lyrid shower is between the 19th and the 23
with the maximum on the 22nd.

Actually this shower is not too well studied and it is a
shame that we don't have enough bodies to cover the
entire duration.

The 22nd is best for me because the kids will have a
chance to get some sleep Sunday. From a personal
standpoint it is not all that convenient as I will be in
Missoula Saturday morning and will have an eight hour +
drive to be back for the activity.

_-*-_

From: TERCBS
To: ALL

The weather in the northeast is CLOUDY AND RAINY...
darn... Had to call 20 students in Wellesley to
cancel.... oh well maybe another time.... looks like
there is some interest in the Perseids even though it is
summer—maybe....... hope others had success!!!!

Bruce as TERCBS /\/\/\/\/\/\//\/\/\/\//\/\/

_-*-_

From: RELYON
To: JCPOTTS

Clouds and rain all weekend in NW Washington State. In
fact clouds will no doubt continue all week making up
for a very dry beginning of the month- 18 days without
rain. That is not usual for the spring.
-*-

From: GLOCKETT
To: JCPOTTS

Dear John,

Our meteor watch was wiped out by a storm.....
-*-

483 27APR90-2303 Meteors
     RE: lyrid meteor shower
     From: JCPOTTS
     To: ALL

All in all the observing session that we had for the
Lyrids was quite successful here in Miles City. We
counted 39 shower members and 14 sporadics. We started
at 11:30 PM MDT and ended at 2:00 AM MDT. We had to
stop early due to cloud cover which was spotty most of
the evening but which increased substantially shortly
after 2:00 AM.

We have prepared a summary of our data in which we have
calculated the hourly count rate based on the 30 minute
time period centered on each 10 minute interval between
11:30 PM and 2:00 AM. The data follows...
-*-

534 17MAY90-0959 Meteors
     RE: lyrid meteor shower (Re: Msg 483)
     From: TERCAW
     To: JCPOTTS

Congratulations on your observations of the Lyrids. It's
a pity the rest of us got rained out. Rain came down
cats and dogs here on the night I planned to watch. I
wonder did you get any results at all from other sites
or was the cloud cover absolute?

I'm interested to see your counts were so much higher
than those in the reference books.

...The bulge about 6.8 hours is certainly an interesting
part of your results. Is there any chance this was

```
caused by the cloud cover reducing temporarily so you
could see more of the sky?
_*_

606 1JUN90-2255 Meteors
    Lyrids
    From: JCPOTTS
    To: TERCAW

    In response to your message (#534) of 17-May I
believe that the peak that we observed at about 6.8
hours was a real result of meteor swarm structure which
was....
_*_
```

Another set of exchanges that were structurally very similar were the messages that arose in the course of the Eratosthenes experiment (see chapter 4 for excerpts and discussion).

Databases

Advertisements for networks tend to emphasize their database capabilities, especially the availability of large standard reference sources, such as encyclopedias. If one reflects on the kind of reference material needed most often in the course of the typical day, these large general reference collections form a valuable, regular, but small proportion of the total resources needed. Much more often one values professional materials of many kinds. For teachers, these include case studies from other teachers, references about sources for apparatus and materials, literature and information about evaluation and assessment, and materials for professional enhancement. West et al. (1989, pp. 12, 30) reported as an important consideration teachers' hunger for specific material, easily transferred to their own classrooms. The database is an important resource in the search for all these tools of the trade. (Specific recommendations for the content of a database appear in the last section of this chapter.)

A database must be a growing repository; teachers as members of the community of practice must be both receivers and contributors. Another important role the database can play is as the archive for public discussions on the bulletin board. This historical backlog can in some measure overcome one disadvantage of the asynchronous nature of the medium—the uncertainty about when a response to a query will come. As the network grows through time, its archives will contain the results of many conversations on topics of perennial interest, and if the database is user-friendly enough, the teacher in a hurry can hunt there for needed resources if a current response on the network does not come in time. Katz et al. (1987, p. 36) felt that their experiment showed the need for this "real-time" backlog for reference, on a system that lacked it.

The LabNet database is of this interactive sort, but it must be said that the databases were not much used, and the only content was posted by TERC staff—this was in marked contrast to the lively, general use of the Forum. The reasons, as noted in chapter 3, are not clear, though we have some hunches. In the first place, the Forum acts as a historical repository, since it is searchable and familiar. In the second place, the Delphi databases are not straightforward to use, and it may be that the workshops did not help people to overcome this. As one teacher, who was also co-author of the evaluation report, observed:

> From my personal experience at the Michigan workshop, I would say that although we were encouraged to use all features, a concerted effort was made to ensure that all could use Mail and the Forum. Staff demonstrations and comments led me to conclude that there were some problems with the...databases. (Gal et al., 1991, p. 23)

Teachers are increasingly using reference databases of all kinds. Despite the limited use of the LabNet Databases, we believe that, for a community part of whose mission is classroom change, it is important to understand how to structure interactive databases, and to stimulate their use. We conjecture that software design and technical support will remove many obstacles that LabNet participants met in trying to use this tool.

Other Services

The Delphi system that LabNet used includes, as a facility separate from the databases, a members' directory. Usage was strictly voluntary, and was sporadic—perhaps as many as 60% of the participants made entries. The directory has often been referred to by others, however. As the network has grown, it has become increasingly important for members to be able to learn who is on-line and who has been recently active (through some kind of log-on record), and to be able to search through people's self-descriptions, in order to establish personal connections based on common interests, geographical location, and similar factors. Such membership databases are common on networks, and are often supplemented by facilities for searching for who is on-line currently. Katz et al. (1987) described similar features for the Common Ground network.

As mentioned earlier, Delphi also has a workspace facility, a member-specific storage area, which serves as the locus to and from which files are transferred for the Forum and Mail. The Workspace also provides on-line text editing.

It is safe to say that the Workspace was little used, except for file transfer. Teachers found it hard to learn, and although they concentrated on the uses of Forum and Mail, they saw little need for the Workspace. As a result, they used their time at the workshops principally to make sure that they understood the network operations and their own software. Many teachers later learned about the Workspace (and databases) at home, by correspondence over the network or telephone calls to TERC or colleagues.

The file-management and text-editing facilities of the Workspace were of essentially no use to the LabNet teachers, who found it easier and cheaper to get the text or other file onto their personal computer and work with it there. The file structure on all on-line facilities was important for the location of items, but each teacher organized the useful portion of that material in his or her own way.

Who Is the Community?

Teachers do not work alone. It is important to ask which of the many other groups that are part of the classroom's context might usefully take part in a teachers' network community. This section considers the role of students and of nonschool institutions, including "professional innovators" like TERC.

Students on the Network

How should students participate in a teachers' network—if at all? The LabNet project explored this question at several points in its history, and the answer depends on one's point of view about telecommunication in the classroom. It has been clear for a long time that telecommunication can be stimulating to students by putting them in quick and personal contact with other students at a distance. It has been harder to demonstrate further benefits from student telecommunication, beyond this "pen pal" feature, which is by no means trivial. Despite the benefits of student engagement— "even if" it comes from a novelty—thoughtful teachers rightly hope to see benefits directly related to learning, and remain skeptical about the value of telecommunication for their classrooms. The skepticism often derives from the teacher's concept of education:

> I teach objective, high-level, college prep physics. I don't want my students to get lost in social interactions or "activities" that do not prepare for college.

In fact, a network has for students many of the virtues that come from conversation and discussion in the classroom. The students find their own voices, test the depth of their understanding as they participate in the discourse, develop their analytical and critical thinking skills by the exchange of information and contrasting opinions.

Furthermore, it is astonishing how rarely students talk about science content (or math content, for that matter). It can be a major breakthrough when a student realizes this, and senses the immediacy and intellectual power such conversation has (see selected responses from LabNet's student questionnaire at the end of chapter 6):

...usually in science we don't communicate with other people, we just learn about it, like astronomy and different stuff. But [when using the network] we got to talk to other people.

...you got to know your classmates better 'cause you worked together and then you communicated over the network to other schools...you got responses back and you would answer questions and stuff.

Our students were excited by the ability and challenge of exchanging ideas and solutions with other students all over the country. They were especially encouraged that they were just as capable (often more) than students in other parts of the country when they have been told that they and their school system are second rate (quotes from Weir, Krensky, & Gal, 1990).

Nevertheless, as we have argued elsewhere in discussing teachers' shoptalk, students' exchanges on most networks must include a lot of peripheral, social discussion. This is especially so because students usually do not have the benefits of direct, face-to-face contact that teachers may get in workshops or conventions. They are quick to notice and explore differences and similarities in their interlocutors, and this gives a sense of reality and richness to the "technical" discussions they know to be their "real" business on the network.

Teachers who are interested in telecommunication are eager to make it available to their students, sensing the role it can play in learning. Teacher interest in students' use of telecommunication has been a prime motivator for developments in educational telecomputing. Student communication played a rather small role on the LabNetwork, however, and this grew inadvertently from the way the teachers themselves used the network. (See Roberts, Blakeslee, Brown, & Lenk, 1990, for an excellent recent treatment of the many factors that go into connecting a classroom with a network.)

At the beginning of the project, there was some expectation that student exchanges of data would play a significant role in communication. The original design for activities was built on the Star Schools model, which at the time was showing great promise in an extensive field test. The Star Schools materials emphasized student exchanges of data, and specified very precisely the timing and duration of the component activities. Some LabNet classrooms profited from this approach during the first phase of the project, but the LabNet community developed a rather different focus, for which the Star Schools model was not appropriate.

As has been seen in other settings, student exchanges are generally most productive in the context of a structure that provides a common subject focus, if not specific activities, and a common schedule. The simultaneous tasks of developing viable ideas for network collaboration, developing and agreeing on protocols for data exchange and group maintenance, as well as commentary and conversation about the content of the study, are almost impossible to accomplish if any large numbers are involved, within the constraints of the classroom and the school year. This is why successful student-oriented networking projects provide (varying amounts) of support structure ahead of time, having thus provided at least tentative answers to these problems, freeing the students to learn the technology and conduct their projects. (For a study of a specific network experiment, see Riel, 1990; for a survey of other examples, see Weir, 1992, and other papers in Tinker & Kapisovsky, 1992b.)

As the LabNet teachers developed their conversations about technology and project-enhanced physics learning, the focus on student exchanges disappeared. Some teachers continued on both LabNet and the Star Schools networks simultaneously; most, however, focused on dialogues with fellow teachers, especially after the network moved to the Delphi system, and bulletin-board (the Forum) facilities became available.

During this period, teachers would use the network on behalf of students not only when organizing projects, such as the meteor watch mentioned earlier, but also when their students undertook projects in areas about which the teacher was not knowledgeable. As one teacher said, "I'm a physics teacher. How should I know about Petri dishes and agar?" In many such cases, the teacher would mention on the Forum that a student wanted to explore a topic, and then mention specific needs—for information, for comments on the proposed experiment, for sources of materials. These were initially answered on the Forum, but then followed up by e-mail.

During 1990, however, several teachers asked how we might include students directly on the network. This raised several logistical issues that to some teachers seemed trivial, but to others seemed decisive. For example, how should one constrain the amount of time students might spend on the network (and thus the amount of money they spent)? What kinds of curbs should be placed on the kinds of messages that students can place on the network? What if an "inappropriate message" got on the network?

There was also less tangible reluctance on the part of some to mix different constituencies with different styles of discourse. Would teachers feel less forthcoming if there were "students in the teachers' lounge," listening in to unguarded talk about the teaching craft, including the admission of ignorance and confusion? LabNet staff were neutral in the discussion. We had thought that teachers would prefer not to have students on, but the network was for them, and if they wanted student participation, we would help it happen.

In fact, the most weighty questions for the teachers were: Can students participate without the network changing adversely, so that we lose what has developed? and Can we ensure that the network will not be overloaded by student messages so that it becomes unwieldy?

The LabNet staff moderated the discussion, and two solutions were adopted; teachers were free to choose which they used. Either a teacher could let the students use the teacher's username and password (or have the teacher upload and download the messages for students, to keep control of on-line time), or LabNet would create a special topic on the Forum for student projects, and give students special accounts that could only read from and write to the student projects forum. In any event, teachers used both solutions. Two or three teachers requested student accounts, and often teachers passed along messages from students.

```
1562  8MAR91-1545 Other
      LINKWAY FOR THE IBM
      From: AEDMOPA
      To: ALL

I AM CURRENTLY WORKING WITH TWO STUDENTS USING HYPERCARD
ON THE MAC SE-30. IS THERE ANY WAY OF DOING THE SAME
THING USING LINKWAY. I NEED GRAPHICS AND SORTING
ABILITY ON THE IBM? ALSO CAN ANY ONE TELL ME HOW TO
INTERFACE THROUGH THE HYPERCARD STACKS ON THE SERIAL
COMMUNICATION'S PORT? AEDMOPA
-*-
```

The striking development, once we had put in place these mechanisms for student use of the Forum, was how little student traffic there was. The total number of messages from students was about 250 (through January 1992). We have no way of knowing how much students used e-mail, of course. The messages were all careful requests for information or project ideas. The following are quite typical:

```
To : All interested parties
From : Brian Riley and Randy Castle, Elmira High School,
       Elmira, Oregon
Re : Student Research Paper on Mitochondria

    As part of an A.P. Biology class project, we are
writing research paper on mitochondria- their
evolutionary origins (i.e.- from primitive bacteria) as
well as diseases that afflict them. We would like to
correspond over the Network with anyone who has any
information pertaining to this topic. Or, if anyone
knows of a valuable source(s) of information for us, we
would greatly appreciate hearing from you. Thanks. You
may send any information through Geriann Walker.
(GWALKER).
-*-

      From: JHARPEL
      To: GWALKER
Gerri, Several groups want to correspond with your
students. We will be posting through next week and
```

possibly after that as well. Our first message is
attached. I will check frequently.

To: The group containing: James Turnbo, Mark Meadows,
and Brett Marcyan. Team Members: Cameron Etezadi, Cindy
Rothman, Sara Banashek. Greetings and thank you for
your letter. Presently we are considering two different
schemes for creating our paper structure. Our two
options are to go "all out:" and build a structure
moderate in mass but with a large descent time or a
smaller structure that has a comparatively short
duration of descent but with a significantly smaller
mass.

Since all competition here relates to a ratio of mass to
time, we are curious as to your opinion of a plan. In
addition, some manner of slowing the ball's descent
without a significant increase in the mass of the
structure. We have read that you have used tape rolls
to provide friction. Any other ideas for things of this
nature would be greatly appreciated.

In the mean time, we continue to evaluate our options as
construction time (next Thursday) draws nearer.

       Sincerely,
       Cameron Etezadi
   _*_

1624 17APR91-1355 Student Projects
       OTHER
       From: AEDMOPA
       To: ALL

KEVIN MAKAREWICZ

HI, I AM A SENIOR AT HAZLETON HIGH SCHOOL. I AM DOING A
TERM PAPER FOR MY SOCIAL ECONOMICS CLASS. I AM LOOKING
FOR ANY INFORMATION THAT I CAN FIND ON NUCLEAR WASTE AND
NUCLEAR WASTE DISPOSAL. ANY INFORMATION WOULD BE VERY
USEFUL.

SEND REPLIES TO MR. EDMONDSON USER NAME AEDMOPA
   _*_

Virtually no student message went unanswered on the Forum, either
by a teacher or a TERC staff member, most often both. Further, many student messages initiated short dialogues that continued over electronic mail.
One interesting feature of these exchanges is that after the opening discussion of possibilities and resources, none of the students reported their results.

```
OTHER
From: AEDMOPA
To: ALL
```

I HAVE A STUDENT WHO IS WORKING ON A SINGLE CHANNEL AD
CHIP FOR AN APPLE II GS COMPUTER. HE HAS BEEN ABLE TO
WRITE THE CODE TO WORK THE CHIP. HE IS TRYING TO
CONVERT SIGNALS COMING FROM A PH ELECTRODE. THE CHIP IS
A 10 BIT CONVERTER WHICH MAY BE CONTROLLED BY THE ANN.
PORTS OF THE APPLE.

I INFORMED HIM THAT I BELIEVE NOISE MIGHT BE THE
PROBLEM, HOWEVER, WE ARE BOTH OPEN TO SUGGESTIONS
CONCERNING THE FACT THAT THE CONVERTER CHIP (LTC-1092)
APPEARS TO GENERATING RANDOM NUMBER SAMPLINGS. DOES ANY
ONE HAVE A CIRCUIT THAT MAY ELIMINATE OR REDUCE THE
BACKGROUND NOISE WHILE AMPLIFYING THE INCOMING SIGNAL
FROM THE PH PROBE? PLEASE SEND ANY SUGGESTIONS TO ADAM
EDMONDSON USER NAME AEDMOPA.

_-*-_

```
1668 29APR91-1524 Student Projects
    student project
    From: JCPOTTS
    To: AEDMOPA
```

The problem that your student is experiencing with
his pH meter could be electrical noise from the
computer. Computers do sometimes generate more radio
noise than they should. This may be solved by placing a
small capacitor across the input leads to filter out the
radio noise.
_-*-_

The students' project ideas tended to be interdisciplinary, and at the margins of the field of physics. For them, the presence of nonphysicists on the network was useful; when, during the third year of LabNet, a biology teacher joined the network, she got several requests for advice, and provided many project suggestions. Students would probably benefit from the network's extending its constituency to include teachers from other disciplines. It is as though the students are not comfortable with "mainstream" physics, and find their own questions being formed in the idiom of other disciplines.

Because the demand was so small, LabNet did not expand nor promote student interactions on the network. The most productive and frequent model for students' profiting from the network exchanges is for teachers to translate the learning they do on the network into their own classroom, as is described in several of the essays in chapter 6.

Fellow Travelers and "Professional Innovators"

How "free-standing" should a network be? It is frequently suggested that educational networks (and other support systems for education) should be developed to the point that they are "self-contained," implying that the members would be only teachers, and that these members would somehow sustain the network's operation for the foreseeable future. Those who make such suggestions often have in mind principally the question of who will bear the financial costs for the enterprise.

On the basis of LabNet's experience, however, we question the concept of a self-contained network in this sense. Considerations of effectiveness and durability argue for other approaches. With respect to the depth of content, the support of innovation, and the dynamics of the community, it is very probable that a network community constructed so as to include only teachers and students is far from ideal.

This was certainly not our starting assumption. We originally expected that the LabNetwork, or any descendent or development from it, should stand alone, with money for its continuation coming from participants, from teacher-enhancement funds, or from school budgets in some other way. We assumed that TERC's role was to develop the experiment, draw conclusions, and make recommendations for (and perhaps participate in) the next stage, whose culmination would be the emancipation of the community, not only from grant funding but also from TERC. In fact, in a follow-on proposal to the National Science Foundation, TERC envisioned the development of LabNet into a self-contained network.

We still believe that the "main event" was the conversation among colleagues—teachers talking with teachers. There is no doubt of the value of this exchange, not only in some abstract sense, but also in terms of the teachers' profit from and enjoyment of participation. Their conversations are the *sine qua non* of the "community of practice."

But the LabNetwork, like almost all others, included many collaborators who were not teachers, and we have come to realize that such collaboration is a characteristic and vital feature not only of networks but of the entire educational enterprise. The very term *self-contained* is misleading, because teachers do not operate independently in any other aspect of their work (except in the classroom itself). What happens in the classroom is supported financially by governing bodies; policies are set by government agencies at various levels, and both these agencies and the public demand accountability for the school's work. In addition, the school is surrounded by a host of contributory institutions—academic, commercial, and others like TERC. The results of all their work is vital to teachers' work, for insight about the educational process, as well as because of their products— curriculum, software, apparatus, and all the rest.

Educational networks have recognized this to various degrees, but they have often been uneasy about the relationship. In the NGS Kids Network and the TERC Star Schools project, TERC and collaborators sought out "domain experts" who would act as resources to the students and teachers when technical questions arose about, for example, acid rain, trees, or radon. (For a discussion of the Star Schools model, see Weir et al., 1990.)

The ETC Common Ground network (Katz et al., 1987, pp. 31-32) included as participants both "moderators" and "guests." Moderators were teachers with strong domain skills, who acted as discussion stimulators, and who in fact turned out to be among the most active participants on the network. In addition to these "officials," whose presence is consistent with a free-standing model, the network included experts in the subjects of each of the topics on the Forum, who would be available for varying periods of time. West et al. (1989, p. 29) have a short and trenchant analysis of the limits of moderators and similar functionaries on a network.

This kind of resource was available to a limited extent on the LabNetwork, in the persons of Professor John G. King of MIT (the project's co-principal investigator, and a prominent physics educator) and Dr. Alan Winter, a physicist and educator from Cambridge University (who appears on the network as TERCAW). Winter especially was an active participant on the Forum in 1989-1990, but was rarely sought out as a resource by the teachers—he commented on other messages, and provided useful information, as well as playing a crucial role in the development and implementation of the 1990 workshops.

Some of the services that TERC rendered to the LabNet teachers are straightforward, and really variations of services that the teachers provided for each other: feedback about ideas, suggestions about resources and equipment, notices about new opportunities for funding or learning, and so forth. Yet when considering TERC's role in the development of the community, it is hard to see how certain features could exist without the participation of some reflective entity, not based in a particular school, but dedicated to innovation and research in the service of the schools' work. West et al. (1989) assumed that specificity of topic is the usual rule, except where personal acquaintance has opened the way for "higher level" conversations. This is true very often, and this kind of discussion is the "bread and butter" of shoptalk in any field, but in the context of educational change it is surely desirable to encourage "reflective practice."

TERC's catalytic role can be seen in settings outside the LabNetwork— for example, in the 1991 conference for Big Idea grantees, where we urged teachers to focus on conceptual issues surrounding project-enhanced learning, rather than on specific techniques and project ideas. Our aim was to stimulate the kind of reflection and conversation that is rare in the pressured workaday environment but is essential for fundamental change to occur. The same kind of effort can be seen in some of the network discussions of the TLCs, and in Shahaf Gal's use of the network to collaborate with LabNet teachers in evaluating the project, enabling these teachers to share in the researcher's reflection and analysis of classroom experiences.

Expert Conversations

The collaboration between researchers and teachers is often at arm's length, channeled by way of reform movements, changes of curriculum, writing of textbooks, and so forth. Our experience (and that of others) is that other, more direct channels are possible, and in many ways makes the division of labor, which is unavoidable, of more value to all concerned. When communication is direct, interactive, and substantive, the expertise of each sector of the community can be shared productively—the expertise and not just the output of the expertise. (For a discussion of the relationship between teacher and researcher, and the ways they can collaborate in educational research, see Duckworth, Easley, Hawkins, & Henriques, 1990, and also the discussion of the LabNet evaluation process in Appendix B.)

In fact, as TERC has stimulated such conversations, they have grown to form a constant, although small, proportion of the network discussion. The following, extended Forum excerpt shows how the different kinds of conversation of which we have spoken are interwoven on the Forum, as they are in the conversation of any group with shared expertise and goals. The variety is productive and vital; it reflects the many concerns of the teachers, and thus is not the monotonic discourse on pedagogy or on science that a professional innovator might long for. After this visit to a week on the LabNet, we turn to conclusions and recommendations for a national science teachers' network.

```
2232 16-FEB 22:53 Student Projects
    Electrostatics
    From: DNASSCO
    To: ALL

    I was recently watching a metal sphere being drawn
    towards a charged Van de Graaff generator when I had the
    following thought: Is there a quantitative lab here
    using a spring suspending a mass?  Can I find the charge
    in the generator without knowing the charge (if any) on
    the test sphere?

    If someone has some ideas along this line, please let
me know....
-*-

2233 17-FEB 09:03 Student Projects
    RE: Electrostatics (Re: Msg 2232)
    From: DTTONOPHS
    To: DNASSCO

If you have an uncharged metal sphere, couldn't you use
the attraction from the rest position as a measure
force.  It would seem to me that....
-*-
```

2234 18-FEB 22:30 LabNet News
     RE: Principles of Technology Workshop (Re: Msg
         229)
     From: RCAPEAZ
     To: LEFCOURT

I had applied to NSF to sponsor or I should say co-
sponsor a workshop which was to incorporate Projects
into the Physics of Technology curriculum. I feel that
the physics of the curriculum leaves a great deal to be
desired but if students can do projects related to
various aspects of the curriculum, there is some
redeeming value....
_*_

2235 19-FEB 10:08 Curriculum Issues
     From: ALTOMMIHOLSE
     To: ALL

I AM INTERESTED IN ORDERING THE NEW VIDEO DISC SET FROM
AAPT/IMC CALLED PHYSICS: CINEMA CLASSICS....
_*_

2236 20-FEB07:16 Student Projects
     Vitamin C testing
     From: AEDMOPA
     To: ALL

I have a young student who would like to know if anyone
has information about testing of vitamin C in citrus
fruits....
_*_

2237 20-FEB 09:33 Curriculum issues
     RE: (Re: Msg 2235)
     From: HLEFCOURT
     To: ALTOMMIOLSE

Tommi: The AAPT videodisc consists of "short" excerpts
from various sources. There are many good segments,
but ....
_*_

2239 22-FEB 13:28 Other
     RE: On Line (Re: Msg 2204)
     From: GLOCKETT
     To: DNASSCO

Hi, my name is Greg Lockett (GLOCKETT) and I teach
physical science, chemistry, and physics at West Valley
High School in Cottonwood CA. In your forum message, you

indicated that you were interested in physics based
student projects. These words mean different things to
different people.

My physics students work on 9 week research projects of
their own choosing. At the end, they usually produce a
very traditional scientific paper that would be suitable
for publication. Occasionally, they produce a piece of
apparatus. Generally, they self-select into working
groups of 3.

Currently students are working on cellular automata, the
properties of water waves with an emphasis on
resonance....
-*-

2240 22-FEB 13:38 Student Projects
    BUILDING A ROLLER COASTER
    From: MJAMEPA
    To: ALL

I AM INTERESTED IN HAVING STUDENTS BUILD A REPLICA OF A
ROLLER COASTER. AS A LAB. MAYBE MAKE IT INTO A CONTEST.
ANY IDEAS?
-*-

2241 22-FEB 13:42 Student Projects
    MAXINE'S LABNET WORKSHOP
    From: MJAMEPA
    To: RSANDMD

HI RICH! WE WERE TALKING ABOUT A LAB THAT YOUR STUDENTS
DID, IT HAD SOMETHING TO DO WITH MAKING AN AIRPLANE AND
FLYING IT THROUGH A TARGET, AM I CORRECT? IF SO, PLEASE
SEND THE WRITE-UP FOR THIS OR ANY RELATED PHYSICS LABS.
THANKS, MICHELE (MJAMEPA)
-*-

2242 22-FEB 17:29 Student Projects
    RE: Electrostatics (Re: Msg 2233)
    From: DNASSCO
    To: DBUTTONOPHS

I think this is a workable way to find the force. What
would the charge be on the uncharged sphere? For an
induced charge, it must follow the inverse square rule,
I'd think....
-*-

2243 22-FEB 17:36 Curriculum Issues
    RE: (Re: Msg 2235)

From: DNASSCO
To: ALTOMMIHOLSE

I am planning to buy the series you mention. I am
presently copying our old super 8 loops to tape....
-*-

2244 22-FEB 17:48 Other
    RE: On Line (Re: Msg 2239)
    From: DNASSCO
    To: GLOCKETT

Thank you for your reply. My name is Dave Nasser
(DNASSCO). I teach physics, A.P. physics, and applied
science at Thornton High, in Thornton, Colorado. Your
projects sound about right for my group...It may be that
the project might be an appropriate task for the A.P if
the product is to be a research paper. Does this work as
well in your general classes? At any rate let me know
what you have in mind....
-*-

2245 -FEB 00:14 Other
    RE: On Line (Re: Msg 2244)
    From: GLOCKETT
    To: DNASSCO (NR)

Hi Dave... Projects are the core of my physics class.
My classroom is a research laboratory. My students are
scientists. Motivation is rarely a problem. My
students are required to choose their own research
topics. This is often very difficult for them. There
is an element of disbelief coupled with many years of
educational training that discourages independence and
original thinking. When they finally understand and
believe, getting them to work is not a problem. Getting
them to stop is a problem.
-*-

2246 -FEB 12:02 Curriculum Issues
    RE: (Re: Msg 2235)
    From: KAUNTUN
    To: ALTOMMIHOLSE

I have played with the discs at local section and
national meetings. I love the accessibility of all of
the old goodies and the price is the cheapest it will
ever be at this time. I would suggest ordering it. Patty
-*-

2247 23-FEB 23:0 Student Projects
    Rubber band projectiles
    From: ESHAUMD
    To: MAXINE WILLIS (R)

Maxine, thank you for suggesting to me in your letter to
try rubber band projectiles....
-*-

2249 23-FEB 14:12 Student Projects
    RE: Electrostatics (Re: Msg 2242)
    From: DBUTTONOPHS
    To: DNASSCO (NR)

I would think that the force on the uncharged sphere
would be zero. I would suspect that the specs that came
with the machine would give the voltage, and then with
the distance away, you could come up with some sort of
force.

I would treat the problem as a pendulum with the force
pulling to the side being the electrostatic force whose
magnitude you don't know. I would then use the
equations for determining the "restoring" force of a
pendulum to figure out what two sides of the vector are
(the weight) being the other. Then solve for the third
side — the electrostatic force you're trying to find.

Others out there!!!! Is this going in the right
direction????? Dave
-*-

2251 24-FEB 17:15 Student Projects
    Mobiles
    From: ESHAUMD
    To: ALL

I have heard of a project/activity where the students
build mobiles. This would give them a hands on approach
towards studying equilibrium. If anyone has some ideas
about how to implement this project, would you please
send me a line.

    Thank you, Ed Shaughnessy
-*-

2252 24-FEB 19:15 Curriculum Issues
    RE: philosophy (Re: Msg 2155)
    From: JCADIAK
    To: WEDDING (NR)

I enjoyed your tome on conceptual physics, Kelly. Although the meager numbers of students I have hardly can be used for anything definitive, I have strong opinions about conceptual physics as a lead-in course. I guess from others comments, it's all pretty subjective anyhow, so I guess my two cents is valid from that perspective....

Anyway, having also taught at university level, my gut feeling is that the totally basal-driven "traditional" approach to PHYSICS IS WRONG, WRONG, WRONG.

As you have found, even those in the higher plateaus of nerdville need to understand WHAT and WHY they do. As you alluded, many can crunch the numbers but lack the faintest feeling for what "the answer" represent. To avoid such a cook-book style of learning physics I feel something like Hewitt's approach is the answer..
_—*—_

ELEMENTS OF A NATIONAL SCIENCE TEACHERS' NETWORK

This final section lays out the critical features that we believe are necessary for building a successful national network in support of science teachers. It builds on the LabNetwork experience, synthesizing the most important learnings; the rest of the book provides much of the rationale behind these reflections. While the tone is declarative, it is meant to be suggestive rather than prescriptive. The elements listed include: software, network structure, on-line facilities, maintenance, expansion, network interconnections, constituency, institutional relationships, and a discussion of infrastructure issues.

General Software Design and Interface

From the point of view of the LabNet constituency, "better software" must include several interface features not always included in software design. For teachers—as for other groups —software should come to the user, and not the other way around: All the "substantive" features one can add will not be used, in fact will be a deterrent, if the software is not accessible to users with many needs and domain skills but little time to spend learning any one piece of technology.

In designing software for educational telecommunication, considerations for future developments should include at least the following, in addition to the more established canons of software design:

1. Educational telecommunication software must pay attention to transitions between modules of the whole system that the teacher may

be using. Uploading and downloading of all types of files should be straightforward, and compatibility with productivity software is crucial—file formats should be easily interconvertible.

2. Telecommunication software should minimize on-line time. The increasing capacity of personal computers can be exploited for information management, allowing the efficient transfer and organization of information from a network off-line. Teacher's budgets for telecommunication will no doubt be straitened for the foreseeable future, but budget cuts may enforce the development of less wasteful systems, reflecting more understanding of users' constraints. That some teachers have found ways to bear the costs required by current systems is a testimony to the need for telecommunication, and the vision of the teachers, not to the quality of the systems that they are using.

3. Software should not be platform specific. Proprietary software development over the past 15 years has been a major hindrance to the spread of computer use, in education as in other sectors of the market. Despite current trends in sales, it is not the case that new model computers are in the majority at all in the precollege educational world. As noted earlier, current equipment still includes computers from all stages of the Apple II series, IBM and IBM-compatibles of several different generations and provenance, Commodore and Amiga systems, Macintoshes of all types, and machines of older vintage as well. If we want to put telecommunication in the reach of all teachers, in the foreseeable future, the software must be designed not for the avant-garde, but for some large proportion of the patchwork that is currently installed.

4. The system should allow for easy transmission of files of all kinds. This has been hampered by the variety of software protocols alluded to earlier, which effectively erects a wall between users of different platforms. For educational purposes, the transmission of graphics and data files (such as databases and spreadsheets) is crucial for full communication about science projects, as well as about evaluation and assessment.

Because the cost of network time remains a major problem, some network projects (e.g., ATT Learning Circles, TERC Star Schools, TERC/NGS Kids Network) have developed software that automates the operations of getting on and using the network, so that reading and responding to mail, the composition of messages, and so forth, all happen off-line. The Common Ground network found similar issues arising, resulting in a preponderance of messages routed through e-mail (63%) rather than the forum (29%). Both Katz et al. (1987, p. 18) and Bull et al. (1992) are skeptical of the "off-line strategy."

This kind of automated system might offer some hope as a medium for the sort of conversations the LabNet teachers carry on, if the network were really resident on the individual members' computers; that is, if the organization of messages and other data were mirrored on my Macintosh. To date, such a system has not been implemented; the networks using this off-line option have built-in constraints on bulletin-board conversations (as opposed to e-mail conversations). Thus, users each must reconstruct a facsimile of the network data structures, and work out their own ways of communicating between their off-line organization scheme and the on-line structure. Until this kind of technical barrier is removed, users need to be able to choose whether to browse on-line or to quickly conduct their business in the shortest time possible.

In summary, the teachers' network that we envision would have a straightforward interface, suited to minimizing on-line time, and allowing most flexible interaction with the system utilities. The interface would include both command and menu options, because well-constructed menus are the most straightforward method of learning a system's structure, but usually not as fast for the practiced user. The system would make appropriate use of the user's personal computer, but there is also a place for a centralized server as well.

Structuring a Network Community

One theme that recurs in the literature on educational networks is the need for the network to serve teachers' "educational goals," providing some well-defined content rather than merely a means of communication. This view recognizes the great demands under which teachers operate, and seeks to further the teachers' work by providing help in as practical a manner as possible. This includes taking care of many logistical issues that arise in the course of developing network collaboration, and this most often has taken the form of shaping the content, or otherwise setting agenda and schedules for the network, or for subsets thereof. Examples of this are the TERC Star Schools, the TERC/NGS Kids Network, and the ATT Learning Circles.

LabNet has taken a different approach, seeking to support a process of professional development that is largely teacher-driven, although with input from an independent entity (TERC), which has helped to set some conceptual goals. We have for the most part relied upon the community itself to provide the practical and organizational structure for specific projects. We believe that this approach respects teachers' role in the creation and implementation of their curriculum, and thus must be an intrinsic element of an educational network. Structured network activities can be of value, and so can access to information services of many kinds. For a network to serve the cause of real, lasting educational reform, however, it must first and foremost give teachers access to each other.

On-line Facilities

These should include:

E-mail

Teachers need to be able to send and receive messages and manage messages received (including creation of a directory structure for the data). They need to be able to create mailing lists easily, and to exchange mailing lists as text files.

There should be good articulation between the e-mail and other facilities on the system, so that messages can pass freely to and from the bulletin boards. This means that the command set should be the same for the same operations, such as creating files, seeing directories and searching through them, and replying to messages.

The e-mail system should make it easy to send all types of files—a prominent feature of most systems already, but of varying ease of use. Finally, the mail archives should be kept on the personal computer of the user, to minimize server demand.

Bulletin Boards

Systems that imitate bulletin boards by using mailing lists or other e-mail techniques are not adequate for the sort of community of practice that we advocate. It is important that those who did not initiate a conversation can follow silently, and participate or not as seems best to them. This functionality can be imitated by large "news groups" and other techniques, but it requires that each user maintain a local archive of the conversation to date, not necessarily shared by others, which will then require the development of protocols for cross-reference to other parts of the conversation. Further, this makes the previous history of the conversation inaccessible to those joining later, unless the messages are archived in a database. A large central database facility containing the bulletin board facilitates searches, back references, and similar use of the conversation as reference material—especially useful for teachers hunting for expertise or advice on a specific subject discussed earlier.

Although this central bulletin-board facility will require some host maintenance, the actual content on the network should be maintainable by members, probably by volunteers who will take on the responsibility (and acquire the technical expertise) to prune, archive, and otherwise support some subset of the total network. Other networks have experimented with paid moderators, and with volunteers, to provide this service. The most that can be said is that the quality of the service depends on the quality of the moderator—results are often uneven, in part because there is a tendency to think of new things for moderators to do. Because efficiency in an enterprise requires the localization of responsibility, it is tempting to load more and more on people already identified for some task. Thus, overload became a problem in LabNet with the Teacher Liaison Consultants (TLCs), who were expressly mandated to provide support to small groups of teachers (12 to 15).

On other networks, such as the Digital Equipment Corporation's internal network, the IGC EcoNet system, or commercial networks, such as Delphi, there is no such onus on the moderator to serve nonnetwork goals (such as classroom innovation, the testing of new technology, or whatever).

Although there needs to be a member watching the traffic on the network, the system should have an archiving procedure that is regular and to some extent automatic. This procedure would move blocks of messages from the bulletin board to an accessible database for reference. It would include using labeling fields from the messages themselves to construct an initial index of the material in the archive, showing date, topic area, subject matter in each, sender identification, and similar information that could then be searched using keywords.

The bulletin board itself should allow for development of hierarchies according to subject matter. The moderator for a topic area should be able to create a subdirectory that focuses a discussion, which may or may not have a long development of its own. A topic area or special interest area on a bulletin board is itself a data structure that users have to manipulate. Because they cannot move through the material on-line as easily as one can scan a book using the table of contents, headings, indices, and other clues to the structure of the content, it is important for users on-line not only to be able to search but to place their area of interest in context of the other content on the network, and to restrict the amount of material they will regularly search through. The building of subdirectories that are coherent with respect to a certain topic allows more efficient use of the forum.

As with the e-mail system, the bulletin board must be fully interactive with other tools (databases, mail, etc.). An individual user should be able to move into and out of those areas on the network easily, and import and export material to and from the bulletin board without having to climb back to a shell or command level, or pass through a tree of menus to accomplish one task and then traverse the system again to take up the earlier task.

Databases

Databases for teacher use should be interactive. That is, they must not only be thought of as reference books, produced elsewhere, from which teachers can draw. The teachers themselves can create much material of direct relevance to their colleagues, in several areas:

- Project ideas, preparatory activities, and sources of related materials.

- Background information (newspaper clippings, references to periodical literature, references to technical information).

- Case studies and teacher reports about specific innovations in the classroom. The process of reflective practice that we advocate, that is necessary to support real change in educational practice, is materially helped by sharing among the practitioners themselves of reports on their experience, on their students' experience, and on their analyses of their experience. As Eleanor Duckworth has long advocated, the teacher can function effectively as an educational researcher; this is especially true in the context of a peer group that is eager to hear reports "from the front."

- Evaluation instruments and assessment tools actually used by teachers. As the latest wave of educational reform has gathered strength, educators have turned their attention to evaluation and assessment as a vital element (some think it the key) for school change and teacher "accountability." As teachers experiment with their classes, and revise or revolutionize their thinking about their work, they will translate their understanding into a wide array of curriculum structures and evaluation instruments. Unless this creative and vital local process is pre-empted by national tests, and similar "top-down" mass instruments, the ingenuity and success (or lack thereof) of individual teachers and school teams will be the most instructive source of supporting information for teachers working in their own context.

- Distance learning materials from introductions to the network system and aspects of computer use, to background information designed to explicate and motivate project-enhanced science. These materials will be built up by teachers, and possibly also by other members of the community (e.g., research and development institutions, such as TERC).

- Practical information about hardware, texts, software, and apparatus.

The database contents must be easily searchable, by keyword and perhaps in some cases by string-search. Directory and index facilities will be important adjuncts to this, but cannot substitute for it.

Support

Unlike computer aficionados of various stripes, teachers are not as a group highly motivated to acquire new technological skills; nor does their work make much room for exploration of new frontiers not traditionally relevant to their duties. Of course, many teachers do desire, and find time for, various kinds of professional development. For a telecommunication-based community to compete successfully for teachers' attention, it must not only recommend itself, but also not repel users. Therefore, a network needs maintenance on several levels.

Hardware and Software

In the first place, there must be people maintaining the software and hardware that constitute the network. During the first phase of LabNet, TERC was already maintaining the Star Schools network for about 600 teachers; the addition 100 plus LabNet teachers made the logistical load even more difficult. The task of maintaining the system was removed when we transferred to the Delphi system.

With the move to an established and stable system, the greatest new challenge was in supporting teachers as they went through the process of connecting to the network. Many teachers needed advice about the acquisition and installation of a computer. Beyond that, however, and continuing throughout the project at a low level, was the need for advice and information about telecommunication software. As discussed elsewhere, the variety of equipment meant a variety of software, and despite our recruitment of teachers with computer experience, the establishment of a reliable software configuration was a challenge to many teachers. The telephone was the usual means of communication; a LabNet staffer then joined the teacher in the frustrating business of long-distance debugging.

As the teachers solved their early problems and got on-line, they were then faced with the task of learning the Delphi system. Once comfortable with at least one of the on-line facilities, the teachers were able to get advice from a wider range of sources—their colleagues who had had to solve many similar problems. During the last 6 months of the project, most queries about software or telecommunication-related hardware were posted on the network, and answered by teachers within a day. The more experienced teachers found occasion to explore the limits of their knowledge about the network, so that they took advantage of more of its possibilities.

Bulletin Board Maintenance

A population of about 150 users (teachers, TERC staff, and colleagues elsewhere) in 2 years on Delphi generated in excess of 2,300 messages on the Forum (February 1, 1990–March 31, 1992), as well as a large but uncountable number of e-mail messages (there were a total of over 22,000 individual "connects" to the network in this time period). Only about the last 100 (at most) Forum messages are "active," in that people logging on are likely to scan the previous messages, either for information or to see what earlier subjects have been covered. Occasionally, however, when a question is posted on the Forum, people will include in their reply a reference to an earlier discussion of the same material. Therefore, it has seemed useful to keep a larger backlog of messages than is commonly seen in bulletin boards. Many such services keep 100 or 200 messages on, at most, and periodically cull them, to keep the numbers down.

What happens then to the removed messages? In a news group or other such bulletin board, "institutional memory" is not a great asset. In the LabNet community, it was occasionally very convenient, if not more. Because the system supported string-keyed searches of the Forum, the Forum history provided a useful way for new members to "catch on" to the general style of discourse, and to acquire the conventions for subject matter, message-size, and so on, that had developed.

Obsolete messages on many network bulletin boards are simply deleted, after a warning is posted. On LabNet, we preserved all Forum messages, both as directly downloaded and as edited. The edited versions were slowly added to the on-line databases. Members rarely referred to these; staff did occasionally, in order to remind users of something, or to reintroduce a topic, or to help a newcomer. Therefore, from most people's perspective, the messages were just gone. The archiving effect of occasional staff references could have been achieved (as seen also on other bulletin boards) by dedicated members keeping their own archives on disk at home and reintroducing material.

"Back numbers" from the network were also used when the network manager summarized a series of messages on a topic (such as the meteor study), and posted it afresh as one long message, among the current messages. On a few occasions, this caused members to revisit the question, and also to remember that there was considerable past history available to them. Again, any zealous member of the network could provide this feature.

It seems reasonable that volunteers could be recruited to do the routine maintenance of the bulletin board, as is done on many other systems. It should be said, however, that LabNet was not successful in getting that help from its members. When the project offered free network time in return for help on the network, few teachers responded. Was this a function of the time of year we asked? Of the fact that teachers have too much to do already, and our teachers were all too busy? We have no information to settle this question.

In summary, routine maintenance of the bulletin board—deletion of outdated or useless messages (e.g., personal greetings, mistransmissions)—could be performed by on-line moderators (volunteers from the community). A more thoughtful "cultivation" of network resources, such as references to earlier discussions, or overviews of people's messages about a certain topic, and so on, would be harder to ask volunteers to do, as a general rule, and on the other hand is the sort of use of the network that a research partner on the network might make, on behalf of the community (and out of curiosity about the dynamics of the community).

Other Resources

We believe that a network is not a community on its own. On-line resources, such as databases and other tools for "distance learning," must be supplemented by workshops and other face-to-face encounters. We return to this with specific recommendations in chapter 8; the following quotation illustrates from a teacher's narrative of his own changing practice how all these factors support each other:

> My teaching has been totally changed as a result of attending a LabNet [workshop] for two years....[I have started] to implement Workshop Physics in my classroom. As a result of this work I applied for and received a GTE grant to place two ULIs (see the glossary at the end of chapter 1), motion detectors, and force-probes in the classroom. I am also working closely with the Trigonometry teacher to coordinate our efforts in our classes...I have been running my classroom with the Workshop Physics curriculum [used] at Dickinson (and Tufts) and adapted by me for the high school....The network is a great support for technical equipment problems. I would never have made these changes so quickly without the support and exposure provided by LabNet. 84 + 9 = 93 students, one teacher, and one student teacher are much happier because of this program.

Interconnections and Multiple Levels

How can a system like LabNet grow in size? Although high-speed, high-capacity public-domain carriers like the Internet (see the glossary at the end of chapter 1) are an important element of the general system, we must stress that the network does not stand alone, and that the kind of interactions we want on the network feed off personal knowledge among some of the members at least; the electronic network is only one manifestation of the actual network among teachers—one that has a unique role to play.

Therefore, the telecomputing network has to expand in a way that keeps in mind its particular purposes and the elements of success from previous systems. Unless some national institution makes such a network a major mission, the growth must assume a minimum of outside support, and therefore its structure must both provide national contacts and local subunits.

The Internet system, and other networks that connect with it and use its design as a model, are based on the idea of distributed networking. The design has much to recommend it on the basis of cost and flexibility, as opposed to the model used by many large network services, such as Delphi itself, in which all traffic is routed through a single server.

In the first place, a single server requires the users to come to it, so to speak. If a network is to serve even a fraction of the thousands of teachers in the country, a single host computer will be inadequate to the task.

Many teachers who undertook Big Idea Grants in 1991-1992 intended their workshops to connect teachers to the LabNetwork, but a few took a different approach, perhaps more productive for the future. Their approach was to build local networks—within their district, within their state, within the school—and to construe "network" widely, to include fax communication, telephone, postal mail, and face-to-face meetings. These networks then could be linked to the national LabNetwork in a variety of ways. (For a description of the Big Idea Grants, see chapter 1, Table 1.1, and the glossary, also Appendix D.)

As the Internet becomes more widely available for users outside universities, this kind of local organization will be more and more feasible. The structure of the Internet will permit the establishment of databases and other resources at particular host computers, echoed to other major hosts, and thus accessible to all users.

The Need for a Network of Networks

Some network projects have focused on large national systems. There are real advantages to this, but such large networks are unwieldy and often expensive. Other networks have been frankly more experimental and smaller by design, and these have not been built with the intention of expanding.

Some "grass-roots" networks, such as FrEdMail and K-12Net, use a structure that makes it possible to add new modules, as new local hosts volunteer. This approach has made telecommunication available and attractive to thousands, but the reliance on volunteers for all purposes, including network maintenance, makes the system somewhat vulnerable. This is a problem if one is trying to build a networked community whose history and stability are part of its value. That is, in a community like LabNet, current conversations are enriched by the availability of previous exchanges and past accumulations of information on various topics. This requires stability and memory.

In the past few years, something has developed that is especially valuable for teachers: the rise of state or county networks. Although as mentioned earlier these often are designed for administrative purposes, creative teachers and administrators have seen that they can be much more.

This context makes it easier and more natural to supply the kinds of support that make a network work—technical advice, personal contact, and the sense that the network conversations grow out of other conversations in other media. This is the direction taken by some of the LabNet "Big Idea" grantees in the third year of the project, and their variations on the basic LabNet theme are of interest.

Jack Cadigan's Alaskan project (see his essay in chapter 6) built on the well-established patterns for distance learning developed for the Australian and Alaskan "outback," which began by using a combination of radio and the postal service, and naturally graduated to television, now aided by satellite link. A telecomputing link with a central teacher is a natural extension of the use of technology to overcome distance. In the case of Cadigan's project, the interactions between student and teacher were augmented by the addition of other resource people, specifically recruited to provide direction in the development of projects and to provide role models for the students as well. Here the technology was adapted to a preexisting model.

In Texas, on the other hand, although there is a factor of distance, Robert Roe's project focused on a different set of issues (see Appendix D). Here the technology was used to overcome the teachers' isolation within a well-defined administrative unit, the county. Roe did not rely alone on network connections among the teachers, but instead augmented the relatively untested telecomputing technology with fax machines. This allowed people who might be overwhelmed by the group of skills demanded by telecomputing to benefit from belonging to a network—and incidentally allowed them to exchange graphic and other materials that the telecomputing network handled with relative difficulty.

Many of these local networks are designed to include connections with university computers, and increasingly this means also the possibility of gateways to the Internet, a group of interconnected networks linking universities, some businesses, and research and educational institutions. Several networks, such as Virginia PEN, are actively linking teachers through the Internet. This addresses financial issues, because such a system can spread the cost over a large number of users on a fixed basis rather than call-by-call. Much more important in the long run, however, is that, by linking local networks to a national community of discourse, the Internet can be a mechanism for more closely relating the teachers and practitioners of science. (For a more extended discussion of the role that NSF and the Internet can play, see chapter 8.)

Constituency

In a network with the kinds of flexibility just described—allowing for e-mail, for a central "piazza" for exchange, and the capability to create subdivisions of the Forum—the system can accommodate a widened constituency. This is essential to the success of such a network, since as we have suggested at several points, the community of practice of science teachers actually includes more players than science teachers alone.

If one were to extend the existing LabNet community (or any similar core group of practice and discourse), one might first include teachers from closely related subjects. This is more problematic than first appears, since the education of teachers, and the structure of most curricula, have enforced strong separations between the disciplines—which some current educational reformers are trying to remove, with great difficulty. LabNet teachers have in fact suggested several such directions in the course of their Big Idea work, and of course others have done so in other contexts.

When the conversation is about pedagogy, very often the discussion is relevant to any age or subject. When the topic is strongly subject-specific—for example, the best way to approach the teaching of electricity, why acceleration is so hard to understand, how to best convey the idea of a half-life—it will be of more restricted interest. Ideally, the system would allow the user to label a message for more than one subdivision of the conference, so that if it is part of a conversation among English teachers, but the user thinks the point may be of more general interest, it can be directed both to the subject-specific area and to some more general area for browsing.

Further, within each general area—science, history, English, and the like—the high school is a late stage of the student's career. By the time the students have reached high school, they have become accustomed to the system's style of teaching, and if the high school advocates a radically different approach, the students may resist as much as anyone. LabNet teachers realized this, and some instituted programs to reach out to teachers and students of physical science from lower grades. The network should enable such exchanges.

In short, teachers working with different subjects and at different levels should find it maximally easy to explore other areas on the network. Educators who are not working in the classroom have the luxury to gather information about practices, problems, and solutions from all parts of the school establishment, and can therefore find connections between elementary work and high school work. There is every reason to believe that teachers would profit from this kind of cross-fertilization as well.

The science-teaching constituency also includes research organizations, such as TERC, and other institutions, such as the departments of education and similar government entities at several levels—and appropriate provision should be made for their participation on the network. These institutions must keep a low profile, since their concerns are with different aspects of the educational enterprise from those of classroom teachers. However, if their participation is respectful of the classroom environment, and aware of the demands and concerns of teachers who are in the end the most pivotal agents for change in the school system, then these "outsiders" can participate fruitfully in the classroom discourse. The perspective on education that can be gained outside the classroom can help teachers make sense of their working conditions and the aims of their work in ways not often available otherwise. Further, these institutions have information about funding opportunities and other resources for teachers and schools that are hardly publicized enough.

Finally, the other major constituency that might make use of the network is students themselves. Many educational networks are designed with the presumption that the most important thing is to get the students talking. LabNet made room for students, but very carefully, because of a concern that the presence of students would inhibit discussion by teachers, and a practical concern about who would pay the bills for student use. As described earlier, various teachers, with and without TERC's help, found satisfactory ways for their students to get on-line and participate.

TERC's experience in projects like Star Schools, consonant with other studies, was that students' discourse had relatively little science in it, and contained messages that critics have disparaged as "beside the point." In the light of LabNet's experience, however, we conclude that student's discourse forms a distinctive type of shoptalk. Just as teacher conversations on a network include personal notes and side topics of various kinds, as well as quite specific and practical points of information, student telecommunication discourse must include such a variety for the interchange to have any sense of reality, once the excitement of novelty has receded. The student exchanges on the LabNet (as the earlier samples show) had a businesslike tone, which was probably due to the students' understanding of the nature of the network—although it was an open channel, it was primarily in the service of science learning. It may be that the determining factor about student participation on a teacher's network is numbers: The teachers' dialogue can just be overwhelmed by their students' messages.

Institutional Relationships

Up until now, this discussion has tended to focus on the network as an independent organism, and to stress the teacher membership. This is, however, an unrealistic picture of a community that among other things seeks teacher change. Our experience (and others') suggests that, just as teachers do not work in a vacuum in their schools, so a "teacher change" network must function in the context of other institutions.

The other components of the educational system can play various roles with respect to the teacher network. In the first place, the teachers benefit from the intervention and stimulus of collaborating institutions for educational research. Earlier chapters have detailed the struggle that is necessary if teachers are to be able to critique and reform their practice in a desirable direction. The first role that such collaborating entities can fill is to support and abet the development of this sense of directionality in the teachers' movements toward reform.

In TERC's experience with LabNet, the teachers who were part of the project were at all stages of thought and preparation for the kinds of changes we were advocating. Many had come to a position like ours years ago, and we were in some ways catching up with them and learning from them. On the other hand, some were motivated by the desire to add to their repertoire of demonstrations and technological skills, with no sense that there might be implications of more fundamental change in what they were doing.

Others came to the group with the sense that they wanted to find some additional dimension for their classes. For all these cases, the intentionality of the community was important to the nourishment they were seeking, and in many ways TERC's contribution was to help the community see some goals that it might adopt, and provide a locale in which to explore the paths there. This was not something that teachers had been doing for themselves very much, nor was it part of their experience from other teacher-enhancement programs. The conclusion is that some such agent as TERC (presumably several in a good case) needs to be part of the community.

All of these changes are happening in the context of a structure, a school system that is itself embedded in regulatory and oversight agencies, all more or less part of the body politic. All these groups are clamoring for change in the way children are taught, especially science and mathematics. They need to hear what the teachers think and confront, and they need to be able to join the conversation about real change in the classroom in a productive way. This means that they should not only be able to tell teachers what should happen, but also hear from the teachers about "ground truth." This has to happen in a context where the teachers cannot be attacked for protecting their wallets, but in the arena of professional exploration of the craft and art of teaching particular subjects. The project-enhanced approach that TERC advocates for science education means that the talk about the classroom need not center only on the "school version" of the sciences, but can include real standards of content and evaluation.

Structure/Infrastructure

New users need technical support. This can take several forms, including but not limited to written materials. We need to remember once again that the network is not a stand-alone institution. The network itself must provide information to help members get in touch with each other, and the first thing that should come to a user is a list of nearby participants, at least with their user-name. The introductory interface should acquaint the new user right away with the way to ask for help, and maybe even have an automated routine, that, when users log on the for the first time, or the first time in some period, gives them the option of sending an "Are you there?" message to nearby people, asking them to call by phone or otherwise get in touch.

Support for the network is not to be divorced, however, from the support needed for the community of practice that we want to continue and grow. Because that community includes teachers, educators of other kinds, administrators, departments of education, students, and so on, the new user should be in touch very soon with these other participants on the network. Also, to realize the promise of LabNet, people should be getting to workshops, making the personal connections necessary to the functioning of a successful network.

The schools need to provide some support as well, and this will mean money as well as new ways of allocating time and other resources. Network interaction does not replace teaching activity, but the kind of teaching we are advocating takes place in the context of a teacher actively improving his or her scientific and pedagogical skills, whose "prep" for class must include conversation and consultation with colleagues, and whose constellation of resources is nationwide, and at several levels of the educational system.

Network connections should be in schools, as they are increasingly in colleges and universities, a utility available to all, and therefore built into the annual allocation of resources. This means creating a whole new category in the budget, and this means recognition of the unique value of telecommunication in the field of education, where it extends an individual's range and can deepen both domain-expertise and pedagogical sophistication. The network expenses themselves are not the only items that belong in this budget revision.

The LabNet experience has corroborated abundant earlier conclusions that workshops—which connect participants to the people of the network, as well as introducing the technology—must be supported as long-term investments in teacher development. The Big Idea experiment of LabNet's third year is one approach to keeping these workshops on a local level, and therefore also containing the costs. As detailed elsewhere, the workshops can take many shapes, to reflect local constraints. A 2-week residential workshop, such as those that the LabNet project ran with its cooperating institutions, has important advantages, but is also a major logistical and financial undertaking.

Big Idea grantees developed variations on this design, which accomplished a large measure of what the residential workshops had achieved. Most alternatives started with some concentrated gathering—a few days, often at a residential setting—followed up by shorter meetings later on, often 1-day weekend sessions. All of these were augmented by telecommunication, as well as other kinds of communication. This kind of approach can be easily replicated. Portions of the U.S. Department of Education's Eisenhower grants and other funds for teacher enhancement should be diverted to support teachers who are willing to give such workshops.

The network, including partners like TERC, can be the locus at which the basic concern for project-enhanced science, and the constructivist-cooperative epistemology that lies behind it, is sustained.

6 REFLECTIONS ON PROJECT-ENHANCED SCIENCE LEARNING—TEACHERS

What follow are seven short essays by LabNet teachers from seven differ-ent states. Each reflects the writer's personal experience with science projects.

We wanted to mine the rich classroom experience of our essayists, so our charge to them was broad: What is your personal definition of a project? How have projects been important in your career? How have projects changed your professional practice? Did you undergo a "con-version" experience that committed you to projects, or was it a gradual process? What is the most successful project you have experienced, and why? What role have new technologies had in your project-teaching ex-perience (computers, MBL, telecommunication)? And what advice about projects do you have for colleagues, and also for elementary schools and teachers?

It is clear that for the teachers who have contributed here, there is no hard-and-fast definition of project-enhanced science learning at this point—although their work shares several common themes: among them the use of MBLs, advice to colleagues, optimism about projects that ranges from cautious to enthusiastic. Instead there is a rich and kaleidoscopic view of what a project should be, and what the best balance is between projects and more traditional elements of the physical science curricu-lum. We have loosely grouped the essays: starting with the place of projects in the larger picture, moving to suggestions for doing projects, and ending with projects as a personal experience. As is seen here, the contributors' response to our broad charge has been both wide and deep.

As a postscript we also give students a voice. We sent a student questionnaire to a subset of LabNet teachers who regularly made projects part of their curriculum. We have selected the student comments that appear here from responses to an array of questions about project experi-ences.

THE MAKING OF A SCIENTIST OR ENGINEER

J. J. Cadigan [1]

It would appear by virtue of a myriad of studies and reports, both objective and subjective, that although we have clearly entered the age of science and technology, we are producing a diminishing number of students with interest and understanding of science. Forecasters claim the national economy in the year 2000 will have a shortfall of about a half-million scientists and engineers in the workplace. Some 80% of girls and 85% of boys in elementary school "like math and science." What happens by the time they enter high school? You guessed it! Interest plummets. Besides subjective tests indicating students' feelings in this regard, the numbers of students taking courses in math and science beyond what is minimally prescribed are far too few.

It should not be surprising that our society is developing fewer scientists and engineers despite open and lucrative job opportunities. As Pogo put it, "We have met the enemy, and he is us." We have developed an educational system that emphasizes rote science "knowledge." We have become more inclined to equate the learning of science to the ability to excel in some sort of "Science Trivial Pursuit," rather than the ability to comprehend and understand things scientific. Through emphasis on rote regurgitation of facts and formulae we have begun to gauge excellence by the capacity to recall rather than by innovation and initiative. Too few at any educational level are the schools that emphasize the "doing" of science. When I speak of "doing" science I mean real "hands-on" or "project science."

Isidor I. Rabi (Nobel Prize, Physics) was once asked the circumstances that caused him to become a scientist rather than having pursued some other profession. He responded:

> My mother made me a scientist without ever intending it. Every other Jewish mother in Brooklyn would ask her child after school: "So? Did you learn anything today?" But not my mother. She always asked me a different question. "Izzy," she would say, "did you ask a good question today?" That difference—asking good questions—made me become a scientist!

Insatiable curiosity is perhaps the hallmark of a good scientist. It has been so from the beginning of civilization when humans first began to discover relationships that existed in the physical world around them. A scientist is always questioning the why or why not of things. When one answer is found, like Rabi, there is always a new question. Project science cultivates the inquisitiveness of a student and hence increases interest in science in the same manner that Rabi's mother unknowingly helped guide

---

[1] Jack Cadigan is located at Central Correspondence Study, Juneau, Alaska.

her son toward greatness in physics. A scientist is not just a purveyor of facts and formulae as found by others, but one who DOES things, applying these facts and formulae to find answers to new questions.

Certainly some findings in science have been random and accidental. Long before Galileo and Bacon quantified the scientific method, countless generations of humans were testing their predictions and stumbling upon new scientific facts. Whether discovery through accident or discovery through design, discovery has always been inherent to science and a precursor to technological advances. Discovery is most often the result of research, and research is usually a blend of library and laboratory. The value of project science is that it virtually requires the blend of those two avenues, and leads the individual student to personal discovery. In those cases where a project may more closely relate to engineering or technology than "pure science," the personal and individual discovery learning still takes place, with the same blend of library and laboratory, and driven by the same impetus of curiosity and challenge.

Science and technology are interrelated. Science seeks answers to theoretical questions, whereas technology seeks answers to practical problems. Technology meets its challenges through application of scientific findings. Both use an existing level of scientific comprehension and understanding to build upon and thereby meet the questions and challenges of the respective disciplines. The expert in technology must first have a complete and thorough understanding and comprehension of an appropriate scientific discipline.

Project science, at least within my definition of the term, provides the means through which comprehension and thus learning readily transpires. It is the medium through which innovation and initiative are encouraged and fostered. It is the fascination that entices and motivates students to excellence, and cultivates a growing interest in science. Project science, with its inherent challenges and quest for answers, can serve as the lure for the Isidor Rabis of the world to choose science as an educational goal and basis for adult career.

Discovery learning is implicit within project science. In one of my classes, an early activity has the students package and mail a "Pringle" potato chip to a specific destination. The challenge is to package the chip so that it arrives at its destination unbroken and edible, and in the lightest weight and least dense package. Clearly, through this activity, students begin to better understand the relationship of mass, weight, and density. Students also learn that there are not "book answers" for every problem encountered. They realize that replication is important, and the success or failure of a single experiment fraught with numerous variables, may well prove nothing. Finally, and perhaps most importantly, those who consider themselves less intelligent than most others learn that their ideas and innovations are of no less caliber than others in their class.

Project science requires an unknown outcome. The outcome may indeed be correctly hypothesized, but the learning takes place by virtue of the process or conduct of the project. This should not be confused with "cookbook-style" school laboratory experiments with teacher-provided and predetermined procedures and outcomes. In project science the students define the procedures and therefore control the outcomes.

As I wrote about this subject (June 1992), I had just completed overseeing an endeavor that I believed was my most successful project. Eight Alaskan high schools, separated by thousands of miles, had collaborated to build a single underwater vehicle capable of maneuvering to the bottom of Prince William Sound and retrieving samples. Most of the students were rural ninth graders, however, the mix also included a learning-disabled science class and an urban Science Club. The collaboration had taken place principally via telecommunication, and secondarily by telephone, fax, and mail.

This collaborative project did not begin at this ambitious level of magnitude. It began with my suggestion to build a vehicle capable of submersing and retrieving a 1-kilogram object at a depth of 2 meters. The students were the ones who escalated the objective. I guess I should be thankful they weren't familiar with the Mariana Trench! In any event, the purpose of the enterprise is project science, or project learning. Although we had originally targeted project completion by the end of the 1991-1992 school year, such a goal was not achievable without degradation of the objective of the project. That objective, or educational goal, was to provide students with the opportunity to learn through project science. This opportunity to learn was indeed seized by the students as they diligently pursued the science involved, and the many practical variables and difficulties inherent in their designs to control buoyancy, provide propulsion and three dimensional maneuvarability, and capture samples.

The process of this project, as with all project science, fostered inquisitiveness as the students sought the answers to their questions in library, laboratory, and from each other—as well as teachers and mentors. All students were first required to identify what they considered were the principal components of a remotely controlled underwater vehicle, and then to design a complete vehicle in collaboration with their fellow students at the local school site. Some schools used computers to enhance design techniques. These designs were of course crude by technical standards and in many cases unrealistic. The technical applicability or correctness is immaterial, of course, because it is the process that is important, and it is the process that has produced a myriad of questions and ideas.

By means of a teleconference with students and teachers participating, each site was assigned a component of the vehicle to design and build. All sites were provided copies of all designs of the entire vehicle from all other sites. Thus, students at each site could also consider ideas from other sites as they set out to design their assigned component. The enthusiasm prevalent at all sites was prodigious and infectious. The overall project included three professional scientists/engineers as "mentors." These persons were specifically selected because of their minority status (Eskimo) and because two of the three are women. One is a civil engineer and is employed in the design and construction of rural airfields in Alaska. Another is a professor of electrical engineering at the University of Alaska at Fairbanks. The third mentor, and only male, has his doctorate in geology and does consulting work in the town where he grew up and was educated—Barrow, Alaska. Thus, the students, and in particular the minority and women students, have role models to whom they can relate.

Although we had all hoped that this project would culminate successfully with the acquisition of samples from the bottom of Prince William Sound before the end of the 1991-1992 school year, as the year passed both teachers and students alike recognized that it would probably take longer, as indeed it has. What has made this particular project exciting was the obvious necessity for collaboration in the design and construction of the assorted parts, as well as the discovery learning experienced. Clearly the designers of the propulsion system and the designers of the buoyancy control system had to collaborate closely with all others in order to know what the total mass of the vehicle was going to be. Unquestionably, students, teachers, and mentors alike experienced "discovery science" at every turn. There was a great deal of learning and understanding that took place through the combination of library and laboratory.

In any event, the purpose of this project was not to simply increase some science test scores, although that might occur as a spin-off. Rather, the purpose was to achieve learning on the part of the student and to stimulate interest and understanding of what science is all about. Further, rather than a competitive environment, a collaborative one was created for the educational benefit of all concerned.

Some might argue that this project is obviously limited to physics or physical science classes. In fact, however, the classes involved included biology and marine science. Removal from the confines of strict curriculum content provided an opportunity for students to learn through the sheer exhilaration of discovery. As in the anecdote about the eminent Isidor Rabi, projects such as this open a plethora of student questions. The answers to the questions they ask may never provide them points on an examination, but the exercise in which they engage will whet their appetites for learning in general and for science in particular.

The idea of collaboration in learning is not the same as cooperative learning. Some students do not learn well cooperatively. Where cooperative learning requires the student to share with others—at each rung, so to speak—on the ladder of learning, collaboration involves periods where the student may work either independently or cooperatively, and then exchange what has been learned. All students have different learning styles, and some simply enjoy learning by themselves. Project and collaborative learning can be fitted to any learning style, and an individual can provide individual input into a shared project as well as collaborate with peers and/or mentors while still learning in an individual mode.

As a professional educator, I am loath to propound what might seem as another educational gimmick being served as the panacea for a very real and very large educational problem. Project science is not a panacea, but an extremely effective principal educational tool. Project science embodies the following assets:

- motivates students to ask questions,
- motivates students to conduct personal research,
- promotes "discovery learning,"
- provides accent on the scientific process,
- encourages ingenuity and initiative,
- promotes collaboration, and
- fosters a thirst for further knowledge.

Those are certainly good "positives." What about the negatives? There are a few, but I submit they are vastly outweighed by the pluses. I would suggest the following as negatives when compared to the conduct of a typical lecture-based curriculum in science:

- requires more time and energy by teacher,
- difficult to adjudge grades, and
- difficult to address in conventional curriculum terms.

As the move to restructure education sweeps the country, it behooves those responsible to take a hard look at what works in education and what does not seem to work. With ever-diminishing interest by students in science, that is an area crying out for help! I submit that ALL science courses need to include heavy doses of project science. I suggest that project science also be a course in its own right. I would leave to the reader the speculation on whether project science as a course should be for freshman in high school to serve as a student motivation for follow-on courses in conventional science disciplines, or is better as a senior course to encourage projects of more academic depth. In any case, I believe that restructuring of the science curriculum should take place in every school in the land, and that project science be recognized as a prime enhancement to the learning of science from kindergarten to graduate school. This may not be the elusive panacea alluded to earlier, but for me it is the next best thing!

THEORY INTO PRACTICE
James David Button, II[2]

I had encouraged students to do "Science Fair Projects" as an adjunct to the regular curriculum for over 15 years. However, the idea of integrating long-term projects into the classroom was one whose introduction by Priscilla Laws, Pat Cooney et al., was most fortuitous (staff at the LabNet workshop at Dickinson College, July 1989). Having moved to a school that not only encouraged, but also supported innovation in the classroom, the time was right for a new idea.

Like most teachers, I was wary of a total commitment to the idea of projects in the classroom. The state, as well as the local school division, has a mandated curriculum with certain objectives that MUST be met for the students to receive credit for the course. Because we deal with young people's lives and futures, it is important that we not do things that could create difficulties for them in their academic pursuits. Because a high percentage of our student body attends highly competitive colleges, it is constantly hammered home to the faculty that we must adequately prepare them for college work.

At the Dickinson workshop, the use of projects as a way to *supplement* the "standard curriculum" took root and began to flourish. Science teachers often tell students, "Science is what scientists do." Yet we often do not practice what we preach because the "laboratory activities" that the students work on are well planned and student-proof. It appears that little real experimenting goes on—rather, a great deal of equipment manipulation is done with extremely predictable results. The students know this; the parents know this; the teachers know this; the administration knows this; everyone knows it, but no one challenges it.

After the Dickinson workshop, with the permission of the local administration, my physics II class began to participate in the Star Schools project. This was like a breath of fresh air to the students. The major "network" projects that we worked on were the descent of the ball and the solar house. The students got really excited about doing the projects for several reasons.

I believe that the primary reasons the students enjoy projects are: (a) the "answer" is not a foregone conclusion, (b) they can share ideas with each other, (c) they see the time as relaxing, and (d) their perception is that they are "doing science." Although the students think that these are four different ideas, I believe that they can all be subsumed under "they are doing science." The enthusiasm that the students generate carries over to their views of "regular" instruction, school in general, and physics II in

---

[2] Dave Button teaches at Osbourn Park High School, Manassas, Virginia.

particular. Parents, seeing the enthusiasm of other students, encourage their children to take the course.

A second component of my conversion to "less teacher talk, more student work" is the implementation of MBL activities as a part of both the project activities and "regular" instruction. Having only one computer in the classroom was at first intimidating, but this drawback forced me to reevaluate how it could be used and to seek ways to use it more efficiently. Up until my introduction to MBL, the computer had served primarily as a number cruncher and a bookkeeper. With the introduction of sensors from the force probe to the motion detector, the range of experiments that could be done quickly and accurately enlarged considerably. Although the use of MBLs started off as part of traditional activities, they allowed students to use the machine at school to obtain results of individual projects that they were working on—"divergent activities," to use a phrase we heard frequently at Dickinson.

The third component, telecommunication, cannot be ignored. Students have always wanted to know what was going on in other classes. They would vie with each other to be the ones to download the mail and forum. The newness of telecommunication as part of the course was a drawing card.

Although often what came over the network was of little or no interest to them, they saw what questions were posed, what was being discussed, and how the system worked. They began to see science as a nationwide collaborative process. They were especially interested when we would put data, such as we obtained from an Eratosthenes lab, out on the network and we in turn would get data for our work in class. They began to see physics more globally. They saw that it was not just mechanics, heat, electricity/magnetism, optics, modern (the "big five"), but that it carried over to other areas of science; it became more and more the foundation of other sciences to them.

Student projects from this year (1991–1992) are going to be sent out on the LabNet Forum as part of their project report. Although this may not be of great interest to others, students will receive the satisfaction of knowing that their research is out there somewhere and may inspire someone else, or give someone else another perspective.

The "Tufts Workshops" of 1990 and 1991 got me thinking more and more about what I was doing with projects. Having been hooked and becoming more committed to project work at Dickinson, I was still floundering over what a project was. I am still not sure that I am as orthodox as some would have it, but my firm, unswerving definition (for today) of a project is, "An activity that is a student/teacher collaboration in defining, in designing, and in executing." I do not mean to say that the student and teacher do it together, but rather the student sees the teacher as a collaborator/guide who has more experience. It is the student doing his research under the direction of a more experienced researcher.

As I "direct" the projects that my students are doing, the following outline could be considered the model.

1. **The student comes up with the idea.** I believe that this is most important. One does not get commitment to an idea imposed on him or her from outside; rather, it comes from within. If the student comes up with the idea, then he or she perceives him or herself to be working on something of his or her own making.

2. **The student and teacher define the study.** Often students, as John King is fond of saying, have great ideas that are too broad for them. They need the teacher to help them focus. The student must, however, be permitted the freedom to reject the advice and counsel of the teacher.

3. **The student and teacher design the study.** Having gone through the previous step, to prevent too many dead ends the teacher and the student jointly design what the study is going to focus on. It is during this step that general procedures might be established for following not a step-by-step procedure, but rather an outline for the work.

4. **The student and teacher execute the study.** In the execution of the study, I see the roles as follows: Student—performs the experiments, gathers the data, analyzes the data, draws the conclusion(s) if any. Teacher—"runs interference" for the student, asks leading questions, suggests alternative pathways for those lines of reasoning that seem to be making no headway.

5. **The teacher gives moral support to the student.** For many students, this is the first time that they have had to do something that does not have a prescribed procedure. When they get "down" on their own work, it is up to the teacher to give an encouraging word.

As examples of this method of operation, consider the following currently ongoing projects:

Jenna and Michelle are the two females in my class. They have joined forces out of self-preservation and to show the males that they are the equal of them. (It might be said that both are planning college work in either physics, mathematics, or engineering.)

For some reason they happened on bubbles. Perhaps they had seen an article in *Scientific American,* or had a younger sibling with a bubble hoop. I don't know; however, I have learned not to ask too many questions. They decided to study bubbles.

That being a rather broad topic, I found some articles for them from *The Physics Teacher, Scientific American,* and so forth, and suggested that they look at them. This they did. We discussed the topic in one of our "catch-up" times, and they had narrowed the topic to what makes a good "bubble soap." They wanted to blow big bubbles, so now with a more manageable topic, they began researching soaps and detergents. They were having some luck, but nothing quantitative. They had discovered that there is some mixture of dishwashing detergent, water, and glycerin that works, but the exact proportions were unknown.

At a conference, I happened upon someone who had worked with students on the topic and got some information. I gave them the information I had about approximate ratios of soap to water to glycerin. They are now working on varying the ratio of glycerin to the other two, hoping to find an optimum for their work.

Peter and Jon are two bright but quite different students who are working together. Peter is more aesthetic; Jon is more mathematical. Peter does not know what he wants to study in college; Jon wants to go into engineering.

They saw the book *Chaos* on the classroom shelf and began thumbing through it. Happening upon a picture of the Mandelbrot Set, they were fascinated by it—Peter by its beauty, Jon by its mathematical symmetry. Because a program to generate the set was available to run on an Apple II, I showed it to them and some magnifications that I had done. They decided that they wanted to play with it.

Two aspects of the project emerged. One, Peter's, is the aesthetics as the magnification is increased. The second, Jon's, is how much magnification can the program be subjected to. Is the limit the program or the computer? To this end, a section for study has been identified and greater and greater magnifications have been made. As of this writing, the area has been magnified 10 times. Although there has been a loss of color, the resolution of the picture taken from the Apple IIgs has not been exceeded. These two young men have begun to appreciate each other's perspective. Peter is beginning to want to know how deep the mathematics can go; Jon is beginning to point out how "schweet" the graphic is.

Either of them alone could have done the project, but would not have benefited from the other's input. As a result of their working together, they are investigating two different perspectives on the same phenomenon.

In each of these cases, and any of the other cases that could be cited from this year's students, I have tried to follow my own advice. I have helped when asked or when I perceived that assistance would not be counterproductive.

Some would say that neither of these is a project. I posit that they are. For these four students, and for the other 19 in the class, they are doing something that is not part of the curriculum, something that is new to them, something that they will know better than anyone else in the school. They will have learned from it. If our goal in education is to have students be independent learners, then that goal will be approached by these projects.

Can I say that I am totally committed to project work? The situation that I am currently in certainly lends itself to project work, at least for my physics II students. With a two-period block so that I can do projects, I am committed to the idea, for the "required coursework," which is stated in very specific objectives, can be done in one period per day.

Am I likely to go totally to project work? I doubt it as long as I have a curriculum imposed from above. Will I work toward it? Yes! We are in the middle of a curriculum revision, and I am most likely going to be working on it. If I am, then if we cannot revise the curriculum to fit the project idea, then I am going to lobby for a "project" course. Under the current central administration and with the known support of the local administration, this sounds like something that will be "do-able."

Were I to advise others about getting involved with projects, I would say, "Yes! By all means." My words of caution would be to:

1. **Read your administration carefully.** If you think that they would be amenable to such an idea, present a careful plan to them. If you think that they would not be amenable to such an idea, get permission to incorporate a "project work" component into your grading scheme. Once your students catch on, they will sell the idea to their parents. Once the parents are convinced, building administrators will see its "High Marquee" value and become your most enthusiastic supports.

2. **Go slowly at first.** Never attempt vast programs with half-vast planning. Project work takes a lot more time than you think. Do one or two well rather than five or six poorly.

3. **Provide class time.** Parents are more likely to support ideas that the teacher is willing to invest his or her class time in. They are more likely to rebel at having students carry out work at home that does not have a teacher time investment.

4. **Be enthusiastic about the projects.** If you don't show that you are excited, the students will not be excited. This means not only in class but with other faculty members. If you have access to other schools, work with them. Enlist the aid and enthusiasm of your peers. Be a local change agent. If you are making the work more exciting for kids, it becomes exciting for other teachers and building administrators.

5. **Have clear, concise guidelines about what you expect.** Students will follow through if they know the rules of the game and the deadlines. If you can, give as much detail at different points in the year about what is due at the next report time. This keeps the project in the student's mind and keeps the amount of stuff to be remembered at a minimum.

One may ask if this has helped or hindered the educational program. The clientele has been small and of high caliber. They are now freshmen and sophomores in such schools as the University of Virginia, Boston University, the College of William and Mary, and Clarkson. They tell me that the project work was beneficial because they had to work some on their own before getting to college. To this end, I can say that it has at least NOT HURT the students.

Can I say that it has helped them later on? The jury is still out.

Has it improved the classroom environment, the students' outlooks, and my outlook? Yes!

Will it continue? Yes! Students coming into the course expect to do project work. Can we deny them the opportunity?

DEVELOPING STUDENT SCIENTISTS
Roger F. Larson [3]

I think that I have always known that the project requirement of any of my courses from grade school through graduate school has significantly contributed to the content of my long-term memory. Of course I remember some of my teachers were terrific lecturers, but I don't recall much of what they said. And yes, I performed some classic experiments in college, such as the Millikan Oil Drop, but I can't say that these repeats enhanced my science curiosity. Unfortunately, a vast majority of my course work has been forgotten. What do I remember? Let's see, building an electric motor in Cub Scouts, putting together a transistor radio in high school physics, giving a speech in college-freshman English on the relativistic time dilation equation, and doing an anthropological study of an inner-city youth as part of a graduate education course. Thus, I have often experienced the project requirement of any course leaving behind a meaningful and lasting imprint.

Like most educators, however, I had been reluctant to make project requirements a part of my science program. If I couldn't come up with a list of appropriate project topics for my students, how could I expect the students to find their own? Of course, I also feared the inevitable task of evaluating more than 100 student project reports.

I now require each of my 120 students to accomplish one project every 9 weeks. How did this transformation evolve? About 10 years ago, the Department of Defense Dependents Schools (DoDDS) began participating in the Junior Science and Humanities Symposium (JSHS). The JSHS provides a format for high school students to conduct original research and then present their findings to other selected students researchers. Each high school was funded to sponsor up to 10 student research projects. For

---

[3] Roger Larson teaches with the Department of Defense Dependents Schools (DoDDS), Yokota High School, Japan.

years, I didn't find the time in my busy schedule to encourage my best students to do a research project as their schedules also appeared to be filled to capacity. In 1984, my wife, a biology teacher, first required students in a second-year biology course to submit a research paper to the JSHS. She took eight students from the DoDDS school in Izmir, Turkey, to London. Needless to say, they had a tremendous experience both in London and at the symposium.

After transferring from Izmir to Okinawa, Japan, I was fortunate to convince the school administration to offer a science research elective for the upper level students. This course required a research paper for the DoDDS-Pacific JSHS held annually at Tsukuba Science City outside of Tokyo. Each year, our science department encouraged a different science staff member to accompany our researchers to Tsukuba. In February of 1988, we decided to require all general chemistry and physics students to perform a project during the fourth marking period to prepare them for a JSHS project the following school year. During that first go-around we all agreed that the students seemed to be truly involved with their projects. We encouraged teams of up to three per group and the projects were presented both orally and in a written format. The most memorable project I recall from that first group was an investigation by a student who wanted to verify that water boiled in a microwave oven was not as hot as water boiled over an open flame. His data did support his hypothesis, which surprised me until I realized that water in a microwave boils first on the surface rather than at the bottom of the container. This is a superb example of an investigation that needed a second look.

In 1989, the advertisements to attend the first LabNet workshop to learn about MBLs and project learning caught my fancy. Much of our time at the Dickinson College LabNet workshop was occupied collecting data via probes connected to computers. In order to prepare graphs of our data, the first-generation Low Cost Interface, sans software, required the use of an integrated package to convert hexadecimal code to base 10. My partners and I used a photogate to analyze the period of a pendulum. With millisecond accuracy we wondered whether or not photogate timers could be used to measure global variations in "g."

At the 1990 LabNet workshop conducted by NWREL on the campus of Lewis and Clark College, the participants were introduced to IBM's Personal Science Laboratory interfacing system and Explorer software. Wow, what an improvement! We were now collecting data and watching the graph line plotted on our monitors in real time.

Our group at Lewis and Clark spent many sessions attempting to describe the nature of a student project and also brainstormed many example topics. It was on the flight home that I began to synthesize thoughts from my LabNet Year 2 experience. I defined project categories and vowed to require a project from each of my science students each quarter:

PROJECT CATEGORY DESCRIPTIONS

1. **Biography of a Scientist**—should emphasize both scientist's accomplishments and insights into his or her personal life (at least two sources with footnotes and bibliography). Specific comments about unique occurrences/characteristics are expected.

2. **Measurement and Analysis of Data**—anything that can be measured is suitable for this project. Results are to be presented in a formal laboratory report containing: Title, Purpose, Abstract, Procedure Description, Data, and Results and Conclusions.

3. **Controlled Experiment**—study the effects of one or a few experimental variables on a test object while holding constant all other conditions that might affect the outcome. Much thought should be given to all variables that can affect the study's outcome. Results are to be reported using same outline as Category 2 above.

4. **Construction of a Model or Scientific Instrument**—build something —buy a kit or parts, start from scratch or repair a broken item. Describe in your report why you chose to build what you did, what new knowledge you gained, and demonstrate your completed project. If you received assistance from someone, give them credit.

5. **Group Design Competition**—for this year is the Descent of a Ping - Pong Ball. In teams of three or four you will design and construct a device [to measure] the amount of time it takes for the ball to descend from 1.0 vertical meter. You can only use 8 1/2 X 11 20# paper and 1/2- inch tape for your construction—which cannot exceed 1 cubic meter. A nationwide competition via the LabNetwork will take place in the late fall. Teams will send an ASCII file describing their device and best time.

6. **Team Project of Your Own Creation**—teams of two or three must reach consensus about the purpose of their project. All members must make a significant contribution to the written and oral report.

Each passing quarter I observed the students had less difficulty in defining appropriate topics. I also noted that the quality of the presentations improved each marking period.

The trick for creating appropriate project topics is to direct each student to identify an area of interest. I will always remember a near-failing physics student who claimed not to have any physics interests. She was only interested in going to the tanning salon. Bingo! Yes, a study of tanning lamps would be an appropriate topic for a physics project. She reported that there were FDA requirements on the amount and type of UV radiation permitted. She even learned that some of the salons in town took the FDA regulations seriously and others refused to discuss them with her. Her classmates learned that physics exists—everywhere.

Another student wondered whether it was practical to invest in window tinting for his car. Would the tint keep his car significantly cooler under the summer sun? Controlling both the interior and exterior colors, he monitored the outside and inside temperatures. The next quarter he analyzed the percent transmittance of various window tints utilizing the IBM-PSL radiometric probe.

Another student team sought to measure the speed of a car by monitoring the Doppler shift of the horn of a passing car. This particular project was inspired by an article titled, "Doing the Doppler," in *The Science Teacher*, September 1990. If you scan your old copies of *The Physics Teacher* and *The Science Teacher* you should find at least one potential project topic in each issue.

When students are encouraged to work in groups of two or three, a class will generate about a dozen projects per quarter. The reading and evaluation of the projects goes quickly on the evening following the oral presentations. About 5 classroom days are devoted to the projects each quarter—1 to 2 days at the beginning to brainstorm topics, and 3 to 4 days at the end for the project presentations. Initially, I budgeted only 3 to 5 minutes for the oral summary report. I now find it advantageous to allow 10 to 15 minutes for reports, which when appropriate include a demonstration of the project.

The class time utilized for the project brainstorming and final reports gives science students the opportunity to participate in the scientific process. Strictly teaching the content uncovered by other scientists via problem-solving sessions and prepared laboratory "investigations" does not allow students to experience the study of the unknown. Scientists seek answers to their own questions by utilizing methods and procedures of their own design. It is time, through projects, to encourage our science students to be scientists!

LabNet challenged, motivated, and assured me of the importance of involving students in projects. The LabNet telecommunication network has developed a team of science educators who now are sharing ideas for improving our product. Such efforts must continue. Project enhanced science learning is yet an infant.

PROJECTS FUEL PHYSICS COURSE
Namie C. Smith [4]

Students were gathered around what looked like a paper castle, watching a small white ping-pong ball appear and disappear among the ramps that surrounded the structure. When the ball reached the bottom, amid cheering, the time of 58.9 seconds was announced. This was the winning time for the slow descent of a ball project, an activity that had been 4 days in planning and execution. Groups of three or four students designed their particular structure, some making adjustments along the way, ending up

---

[4] Namie Smith teaches at Ridgewood High School, Ridgewood, New Jersey.

with a totally different structure than their initial idea. Others were divided on what they wanted their structure to be, only learning too late that compromise and cooperation were necessary to get a finished project in on time.

The basic rules had been fairly simple: construct a paper structure within a 75 cm by 75 cm by 75 cm space. Place a ping-pong ball at the top and measure the time for it to reach the bottom. The team achieving the longest time (slowest descent) would win. Supplies included 8 1/2 x 11 sheets of paper (I use recycled paper, which I collect all year long), scotch tape, and staples. In the course of the 4 days, the students learn about the strength of paper (folded, rolled, or placed on its edge), the difference between a small scale model and the larger structure, and most important, to be creative, cooperative, and competitive. The project is a great advertisement for physics—friends stop by to see what's going on, other teachers stop by to see what their students are talking about. Enrollment in physics has increased from 7 sections to 10 in 3 years. This activity is not the only reason but it is a good indicator of the transition that has taken place within the last 3 years as a direct result of the LabNet experience.

Before I had attended the 3-week introduction to project physics, my course included a heavy dose of demonstrations and what I would call canned experiments: exercises where the outcome demonstrates one of the fundamental laws of physics or at least a corollary. A term project where a selected topic would be studied in some depth might be included if time permitted.

Timing is everything, someone once said—at the time I was getting involved in LabNet our school district was involved in a series of different teaching techniques, one of which was cooperative learning and another was the "4MAT" system—customizing teaching techniques to different learning styles. The 4MAT premise is that there are two different ways by which we learn: the way we perceive and the way we process information. Some are doers who need to try out new information immediately. Others are watchers who reflect on new ideas and need time to synthesize what they have observed. To reach all the different learning personalities involves incorporating a variety of teaching techniques, one of which fits closely to the project-based approach of LabNet. By including the project idea into my class I was also fulfilling a curriculum goal set by the school.

After the first slow-descent project, I was hooked. The second time, I started with a project to construct the tallest tower from a single sheet of paper. As a one-period activity, this introduced the students to creative thinking and was short enough to avoid any frustrations. It also set the stage for working with paper, learning about its strength and the strength of different cross-sections.

Now I wanted to see how a project could fit into a specific curriculum topic. Because energy conservation is a major current events issue, I incorporated the building of a model solar house as the culmination of a unit on energy. This became an interdisciplinary project with the drafting teacher, who explained drawing floor plans, solar-house specifications, and zoning laws, and provided other technical assistance as needed. Models scaled at 1 cm to the foot (larger than the architect's traditional 1/4 inch per foot) were a manageable size. Not only did the students build their models but they were tested for thermal properties. A home designed to be in the side of a hill was the most thermally efficient. (Yes, the student used real topsoil to cover three-fourths of the house.)

The natural progression was to try student-initiated projects. With much trepidation I okayed a variety of projects from studying the insulation efficiency of the school building, to sound pollution in the community (along a major highway), to hydroelectric energy production (a student built a water wheel to use in our local creek), and comparisons of acceleration efficiencies of two models of cars (my hot-rod experts). The most difficult aspect of these projects was the evaluation process. Using a suggestion from Greg Lockett (a LabNet teacher from Cottonwood, California), I had the students make presentations to their class, with their peers grading them using a set of standard criteria. This evaluation included content, relevance to science, clarity of presentation, visual aids, and overall impressions. The evaluation, weighted as 25% of the total, was on a scale of 1–10, which I combined with my own evaluation. By including the students in the evaluation process, they had to be attentive during the presentation and validate their scoring with an explanation.

In retrospect, I would have been more specific about the parameters of the project, requiring experimentation and the collection of data and a review of the progress midway through the project. Some students did essentially nothing but a literature search with xeroxed figures for visual aids. On the other hand, some projects were well thought out and executed.

The amount of time that was required on my part to monitor the projects was much greater than I anticipated and was part of the reason some projects were not executed as well as I would have liked. In the future I plan to spend more time explaining the criteria for evaluation and stress data gathering to substantiate conclusions.

The three types of projects did a great deal to enrich the physics course and much to publicize the course in the school as well. The final exam grades were about 5% lower overall than in previous years but this reflected more the change in content than the inclusion of projects. (The same exam is given each year as a criterion reference test to monitor teaching rather than student learning.) Other departments also noted a drop in the final test scores, which probably indicated the general aptitude of the student body. If a different type of test were administered, the grades would reflect the advantages of project-based physics.

Besides the projects, the laboratory experiences of the students have undergone a major revision based on my LabNet experience. With support from the assistant superintendent for curriculum and the principal, I was able to obtain six Apple IIgs computers, the HRM sonic ranger, sound microphone, and Pasco Smart pulley hardware. Three rotational motion rigs were purchased for the Advanced Placement courses as well. Using the Project-Based Physics manual prepared by Priscilla Laws of Dickinson College, and the Motion manual prepared by Ron Thornton of Tufts University, my colleague (who teaches the AP physics course) and I revised the kinematics lab exercises to include computer-aided acquisition of data.

The students spent more time exploring the concepts that they could quickly observe, rather than laboriously cranking out the data by using the ticker timer. They see the computer as a viable tool for data collection as well as data analysis. When students went to the computer independently to generate graphs of their data without being told to do so, the time spent teaching the use of the spreadsheet became worthwhile. When students figured out how to use the programs in more appropriate ways than my simplistic directions, they learned the value of the computer. Before attending the 3 weeks at Dickinson, my only computer experience was using the word processor and spreadsheet, and although I still have a long way to go, I can now expose my students to the merits of computer technology.

The telecommunication aspect was the most fun for my students during the first year when they were involved with the Star School projects. The exposure to students from rural areas was an eye-opening experience for the eastern suburbanites whom I teach. They enjoyed the chance to talk to them, not only by computer but also by phone and even called Iowa one morning at 8 a.m. However, the software was limiting. The LabNetwork through Delphi has been better for communications but has curtailed telecommunication for my students. Reading the Forum has enriched my teaching as I incorporate suggestions from fellow physics teachers. I would like to see more interaction between students doing projects with telecommunication as a link. Expressing ideas concisely is an important aspect of survival in the scientific and engineering communities and we should do as much as we can to foster such attributes among our students.

Projects as simple as the paper tower or as intricate as a Rube Golderg do a great deal to foster creativity and critical thinking skills for students. Any project at the elementary level is providing the experience necessary to build a foundation. I encourage elementary teachers to incorporate projects into their curriculum. Having students work in groups and providing them with concrete objectives is the first step. Just as I found with my own experience, projects with a well-defined task are important in setting the stage for more elaborate efforts. Learning to complete a project has a value as a goal in itself in addition to the content and process learned.

The last 2 years have been the fullest years of my teaching career, in part due to the inclusion of projects into the curriculum. I recommend this invigorating experience for everyone.

SOME THOUGHTS ABOUT PROJECT SCIENCE
Norm Anderson [5]

My first thoughts go back to the first years of my teaching career. It was in the mid-1960s. The space program was in full swing—the president committed to sending a man to the moon by the end of the decade. It was very easy to find the majority of science students eager to do projects. Of course there was a great deal of enthusiasm for building rockets and this became one of our first enterprises.

I recall one student who wanted to continue in this effort, but rather than purchasing the rocket and engine elected to build his own. Having had experience with metal-turning lathes, we convinced the industrial arts teacher to allow us the use of the metal shop after school and on weekends. Being in a small school system, I taught chemistry as well as physics. So with great care the solid rocket fuel was manufactured in the laboratory. Only static test firings were allowed and these were carried out in the country with both student and teacher hidden behind a large boulder. The result of all of this was a second-place finish in a regional science fair. From the simple launching of these first rockets this student was involved in a multitude of learnings—using the lathe, designing the rocket body, the chemistry experience, testing the rocket fuel, collecting data, calibrations— but above all the satisfaction achieved from the experience.

More recently, I introduced my physics classes to the fundamentals of producing reflection and transmission holograms. I had a student who wanted to use the laser to produce holographic images of objects, as seen through a microscope, using optical fibers as the transmission medium. He also wanted to try to produce a method of using the laser as a scanning instrument for finger printing. Some very lofty goals indeed, I thought. Suffice it to say the projects turned out to be unsuccessful. Today that same student, now in his second year in college, has just completed working on a project this past summer through a grant received from NASA.

These are two contrasting experiences of the success and failure that students are certain to encounter when working on projects. But the experience gained is far more important than the results.

Projects in the classroom. How does one get started doing project science in the classroom? My suggestion would be to start with a project for the entire class. Do this early in the year. Start the first week of school

---

[5] Norm Anderson teaches at Cedar Falls High School, Cedar Falls, Iowa.

if at all possible. Pick a project that is not too difficult, and something that will be relatively successful for everyone involved. Have the students work with a partner and choose a project that requires no more than a couple of weeks to complete. Toothpick bridges, Lou-Vee AirCars, mousetrap cars, paper airplanes, an egg drop are some that I have used. The culmination of all of these projects involves lighthearted competition between all of the students and they thoroughly enjoy it. You may even award a small prize to the winners.

If this is a first attempt at doing projects in the class it will give you a clue as to the students' receptiveness for doing project work. By doing this early in the year it gives me the opportunity to feel out my classes and decide what to do for our next effort. If this is a first in project science don't make the mistake of tossing out a multitude of options that cover all areas because it will drive you right up the wall. I tried it once and believe me, that after years of doing science fair projects it was much more than I had bargained for. You will find that you will only get to a few students at a time and the accomplishments will be much less. I do many different projects at one time, but they are limited to a specific area. The biggest thing that has changed for me is the aid of the computer in the work that we do. It is no problem doing a dozen different projects that involve electronics, because one can use the computer as a measuring instrument for all of them. If you don't have access to some of the more sophisticated interfacing devices (MPLI, ULI, PSL, etc.) the Apple gameport will do very nicely and one can find many programs written for interfacing a number of projects.

How do I know that these projects are of any value to my students? Do they really help when they go on to college? Many of these students somehow find their way into similar situations when they get into college. Many are working as undergraduate assistants in a variety of disciplines. I don't believe they would be in those positions were it not for the project work they had done while in high school.

The most frequently asked question by other teachers is: What do you leave out because of the project work done during the year? My answer is: Nothing. What I do is to omit all of the repetitive teacher-centered problem solving that I used to do. The students are forced to do more work on their own and in cooperative learning situations with other students working in small groups. They perform just as well on their quizzes and exams as they have in the past and I still manage to cover as much material as I ever did. I haven't changed my style of teaching (I still use the PSSC text that I've used for many years). The basic experiments that we do are similar but the method has clearly changed. This is in large part because of the integral part the computer has played in the lab over the past several years. This has also allowed for increased time for projects in the classroom.

All of this has been a gradual change for me. I have always had a certain number of projects going on in the classroom, but not to the extent that I do now.

I don't know that there is any one project I could single out as a favorite. Last year, for example, we built a rocket assembled from plastic liter bottles and a few wood scraps. This is a rather involved project using a one-liter plastic bottle partially filled with water, pressurized with a tire pump, and released from an apparatus built from a 2x6-inch piece of wood. I mention this because it was a project where everyone in class really became involved. We'll be doing this one again in the spring with many improvements. Perhaps what I just mentioned is the most important part of a project, that is, total class involvement. It should be an enjoyable experience.

What advice would I give to those who have never attempted project work in the science classroom? As I mentioned previously, begin with something simple that all individuals will feel comfortable with and not become frustrated in doing.

Probably the most difficult thing to decide is just what exactly constitutes a project. At the very least it should be something beyond the realm of the typical experiment one would normally do in the laboratory, but it certainly may be an extension of it. We should not turn down a project simply because it's been done a thousand times before. Quite often these seemingly simple projects lend themselves to more questions and research on the students' part. Most projects I do are rather extensive and students spend several hours each week both in and outside the classroom during a 9-week period.

TO MOTIVATE, TRY PROJECTS
Sandra J. Rhoades [6]

I have used projects in my physics, physical science, and chemistry classes for 10 years. I began with one project per year and progressed to more fully project-based courses with projects done whenever applicable to the concepts being taught—usually about one per month.

The first project I did with my classes was one in which physics students are required to design a mobile, determine the placing of the pieces by using the equation for calculating torque, draw a detailed diagram indicating measurements, then construct the mobile. Students are given the latitude to develop any theme of their choosing for the mobile; however, they are required to construct at least three branches, all of which must be

---

[6] Sandra Rhoades was teaching at North Cobb High School, Kenneshaw, Georgia. She has since moved.

free to rotate about each other in a space no larger than one cubic meter. The fundamentals of sound design are introduced by the art teacher, who shows slides of some mobiles done by Alexander Calder, a former engineer and the originator of this art form. They are told that the project will be graded on its artistic merit by the art teacher and on its design and adherence to calculations by me. The completed mobiles are hung in the physics lab, other science classes, the media center, and administrative offices. The finished works began to attract a lot of positive publicity for the science department.

The project has been popular with my physics students, is interdisciplinary, and applies to areas of our lives other than purely scientific pursuits. The students gain an appreciation for the problems and challenges encountered by architects and engineers in designing structures that must be technically sound, structurally strong, and pleasing to the eye. After the first few years, I began to see a pattern emerging in my students' performances on the project. The best mobiles were often the work of students who were struggling with physics and whose grades were not high. This was an area of success that they would never have experienced if I had followed a purely traditional approach to teaching: lectures, typical physics lab activities, written problem solving, and conventional testing. It was then that I began to search for other project possibilities.

What constitutes a project? What distinguishes a project from an activity? I believe that a project is anything that requires problem solving, creativity, planning, and self-direction. It is not defined by the length of time it takes to complete. Some small projects can be done in a single class period; others require months of work. They all constitute a process of struggling through a problem. Some can be done as competitions. The science olympiad and physics olympics events are excellent examples of projects that are competitive in nature. Some projects require original research and are less competitive.

Projects have substantially changed my classroom practice. Once I became convinced of the value to all students of participating in projects that required original thought, creativity, and innovation, I began to design many of my lab activities around a project approach. I made my labs more open-ended—more conducive to inquiry and cooperative effort. Projects seem to naturally follow the learning cycle of exploration, application, and extension of concepts. Most exploratory lab activities are really mini-projects in that the students have freedom of choice in approach to the stated question or problem; they can use whatever procedures and measurements are necessary to solve the problem and they can draw conclusions from their own observations. Making lab activities more project-oriented has freed my students from a cookbook approach to science. They are more responsible for their own learning than they have ever been before.

Over the years, my students have responded most favorably to projects. At the end of each semester, I ask my classes to write a brief description of their favorite activity in the course, whether it be a lab, project, or class activity, such as problem solving. Almost every student cites one of the projects as their favorite activity in the course. Many list the long-term, design-oriented projects as their favorites, even though these are often the activities that caused them the greatest frustration. Examples are the Descent of a Ball Contest, hologram design and construction, amusement park physics, Rube Goldberg Design, mousetrap racer, hovercraft design, and—for chemistry—analysis of food spreads for fat content, popcorn analysis, hydrometer design, and UV blockage analysis of suntan products. My students have written poetry, music, and plays based on scientific principles. They present an annual Science is Fun demonstration assembly, complete with a laser show, for elementary students. Last year, we hosted more than 2,000 elementary students. One of the most ambitious projects is one on which my students are presently working. They are building a Discovery Center in a science lab for middle school students. My students will be responsible for presenting the activities, explaining the concepts, and fully maintaining and staffing the Discovery Center.

Projects take time. Some of the work is done at home, some is done during class time so students can ask questions and solve design problems. When I arrive at the end of the year now, I have not always "covered the book." However, my students do as well as they have ever done on standardized assessments, such as the achievement tests and AP exams. More of my students than before are taking these tests, and I have many more students who are pursuing science and engineering majors in college. Projects have significantly heightened student interest and motivation.

The most successful project I have experienced has been the Descent of a Ball Contest—a national project for physics students initiated by teachers in New York State. This effort involves designing a structure of paper and transparent tape, limited to a volume not to exceed 0.5 meters on edge, which allows a regulation golf ball to fall a vertical distance of 0.5 meters in the longest time between 15 seconds and 30 minutes. The most successful structure is determined by dividing the time of fall in seconds by the mass of the structure in grams. Last year was the first year of the project. My students' structures ranged from heavy "parking ramp" designs to a simple tube, with times of fall varying between less than 15 seconds to more than 30 minutes. The winning structure massed 14 grams with a descent time of more than 22 minutes. Many students experienced great frustration during this project—some wanted to give up. I showed them a videotape of the fall of the Tacoma Narrows Bridge to show them an example of frustration on a grand scale from the real world. It seemed to help their outlook on what they were experiencing, and not a single group gave up.

The students were given an opportunity to telecommunicate their results to the project originators, which was motivational in itself. They were very much excited about communicating with students and teachers from another state. It added a positive dimension to an already successful project. Students have also been able to seek data and advice from teachers around the country through the network. My physics and chemistry students are currently involved in a heating degree days project in which they determine over a 3-month period the amount of heating fuel they use per square foot and the cost. They send their data and compare it to the data received from students in seven other states.

Projects provide excellent vehicles for incorporating technology into the classroom experience. We use microcomputers in several design projects for measuring time, distance, velocity, and force. In chemistry projects, we measure temperature and pH with computers. One project involves designing and constructing a musical instrument and tuning it by using a computer interfaced to a frequency meter.

I would strongly encourage teachers at all levels, pre-first to college, to try a project-based approach to science. It takes time, energy, and much planning. But the results are worth it! Student leaders emerge who have never before assumed a leadership role; cooperative learning is at its best during project work; students have an opportunity to be creative and innovative. Science can be made interdisciplinary and more relevant to students' daily lives. Science can be integrated with art, music, writing, sports, dance, consumer interests, environmental concerns, technology, invention—the possibilities are endless!

My colleagues and I have incorporated project-based science in every workshop we have conducted for elementary and middle school teachers, as well as high school teachers. Participants are unanimous in their excitement about project-based science and their determination to incorporate projects into their curriculum. Projects allow students to make decisions about their own learning process; it gives them experience in higher level thinking and in relating concepts to concrete problems. It will add a flavor to any science course that cannot be matched by any other vehicle. Try it—you'll like it! (see Rhoades & Franklin, 1989).

LEARNING TO THINK THROUGH PROJECT SCIENCE
Kelly A. Wedding [7]

My "conversion" to project-based teaching occurred in a very short period of time while at the second summer session of the LabNet program. In only a few hours, I was convinced about the value of hands-on teaching in

---

[7] Kelly Wedding teaches at Santa Fe High School, Santa Fe, New Mexico.

the physics classroom. During that session, I had the opportunity to talk to and work with teachers who had ideas and experience in teaching at least some projects. Their enthusiasm was infectious and a sure sign that something they were doing was very right!

The next year, I added some simple projects to my classroom schedule (really just lab experiences with less teacher direction), and found that my students not only learned more, but enjoyed themselves a great deal more. One basic type of project is the building of a device or structure within specific parameters or with a certain amount or type of materials. In my classroom these include the construction of a paper tower, a bridge, and personal timers. Students work together in groups. Evaluation is usually in the form of a contest—against each other, against the clock, or against a specific set of criteria. The second type of project is one that is student-initiated. These are usually selected by the student due to a prior interest or are efforts to answer a specific question that they have formulated. They vary greatly and include projects on sound, the architectural soundness of adobe structures, investigations on various types of motion, and environmental studies. Students typically work alone. They choose a mentor, usually an adult with some degree of expertise in the field, and spend a significant amount of time (9 weeks) on the project. Students write up their experiment in the form of a scientific paper.

The project approach is a significant change from my earlier methods of presentation and classroom style. I still do some "traditional" laboratory experiments, but I have discovered that students learn much more when they have a part in the design of the lab, when they choose how and what to measure, and when they look for the physical relationships from *their* data. I have successfully integrated projects with a regular class. I have had to accept a certain amount of chaos and noise in my classroom, a level that I would not have tolerated in previous years, but a careful ear will quickly assuage any belief that learning is not occurring. Students learn the value of peer teaching and I no longer act as the primary source of information or techniques. In a project classroom, students work together to come up with solutions to problems; the teacher simply acts as a catalyst. In my own classroom, I enjoy hearing students *teaching* each other. What frequently sounds like an argument ends in, "Oh! OK!" and the students continue with the project. If you were to visit my classroom on any given day you would observe peer teaching: students explaining, drawing diagrams, and demonstrating concepts.

One of my favorite stories in this vein involves a group of students arguing over acceleration due to gravity. One student was convinced that a heavy object would hit the floor before a lighter object (they weren't talking about mass although that was exactly his point). This student bet a soda that he was correct. The group came to me for objects and I gave them a bowling ball and a block of wood. Over and over they dropped these and an assortment of other things in the classroom. The skeptical student finally bought the round of sodas. It was a lesson he never forgot, not because he lost, but because they did the experiment to prove the concept.

The opportunity to work as part of a team toward a common goal gives students a sense of responsibility for the results. It initiates a change in attitude about working in the laboratory and teaches students to listen, *really* listen, to what others have to say. In a project-based classroom, students take responsibility for their own learning; they take ownership in the process of learning. My experience has been that when I hear students asking each other how they are going to solve a problem or build something to meet specifications, learning is occurring. An argument is a definite sign that ideas are being tossed about, that some thought is going into a project and that it is not simply a collection of data or a regurgitation of something I have told them.

Students also enjoy the opportunity to be creative in the science classroom. They determine the approach to a problem, and try several methods of solution—reworking or redesigning as necessary. This does not necessarily require a trial-and-error approach, but many students begin with that method in the early stages of a project-based lab.

In my physics classroom, groups of students usually use the trial-and-error method early in the year. Gradually, a shift in their methods begins to occur as they form a hypothesis earlier into the project and develop a plan of attack that is more scientific *before* beginning the project. I believe this is typical of most project-based science classes. Students who are used to the "chug and plug" type of lab are usually surprised and pleased with the opportunity to make choices, but sometimes find it overwhelming in the beginning. There is no "set" way to do a particular experiment and students have the opportunity to see several approaches to the same problem.

An important result of the project-based physics experience is that students end up with a better understanding of the subject. This includes the ability to (a) solve a problem using the principles studied, (b) develop a theory about how something works or happens, and (c) see beyond the project itself. My students have come to me to say how a particular activity cleared up misconceptions about a topic in mechanics or to express a general disbelief in a theory I was teaching. Students understand the subject more thoroughly and have a better degree of success because of it.

When students make statements like "Why? I want to know why the forces aren't equal," or "I think you are wrong and here's why," we have made a difference. Traditional laboratory experiences do not invite or encourage students to want to know more. They are simply a method of getting from here to there and only a few of our students really get the point or develop an understanding of the laws we intended them to investigate. While working on a mobile for a project on torque in my physics class, I heard two students discussing the art forms that require a knowledge of the topic. In a class period of about 1 hour, they involved almost every student in the room in a discussion (including diagrams on the board for illustration) of everything from sculpture to how art was displayed (hanging pictures and textiles, balancing furniture, etc.).

Finally, students experience an increase in self-esteem that encourages them to tackle the unknown, encourages them to think on their own, and gives them a sense of accomplishment in a difficult class. The attitude that "I can do hard things" is certainly beneficial to a student and helps ensure future success. This single factor is vital to the development of the idea that *they* might be able to go into a scientific field of study in the future.

In my own teaching, experience has led me to believe that self-confidence and positive self-esteem, second only to interest, are the most important factors in whether students will pursue a scientific career. Once again, the belief that "I can do hard things" is essential to scientific success. This is certainly not the only reason we would want our students to take advanced sciences. However, the ability to motivate these young people lies in making the science interesting, and getting the principles so thoroughly ingrained that students think about physics on a day-to-day basis. Students are more interested in physics when they are involved in projects. When they choose their project topics, they can investigate something they find intriguing.

Students learn a new approach to problem solving that is not a regurgitation of information from the text. They learn to plan, implement, alter, and try again. This method is real science, something for which lab manuals do not allow.

Students learn to respond to situations that demand a reaction to change. There is no longer a standard format in the laboratory. The experiments are open-ended and "what if's?" are encouraged. When the computer did not respond as expected in my AP physics class while we investigated the coefficient of friction with a force probe, our mistake was as much a learning experience as the labs we did later. My suggestion was to go on and we would figure it out later because we knew what should have happened. The students refused to accept that and insisted on finding our error or accepting the force probe's findings and changing the laws of physics!

Each component of learning takes them into new areas as they explore the possibilities in the project-based classroom. My students tell me that experiments are now fun and interesting. In previous years students would groan when I would announce a lab day. In general, students perform better than their nonproject-based counterparts on tests. They have a better grasp of the concepts and do well in the area of problem solving.

As advice to teachers who want to implement projects in the classroom, I would like to offer the following:

1. **Implement simple projects first**. Student performance will not be
   terrific and you will wonder why you are doing this, but remember, students are not used to *thinking* in the laboratory. They are
   used to filling in the blanks with "appropriate" responses.

2. **When students do personal projects, monitor them over time**. I
   give out a progress report every 2 weeks. On this sheet they tell me
   what they have done, what they are doing and they ask questions
   or request equipment. The forms allow you to follow a project and
   they take very little time to "grade." If nothing else, you have poked
   them several times and reminded them about their projects. I have
   discovered that students turn out much better projects because they
   do a little bit over a continuous period and identify problems in
   time to correct them. They frequently do some real research!

In addition to the projects we do in class, my students are performing
research on their own. I have taken some of the hysteria out of the assignment by removing the horrifying phrase "science fair," but I plan to ask
some students to compete when the time is appropriate. Students have
chosen their topics and are in the process of collecting data, changing their
direction, and finding mentors. Some of their subjects are as follows: Basketball training shoes—do "jump" shoes improve your performance? Are
static mats really useful or necessary for computers? Why lean forward
when skiing? Is the greenhouse effect going to cause more intense electrical storms? and, How do dancers shift their center of gravity? *The Physics
Teacher* has proven to be an excellent resource for project ideas, along with
the "Amateur Scientist" in *Scientific American*.

Whenever a student asks a question for which I do not know the answer, there is almost certainly a project there!

The major problem I have encountered in implementing projects involves lab partners. I make a point of pairing up a male and female as lab
partners for a number of reasons; they tend to learn more from each other,
it seems to limit the "testosterone poisoning" that leads to dangerous experimentation, it reduces the amount of silly giggling that sometimes occurs, and it provides an opportunity for a better interaction between
partners. One problem with students in the laboratory (either gender) are
the young people that fall into the category I call "lab leeches." These are
students who wander from one lab group to another specifically to steal
data, or who cling to their partner with no intention of doing any real work.
These are students who would prefer to get equipment and take a secretarial role than chance failure. The fortunate characteristic about these students is that they are relatively easy to identify. They also usually turn out
to be good experimenters when they are paired with one of their "own

kind"—another "leech," basically forcing them to get involved with the experiment. In essence, I choose students' lab partners for them; later in the year I allow them to select their own partners for some projects that require out-of-class time, like the golfball catapult. Because projects allow for a wide range of creativity, I have found it best to mix up the partners frequently. This is based on my personal philosophy that people need to learn to work with all kinds of people and that we learn about ourselves by working in groups with persons who are different from ourselves.

As a result of the pairing just discussed, I have found that a mixed-gender group seems to work best, but that personalities have a strong effect on the project. Groups with two females or two males do work, but I feel that some creativity is lost. I believe that pairs of females are not as creative due to a fear of failure. They tend to watch the methods of groups around them and to modify their attempts to match those rather than try something out of the ordinary. Male pairs sometimes get so caught up in being creative that they miss the point of the project altogether. The content of arguments that occur between lab partners is a good indication about what type of collaborative effort is taking place. When the discussion (heated though it may be) concerns the physics involved, then both partners are usually involved in the experiment. When the disagreement occurs over who is doing what, then it is typically caused by one partner treating the other as a go-fer. I monitor the laboratory to be sure that no one partner is so aggressive that the other acts as an assistant. This method has worked well for me, by eliminating the opportunity for females to take a subservient role in the laboratory, and reducing gender differences in performance in the classroom. Projects are much more conducive to this change in gender attitude than are traditional physics labs.

The advantages of the project approach are that students do real science in a real environment. They are allowed to be creative in their search for a solution to a problem. They learn to use the information they have gained in the classroom and not see it as a body of knowledge with little practical use. The classroom becomes a place of relevant learning. Any topic covered in class can become a point of departure for a project, which is only limited by the imagination. Finally, students accept responsibility for learning. They "buy into" the need for knowing physics and learn that science is not only valuable, but fun. Fun produces interest and interest leads to study, which can lead to a career in science.

POSTSCRIPT: LABNET STUDENT COMMENTS

This postscript contains unedited quotes from 14 LabNet students from six states on their thoughts about being involved in physics projects. The data are drawn from 54 responses to a questionnaire sent via selected LabNet teachers in June 1991. The students, primarily juniors and seniors, were given the survey with a stamped envelope with return address so they could respond freely. We include here selected students' responses to the following open-ended questions:

- Describe the last project you completed in your physics or physical science course.
- What will you remember most from this project?
- Was doing the project different than your typical science activities? Can you give an example?
- Did working on your project challenge you to explore different areas of science? In what ways?
- Do you think the projects in your science class have helped you to understand science better? Please explain.

The responses are organized into three groups: four individual projects, six small-team projects, and four all-class projects.

Individual Projects

A Female Junior From Colorado

Project description. In my last physics project I built a generator from a kit. I wrote a program on my computer to predict the voltage output, but it only worked a couple of times because the magnetic field was either too strong or too weak.

Remember most? The hard time I had trying to make it work.

Project different? Yes, because I had to use tools to make a generator work, but could apply physics to it.

Challenge? Yes, I didn't know physics had anything to do with motors.

Understand Science? Yes, because projects showed how science can help you in everyday life.

A Male Senior From California

Project description. Logarithmic changes within a vortex.

Remember most? I will remember the common gas law, how and what really happens in frontal cloud systems.

Project different? Yes—because I feel that I learned more. I think a regular class is important, but I've had science classes ever since I can remember and I know that I have a general idea of what science is. With projects I can investigate what I found interesting in the science....

Challenge? Yes—I started out with just the idea of exploring the common gas law through pressure and temperature changes, but I ended up learning a lot about meteorology.

Understand Science? Yes—I learned the basic concepts of how scientists apply theory to make experiments. I learned the scientific process—something books cannot provide.

Additional comments. This year has been a great learning experience. The only problem was that I wish that I could have learned more in the field of relativity. I would just suggest that maybe a 9-week brief theory course be taught before projects begin.

A Male Junior From Georgia

Project description. Using the physical principles of torque, I designed and constructed a mobile with two free arms connected to a main arm that hung from the ceiling.

Remember most? Half of engineering is fine tuning once the basic equations tell how it's supposed to work!

Project different? Yes, this was a matter not of serving a new principle but of taking an understood concept and making something which was beautiful to me.

Challenge? This particular project did not precipitate independent exploration but I personally spent a lot of time in self-reflection designing and enjoying the finished project. I wanted my mobile to reflect me as a member of a community of people and of the story of life on earth...

Understand Science? Projects have definitely calmed some of my fears about technology: certainly science/engineering are complex, but the principles are based on observed fact that with the right insight can make perfect sense.

A Male Junior From Colorado

Project description I wrote a program to simulate the motion of the planets using ag=G. I used a time iteration one day (8.61E4s), calculating total acceleration for each planet as it circles the sun and adding that multiplied by 8.61E4s to get it into velocity to the current velocity and adding that then to the position.

Remember most? Debugging the #! @#s program.

Project different? It was very different in that I actually wrote a method to explain and use a formula.

Challenge? It required me to explore mathematics, specifically trigonometry and Cartesian vectors.

Understand Science? I feel that my project helped me understand science more than any other approach, because it took science out of the realm of abstract and unconnected concepts and unified them into an understandable system with real purpose.

Small Group Projects

A Male Senior From California

Project description. I was involved in the development of an accurate model of a future Mars colony including living structures forming experimental structures, located in the Coprateses Chasma canyon on Mars. Oxygen would be obtained from heated Mars soil.

Remember most? That it is possible to colonize Mars without any new technological advances.

Project different? No, because this is the main ideas of this class, basic science is a common part of the class.

Challenge? Yes, we did a lot of research in astronomy, to find out how colonization would be possible.

Understand Science? Yes, a lot, I believe experience is the best way to learn—much better than just a textbook. This is hands-on work you can understand and use in life.

A Female Freshman From Oregon

Project description. Truss bridges. We made truss bridges out of balsa wood and Elmer's glue. We had to draw out plans, and cut the pieces ourselves.

Remember most? The experience that I shared with my partners. The chance to really work at finding something out yourself, to feel good about yourself and your work when you have accomplished your goal or understand the topic.

Project different? Yes, we didn't have to sit and listen to any lectures, or read. It was great.

Challenge? Yes, actually it did. It got me interested in how such flimsy structures can hold so much weight and pressure.

Understand Science? Yes, I do think projects have helped me to a full extent. I mean, when you do a project you get to work hands-on with the things you are supposed to be learning, instead of just reading or listening to a boring lecture.

Additional comments. I think this questionnaire is a great idea. It gives students such as myself the chance to express how we feel about what we do in our classes. Please help our teacher.

A Male Junior From Colorado

Project description. The last project I completed consisted of recording and comparing the frequency, amplitude, and period of sound waves from a trombone, a tenor sax, and an alto sax at different ranges of each instrument.

Remember most? I will remember that the trombone has a purer sound than the saxophone no matter how poorly the trombone is played or how well the saxophone is played (for our instruments).

Project different? Doing the project was a lot different than my other science classes because I had to figure everything out myself (with my partner) and I learned a lot more that way. It was only a little different from my regular physics class because [our teacher] always allowed us to figure things out on our own.

Challenge? Yes, working on the project opened my eyes to many different fields of science. I learned there were many things that traveled with waves, and that there were many things to still be explained, one of them being light.

Understand Science? Yes, I do think the projects helped me to understand science better. I learned how the principles of physics tied into everyday things, which helped clarify the principles I never really understood. It proved to me that even physics has a place in the everyday world.

Additional comments. I recommend doing projects for all physics classes because it helped me so much.

A Male Senior From Pennsylvania

Project description. A detailed model of a bridge with working arc lights and a full set of blueprints.

Remember most? The fun I had drawing up the blueprints and making the actual model.

Project different? Yes, because most science courses just use the book, but this gave us a hands-on experience.

Challenge? Yes, because with the bridge project, we were required to calculate stress loads of materials and the bridge itself to see if it was stable enough for driving.

Understand Science? Yes, because we do a lot of different experiments (which tie in with what we are learning), but most important, it makes the class interesting.

A Female Junior From Colorado

Project description. Our last project was designed to test our cumulative knowledge of physics. We had to find the force needed to throw a baseball 30 yards. Using stopwatches to measure time, we went out onto the school football field to do the experiment and collect data.

Remember most? The feeling of success when I used limited information to find the force to throw a baseball is what I will always remember about this lab.

Project different? This project was different in that we went out of the classroom to collect data and the teacher was not available (on purpose) to help us.

Challenge? This project, specifically, didn't deal with other areas of science. Other projects of the year have, however.

Understand Science? Yes, they have definitely helped me understand. Most science classes are lecture oriented, where formulas are stressed. Labs help students apply their knowledge to real, tangible objects. It's much easier to remember information from projects than from textbooks and movies.

Additional comments. Our physics class was very nicely structured, I believe. All of the lectures gave background information for a project. We learned the concepts, then applied them to solve a specific problem.

A Male Senior From California

Project description. I attempted to produce a visual representation of the vibrations of an electromagnetic speaker. To do this, I attached a very small mirror to the center of a speaker, such that the mirror would vibrate just as the speaker surface did. Then I reflected laser light from the mirror onto a screen. The result was unique patterns of laser light seen on the screen.

Remember most? That it requires a great amount of self-discipline to work on the project every day. It was very easy to take project time to take care of other business, such as making up tests or working on other homework.

Project different? Our project lasts one quarter, and it doesn't necessarily relate to the lectures or readings or class discussions.

Challenge? I found that we had to go to literary sources to learn the background on our project.

Understand Science? Yes, definitely. The hands-on experience solidifies conceptual issues for a better understanding of the topic at hand.

Additional comments. I would only suggest that teachers have students accomplish certain subdivisions weekly, because some students procrastinated so much that the last few days were a mad scramble for finding research.

All-Class Projects

A Female Junior From Colorado

Project description. The last project we completed was a lab on vocal sound waves. We used Apple IIe computers connected with a microphone so as to see our graphed sound waves from our voices.

Remember most? I will remember the fact that by observing two (supposedly) unlike things, you can discover relationships between the two and thus discover more about both.

Project different? We did it all on our own. We were able to run the computers by ourselves. Most teachers go through step by step. [Our teacher] let us figure it out on our own.

Challenge? Yes, it challenged me to explore different areas of science. It challenged me because I realized that there are so many everyday things which I take for granted which I could know so much more about if I worked harder.

Understand Science? The projects have made me understand science much better because I learned the math is directly connected to most things in science.

Additional comments. My ability to understand physics has grown immensely this year due to the fact that I trust my capability to learn better. Physics started coming together for me at the first part of second semester. From then on, I have learned to keep an open mind and realize that everything is relative.

A Female Senior From Georgia

Project description. Paper tower.

Remember most? This may not seem very scientific, but it made me realize that everyday science, such as building, involves fun. But you also have to know what you are doing in order to succeed.

Project different? No, because it involved deep thinking to solve a problem. Most of our labs are like this.

Challenge? Yes, you had to gather all of your knowledge of physics and try to bring it together to solve a problem.

Understand Science? Yes, they give you an understanding through hands-on experience. You seem to grasp the concept/idea.

A Male Junior From Missouri

Project description. In the most recent project, we went to the St. Louis Six Flags Theme Park and measured nine forces, calculated speeds, height, periods, of various rides.

Remember most? The effect of normal force on the human body (i.e., what it feels like to pull g's).

Project different? Yes, very different. Typically a class is not held in a park! Further, this was an opportunity for many students to see physics at work and not just look at it as a bunch of formulas on paper.

Challenge? Yes, for a bumper car ride we had to use our knowledge of chemistry to determine the flow of electricity from–to.

Understand Science? Yes, this experiment allowed me to personally experience and not imagine many of the laws and theories talked about in class.

Additional comments. In addition to the educational value of this experiment it was also a lot of fun and a pleasant change from the typical day.

A Female Junior From Pennsylvania

Project description. Heating Degree Day Project. Our class calculated the area of our homes, recorded and averaged temperatures, calculated heating degree days, and calculated how much heat our homes used over a 3-month period.

Remember most? I found out what r-ratings are (type of insulation). I also found out that the type of heat you use and the insulation you use can help you conserve on the amount of money you spend.

Project different? It was very different. It gave the students a chance to do something interesting outside and inside of the classroom.

Challenge? Yes, we used thermal chemistry, and dynamics, and meteorology.

Understand Science? Yes, it made me realize how much science helps you in your everyday life. I think that this project was excellent because it not only helped one now, but later in life it will help me to conserve and save money.

7 Reflections on Project-Enhanced Science Learning—TERC Staff

LabNet's two co-principal investigators provide bookend essays for this chapter. Bob Tinker, a physicist who is TERC's Chief Scientist, contrasts the science that students regularly see in school with science as actually practiced, concluding with the role of projects in correcting this discrepancy. John King, who has taught undergraduate physics at MIT for many years, gives us a "compleat guide to projects." His essay includes almost everything you wanted to know about projects—certainly enough curriculum ideas to last a teaching lifetime—the right way to end these two chapters of reflections by working project users.

Between the bookends are five thought pieces by senior TERC researcher/developers. The work at TERC is divided into two centers, mathematics and science. Chris Hancock and Ricardo Nemirovsky write from the first center, Candace Julyan, Nathan Kimball, and Deborah Muscella from the second. But the pieces cross nicely. Muscella and Hancock muse about some of the difficulties of doing experimental project work in the elementary classroom. Julyan reports on the success of such an effort. Kimball looks at MBL from the perspective of many years designing and programming MBL software. And Nemirovsky considers the relationship between projects and a sense of wonder.

Learning About the Scientific Method
Robert F. Tinker [1]

Many teachers would say that the responsibility to acquaint students with science practice is largely discharged by giving students lab experiences. Superficially, this sounds good, but, on closer examination, it is quite wide of the mark. The lab is where we give students a chance to try out science, but most standard science labs give a misleading view of science. Too often the form of scientific study is slavishly followed, while including none of the substance of scientific adventure and thought. Perhaps an example would be helpful in showing how misleading standard science labs can be, and what student research can mean in science education.

---

[1] Bob Tinker is a physicist by training. A long-time advocate of engaging students directly in doing science, he has been a leader in the project movement and in the development of powerful microcomputer-based tools like MBLs and telecommunications.

The Science Students See

A perfectly normal science lab would have students understand the relation between a liquid's vapor pressure and boiling temperature by measuring the boiling temperature of water under different reduced pressures. A typical lab for this requires detailed procedures that someone spent hours developing to ensure that the lab "worked." There would be instructions for using a manometer, a thick-wall, side-neck Erlenmeyer flask, a vacuum manifold, tubing, thermometer, and hot plate. Detailed instructions would cover safety, operation, and data collection. Students might be instructed to heat distilled water to 100°C and then remove the heat and start reducing the pressure. As the water boiled and cooled, temperature and pressure readings need to be taken every minute.

Students can "do" this lab without too many mistakes in the limited time available and return a lab write-up that starts with "Hypothesis: The boiling point of water decreases as the pressure is reduced." The write-up would include a nice graph of boiling temperature as a function of pressure, with error bars and a fit curve that nicely summarizes the results.

What does a student take away from such an experience? Some lab skills, certainly—safety and use of the apparatus. But most teachers would be shocked at how little *science* would be learned. Educational research shows that in similar situations, students learn almost nothing from such a lab and can get through it without altering fundamental misconceptions about the most basic concepts supposedly elucidated by the lab. Instead of supporting the idea that there is only one boiling temperature at a given pressure, students could easily slip through this lab reinforced in the common view that water at atmospheric pressure will boil at different temperatures depending on how much you heat it. Students would also probably get through this lab unchanged in their belief that the bubbles and the space above the water are filled with air, not water vapor, and that boiling only happens when a liquid is hot.

Students would also learn little from this lab about the conduct of science; it would probably reinforce the idea that science is dull, procedural, and thoughtless. They have no particular reason to study this topic except to pass the course; they did not participate in planning the experiment or developing the procedures; nor was the stated hypothesis really a question they had. Because there was no internal motivation to study this, they would probably not attend to the results or attempt to internalize the consequences.

The lack of student learning in labs like this is directly related to the lack of active thinking it requires. The careful procedures, the concern for safety, and an atmosphere that all too often penalizes errors, all militate against questioning, risk-taking, thinking, making mistakes, and real learning. It is as though both teachers and students subscribe to a mechanistic model of learning, which posits that going through certain steps without thinking will somehow magically result in learning. This is antithetical to all that science is about.

The Science Scientists See

I studied liquid helium evaporation for my PhD thesis, and it is useful to contrast this experience with the student lab. The importance of this tale is how I, as a typical graduate student, went about learning about experimental science, which is so different from the model presented in school.

Superfluid liquid helium is fascinating. It is the only substance that is liquid down to absolute zero. Below 2.17 K (–271 C!) the common isotope, He-4, becomes a superfluid with amazing properties. For instance, if you put superfluid helium in a cup, it will creep up the sides, over the rim and out, emptying in no time. It conducts heat thousands of times better than silver, the next-best thermal conductor. It pours through molecule-size holes (super-leaks) that block all other substances, including liquid He above 2.17 K. Who knows what practical applications might result from a better understanding of such a remarkable substance. It might bathe future computers, keeping them cold and removing the heat they generate.

When I was a graduate student, the theoretical reasons for these odd properties were only beginning to be understood. Part of the answer lay in the thermal vibrations in the liquid. When they interact, these vibrations had to be thought of as particles—phonons and rotons—in much the way light waves must be considered as particles—photons—when they interact with atoms. If some wild guesses were made about the properties of these thermal wave/particles, then many of the unusual properties of liquid helium could be calculated. But the calculations were esoteric and many questions remained. Experimental evidence about phonon and roton interactions was needed before there could be much advance.

Finding a good experiment that would contribute to this emerging theory was an enormous challenge. (For another tale of a fellow graduate student's difficulties in selecting an experiment, see Cohen, 1974, pp. 12-14.) The experiment had to be theoretically interesting and experimentally feasible. It had to provide valuable information whether or not some breathtaking new result was discovered. We (there was a team of graduate students in my group all on the prowl for good experiments) explored many ideas that led nowhere. Either the effect was immeasurably small, or the experiment far too complex, or the result unremarkable. I felt like we fooled around a lot, just wasting months as we played in the shop and speculated about many areas of physics; this was amusing but a bit scary because the end was nowhere is sight. In retrospect, we were sharpening a wide range of skills and giving ourselves enough background to recognize a good project. But this was not a conscious plan, and I was worried because there seemed to be no script we were following like the comforting "scientific method" I learned in school.

If there were a good experiment to be done but not already performed by the legions of other researchers, perhaps it would rely on the particular strengths of our group, which lay in measurements on "beams" of atoms streaming through a vacuum. So, while inventing and discarding experiments, I stumbled into the craft of atomic beams, metal machine-shop skills, soldering and brazing, drafting, creating and controlling a high vacuum, electronic instrumentation, and atom detection. One of the arts involved forming ultra-sharp needles using electrochemistry and observing them using microscopic techniques borrowed from biology. I also pursued the theory of helium and shopped around for mathematical techniques used in other fields that might be applied. In retrospect, all these activities seem purposeful and coordinated to support the experiment I did. But in reality, the experiment was determined by what skills I learned, and that learning was haphazard, at best.

This was a time of waiting and deep personal doubt and frustration. What was THE experiment going to be? What if it revealed nothing? Who cares anyway? Is this a sensible way to spend one's life given the social crises erupting around us (this was the late 1960s)? I increasingly saw the graduate school life as unnatural and cloistered; difficult primarily because of the sacrifices it demanded.

The final choice of experiment did not appear in a flash of inspiration but slowly emerged as the best of many contenders. In a way, it was disappointing because it was so obvious; none of our wilder speculations developed into a breathtaking experiment. A hunch that the rotons should influence the speed of the evaporating atoms seemed reasonable. There were supposed to be a lot of energetic rotons in the superfluid and this might directly influence evaporation, causing an abnormal number of energetic evaporating atoms. This hunch was confirmed by increasingly sophisticated calculations that indicated that unusual evaporation around .3 K could be measured and would yield a clear answer to the hunch.

The measurement fit all the criteria. Even if my hunch was wrong it would be interesting to understand why. It suggested an experiment that used many of the traditional molecular beam approaches and equipment, so I could be fairly confident that the measurement could be done. Measurements could be made on both He-3 and He-4 yielding two theses, so I could team with another student who was weaker theoretically but a better experimentalist.

It still took years to design the apparatus, get it perfected, redesign it, and get it working. The extremely low temperatures were a challenge, the evaporated helium generated a fierce background signal, the rotating beam chopper just above the helium surface vibrated, and the apparatus generated too much heat to run the experiment long enough. We had to come up with numerous inventions to overcome these and other problems.

But eventually, the experiment worked and yielded results; not all at once, but in fits and starts separated by months of repairs. Unfortunately, we saw no sign of the rotons in the evaporating atoms , but it did not matter; the result was original and significant, and the thesis was quickly written.

I dwell at some length on this experience for two reasons. First, note that there is hardly a hint of the usual hypothesis-experiment-deduction paradigm in this story. There was a hypothesis—rotons influence evaporation—but it completely fails to encapsulate the thought process. A better description of our thinking was total immersion in a fascinating problem, permitting us to eventually find a niche where our skills and persistence helped uncover something original and valuable. Second, note the broad nature of what I learned while following this narrow, arcane specialty: construction, plumbing, electronics, drafting, microscopy, electrochemistry, mathematics, and invention itself. I learned about heating and cooling, properties of metals, machine-screw sizes, sharpening a metal lathe tool, and different kinds of solders. I also learned about boiling under reduced pressures, since the way we reached these low temperatures was to boil He-4 and He-3 in a vacuum. A similar breadth of learning through immersion in focused experimentation can be brought to almost any classroom.

The Real Scientific Method

The "scientific method" is often held up as a script scientists supposedly follow. As a child, the emphasis on scientific method at school—a seven-step sequence leading inevitably to a conclusion—led me to believe the way scientists proceeded was alogical, outside the realm of normal thinking. This is a perversion of the truth. You could map my graduate school experiences onto the scientific method: My hunch can be described as a hypothesis, I certainly had a method that was described in my thesis, and I did conclude something. It is just that converting my bumbling around in the lab to a rigid, semi-mystical, desiccated scientific method gives a completely wrong impression.

In reality, there is nothing mystical about the scientific method; scientists approach their problems much the way a carpenter approaches the problem of designing kitchen cabinets or a teacher devises a teaching strategy for a difficult student. In each case, you think about the problem, draw heavily on your experience and intuition, perhaps consult some references to see what others may have done in similar situations, develop a hunch or two, devise a plan of action using that hunch, and see whether the plan was effective. In each case, it is just common sense.

The Lab Notebook provides a perfect case study of the erroneous impression of science that schools convey. Most science students are compelled to keep a lab book consisting of a series of experiments, each starting with a hypothesis, detailing the apparatus, method, observations, and ending with a conclusion. All the best notebooks are virtually identical; the poorer ones have parts missing that should be there. The hidden message is that the lab-book regimen is part of science; after all, one of the justifications for subjecting all students to science is to convey a sense of its intellectual traditions. And, of course, the intellectual tradition embodied in a school lab notebook is deadly; from it any student would conclude that in science there is no thought, no originality, no half-baked ideas, no departure from the norm.

Again this is a perversion. Most scientists do keep notebooks, but they read much like the personal journals a writer might keep, except with more math and equipment thrown in. Notebooks are used to help scientists remember things too easily forgotten—where to order special tools, what solder worked best at low temperatures, bright ideas, notes from interesting articles. They do also contain information about experimental apparatus and procedures, so again, school has conveyed a partial truth, but one that has all the juices squeezed out of it.

The common thread in all of science is the *search for simple, mechanistic explanations that tie together the largest number of observations possible.* The word "simple" may seem surprising here because science is so often perceived as "hard." This is unfortunate, and probably derives more from bad teaching than from the underlying concepts. The teaching about science too often emphasizes mathematics because it seems to simplify the concepts to the lecturer although, unfortunately, it usually obfuscates them for the learner. "Mechanistic" is also important in this definition to distinguish science from other perfectly valid human pursuits, such as art, poetry, and astrology, that do not put a premium on objective, verifiable chains of cause and effect. Finally, the idea that scientific explanations have power, in the sense that they tie together the largest number of observations, is an amazing comment on the world in which we live. It could be that general laws did not exist, or that huge numbers of scientific principles were needed. The remarkable fact about our reality is that a very few laws and principles have very broad applicability. Hence, we owe it to our students to convey an impression of this, that the search for general principles is often rewarded with understanding that brings order into our lives.

Science progresses through the *application of common sense and involves communicating ideas that convince critics.* There is no special thought process scientists use. They are careful in their own work and critical of others' because they want to be right and have learned that it is easy to make mistakes. They eschew arguments from authority because the authority might be wrong, and they assume that their audience is as cranky as they are, only believing statements that can be reproduced by an objective observer. A consequence of this that surprises scientists and outsiders alike is that the ability to communicate is essential to success in science. The scientist must be able to present his or her views and defend them, often using persuasive writing and speaking skills that go beyond pure objectivity.

A final observation about contemporary science is in order: It is *collaborative*. The pervasive image of an Einstein independently inventing general relativity is highly misleading. Although there continue to be a few isolated Einsteins, the vast bulk of science is a collaborative affair, in two senses. First, much of science is undertaken in groups, with the result that original scientific papers usually have multiple authors, sometimes dozens. My thesis work is a case in point, where the initial ideas were tossed about in a group of 5 to 10 colleagues and the actual research was done with one other graduate student. This is a commentary on the scale of much of science, requiring expensive equipment, big labs, and team funding. It is also a commentary on human nature, which is stimulated by others with similar, but differing, outlooks, sharing an environment and goals. But, in a second sense, the collaboration extends even to the isolated researchers who, while working alone, must read the literature, attend meetings, obtain funding, and communicate results with the society of peer scientists.

This view of the work of scientists as simple, careful, common sense, and collaborative is quite accessible to students and must not be transformed into some mystical, incomprehensible, and illogical scientific method. It should be easier for students to imagine becoming scientists using this demystified view of science. Still, it seems a long way between a simple lab on vapor pressure to thesis research on helium vapor. Fortunately, it is not necessary to be a graduate student to ask scientifically interesting questions. They are everywhere about us and accessible to all students.

Student Projects and Real Science in the School

Student projects are the place where students can meet the science that the scientist sees. By focusing on the goal of thoughtful student participation in original work, we fall back on mathematics and science for inspiration, a strategy that we hope brings to education the excitement of discovery that motivates anyone to get engaged. This strategy also emphasizes the importance of the learner in constructing understanding that comes from a self-motivated need to know.

Of course, like most ideas in education, this is hardly new. At the end of the 19th century, Dewey (1897) stated, "I believe that education, therefore, is a process of living and not a preparation for future living" (p. 79). In 1963, Philip Morrison in the article *Less May Be More* said, "...I am speaking for...a laboratory involvement that may be painfully slow, that 'doesn't get anywhere.' You don't 'cover the material,' but you spend a good many hours of the week doing something" (p. 448).

When student projects are tried in schools, too often they result in activity without learning, motion leading nowhere. Of course, students have to be thoughtfully engaged. As Morrison continued: "That's what I'd like to see....the free use of simple materials, ...[with] *analysis*" (pp. 448-449). Dewey in 1938 said: "But observation alone is not enough. We have to understand the significance of what we see, hear, and touch....The crucial educational problem is that of procuring the postponement of immediate action upon desire until observation and judgment have intervened" (pp. 79, 81).

Student projects are most widely used in the very best schools and perhaps this is why project-oriented instruction has gained an unjustified reputation as being only for elite and academically advanced students. A study by Warren, Rosebery, and Conant (1989) of a seventh-grade bilingual Haitian Creole class belies this view and clearly shows that a broad range of students can learn through participation in projects. The best of these students were performing two grades below level; some were illiterate in Creole, spoke English only with difficulty, and had little idea about Western science.

After an animated discussion about what to investigate, the class decided to study something it really cared about, the quality of the water in the drinking fountains on the different floors of the school. The students were sure that the water on their floor would be much better than that on the first floor used by "little kids." The students transformed their feeling about "better water" into a taste test and thought about the problems associated with a subjective test. They developed the idea of a blind protocol to protect the results from accidental operator bias, although they, of course, did not use these abstract terms.

When they ran the test, they were appalled that the data gave what they felt was the wrong result—the first-floor water tasted better! Convinced that this was wrong, the students then decided to do what any reasonable researcher would: They repeated the experiment more carefully with a larger sample. This time, they decided to use other students' opinions, so they picked a day to test water at lunchtime in the cafeteria using an improved taste test. The results of the larger test only confirmed the earlier, inexplicable results: The first-floor water was better! Then the students had to begin to understand why. They came up with all sorts of interesting hypotheses: temperature, lead, pH. This involved quantitative measurements, which they eagerly undertook.

Were these students learning mathematics or science? Clearly, both were integrated in the students' research. To determine which water was better they had to use mathematics and intuitive statistics. To design the test, they were doing science. Their further studies involved measurement, averages, dissolved ions, pH, and temperature. These involved the natural fusion of mathematics and science ideas, not a force-fit determined by curriculum designers.

Incidentally, the students learned more than just mathematics and science. The students had to communicate with the larger community in English, and they actually became the experts and leaders about anything concerning the test. Warren and Rosebery, particularly interested in communication, saw major advances in student use of language. The confidence and autonomy conveyed by this project seemed to generalize, so student interest in other subjects increased and absenteeism dropped.

By emphasizing thoughtful original student investigations—projects— I do not intend that mathematics and science education should be composed of nothing else. Were students doing nothing but projects and not gaining any systematic understanding of the fields, I would probably come out strongly for some "book learning." However, student project activities are all but absent from mathematics and science education, and with that absence there is a lack of reality to mathematics and science education, a lack of connection to problems of concern to students and, necessarily, a lack of interest, solid learning, and desire to learn more.

A school that makes a real commitment to student project activities must re-think the entire mathematics and science curriculum to both create time for a healthy injection of project activities and to re-orient the remainder of the curriculum to support project work. Both changes are healthy but difficult. The former change requires new and interesting project activities that do support "observation and judgment." The latter change requires schools to determine how the remainder of the curriculum should be altered to prepare students for progressively more sophisticated and independent project activities that become closer and closer approximations to what mathematicians and scientists do. And of course, these changes force schools to come to grips with new approaches to evaluation appropriate in a project-oriented learning environment.

Project-centered instruction places extra demands of time and imagination on teachers. Instead of lecturing, you have to juggle multiple student groups, providing encouragement, guidance, ideas, and criticism in just the right measure and at the right time. There is always a temptation to help out by checking out a reference, acquiring a needed piece of apparatus, and so forth. These only add to the burden. Then students get frustrated because their ideas cannot be realized because you do not have the measuring equipment needed.

Are there ways technology can help support project-oriented science? There are three technologies that seek to offer help: telecommunication, microcomputer-based labs, and analytical tools. Telecommunication and microcomputers can give students the tools they need singly and in groups to begin to experience investigations that are original and important.

Telecommunication provides unique opportunities for students to collaborate and share ideas, techniques, and data. Inexpensive microcomputers can be versatile instruments giving students the functionality of racks of electronics that not long ago were reserved for advanced research. With these microcomputer-based lab (MBL) interfaces, students become better experimenters, able to explore first-hand a broad range of phenomena on which science is based. These same microcomputers can be used for computations and data analysis, allowing students to be theorists and to move between theory-building and experimenting with ease. In such situations, there is no distinction between mathematics and science.

The benefits and the struggles that come when a teacher begins to incorporate projects in the science classroom informed the shape that the LabNet project took, and are vividly portrayed in the teacher essays in the previous chapter—testimonials from the field. The effort to incorporate real science into science learning and teaching is at an exciting, pioneer stage, with every classroom a frontier.

DATA ANALYSIS PROJECTS[2]

Chris Hancock[3]

Using the records kept in the school office, a class of fourth graders looks for patterns in the accidental injuries in the school playground over several years. The students devise many ways of categorizing, tallying, and graphing the data. After much work and discussion, they reach some interesting conclusions: High injury rates are associated with (a) fewer teachers being present on the playground, (b) large numbers of classes having recess at the same time, and (c) a particular jungle gym whose bars were too wide to be securely grasped by young hands. These conclusions in turn suggest practical changes in recess policies at the school.

The playground injuries activity was developed by TERC's Used Numbers project (Corwin & Friel, 1990). Although I did not witness it myself, I have always thought of it as a good example of how a data analysis project should be. Students begin with a problem that matters to them and, with the facilitation of the teacher, devise a plan to collect data that will help to

[2] The theme of this essay is presented together with other lessons of our year of classroom work in a longer paper (see Hancock, Kaput, & Goldsmith, in press).

[3] Chris Hancock directs TERC's Hands On Data project, which is funded by the National Science Foundation, grant # MDR-8855617. The classroom work discussed here is done with the collaboration of the Cambridge Public Schools and with the support of the Apple Classrooms of Tomorrow. The opinions expressed are the author's and are not necessarily shared by the participating and funding institutions. Special thanks to Bill Caragianes, Joan LaChance, Phyllis Kalowski, Ned Rice, and Rita Jayne Shiver.

solve the problem. A first round of data collection yields some partial answers: possible trends that weren't expected; clearer questions that require revised and extended data collection. Rival interpretations are debated and evaluated. Finally, the data, graphs, charts, and explanations are assembled into a presentation that is persuasive to others and leads to a tangible impact.

Why is this a good way to do mathematics? First of all, every number and every computation, every ratio and every percent in a project refers to something real. Furthermore, if the mathematics is being used to address a real problem, students become concerned not just with carrying out computations correctly, but with thinking critically about which computations are the most meaningful and relevant—this is the important idea of mathematics-as-modeling. Finally, through such projects students can experience mathematics and data analysis as tools for finding out the truth and exerting influence in their community.

Together with a small group of teachers and researchers, I have worked for the last year and a half to foster data analysis projects in fifth- through eighth-grade classrooms in an urban Cambridge, Massachusetts, school. We began with high hopes, fueled by our belief in the great potential value of project-based curriculum and by the fact that we have a very powerful and intuitive computer-based data analysis tool.[4] In one year, we developed and tried out quite a few investigations: personal information about students in the class; the color distribution in packages of M&Ms; the scientific properties of six mystery powders; patterns of school attendance during the week; famous African-Americans; temperature change during a day; a taste-test showdown between major brands of cola; market research for advertising; and consumer research comparing portable radio/tape decks.

There was a lot for us to learn. We gradually got better at organizing units and at developing interesting topics; the students got better at designing databases and at thinking about what a graph means. However, the playground injuries example has remained an unattained ideal. We have found it hard to bring projects to a conclusive and satisfying end, one in which the starting questions are answered, or at least reconsidered in the light of the data. Projects often began without clear questions, and ended without clear answers. And our efforts to generate projects that are meaningful to students, where the students care about how it turns out, have been at best partially successful. It seems that the kind of data analysis project that we envision does not happen easily in today's schools—at least it hasn't for us.

---

[4] The Tabletop uses animated visual representations to let students build and modify Venn diagrams, bar charts, scatterplots, crosstabulations, and other graphs. A prototype version of the Tabletop has been developed by TERC.

Part of the problem certainly has to do with relevant mathematical concepts. By and large, students of this age do not have facility with thinking about trends in data: For example, they know how to compute an average but they don't have a good sense of what it means (Mokros & Russell, 1992). They do not know much about ways of organizing and transforming data. So one thing we need to do is work on these concepts and skills. Also the choice of good problems is a fine art: Playground injuries is an example of a topic that can be very interesting to students. We want to get better at working with students to choose good topics. But the deepest problem may be with the very notion of a meaningful, goal-oriented project. This way of organizing activities, although it holds so much educational promise, seems to be at odds with patterns of thinking and activity that we see in classrooms. What is the conflict, and how should it be dealt with? What kinds of data-modeling projects are truly meaningful to younger kids, and how can we help to make them happen? Are students not yet able to engage in such projects; if so, how can we help to prepare them? Does the culture of school need to change, and in what ways? And how does our own ideal of data-based inquiry projects need to be altered?

The "Advertising" unit provided an interesting example of the kinds of complexities that can arise. This was the last project of the school year for a fifth/sixth-grade class, and its various phases spanned 2 months. The teacher's initial conception of the project was that students would begin by collecting data about the different kinds of products that are advertised in different magazines. Then groups of students would take on the role of an imaginary advertising agency and design an ad campaign for an imaginary product. They would do survey research about consumers' interest in the given kind of product, design an advertisement based on this information, and decide in which magazines to place their ad. Finally, they would present their work to the class.

In practice, things began to get complicated when the students formed their imaginary ad companies, because it also fell to them to choose what kind of product to advertise (there was no one to play the role of the ad agency's client). Some of the choices were sneakers, perfume, dog food, and fast-food restaurants. One group, working on a restaurant, designed its questionnaire as though the restaurant already existed, and as though the respondents knew about it. Their survey asked: "What do you like best about our restaurant? (a) clean and comfortable, (b) good food, (c) fast and courteous service, (d) comfortable, spinning chairs, (e) other."

Many groups used their surveys to change the design of the product—something that an ad agency doesn't usually do. For example, the dog food group found that most people (!) prefer moist dog food over dry, and chunky over nonchunky; accordingly they decided that their dog food would be moist and chunky. In some cases, tailoring the product to survey results went beyond the believable, as when one fast-food group set the price of all its entrees at $1 or $2, because that's what most people preferred to pay. When another student was challenged that the carpeting in his oceanside restaurant might get wet, he countered by saying that the restaurant would have an adjacent factory that made special waterproof carpets!

In these shifting sands of make-believe it is hard to identify, much less hold constant, the problem that is to be solved by the collection and analysis of data. This kind of activity does not seem a good way for students to learn about data analysis as a way to answer real questions and solve real problems. But should we then discourage all data analysis projects built around make-believe projects? Probably not. Make-believe offers many advantages in data analysis activities: for one thing, make-believe situations do not have real-world "messiness" and are thus more easily modeled by data. (Of course, we do want students eventually to deal with the complexities of real-world problems.) An important distinction can be made, however, between make-believe projects in which the problem is well-defined, and projects in which it is not. Many of Tom Snyder's software packages, for example, succeed in engaging students in role-play situations where the problems to be solved are challenging and clear. What distinguishes the Advertising unit is not make-believe per se, but that the problem—the rules of the game—was not well enough defined.

It is worth noting that this "flaw" did not appear to bother the students. They carried out their questionnaire design, data collection, and graphing busily and with enthusiasm. The project seemed coherent and sensible to them—more so than it was to us. How should we interpret this? Certainly it is well documented that children can engage in role-play games that focus more on what people do than on why they do it, and that much is learned through these rehearsals. Children enjoy going through adult motions—carrying a clipboard and administering a questionnaire, for example. But I see no reason why this enjoyment should be incompatible with having a clear understanding of what problem is being solved and how each activity is helping to solve it. I suspect that the reason that these students did not show such an understanding is not that it conflicts with the pleasure of role-play, nor that it is inherently too hard for children of this age; I think the students were simply unaccustomed to school activities in which it is important to keep the end goal in mind.

The Advertising project exhibited a principle common to many school activities, which I call *divergence*. This is an alternative conception of projects in which the idea is not to coordinate activities toward a single goal, but rather to conduct a variety of activities all related in some interesting way to a central theme. A tour of the bulletin boards in any elementary school will yield examples of this paradigm. The various pictures, graphs, constructions, writings, and other products that emerge from such a project are not meant to be logically unified; rather, the guiding principle is one of inclusion, with the implicit message that everyone's contribution is welcome. That is a fine message, and I would hardly argue for the abolition of divergent projects; on the other hand, it seems that the predominance of divergent projects is part of the reason why both students and teachers are unaccustomed to questioning how a particular lesson is furthering the overall goal of the project.

Adults' Games with Data

Schools are not the only places where people do data analysis without solving a clear problem. I have a database of information about 24 industrialized nations, which I sometimes use to introduce our data analysis software. Playing with the software's ability to make lots of graphs easily, adults often become enthusiastically engaged in a conjecture-making game: "Maybe there's a relationship between the divorce rate and the number of installed telephones. Hmm, that only seems to apply in countries with a large agricultural sector. Now why would that be?" In this game one does not ordinarily ask *why* they are so interested in the relationship between the divorce rate and telephone installations, and, if they really are interested, whether this database is likely to yield reliable insights into the relationship. These are not appropriate questions because the game being played is: "Look at all the interesting things we can find out through exploring data on the computer."

A researcher visited our classroom during the Advertising unit, and looked at one group's survey data about sneaker preferences. He said to the students: "Maybe you could use this data to find out about differences between why boys and girls buy sneakers." The students did not take up this suggestion, largely because they felt that they already knew who was a boy and who was a girl, so they didn't think they needed to put that in as data. In fact, because the survey had only six respondents, the likelihood of finding significant or even noticeable trends was low. The researcher's suggestion reflected a background not shared by the students, including a long schooling in the literature of gender differences. It also reflected a habit that is instilled in social scientists: the suspension (or at least the bracketing) of personal knowledge when reasoning about data. This is what we do when we pretend that we don't know anything about differences between boys and girls, and look to the data to inform us. This is a valuable part of the process of maintaining rigor and developing shareable knowledge in a community of inquiry, although it can be carried to an extreme of academic myopia.

My main point here is that adults who already know what it is like to use data to solve a real problem, and who are schooled in scientific discourse and the researcher's stance, often play games with data analysis in which they are not really solving a problem. We may have good reasons to play such unacknowledged games, but if we try to get kids to do what we do, the basis for the pretending will not be apparent to them, and authenticity will suffer. Becoming more sensitive to our own game playing is an important part of learning to facilitate inquiry and problem-solving activities that make sense to students.

Whose Project Is It?

Although they have value in their own right, I think that divergence and make-believe are more prevalent in schools than they should be, because they are adaptations to the disconnectedness of school activity from the goals and constraints of ordinary life. Children spend much of their time prevented from pursuing agendas of their own; nor are they asked to help with authentic adult agendas (a true shame, when children are often so eager to help). Make-believe and divergence are then just ways of filling the meaning gap.

In the year following the Advertising unit, we have given some students the opportunity outside of class to pursue any data collection project that interests them. Sheila, who participated in the Advertising unit, designed the following questionnaire:

We decided to do a survey about hats...

1. Do you like hats? **A**. Yes **B**. No **C**. I don't know.

2. Why do you or don't you like hats?

3. What is the best color for a hat that you would like?
   A. Green **B**. Black **C**. White **D**. (your choice)

4. With or without words would you like on a hat?
   A.With **B**. Without **C**. Don't know

Sheila is known as a good student. She designed this questionnaire and collected the data methodically. With sober competence she produced and labeled a variety of not-very-informative graphs, such as a Venn diagram intersecting the set of people who answered "A" to the third question with the set of people who answered "B" and the set of people who answered "C." When asked why she had designed the questionnaire that way, and what lesson could be drawn from this graph, and didn't it seem strange that so many people chose black hats—she resisted being drawn into discussion, as though such questions went beyond the social contract of the activity.

In fact, it seems likely that Sheila wasn't really doing a project that interested her; rather, she was trying to do a project that would meet what she surmised to be our expectations. This style of "make-believe" verges into a sort of mindlessness adapted to the dull labors of school. Other students manifested the same problem in a more direct way: When we asked them what kind of a project they would like to do, they simply couldn't think of one. Some of them chose topics, such as sports teams or

TV shows, but none of them had an idea for a clear problem or question that they might solve by collecting and analyzing data. Clearly, we have a long way to go in bringing students to the point where they can envision ways that a data analysis project could address an issue that is meaningful to them. The difficulty of doing this most probably relates to some rather fundamental facts about school:

- It is rare for students to participate in any kind of purpose-driven project in school.

- It is still rarer for students to be asked to choose and manage such a project. Students do not expect to have this kind of responsibility.

- In fact, students have almost no responsibility or decision-making power in schools—this rules out many of the contexts where reasoning supported by data might be genuinely useful to them.

Given this, perhaps we should not be surprised if students' ability to choose and pursue meaningful academic projects is severely stunted.

We are not giving up. We are working on refining our pedagogy in modest ways. For example, we are trying to speed up the turnaround in activities so that data analysis yields answers while the questions are still fresh in students' minds. Through various forums, such as the school radio station, we are trying to sow the seeds of a culture of inquiry in which it is normal for data-based arguments to be presented and debated. We are finding our satisfaction in each small advance that we can make.

We believe in the educational value of project-based curriculum, but projects cannot be simply "installed" in a classroom. The problem of meaningfulness in pedagogy, once raised, leads not to quick solutions but to a widening set of questions about students, classrooms, and schools. In the past couple years, my view of projects has changed slightly: I still believe, as I did before, that projects are a great way to learn almost anything—facts, skills, processes. But now it seems to me that developing the ability to do projects, for students and for schools, may itself be the biggest challenge, and the most valuable accomplishment.

CONVERSATIONS: THEIR IMPORTANCE
IN PROJECT SCIENCE
Candace L. Julyan [5]

For many, science was, and still is, a dreaded subject. Memories of science classes conjure up malodorous dissections, esoteric laboratory procedures,

---

[5] Candace Julyan is a TERC Senior Project Director, currently directing the NGS Kids Network project. For two decades she has explored science education from various perspectives. Dr. Julyan is particularly interested in knowing how individuals make sense of scientific ideas and how this knowledge can be used in redesigning classroom activities.

and endless lectures filled with long and unrecognizable vocabulary words. As an adolescent, I spent a great deal of time investigating life in a ravine behind our house. Was that science? I never thought so at the time. The scientific information memorized in school was so rarely of use in my numerous out-of-school investigations. My ravine studies were free-form, of my own design. Different months involved different investigations. One month's inventory of all the stream critters led to a similar study of all the land critters that shared my special spot. Another month, my study involved sound, lying on the smooth warm rocks next to the stream and considering the distances traveled by various sounds, from water moving over the rocks to birds' songs to the air moving through the trees.

But were those investigations science projects? My "findings" never found their way into any of my science classes, nor did I expect them to. The majority of these studies were quite private. I spoke about my inquiries with no one, short of a few timid questions to my biologist father. As I think back on it, I regret the solitude of those studies. I think of how much more I could have learned if I had opened my curiosity to conversations with others. It never occurred to me that others might be interested in my observations or that their ideas might deepen those studies.

Despite that silent entry into science, my work for the past two decades has involved some aspect of science, from research studies to science education. During that time I have had many conversations with a variety of people, from scientists to school teachers, about topics of shared import. My views have developed as I opened my ideas to the scrutiny of others and listened to their ideas. These conversations have shaped my thinking about scientific information, as well as my thinking about science classrooms. This essay details the scientific investigation of one particular class of sixth graders, an investigation filled with conversations. These students' work reveals many important components of student-initiated projects: interest, accuracy, reliability, curiosity, and most particularly conversations. Working with these students over 3 months taught me a great deal about the importance of well-timed, thoughtful conversations in science projects. This essay explores our joint learning.

For the past 5 years, I have been working on TERC's NSF-funded, elementary-science curriculum, the *National Geographic Kids Network* (Julyan, 1989a, 1989b, 1992). Most of the units in this curriculum involve predesigned, local studies in which students collect data and then share their data on a computer network. We encourage conversations among classes about these collected data, but we have been disappointed by the scarcity of those dialogues. We were curious what sorts of conversations would arise if students designed their own projects and solicited involvement from other network schools. Although the required structure for this particular curriculum ruled out student-designed projects, we were curious about the ways in which we could support student-designed project on computer networks.

The result of this curiosity became an experimental, unpublished unit that gave students an opportunity to gather data about their questions first in their own community and later in communities around the country. As is the case with other units in this curriculum series, we assigned classes to a small research team of 8 to 12 schools around the country that were able to share data and letters via a telecommunication network during a specified time period. Unlike other units, we did not design a set of prescribed activities for teachers and students to follow, but rather offered suggestions for creating and executing their own investigations through a series of research phases. We organized the investigation process into five phases of activity: topic selection, design of reliable data collection procedures, explanation of study to network colleagues, collection of data, and finally, making sense of the data and reporting findings to network colleagues.

We worked with eight schools in this experiment. Throughout the 10-week unit, students were engaged in many conversations. Some took place in the classroom; others took place on the computer network. In each phase of their investigation, these conversations helped to shape and direct the students' work. Although each study had its own interesting findings, one class stood out both in terms of the amount of data generated and the thoroughness with which the students conducted their study. This most remarkable Wisconsin class taught me a great deal about the importance of process and content in science projects and the value of dialogue to both. In the beginning of their investigation, these students talked primarily with one another and their teacher about the logistical details of the study. As their study became clearer and they began to generate data, they reached out to have conversations with others to discuss their procedures and share their findings. Each of these kinds of conversations, classroom and network, had an important role in their thinking. Both provide an intriguing look at the types of conversations that are vital for project science.

Classroom Conversations

Appropriately, this class' investigation began with a discussion about potential topics for the investigation. These students were unanimous in their desire to conduct a study that was in some way related to a current issue in their town—recycling. The students felt strongly that they wanted to conduct a scientific investigation that would further the community discussion on this topic. The neighborhood surrounding the school was involved in an intensive recycling experiment involving the usual paper, metal, glass, and plastic material as well as organic waste. Residents had agreed to eliminate all food and lawn waste from their disposable garbage by contributing to either an individual household or neighborhood compost pile. Students were personally involved in this study at home and were curious about how they could learn more about recycling through a study at school. Given the focus on compost, students decided to concentrate their investigation on the food waste generated in their school lunchroom. They knew they wanted to collect data about food waste but were uncertain as to what their research question could be. For several days students stationed in the lunchroom took notes about what they saw.

> Kids don't eat their food. Leave lots of stuff. Kids took one bite and then threw it away. Open milk then threw it away!

> Pizza, more people ate hot lunch. I saw a kid throw his whole pizza away.

> Five whole apples, whole bags of chips, pretzels. Waste a lot. 15 milk cartons not even opened.

> We found that kids throw away whole sandwiches, apples, oranges, cans of fruits, unwrapped granola bars, chips, and twinkies from cold lunches. It seemed that kids threw away more bread products than anything else.

Different students had made different observations. All were amazed at the amount of food wasted. Some had taken notes about the school menu; some had counted particular food items thrown away. Classroom conversations that included all the various observations helped the class shape its research question: Which lunches produced the most waste— lunches from home or lunches purchased from the school?

Once they had their research question, the students' next step was to determine what sorts of data made sense to collect. This decision required more sharing of ideas and testing out those ideas in the lunchroom. At the beginning of the week, one group collected data from each lunchroom table but found this method was time-consuming. Students decided to collect data at the trash can itself. Another group carefully noted the contents and weight of the trash cans, but failed to count the number of students. Another group noted that pounds were too gross a measurement and suggested that all the weights be converted to ounces. Through trial and error and many conversations, by the end of the week the class had developed both a procedure and a data collection form that assured that all the necessary data would be collected each day in the same way.

For the next week, two students with clipboards were stationed at each lunch period to record the number of students throwing refuse in the can. Further, they designated a can for each of the sources of refuse—home and school—and requested that their fellow students assist in the study by throwing their waste in the appropriate can. At the end of the lunch period, the student-researchers weighed the cans and noted the number of students who contributed to each. After the first few days, they began to add more data to their clipboards. For example, they became interested in recording the menus for each day, as well as the weight of the waste. This additional information led to the further observations.

> The greatest number of kids (374) ate hot lunch when pizza was served, but this meal also generated the most waste (880 oz.).

> "The greatest number of kids (150) chose to eat cold lunches rather than hot lunches when batter dipped fish was served for hot lunch."

Each of the classroom conversations gave students an opportunity to report their observations, propose a plan of action, or consider the ideas of their peers. By sharing ideas as a group and testing the validity of those ideas, the students were able to design a clear, well thought-out study from the research question to the procedure for collecting data. By the time students began their network conversations, they felt confident about the strength of their plan and eager to hear what others thought.

Network Conversations

Filled with their questions, discoveries, and a significantly more reliable procedure for collecting and recording their data, students were now ready to explain their research question and procedure to others and were curious to see how their data compared to that of other schools across the country. They had also come to appreciate all of their work in refining their study and were careful to convey their learning in an organized way to their network colleagues. In addition to sending a copy of their data collection form, the class began their conversation with other schools with the following description of their study.

Our school and homes are in a section of the city which is piloting a new recycling program. We sixth graders are helping the city by learning about and educating the public about waste management—specifically composting yard and food waste.

Our question: How much food waste is generated in your school's lunchroom in 5 days?

Data collection: Students will determine the total weight of solid food (excluding milk, pop, etc.) waste generated in the school's lunchroom. The data will be collected separately for both cold lunches (lunches brought from home) and hot lunches (lunches prepared by the school)."

Kinds of data: Each day data should be recorded on the lunchroom food waste data collection form. We want you to collect six things. 1) total weight of hot lunch, total weight of cold lunch. (weight in pounds—convert to ounces) 2) Number of kids eating hot lunch, number of kids eating cold lunch.

Materials needed: 1 scale, 2 garbage collection containers, 2 garbage collection liners, 1 data record form.

Procedures: 1) Monitors should be on duty 5 minutes before lunch is served. 2) Students need to monitor the food waste containers. 3) Monitors should be changed each day so that every student gets a chance to collect data. 4) Monitors are responsible to get the correct number of students that ate hot and cold lunch. 5) Be sure that paper, plastic, and liquids are not accidentally mixed with waste. 6) At the end of the lunch period, place containers of food waste on the scale. 7) Find the weight and subtract the weight of the containers. 8) Record data: a) weight—convert lbs. to oz. b) number of kids that ate c) average per student—divide total ounces by # of kids.

Sporadically during the first weeks of refining their study, I had conversed with the students on the computer network acting as their scientific consultant and listening ear, querying students about their data and procedures. Once they composed the letter to their teammates, our conversations began to focus on the substance rather than the form of their data. For example, after they reported that sack-lunch waste was definitely heavier than school-lunch waste, I questioned whether there was more waste or just heavier waste, given their finding that lunches from home often included heavy (and frequently uneaten) fruit. Sometimes these questions were used by students to clarify their main investigation as in the case of my question about whether or not they included milk in food waste. Other times, these questions led students to conduct their own investigations while the network classes were collecting data for them.

For example, my question about the weight of the fruit as a problem for their sack-lunch data led one group of students to investigate fruit waste further by gathering data about the number of apples discarded in the school lunches. Although not the intent of my question, this investigation led to an interesting discovery, which students shared with me:

> Students had a choice to take an apple with their hot lunch because apples were listed on the menu. Seventeen percent of the students took an apple; 83% of the students didn't take an apple. What do we think the data tells us? Not many people eating hot lunch took apples. Out of those that took apples, over half were not eaten and they were thrown in the garbage. We now believe that students at Riverview School do not like to eat apples for either hot lunch or cold lunch. They do not like to eat apples for lunch— PERIOD! It doesn't matter if the apples are bought in grocery stores by their parents or provided by the school district.

The milk question also sparked a separate study on milk, again unrelated to the intent of my question. In this instance, the question led students to wonder about the significance of the data that they had collected:

> We concluded our study on milk waste today. Our prediction was for more milk waste today because of only having white (milk) on the menu, whereas yesterday students had a choice between white and chocolate. It seems that kids like chocolate milk better than white. Even yesterday there was more white milk wasted than chocolate. We were surprised at the milk waste amount.
>
> MILK DATA: (Monday 7.5 gallons, Tuesday 12.1 gallons, Average 9.7 gal.)
>
> We had one of our students who lives on a farm call her dad and find out how much milk one cow produces a day? The whole farm of cows? She told us that one cow produces 6-7 gallons of milk a day and that the whole farm produces 500 gallons a day. Our school waste at lunch (this doesn't include milk breaks at recess for the kids) is about 9.7 gallons a day, about 1 1/2 cows production a day. In a year, our school wastes almost the same amount as a dairy farm of 80 cows' entire production for 3.5 days— 1,740 gallons of milk waste.

Although interested in their own school's data by itself, students were particularly eager to compare their data with those from the six other participating schools. Their findings and final report show a mastery of understanding how to make sense of complicated data and a sophisticated (and humorous) way of helping others less familiar with the lunchroom data understand the significance of the findings. In addition to numerous tables and graphs that detailed their findings, the students made the following summary statements.

> It appears that hot lunch is more popular in all network schools since the data shows that three times more kids ate hot lunch than cold. The network average is approximately 3 ounces of food waste per student for either hot or cold lunch.
>
> Washington had the highest average of food waste per student for hot lunch and West Virginia had the highest average for cold lunches. Arizona had the lowest average amount of waste per student for both hot and cold lunch. The other schools (Wisconsin, Indiana, and Michigan) all had similar averages which were only slightly higher than Arizona.
>
> In 1 month, there was approximately 10 tons (20,173 lbs.) of solid food waste for hot lunch and about 4 tons (8,540 lbs.) of food waste from cold lunch generated in six NGS Kids Network schools. In 1 year, these schools generate approximately 90 tons of hot lunch waste and 36 tons of cold lunch waste. The total weight of solid food waste of both hot and cold lunch for 1 year is equal to the weight of about 32 four-ton ELEPHANTS!!!

This report certainly demonstrates the ability of these students to design and conduct a complicated class project requiring clarity, accuracy, and cooperation. It also demonstrates the ways in which their numerous conversations shaped their thinking. Central to their investigation were their conversations with one another, with their teacher, with me, and with their network colleagues. These conversations helped students shape and sharpen their study, initially in their class discussions about the logistics of the study and later in their ability to engage me and other adults and students in the content of their findings.

In addition, conversations with those outside of the classroom and the network caused students to reconsider their data by exploring a variety of ways to present their findings or isolating data that was particularly significant for specific audiences. For example, toward the end of their investigation, the students were asked to present their findings to the school committee. By this time the students were quite concerned about the amount of waste in their lunchroom and were interested in using their data to reduce that waste. A portion of the students' presentation focused on the ways in which lunchroom personnel can use the data to change wasteful practices. As one student explained, tartar sauce was always automatically provided with fish; however, the tartar sauce was always thrown out by students. This finding led students (and the school committee) to question further purchases of this condiment.

The conversations from this study were rich and varied. Peers and adults frequently offered advice regarding various aspects of the study from data collection to the final analysis. As the study developed, so did these conversations, from logistical to substantive. Equally important was the students' eagerness for these conversations, eager to share their ideas with others and to integrate new ideas into their investigation. Unlike the silent studies of my adolescence, this investigation was shaped by a lively exchange involving students, teachers, and outsiders. These conversations strengthened both the process and the content of this study. Through this dialogue the students learned about the scientific process, the garbage problem in their lunchroom, and their own ability to use data to clarify a problem and suggest change. The conversations that grew from these studies helped students see the significance of scientific studies in real life situations.

> "Before our investigation, kids threw their whole sacks with the food they didn't eat into the garbage containers. Therefore nobody ever saw the food waste because it was always inside the sacks in the garbage container. We used to think just a little food was thrown away every day, but now we KNOW a lot is thrown away. We never paid attention to this, but now we think about it."

Unfortunately this investigation is not indicative of what takes place in many science classrooms. It certainly differs from the science classrooms of my adolescence. Rather than memorizing facts that were unrelated to their interests, these students pursued questions of their own design in a systematic and scientific manner. Rather than remaining silent during their study, these students actively conversed with many different people and gained confidence and knowledge through those dialogues. For these students, the study revealed previously unknown data, raised awareness to a serious problem, and perhaps even changed behaviors. These results came not from the findings alone, but rather grew out of the many rich and varied conversations. Was this science? Absolutely.

ESSENTIAL ELEMENTS OF MBLS
Nathan Kimball [6]

I started designing and programming for microcomputer-based lab (MBL) software with both great enthusiasm and naiveté. If kids just see this beautiful *real-world data* flying onto their screens they can't help but learn science. I believed that MBL could be taken like a magic pill as a prescription to cure the ills of science education. Being a visual learner, I find the power

---

[6] Nathan Kimball is a senior programmer and software designer at TERC. He was project director for the development of the PSL Explorer, IBM's microcomputer-based laboratory, and is presently researching and designing new MBLs.

of an MBL's graphic presentation absolutely compelling. Four years designing, building, and testing MBL software with children has not diminished this enthusiasm, but my naive notions have been pushed aside by experience.

Watching students work with MBL and listening to insightful colleagues has made my working hypotheses of learning with MBL grow into an *ad hoc* theory. The theory itself is not about software. It's about learning science. I need this theory to guide my software design. To the extent it is valid it will be useful to teachers and developers of curriculum who work with children to help them gain scientific understandings and a scientific approach to problem solving.

I offer this MBL theory with these motives. First, I want to give my perspective on the state-of-the-art of learning with MBL. With this I hope to intrigue the novice to try MBL or spark the experienced to think in new ways about working with it. Second, I hope to raise questions from seasoned practitioners and invite contrary points of view. I ask them to discuss with me or their colleagues how and what children learn using MBL. Third, these notions may prove useful to teachers and students as they go about the daily business of teaching and learning. I would love to hear which ideas make sense to the people who use MBL for whom all this matters the most.

The main ideas of early MBL work still provide the basis for my MBL discussion. First, the essential traits of the software have remained unchanged. The data must appear on a graph in real-time, and it must be simple enough to operate to be unobtrusive in the learning process. Second, in the classroom, the early MBL work emphasized students messing about with the probes, software, and materials to gain an intuitive understanding of how they workedthen using MBL to answer their own questions. Students making predictions become invested in the outcome of experiments. This has always been an effective technique.

I present my theory in two sections. The first section is slightly philosophical. The three principles here are guiding lights for mewhat I fall back on when things go amiss. The second section contains six tips learned from experience. It is more practical and, I hope, useful. I claim that my principles hold for students from third grade through high school. My approach here is most concerned with MBL course work that could be introductory to a project-based approach.

MBL Principles

Principle 1: MBL Learning Must Start With Children's Ideas

What components comprise MBL? We know about probes and software with real-time display of data in graphic form. We also know using an MBL implies a learning style based on discovery and doing. However, it is helpful to view the child's set of scientific beliefs as an integral part of the whole. When a child starts to work with MBL those beliefs shape his or her perceptions of the data. It is essential to both students and teachers to capture and understand these perceptions. They are what we seek to enhance. As children annotate their MBL graphs with words and pictures we gain insight into the way they see the phenomena that produced them. This process of annotating their graphs makes students aware of their own understandings, and allows them to assemble their thoughts. For teachers, it provides a window into children's scientific mind. They can follow their students' progress to better aid and assess them.

Principle 2: The MBL Experience is Another Way of Knowing

Initially, we learn how the world works by touching, seeing, and experiencing it with all the senses. We gradually develop the ability to abstract these experiences and use words, symbols, and pictures to convey knowledge. Children (of all ages) working with MBL cannot do better than begin with what is readily perceptible, relating it slowly with the abstraction of the graph. The real-time control and creation of graphs through MBL does demonstrably speed students' insights into a graph's meaning. However, only after a great deal of experience can students understand new phenomena by seeing a graph of it. Therefore, we should not use MBL graphs as proof of any phenomena, but merely one more piece of representation, of evidence, for consideration. Students must reconcile their past ideas and perceptions with the experiment at hand and the graph it produced.

An enormous number of skills are called into play when a child interprets a graph he or she has produced from a real-world experience. A feeling for what and how the probe measures is necessary along with an idea of what data to expect. It is usually a small matter to simply read a graph for highs and lows, but to understand physical events based on graphical representation requires judgment that is born only from experience. Observing a phenomenon, measuring it, representing it in a graph, and understanding it are all tightly linked. The graph allows the student to know more about the phenomenon, and the direct experience with the phenomenon allows the student to know more about what the probe measures and the graph that is generated.

Principle 3: MBL Learning Takes Place in a Social Context

MBL in the classroom is best as a shared activity with three or four students. With a small group, every experiment provides an active and separate role for each student. The study of science becomes an endeavor in communications that requires students to organize their procedures together, make plans, and share their ideas. Students develop the methods and language to solve their scientific problems, peer to peer. After small groups have conducted their investigations, class-wide discussions and presentations can bring out the diverse approaches, and the range of ideas. The classroom becomes a model scientific community, where ideas rise and fall on the basis of evidence, investigation, and communication. Students' involvement and trust in this process is the most important outcome from science study. Of course, this process transcends MBL curriculum, but by efficiently gathering and presenting data, MBL facilitates children investigating, communicating, and building their own scientific community.

MBL Practice

Any single graph produced by MBL presents a sea of information about the physical events that produced it. For instance, the data in a line graph captures the range of measurement, the rate of change of it, and the magnitude of each moment. Most important, each point on a graph is caused by some physical event (even artifacts usually have external causes). Students may or may not relate the shape of the graph well to the events that created it. I have seen students differ widely in what aspects of a graph intrigue them. They need time to satisfy their curiosity about the details of a graph and all the elements of creating it. But how can lesson objectives be met in such a free-flowing environment? Practically speaking, what is the balance between freedom and structure for learning to take place? I offer these tips.

Tip 1: Students should physically control the making of the graph in their first MBL activities.

Making the causal link between physical events and the graph is what makes MBL potent. For some reason, this link must initially be forged by using the body, by touching, or otherwise physically affecting the data and controlling the graph. Onlookers never quite get it. We have often discussed the reason for this by stating the importance of kinesthetic experiences. I believe using the body is an essential way of knowing. Age is not a factor here. Trusting sight and intellect alone is not enough no matter how young or old you are.

Often students first using MBL will want to play with the probes to make designs with the graphs. This is an important part of the initial phase. It reinforces the causal links, and releases students' unbridled creative energy, positioning them well for more investigation. The games that we have invented for students to control graphs, such as slaloms and challenges, are used effectively at this time.

Tip 2: Practice correlating the event and its result on the graph Is very important.

Despite our efforts to get students to see and feel the causal link between external events and the graph, they can still miss the connection. This is where annotating graphs and discussing them will help. Writing about all aspects of an experiment, telling the story of the graph, can provide us insight into students' thoughts. Sometimes this story will reveal that students are seeing what they expected to see and are blind to the actual data. Usually this means that things are happening too fast. The materials of the experiment may be so absorbing that the probes and graphs are a distraction. Students need to have time to enjoy their new experiences and formulate some initial ideas. They will never correlate events and graphs well until they have some intuitive understanding of the system they are investigating. More time is needed messing about with the materials. Add MBL and the probes as they are able to build on students' intuitions.

Tip 3: It is often wise to constrain the experimental environment.

Simple systems can reveal remarkable things. Until students have become comfortable with MBL, it is best to find experiment environments rich enough to be interesting, but not too complicated to be overwhelming. Furthermore, limitations of the probes can require simplified setups. The motion probe, for instance, needs a clear, straight path to "see" the object of interest. Temperature probes require good thermal contact and time to equilibrate with what they measure. They are best suited to measuring air temperatures and liquids. Other phenomena, such as the response of a light probe to the 60 Hz "flicker" of standard room lighting that is invisible to the eye, may interject a bewildering complexity into students' investigations. Students need to decide if experiments are fair and if variables are controlled. Systems that are too complicated may be very difficult to control or to even know if they are controlled. The systems students work with should at least be able to produce fair tests. Good discussions can form around the question of what is a fair test.

Tip 4: MBL data is valuable, but not too valuable. The really valuable thing is doing experiments.

Particularly in the early stages of working with MBL, teachers need to emphasize experimenting with the purpose of forging the causal link between the event and its graph and answering students' questions. Because of the immediate response of the probes, the times that students spend gathering data with the experiment materials and real-time graphs are magical learning moments. The special work of MBL learning is done right at the computer with the materials at hand. Students must catch the feel of the experiment and the feel of the data. They do this by seeing events affect the data on screen. At first they should not be encumbered with too many procedures for recording their experiments, or spend too much time printing their graphs. They need to reflect on their work, but if they have not internalized the experience first, they may be reflecting on misperceptions.

Now, saving and printing data is important and necessary. Students must have a record of their work to think about, annotate, talk about, make presentations with, write about, and keep a log. Record keeping is an essential part of the scientific process that we wish students to learn. It is also necessary to manage and assess students' learning and keep them organized. As students become more comfortable with MBL and the language of graphs, its use as a scientific tool of inquiry will increase. Careful record keeping must then become a matter of habit.

Tip 5: MBL is a unique medium. Proficient use of it must be cultivated.

Several MBL hardware and software packages designed for students of different ages allow them to pursue science effectively. Some do it better than others. However, all packages have limitations. Data rate, the effects of filtering, probe range, and the inevitable artifacts in the data are just a few of the realities of measurement that can affect the graph. Most of these problems can be addressed with adequate time spent experimenting with the probes, understanding what they can do as well as their limitations.

Tip 6: Sometimes using MBL an experiment will go awry. This is what you want to have happen.

Students work with MBL to solve problems, not find pat answers. Problems encountered give opportunities to rethink the process that can lead to adjustments and new approaches. A teacher's role should usually be to bring together students and let them try to solve the problems themselves, not attempt a quick fix that demonstrates a certain scientific outcome. The topic or "objective" of the lesson is less important than the process of solving the problem.

What Is the Objective of MBL?

MBL is designed to help broaden and deepen children's ideas about science. This deepening requires cultivating an intuitive sense of the area of science under study. My "MBL principles" emphasize changing children's ideas by providing direct experience, by giving them a mode of scientific expression in the graph and annotations of it, and by communicating the experience to their peers and teachers. Teachers can better understand their students' thoughts, and students have tools for expressing them. This process builds students' confidence and scientific perspective.

As a designer of MBL software, I need to be aware of all aspects of its use in the classroom. Many of the educational dimensions I have mentioned are not amenable to technological fixes. Teachers create and nurture their students' educational environment. However, my understanding of this environment is essential for creating a usable software tool. Only with constant checking with students and teachers can these needs be met.

FINDING AN AUTHENTIC VOICE

Deborah Muscella [7]

Grace Paley, an author of short stories, described writing as finding a voice, a voice shaped not by genre, but from which a form emerges. What did she mean? When I read her stories, I find myself listening to her characters, hearing echoes of my life in theirs. At the same time, her stories allow me to step outside of myself, to think about grief, love, or friendship in ways I had not yet imagined. Sometimes I read her stories as I would a poem—looking for meaning in elliptical phrases, finding new metaphors for familiar scenes. At other times I read to find out the when, where, and how of the characters in the story. I can read her stories as poetry or prose because Ms. Paley has not confined herself to any particular form. Rather the genre is simply a platform from which she and her characters speak freely and authentically.

Learning, too, is a process of finding a voice. What does it mean to find one's voice as a learner? When I am learning something new—to speak Spanish, to play the flute—I juggle the knowledge of the discipline and my own understandings. What I need to know is both within and outside of myself. When I can ask a question spontaneously in Spanish or play a chromatic scale with musicality, I begin to sense my own voice emerge in the learning. It is not until I find my own voice—no matter how primitive—that I begin to feel that learning is authentic. I am no longer confined solely to the teacher's knowledge. Rather, the teaching and learning interact, allowing me to deepen my own understanding.

When learning echoes what children know and prompts them to look at ideas from another perspective, their own voices emerge. How do children find their voices in learning? As a researcher who studies how young children learn, I continually search for ways to hear their emergent voices. I recently realized that to listen and hear children's voices sometimes requires me to look at teaching and learning from the child's perspective. I came to this understanding during a research project in which first graders explored motion and distance with a microcomputer-based laboratory (MBL). I was perplexed about how this tool-based software could be useful for young children's learning so I asked myself: *How will first graders use this technology? What sense will they make of the MBL? Is this even a viable tool*

---

7 Deborah Muscella has spent the past 18 years as a teacher, researcher, instrument designer, and staff developer. Her current work focuses on research and evaluation in school settings. Dr. Muscella has designed qualitative research that examines classroom learning environments for minority children. Most recently, Dr. Muscella has developed an assessment framework for a technology-oriented science curriculum.

for young children? Answering these questions prompted me to watch the ways that young children explored an MBL technology.

These questions were a richer genesis for deepening my own understanding of children's learning than I ever imagined. Not only did I gain new insights about how children made sense of the technology, but I also developed a deeper understanding about my own work as a researcher. My skepticism led me to hold my own beliefs about learning in abeyance and so I heard the voices of children a little more clearly, and my own voice as a researcher emerged with more clarity.

I began the research in the summer of 1990 with a group of first graders. We were exploring the ways in which an MBL could give children another vehicle to explore rather complicated ideas in science. Could the temperature and motion probes, with their accompanying real-time graphical display of data on the computer screen, reveal concepts about motion and velocity and heat and temperature to young children? I was doubtful of an MBL's usefulness as a pedagogy for youngest primary grade children to learn science.

In fact, I wondered if an MBL was even appropriate. Could it encourage active exploration? If children did not understand the relationship between the data that the probe gathered and the resulting graph, then how could they ever use the tool purposefully? How would children use the MBL's graphical data—already quite a sophisticated pictorial representation—to interpret science concepts that educators already believed were too difficult for first graders to grasp.

After spending several months observing first graders use the motion probe, I now think that an MBL naturally leads children to ask questions, challenge their beliefs, and engage in projects of their own design. The technology creates an environment for children to explore their intuitive understandings of motion, distance, and speed. Let me describe some of the things that happened that led me to these assumptions.

We began our work with first graders in the summer of 1990. We designed some activities for them to use with the temperature and the motion probes. Although the children were intrigued by the activities, our observations reminded me of Eleanor Duckworth's (1987) essay: "Either We're Too Early and They Can't Learn It or We're Too Late and They Already Know It." To only read the title of her essay is misleading, however. In it she argues that for learning to expand children's understanding, experiences must puzzle children enough so they begin to look at problems differently. After our summer work with the children, I had a hunch that an MBL motion probe might puzzle first graders just enough.

Kate, a first-grade teacher, and I pursued this hunch in her classroom in the fall. Kate and her students began to experiment with the motion probe while I watched with an eye behind the video camera. After each observation, I reviewed the videotape. My preliminary analyses supported my skepticism. Children danced, skipped, hopped, jumped, and did cartwheels in front of the probe, paying little attention to the line graph portrayed on the computer screen. I returned to my initial suspicions—an MBL was too complex for young children

After a few sessions I noticed a change in what the children were doing. Actually, I noticed the change first with Franklin. When it was his turn, he seemed to have a plan in mind for moving in front of the probe. He walked backward and then forward. I was intrigued by the next thing that he did. He walked to the probe and turned it toward the ceiling, immediately causing a straight line on the graph. I was convinced that Franklin knew that pointing the probe to the ceiling would produce a straight line on the graph. What I found more intriguing was that he used this knowledge to construct a particular graph pattern. I suspected that if Franklin had plans for making graphs, other children must also. So Kate and I began to ask children of their plans before they began to move in front of the motion probe.

And plans they had. Rosie would make two big mountains and two small mountains; Dan a mountain and then a straight line; Ami three small mountains. To execute these plans the children had to know how to time their movements for the 60-second data collection period, create a straight line, judge their distance from the probe. They had constructed quite a bit of knowledge about the probe simply through their own explorations. Now I was not so sure that I could dismiss an MBL as a learning tool.

A few weeks later, Kate had a conversation with the children that began to convince me that an MBL technology was offering these first graders a venue for learning that we had not imagined possible. She had asked them to think about what the motion probe could see. During this conversation, the children asked the question, *Can the probe see us dancing?* I listened closely to their evidence as they answered the question. Rosie and Holly offered a convincing argument.

Rosie: *The probe can't see us dancing because it can't see us turn.*

Holly: *It could see Lori turn when she did the Hawaiian dance.*

Rosie: *No, it doesn't see us turn. If it did, it would make circles.*

Holly: *But what if it could make circles?*

I suddenly realized that the children had been building up their knowledge about what the probe would do by exploring its parameters. What I considered to be primitive movements and ideas had been their departure point for learning what the probe could do. They also imagined other graphs that would represent their more intricate movements like dancing. I remained puzzled, however, about how, if at all, an MBL was contributing to their learning. The technology was, paradoxically, too simple to portray the running, jumping, hopping, and skipping about which young children knew a lot. At the same time the graphical displays of velocity and distance and time were too complex for first graders to make sense of.

As the children were constructing their knowledge about what the probe "saw" and how it showed what it "saw" on the screen, I was developing new ideas about how children made sense of graphical language. Now I asked: How could a technology like an MBL open a new window for us to explore children's learning? I had two parallel ideas. I approached the problem by asking if the real-time data of an MBL could help young children learn to read a two-dimensional language that was new to them, and if the motion probe could tap children's intuitive notions of motion and movement.

As I observed the children working, I continued to explore theoretical perspectives that might offer explanations for my observations or suggest other paths to explore. In reading Piaget's studies of how children view movement, it was evident that children's ideas about motion evolve considerably from the time they are 5 until they are 8 years old. In most of his studies, Piaget found that children who were 5 and 6 do not understand that speed has something to do with distance and something to do with time. But the evidence that we had gathered with Kate's first graders seemed contradictory. They timed both their movements and the speed at which they moved to create graph patterns with an MBL. But, were we really tapping children's intuitive ideas about motion as Piaget had been? One day as I was walking up the street to Kate's school, I noticed kindergarten and preschool children on the playground. They were on swings, slides, jungle gyms, running, skipping. I suddenly saw the swings as pendulums, the slides as inclined planes. I realized that to choreograph such intricate maneuvers with so little forethought, the children needed an intuitive sense of movement. I decided that Piaget was absolutely right and absolutely wrong. Of course young children could not predict which of two cars, traveling at the same speed, on tracks of different lengths would arrive at the end first. The logical reasoning was too complex for young children. Their own experiences on playgrounds and in learning how to walk, run, jump, and skip, however, had given them a storehouse of knowledge about movement.

In re-reading Howard Gardner's (1983) chapter on the intelligence of kinesthetic movement in *Frames of Mind*, I was struck by a quote by Isadora Duncan, "If I could tell it, I would not dance it" (p. 224). Aha, I thought, children's knowledge of speed is tacit. I began exploring what others might know about movement. I found Isomu Noguchi's playground designs. As a sculptor, he has spent his lifetime designing structures, outdoor spaces, and sets for works of Martha Graham, the choreographer and dancer. He brought his knowledge of how structures can convey a sense of movement to his playground designs. Swings on the same balance pole hung at different lengths; slides were straight and curved; tunnels gave way to paths that were suddenly visible. The structures that he designed invited children to explore their movement through space. I was now convinced that there was a language of movement that was more sophisticated than I had imagined, a language the first graders understood better than I.

In thinking about the language of structures and the language of dance, I looked at what the first graders had done with the probe in a new light. I developed two new hunches. The MBL graph gave children a two-dimensional language for them to explore their movements in a three-dimensional world. The graph also gave them a language to describe something they knew about only intuitively. I was not sure, however, how to explore these ideas in the classroom.

The children themselves showed Kate and me how to proceed. A group of children had been building ramps and testing out the speed of balls, cars, and tubes on the ramp. The children called themselves the "speed group" because they were testing how fast things rolled down the ramp. Again we began by watching the children work.

We noticed that the children experimented by rolling wheels, cylinders, and balls. They asked the question: "Which things roll fast?" Each time they rolled an object down the ramp, they proclaimed: "It rolled fast." Whether objects rolled 3 feet beyond the end of the ramp or stopped in the middle of the ramp, they rolled fast. Kate and I were puzzled by this. When Kate and asked them how they knew it rolled fast, their reply was always the same: "We watched them roll fast."

The next day, however, I noticed that children began to test various attributes of objects. They isolated things by color, size, weight, things with wheels, and "feelington" or texture. Through their tests they eliminated color and "feelington" as things that made objects roll fast or slow. They decided, however, that heavy things, things with wheels, and small things roll fast. Although all the things that they rolled were round in some way, they never talked about the need for things to be round to roll. Nor did they consider differences between wheels, cylinders, and balls.

Once again, there was a paradox. These first-grade children were able to pose questions about variables that influenced speed. Was it the size of the object? Did color make a difference? Did heavy things roll faster? Was it how an object felt? The children were experimenting with ideas of how weight, surface tension, and size affected speed. It was as if they had a tacit understanding of what made the objects roll fast. But, at the same time, the children continued to test speed by simply watching. When judging how fast things rolled, the children did not consider the time that an object took to roll down the ramp or the distance it rolled. What sense did they make of speed, distance, and time? Did they even see that speed, distance, and time were possibilities? Now I wondered if an MBL technology could be useful in helping children articulate their intuitive understandings of motion.

Once again I thought Piaget was absolutely right—and absolutely wrong. Children's intuitive notions of speed were emergent. Yet, their approach to testing the speed of objects was more precise than I would have imagined. I suspect that the children might have known more about motion than they could say. I think that technology could help them to experiment with their primitive intuitions about speed and motion. I wonder if translating the three dimensional language of the probe into a such pictorial language as a graph or speed gauge on the computer screen would give voice to children's intuitive notions of motion and speed?

We have not answered this question yet. George Forman's (1988) proposals for such future technology as stop-action video and Logo-like robots that run see-saws and trains would present the motion of the objects with analog and digital displays. He suggested that such displays would allow children to focus on the path of the object and not simply on the action. But, it is the action and the path that children know intuitively. For technology to help children make their tacit knowledge explicit will require that they can explore many dimensions related to speed. As children pursue these explorations we, as researchers, have the unique opportunity to observe children and listen for their emergent voices. If we let the children find their own voices in such future technology, then as researchers we will discover more about learning than we had imagined.

In another context, Linda Delpit advocated the need to value the perspectives that learners bring with them. Although the context she described is that of teaching from cultural perspectives that may not be our own, her comments resonated with the voice I had found when these first-grade children asked me to stop and listen.

> We must keep the perspective that people are expert on their own lives. There are certainly aspects of the outside world of which they may not be aware, but they can be the only authentic chroniclers of their own experiences. We must not be too quick to deny their interpretations, or accuse them of "false consciousness."...And, finally, we must learn to be vulnerable enough to allow our world to turn upside down in order to allow the realities of others to edge themselves on our consciousness. (Delpit, 1986, p. 297)

What I know now is that it is not just this once that I must allow myself to be turned upside down, to radically change my mind. No, I think that every time I enter into a classroom, I must be willing to suspend my beliefs and listen to the voices of teachers and learners. I think that it is only in this way that I will continue to find my voice as a researcher, and as a learner.

DON'T TELL ME HOW THINGS ARE,
TELL ME HOW YOU SEE THEM

Ricardo Nemirovsky [8]

The teacher had set up today as a deadline for each team of students to decide on a project to develop. But it turns out that most of the teams have not decided yet. Team A, for instance, is discussing several possibilities that it found in different books: a demo about magnetic damping, a demonstration of how an electric motor works, and an electronic circuit to generate waveforms. But all of them seem uninteresting or too mundane. The students in Team B are excited about the possibility of constructing a laser. They got the idea from an article in *Scientific American*. But they do not quite understand how to do it.

This essay was originally conceived as an analysis of common difficulties arising in project learning. More specifically, as an exploration of some patterns in students' attitudes toward the selection of "what to do," as an attempt to unfold what these attitudes may be expressing. They are exemplified by the Teams A and B in the scenario just described. As I wrote and articulated my ideas, a theme emerged as the center of this inquiry: the sense of wonder about the world around us. Slowly I began to envision the critical relationship between project-enhanced learning and the sense of wonder about the world

Each time a teacher decides to organize project-enhanced learning, she or he is reflecting a particular perception of science education and of her or his students' needs, namely, to create a learning atmosphere that resembles how scientists work. One of the most widely shared hopes behind the organization of project-enhanced learning, is to foster intellectual autonomy in students. This goal highlights the importance of giving students the freedom to choose what to do. To the naive observer it seems really straightforward: You provide some guidelines and just ask the students what they want to do. What happens next? A few students are very responsive. They have clear ideas and some can lead their team of classmates. But for many students the situation is very unsettling. Some of them may be characterized as the "Bored" ones. Nothing seems to trigger their commitment, and every idea that is discussed ends with a "nah." Often they are driven to an "I don't care" attitude, selecting whatever looks simple and easy from books or teachers' descriptions.

---

[8] Ricardo Nemirovsky studied physics at the University of Buenos Aires. He is now completing a doctoral degree in education at Harvard University. He worked in educational projects in Argentina, Mexico, and the United States. His current research focus is on how people without background in calculus think about calculus problems.

Others may be called the "Spectacular" students. They are only moved by sensational projects that will impress the audience during the final presentation. Sometimes their ideas are unfeasible. They have a hard time assessing the cost, time, and expertise demanded by the ideas they want to pursue. Other times they have difficulties infusing their impressive performances with science content and are forced to add some irrelevant explanations alluding to "Newton's laws" or "electrostatic forces." Among all the patterns in students' attitudes toward the selection of a project, I believe that the Bored and the Spectacular ones reflect two sides of the same coin, which is: How hard it is to wonder about the world around us.

On the Sense of Wonder

Every child, until she or he is 5 or 6 years old, shows a never-ending sense of wonder about the events that affect her or his life. Something fundamental changes along the path toward adulthood. A gap grows between child-like and adult ways of knowing. When a child asks why the trees do not walk or why the moon is white, something magic is triggered in an adult's mind. It is like an awakening from a dream, because we sort of know that trees do not walk but...how come one can wonder about that? A more unsettling feeling may follow as we realize that we don't have good answers. Children help us to shake what we take for granted; in a way this "taking for granted" is a key to understanding the nature of the child–adult gap. We adults learned to see the world around us without the perception of strangeness. Strangeness recedes into the distant and the unusual. The everyday world becomes obvious. The common experience moves to an invisible background.

However, when we become adults the 5-year-old child does not disappear. Howard Gardner (in preparation) said that in every adult there is a 5-year-old child struggling to emerge. Moreover, he claimed that this struggle is behind some of the most extraordinary creations of the arts and the sciences. It takes an enormous effort to become aware of the strangeness of the everyday world, an achievement that has been described as the recovering of the child's vision. I do not see any role for science education more important than the preservation and enrichment of this childish perspective on nature, of the ability to develop a fresh look at common things. When this does not happen, when we become incapable of wondering about the world around us, our search for amazement and excitement necessarily lead us to the distant and the unusual; the immediate comes to be self-evident and ultimately invisible. A new dichotomy begins to encompass our relation with nature: boredom or spectacularity, the triviality of the immediate or the hard-to-believe behavior of the remote.

There are basic differences between amazement and wonder. In pondering the nature of something it is very different to say "I wonder" than "This is amazing." The locus of wonder is in the knower, whereas the locus of amazement is in the event or thing. Amazement is a reaction to an unusual event that happens "out there," whereas wonder is born from our inner perception of puzzlement. In trying to revitalize the students' interest in science there is a trend to substitute the feeling of amazement for the sense of wonder. Sometimes they are connected. Amazement may elicit wonder, but this link is not a necessity. Amazement can dissolve without wonder. This is evident in many science museums' exhibits. It is not unusual to see people running from device to device, pushing buttons compulsively expecting to see something amazing happen. If this does not take place quickly they run to the next. I was told by a science museum officer that the rule of thumb is 30 seconds. If, after 30 seconds, nothing amazing has taken place then the exhibit has failed to catch the attention of visitors.

An element that suffocates the sense of wonder is the pervasive perception that things are explained by theories. Polanyi (1964) was a very eloquent critic of this perception. He argued that things are explained by people. Science is not in the books, it is in the human activity of making sense. Moreover, he articulated the point of view that science resides in the personal knowledge of its practitioners. Personal knowledge does not refer just to what individuals have "in their heads." Personal knowledge is acquired through immersion in social practices, through apprenticeships, communication, and the use of the tools and symbols that are built in a cultural environment. Through participation in scientific communities, the tools and symbols of scientific discourse become transparent, subsidiary, and therefore "personal." In other words, personal knowledge thrives through one's participation in cultural forms of knowing.

Large domains of personal knowledge are necessarily tacit. An example may help to clarify this notion. The example that I use (that is common in the literature) is our knowing what is an appropriate physical distance between people. We express rich knowledge about this issue in our day-to-day interactions. We know how to adjust our closeness according to the situation: if the relation is more or less formal, if the environment is more or less noisy, if we are in a group, and so forth. We also may interpret some attitudes from "the other" as telling us that we are too close, or too far. This body of knowledge is tacit. We can talk about it, we can make theories about it, but our acting out of distancing from others cannot be reduced to our talking about it. Actually, our talking is a reflection on our experience of what it is like to behave appropriately. As we become skilled, as we enrich our personal knowledge full of tacit components, our talking becomes more and more meaningful.

To learn science or mathematics implies the construction and refinement of many tacit components of knowledge. For instance, the grasping of what it means to prove something, what are pertinent science questions, or how to make sense of an experiment, are largely tacit. Sometimes we expect the contrary, namely, that being exposed to formal descriptions and explicit accounts of theories, are the bridges toward the thriving of personal knowledge, rather than the latter being the condition for a meaningful discourse. David Goodstein, in an issue of *Physics Today* devoted to the memory of Richard Feynman, recalled:

> In all those years, only twice did he teach courses purely for undergraduates. These were the celebrated occasions in the academic years of 1961-62 and 1962-63 when he lectured...on the materials that were to become *The Feynman Lectures on Physics*.. As the course wore on, attendance by the kids at the lectures started dropping alarmingly, but at the same time, more and more faculty and graduate students started attending, so the room stayed full, and Feynman may never have known that he was losing his intended audience....The lessons in physics he prepared, the explanations of physics at the freshmen level, weren't really for freshmen, but were for us, his colleagues...It was more often us, scientists, physicists, professors, who would be the main beneficiaries of his magnificent achievement, which was nothing less that to see all of physics with fresh new eyes. (Bartlett, 1992, p. 67)

Feynman's lectures, rather than explaining physical phenomena to novices, deepened the physicists' understanding of their own practices.

However, there is a common view that scientific ideas can be explained beyond practices, beyond human activity, and that they dwell in the statements printed in books and journals. This has led people to think that there is something that we may call the "Official Explanation of Things" (O.E.T). When the students' personal knowledge is inconsistent with the O.E.T, science education is supposed to fix it. For example, during the 1970s and 1980s researchers discovered all sorts of inconsistencies of the kind that are extremely difficult to overcome. They were called "misconceptions." This research movement produced compelling evidence that naive approaches to natural phenomena are sensible, structured and complex.

One of the pictures that grew out of that research movement is somewhat grotesque: Students stubbornly resist adopting the O.E.T., preferring to use their own, often mistaken conceptions. Consequently, the role of the teacher is to convince students that the O.E.T is the right way of thinking. Teaching in this mode is interpreted as convincing, as an effort to undermine students' arguments for holding their misconceptions.

The focus of science education on students' internalization of the O.E.T weakens the sense of wonder, just as the focus on amazement does, because it frames science as external, in the things or in the books. The knower's activity remains legitimate to the extent that it fits the established truths of the O.E.T. Seymour Papert (1980) analyzed a mathematical problem that may illuminate some of these issues. Suppose we pose the following problem: A string forms a circle whose radius is 2 inches. Imagine another circular string with the radius of the earth. How much more string do you need to enlarge the radius of each circular string by 1 inch?

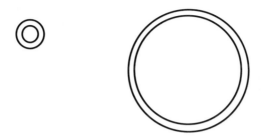

The fact that you need to add the same length of string in both cases is extremely counterintuitive. It is not hard for another person to convince us that it is the same. She or he can use some basic facts, such as the formula for the length of a circumference, to show that the length of string that has to be added is independent of the radius:

$2\pi\, r = 1$

$2\pi\,(r+\Delta)=1+2\pi\,\Delta$ —> the difference is $2\pi\,\Delta$, for any radius r.

The only thing that matters is the change of radius. But even if she or he is successful in "convincing" us, still the issue is unresolved: What is it about our way of thinking the problem that leads us not to expect such a result? Without pursuing this inquiry, without exploring the nature of our personal knowledge, it is likely that a change of the conditions of the problem will elicit the same initial expectation. It is possible that many "convincing" demonstrations affect the students' sense of their own abilities to understand science more than students' actual understanding of science. It is not a matter of "stubbornness" or not wanting to accept the O.E.T, it is the fact that we do not have any way to know beyond our personal knowledge.

If the hard-to-believe demonstrations, or compelling O.E.T pronouncements do not help to nurture the sense of wonder, what does? I believe that the sense of wonder is activated when our own way of thinking about the world becomes an object of our inquiry, when we become aware that things may cease to be obvious as we change our "knowing" perspective, when we recognize that it is not just a matter of how things are, it is also a matter of how we envision them. I describe an episode with a high school student who is puzzled about different aspects of water flow. It shows a student experiencing the obvious becoming unexpected. No galaxies, no black holes, no quarks, just water flowing out of common containers.

This was the fourth session during which Elisa, a high school student, had worked with water flow. She had experimented with different containers, measuring different regimes of inflow and outflow. In this session,

Elisa predicted that the curve of rate of outflow versus time for the water flowing out of a cylindrical container would display this shape:

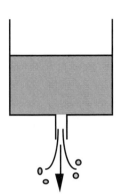
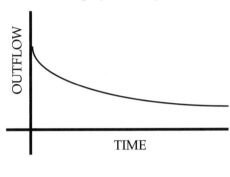

Her prediction was based on the notion that the water inside the container "pushes" the water flowing out, so as water flows out, and the water level decreases, the "push" will be smaller. On the other hand, she predicted that the water level would decrease linearly. That is, the curve of water level versus time would look like a descending straight line. This intuition was elicited by noticing a symmetry. She had observed that the funnel and the Erlenmeyer flask produced the following graphs:

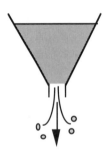
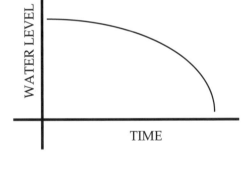

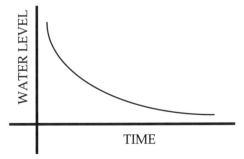

Therefore, a cylinder, which is in the middle between a funnel and an Erlenmeyer, would produce a straight line.

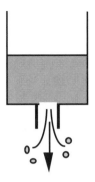
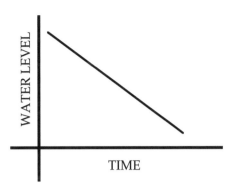

We were discussing the process by which she calculated the outflow taking differences of water level:

Ricardo: Then if you have a straight line, what would you expect, taking differences at regular intervals?

Elisa: That it would be the same....If it wasn't the same, then...the difference should be the same. It's supposed to be. Is it? If that one [water level vs. time graph] is really a straight line, then, if that one is really a straight line, then the other one [the outflow vs. time graph] is really a straight one [gesturing a horizontal line], basically, because if it makes a difference in the outflow, then it has to make a difference in the level versus time, because then it would make a difference in how much water's going out at each point

Ricardo: That's important then.

Elisa: So then, one of them has to be wrong. One of our predictions has to be wrong...if the outflow is first high and then gets leveled...then the level can't go straight like that.

Ricardo: Cannot?

Elisa: No, it cannot, because if the outflow's high, then the level has to decrease fast. When the outflow gets less, then the level has to decrease slower....Either this one or this one [of the predictions] has to be wrong...or both of them.

The heart of Elisa's puzzlement about the behavior of water flowing out of a container is in how to think about it and in her awareness that two conflicting intuitions, the water push and the figural symmetry, struggle to emerge in her attempt to make sense of the situation. Her wondering is part of an ongoing process of reflection on the unintended results of our joint experimentation with water and containers. A measurement of the "real" curves of water flow and level versus time, won't be the end but the beginning of new reflections. Suppose that she measures and gets an experimental curve indicating unambiguously that her prediction of outflow versus time is "right." What to do with the idea of symmetry? Just forget it? No, there has to be (why am I so sure?)—a certain shape for the container such that the water level decreases linearly, which one is it? Moreover, how does the shape of the container affect water flow?

Elisa, like most of us, has plenty of experience with water and containers. It is this expertise, sharpened by the work that she did during the previous sessions, that stands behind her intuitions. This kind of expertise is an essential part of the wondering about something. We wonder about what we know. What could I wonder about quarks? Nothing. I do not have expectations about them. Usually the media identify things like quarks, or any other exotic entity or procedure, as dwelling on the "edge of knowledge." But this way of labeling ideas conceals the fact that each one of us has different edges of knowledge. For example, Elisa, as she articulates her expectations about water flow, is experiencing one particular edge of her knowledge.

This reminds me of something that happened to me recently. I was eating an orange and I noticed that it was seedless. I had eaten seedless oranges before, but this was the first time I wondered about them. How do they manage to grow orange trees that do not produce seeds? How do those trees reproduce? Or how can they inhibit the tree from creating seeds? My experience with fruit and my expectations about the role of seeds in the reproductive cycle made me realize, as has happened to Elisa in the former episode, that there was something to be revised in my way of thinking about this matters, something important to be learned. The following day I asked a colleague who is a biologist about seedless oranges. He helped me realize that there is a possibility that I had not envisioned before: Fruit can grow before the seed is born. Perhaps the fact that seeds are usually inside a fruit had induced me to assume that it must grow around a seed, and therefore after the seed comes to be. In any case, the point is that the seedless oranges were at the edge of my knowledge. Edges of knowledge can be found around anything we know something about. Because in the end nothing is trivial. Triviality is an illusion that we adopt whenever we take something for granted.

Genuine Inquiry

At some point in our lives we all have the insight that when someone asks something, teachers in particular, often it is not because she wants to know the answer, rather it is because she wants to check whether we know what she assumes to be the correct answer. I will call "genuine inquiry" a mode of engagement in which his insight is *not* enacted; in which there is no sense of "simulation" and any question that is uttered reflects a personal wish to learn something from the other's perspective. I want to claim that genuine inquiry has a fundamental role in fostering the sense of wonder about the world around us.

There is an intimate interplay between wondering about the world around us and wondering about how we understand things.

> The general form of propositions is: "This is how things are"—This is the kind of proposition that one repeats to oneself countless times. One thinks that one is tracing the outline of the thing's nature over and over again, and one is merely tracing round the frame through which we look at it. (Wittgenstein, 1958, p. 48e)

This movement from "how the things are" to "how we frame things" triggers the sense of wonder. Wondering about our ways of understanding thrives as we deal with how different people, including ourselves, come to understand something. Genuine inquiry creates a communicative atmosphere that promotes the flourishing of these attitudes.

One may ask oneself: How is it possible to nurture genuine inquiry when one *knows* something? For example, if I ask myself whether a student knows Newton's first law, I cannot act as if I myself want to learn Newton's first law—it is too late, the question *cannot* be genuine. I think that this is true. The question "What is Newton's first law?" from someone who is a "knower" of Newton's laws, is not genuine. However, and this is central, it is certainly not genuine if the questioner refers to the statements of the O.E.T, that is, to what the textbook states under the title of "Newton's First Law." But if we shift our inquiry to how one can come to make sense of "Newton's First Law": How can one be sure (or not) of its validity? What does not make sense about it, or why it is so difficult (or trivial) to grasp? In other words if we move from "this is Newton's First Law" to "how does the Newton's First Law play in my understanding of things" AND if we realize that no two people make sense exactly in the same way of Newton's First Law, then the inquiry may become genuine.

Why do I say "it *may* become genuine"? First of all, because there are no recipes: It is not a matter of the *form* of the questions. It is a matter of really wanting to know how the student imagines things, and it is also a matter of throwing oneself into the scene. That is, of sharing our personal knowledge as such—as personal knowledge. Let me elaborate. It is common to hear conversations among teachers about what to do when a student asks something and you do not know the answer. It is a typical statement of progressive education that the teacher should honestly be able to say "I don't know" without feeling that something wrong is going on.

But it is much less common to hear about the broader issue, about the importance of personalizing knowledge. To answer "I don't know" is an act of personalizing knowledge, but as an isolated response it is reactive rather than proactive, it is not part of a general attitude. Personalizing knowledge involves talking about ideas manifesting their genesis ("I have not always thought in this way"); their tentativeness ("let me try to envision other possibilities"); their images ("I see it in several different ways"); and, their limits ("It does not help me to..."). Personalizing knowledge is a way of talking that situates expert and novice approaches in a continuum, rather than in the two opposite sides of a gap.

By saying "it is a matter of really wanting to know how student imagines things" I imply two things: First, that one does *not* know a priori how a certain student imagines things. Second, that one may learn something *new*, about us and about science or mathematics, by knowing how a student imagines. Some people who are familiar with the literature on students conceptions act as if all that is needed is to master the published taxonomy of conceptions. It is as if, say, you should ask the student to draw the forces acting on a flipping coin and then you categorize the student according to the answer A, B, or C. I think that it is useful to know about the research in this field, but not in order to substitute genuine inquiry, not in order to adopt published results as an O.E.T. Suppose that you ask a European his nationality. You can categorize the possible answers (Italian, French, etc.). He tells you that he is Italian. Would this "test" obliterate the need to talk about his personal experience? Would you assume that you know all about him? No two people arrive at the same answer A or B through the same personal experiences.

I do not deny that some techniques, such as how to word certain questions, may be of some help in fostering genuine inquiry. But there is a latent conflict in focusing on techniques because some readers will take form for substance and the message will be totally misunderstood. Because the same question, even the same words, may convey profound differences in what Carl Rogers (1969) called "attitudinal qualities." Let me introduce an example: In teaching there is an extremely common attitudinal quality that we may call "guess my mind." The teacher poses a series of questions and clues to "guide" the students toward a specific idea or answer that she or he has in mind. The students get involved in the communicative game trying to guess the hidden idea. This attitude may be of value in many circumstances but it does not help to promote genuine inquiry. It tends to structure the whole activity around a fixed piece of knowledge owned by the teacher.

When I *find myself* in a "guess my mind" stance while I am trying to encourage genuine inquiry, I tend to do one of two things (sometimes I do have this attitude but I do not find myself doing it, so I keep doing it): First I might speak my thoughts and say things like "you know, to me this is so and so, what is it for you?" But often if I state my own perspective it may prevent the other from pursuing her or his own approach. An alternative that I use is to *go beyond* what I have in mind, asking myself something like "What is it about the situation or about our prior experiences that we see it differently?" Exploring this question helps me to come up with overt questions, observations, and gestures that engage both of us in trying to understand what moves us to see things in a certain way.

Now I can use this example to illustrate the initial point: The same word may convey different attitudinal qualities—for instance the word "why?" In a "guess my mind" attitude, "why?" may mean: "I know why this is so and so, but I want you to figure it out for yourself. Look at what I'm pointing at, that is a clue, so tell me...," whereas in a genuine inquiry attitude it may mean: "Why do you see it in this way? I see it in a different way and I cannot picture your point of view, so, try to help me" These two meanings may be discriminated by the tone of voice, facial expression, gestural movements, and so forth, but rather than elaborating on facial expressions it is much more productive to talk about the kind of feelings that move us on to genuine inquiry.

With some people it is much easier to engage in genuine inquiry than with others. Through my experience interviewing students I have noticed that this is not related to school performance. I believe that a major determinant is to what extent the student feels that her or his own personal way of approaching something is worth looking at. When one strives intensely to articulate what "goes on in my mind" we become immediately aware of how distant it is from the closed and neat discourses of the kind that shape textbooks and lectures. Ideas and images seem to come from nowhere faster than we can keep track of them; understanding appears fragmented and partial; moments of insight alternate with feelings of being lost; and, frequently one gets caught in the middle of saying something that, suddenly, means nothing.

Some students, instead of interpreting these disjunctions as a manifestation of how subtle, rich, and complex is our sense-making activity, take them as showing ignorance and incompetence. They do not grasp that books and lectures in closed form result from an intensive struggle to *deny* the fleeting nature of human thinking. Even though there are many very good reasons to pursue such a denial, the permanent exposure to these "models" of good thinking has secondary effects that have been dramatically exacerbated by misuse. One of them is a tendency to deny our own ability to think. Our self-esteem, as beings that are able to make sense of the world around us, drops because knowledgeable discourse seems to be out of reach. Reliance on experts, textbooks—on the O.E.T.—emerges as an inescapable substitute of making sense by ourselves.

Sometimes the difficulties in creating genuine inquiry go beyond the individual participants, because in any relationship there are expectations given by the social context. Brousseau (1986) coined the term *didactical contract* in reference to a series of tacit expectations that guide the classroom behavior. They are written nowhere but they are still there. It may be part of the contract, for example, that the teacher will define what to do, that the students should tell the teacher what they know, that the teacher will determine how well the students are doing, and so forth. Some didactical contracts include expectations that are incompatible with genuine inquiry and, if that is the case, genuine inquiry may happen only as part of a renegotiation of the contract—at least a temporary one. A teacher cannot always renegotiate the contract. Lack of support from the system or lack of tradition may pose serious obstacles. Sometimes the organization of project-enhanced activities opens opportunities for a temporary predominance of an alternative contract.

It is clear then, that there are many possible reasons for the fact that genuine inquiry is unusual in the school practice. I believe that to talk and reflect about genuine inquiry is so important because it is so uncommon. Should genuine inquiry be the only, or permanent, mode of interaction? I do not think so. This reminds me of Peter Sullivan, an Australian researcher in math education who is working on an investigation about the role of open-ended questions in the learning of mathematics. He was reporting many interesting findings and one of his marginal comments was, "after a while the kids got sick of open-ended questions." Learning seems to require all kinds of modes of engagement. Closed questions also have important roles to play. Recipes are often powerful means to get unstuck, or to begin something new. A "guess my mind" attitude may trigger intriguing games. Genuine inquiry is a fundamental way, but not the only way, to help each other to learn.

Among all the modes of engagement for learning, genuine inquiry offers a unique contribution. One that goes beyond the learning of particular aspects of science or mathematics. It helps us to grasp the human dimension of knowledge. By noticing and sharing how we come to understand something, the shallowness of triviality dissipates, letting us to recognize how strange and wonderful is the world around us.

PROJECTS AND EXPERIMENTAL EXPLORATION
John G. King [9]

What is meant by "projects"? It depends on who's talking, because the word describes so many things, from NASA putting a man on the moon, through housing developments, to making a mahogany coffee table in 6 evenings. Projects are meant to be well defined, with a beginning and an end. A better name for what we mean in the context of science teaching would be "experimental exploration," which suggests the mixture of adventure, ambiguity, and uncertainty that is usually so energetically avoided

---

[9] John King is the Francis L. Friedman Professor of Physics at the Massachusetts Institute of Technology. He has a long and distinguished commitment to education at all levels. He was deeply involved in the PSSC physics curriculum development effort. Through the Commission on College Physics, he played the leading role in popularizing the idea of an instrumented project laboratory, which he has implemented at MIT.

in science education and is so prominent in real life. This is not to say that we want chaos in the classroom; we just want each student to undertake some work that is interesting, needs to be invented, and whose result is not known in advance.

It has always pained me that when an English teacher asks a student to write about "my summer vacation," the result, however lame, is a more original product than anything done by most students in their science course. So the message to the student is: Learn what is known as presented in text and class, do the problems, pass the tests, but also try to use that learning (and more, as needed) to answer questions of your own—find or invent a problem or a project turn it into an experimental exploration, or Exp^2 as we'll abbreviate it from now on. Another important aspect of Exp^2 is that it should involve measurements, data, analysis, and written and oral presentation of results. This stress on the quantitative in Exp^2s is vital; we can take as a motto the famous (if reductionist) remark of Lord Kelvin, which can be paraphrased in short form as "show me the numbers; without them you don't know much."

Any educational situation has five elements: students, teachers, subject matter and equipment (or software and hardware), format (matters of schedule and working space). We discuss each of these overlapping elements, interacting as they do in complicated, nonlinear, inconstant ways, as clearly as we can in terms of achieving successful Exp^2s.

Students

Students, like everyone, can be characterized well enough by, say, a few hundred parameters or adjectives starting with noncontroversial things like age, height, weight, physical strength, coordination, and endurance. Then there are more questionable indices like IQ or the MMPI. There are hard to measure but important qualities such as initiative, energy, originality, persistence, intellectual power, memory, ability to communicate, cooperativeness; as well as even more subtle aspects of personality—spirit and soul. The point, of course, is the marvelous and stimulating variety of human beings, each with qualities from some imaginary ensemble of likely bell-shaped distributions; people who should not all be forced all the time into the same science educational Procrustean bed.

As far as doing Exp^2 is concerned, we can imagine our students grouped according to interest in science, skill in dealing with the abstract (including mathematics), and skill in dealing with the concrete (building apparatus and making it work). The rare person who ranks high in all these, and has energy, character, and personality needs only a little guidance and some inspiration and encouragement; otherwise stay out of her way! Less rare are students who are great instinctive fiddlers with gadgets and machines, and, at the opposite extreme, people who never touch them but delight in puzzles, chess, programming.

One of our tasks as teachers is to use Exp^2s to develop skills complementary to those that come naturally. The fiddler will make measurements, analyze them, and draw quantitative conclusions instead of simply hypnotically admiring the apparatus working. The "hands-off" type will learn to solder, drill, assemble, and make it work instead of hovering at a distance, almost proud of his klutziness. Both will learn to present their results as if to the critical audience of a professional meeting, such as they may well face in only a few years. What to do about the many students with seemingly neither aptitude nor liking (or even antipathy) for science? By devising an appropriately tailored Exp^2 based on their interests—at the least they will get an idea of the process and methods of science and at best they may experience an epiphany, often expressed as "this is cool." They will have become experts in a collection of topics relevant to their Exp^2 and that feeling can last a lifetime: "I once did an experiment where I understood everything."

Opposed as we are to coercion, we nonetheless feel that everyone should be required to try an Exp^2. It may not succeed with those who hate or fear science and math, but it'll likely leave them with better memories the ones of all the problems they couldn't do. Just as any responsible parent tries to get the kids to eat "funny, gross" vegetables, any responsible science education program should contain Exp^2s for everyone.

Teachers

Teachers were once students, and most of them were once students of the subject they now teach. Let's hope that they were and are enthusiastic and knowledgeable about it, certainly the basic requirement for effective teaching. How impressive and admirable is the teacher who maintains and develops these qualities year after year in the face of long hours, large classes, administrative hassles, and low pay. What else is needed from the teacher if he or she is to introduce Exp^2? Our answer will show a hardly surprising bias towards physics, but not so bad since most of science and engineering now depend on sensors, electronics, and computers, which in turn are explainable, at least at both the introductory and fundamental levels, by physics.

Now, because Exp^2 involves the quantitative study of some system or situation of interest to the student, which, while starting simply with crude instruments, is likely to become quite sophisticated in order to reveal a degree of detail that needs imagination to explain and to show the next steps in the exploration, the agility and sensitivity of modern data acquisition, processing, and display methods should be exploited. Therefore it is immensely helpful for the teacher to know about sensors, electronics, and computers—how they work and how to make them work.

The teacher's knowledge will grow along with that of the students in Exp^2. Unlike the prototypical situations of the problem with its correct answer, obtained and to be obtained by legions of students, past and future; or of the prepared, "set-piece" experiment where the only variety comes from the occasional equipment failure or a novel adaptation by an ingenious students, Exp^2 is a daring foray along a road not traveled. There will therefore be times when neither teacher nor student knows what's going on or what to do next. Hardly surprising, because ignorance and error are bound to be a part of any genuine exploration. The teacher, usually in control and seemingly omniscient, has much more (and much more varied—see "mulch" later) experience than the student and by working hard and honestly and openly can invariably find a way to go on. Seeing that happen is a valuable lesson, which occurs all the time in Exp^2 but is otherwise rare because we usually hide the gropings and false starts of serious creative or intellectual work in the real world.

Here are random remarks on useful ingredients of Exp^{2}s: Besides the valuable sensors that are part of MBL or PSL, which make it possible to measure temperature, displacement, force, sound pressure, and light intensity, there are many homely low-cost items, some household and some deriving from consumer devices. A glass thermometer is a good way to start experiments with heat and temperature—How does it work? How and why accurate? How fast? How calibrated? Try preliminary experiments before going on to the resistance thermometers, thermocouples, thermistors, which may be convenient and appropriate. Besides professional humidity sensors, there is the human hair, or could one arrange a color-sensitive photo-electric way of reading the change with humidity from blue to pink of cobalt chloride? That sounds like an Exp^2 in itself.

If you can stand the friction, a 10-turn potentiometer is an OK displacement measuring device with pulleys and string attached to, for instance, a float to monitor water level in a well or reservoir. A speeding cyclist can unwind line from a fishing reel whose clicking ratchet reveals speed, with correction for changes in diameter of the wound-up line and the drag. The permanent-magnet DC motor is a good speed sensor (and actuator), and then there are items of consumer electronics, low-cost microphones, the no-longer-commonplace stereo phono cartridge as a sensor of vibrations, the microphone and loudspeaker as reversible transducers, the latter a basis for a seismometer. There are LEDs and photodiodes and, since the CD, lasers in cheap profusion. Audio equipment is also everywhere—one can drive two-phase AC motors at variable speed with an oscillator and a stereo power amplifier, and there is the transistor portable: cheap amplification for modulated signals at 1 and 100 Mhz. This only scratches the surface of the vast lode of either cheap or scroungeable stuff adaptable to Exp^2; whenever in a hardware, junkyard, electronics store, we try to find the leisure to examine every item—it takes a few hours—and ask ourselves: How could we use this in some future Exp^2?

Knowing some electronics greatly extends the range of Exp^2 beyond the prepared stuff and can also teach generalizable troubleshooting skill, which is partly an extension of the childhood game of finding "What's Wrong With This Picture." There is a mosaic of complementary ways of learning electronics: formal courses, assembling kits of progressive complexity, and studying books. Among the wonderful and useful books we have found are *The Radio Amateur's Handbook* (ARRL, Hartford CT), the collected pamphlets on electronics by Forrest Mims III (available from Radio Shack), and *The Art of Electronics*, by Horowitz and Hill (McGraw Hill). Communications and elements, valuable and simple gizmos, and the full professional treatment in readable form; they complement each other beautifully. Most important, never do anything electronic without using an oscilloscope to observe the progress of signals in any device; only in this way will you develop insight into how things work. The goal is to be able to match sensors and transducers, condition and amplify signals, minimize hum, noise and distortion, and calibrate or otherwise characterize the entire system.

Then there are computers. Despite their advantages of speed, up-to-date, hi-tech feel, and the satisfying sense of control they give, we don't all agree on what their role should be in Exp^2. There can be no doubt that everyone should have first-hand experience of everything to do with computers, including the essentials of how they work, some programming experience, familiarity with a large repertoire of standard programs and applications, and data handling and simulation. Everyone should appreciate the dazzling increases in productivity and precision that computers have brought to such diverse areas as word processing, accounting, airline reservations, aeronautical engineering, design and drafting, weather. . .

Now Exp^2 gives students a chance to report on their work, orally and in writing; but important as this is it's not central. With rare exceptions, computers should not be central either, because at the heart of Exp^2 is direct contact with things and phenomena that at the beginning at least can be completely understood. The goal is to find out and understand with the least amount of prearranged special purpose instrumentation, programs, and so forth. Computer-assisted instruction and simulation and even MBL all do good things in teaching all sorts of material, but the kind of exploration possible with them doesn't have the freedom, detail, degrees of freedom that some of us think is essential.

Consider a neatly packaged thermistor appropriately interfaced and calibrated so as to show the temperature of some object as a function of time. It is dazzling, particularly to the older generation of teachers, and the student can learn about and explore heating and cooling. But he should take some curves by hand, and be aware of the response time of the thermometer, so that if he wants to measure temperature rises with millisecond resolution he might choose a themocouple made of thin wire, or a thin film resistance thermometer. Making these, and arranging amplification for the small voltages involved, and figuring out how to display them is all a vital part of the Exp^2, so the student really knows what she's talking about rather than reporting on things she couldn't afford or build and doesn't understand.

So we are arguing that in this example the student should not only learn about energy content and flow in cooling and the differential equation and exponentials that describe it, but also about temperature measurement, and if it's thermocouples, make them and learn something about electrons in metals, and build amplifiers, and learn how an FET amplifies, and electrons moving in vacuum, and the CRT, and fluorescence, TV, and so on. Nothing on the lab table should escape scrutiny and dissection and discussion. This is the way to avoid passive learning, good for narrow cogs in the machine. We may succeed only with a few but everyone must be given the opportunity; hence our radical belief in compulsory Exp^2!

Finally, there's a problem that parallels that with pocket calculators, namely the idea that without it nothing can be done, no mental arithmetic, no long division. We shouldn't give the idea that you have to have a PC with AD conversion to experiment.

So introduce computers with care and use them sparingly. If we were in a society full of students with the sort of miscellaneous hands-on background that one romantically imagines was acquired on the farm from seeing and helping with fixing the fence, the motor, the carb, the pump, the well, the leaning shed, the separator, the baler, and all that, we'd be pushing simulation and theory, even though there would still be no substitute for hands-on fooling with the real stuff. Our students would simply not be so pathetically deficient in that kind of experience.

Teachers might say: How can I invent projects? Here are some remarks that may be helpful: Exp^{2}s need not be on grand topics, like looking for the top quark. Looking at the most insignificant phenomenon invariably requires every kind of skill as one expands and deepens the investigation. Everything has properties—mechanical, electrical, optical, for instance. Take peeling paint; what is paint? How does it stick? How strong and abrasion-resistant is it and why? What makes the color and the gloss? How good an insulator, thermal and electric is it? Devise ways of measuring these properties. Keep on observing, searching, noticing things and situations that might be the start of Exp^2, perhaps write them down, but avoid working them out too much in advance, or they'll lose the freshness that is so essential.

Naturally, one will present old topics of Exp^2 as examples of what's possible. Miscellaneous knowledge of all kinds, often unrelated and no item of which is especially important or essential, is, in aggregate extremely valuable in guiding Exp^2; we call this "mulch," in analogy with the heterogeneous organic matter from which flowers grow. Another name might be "a thousand trivia," remarkably valuable all together and part of what makes it possible to know one's ear from his elbow. It is certainly impressive how the mind can learn to combine disparate elements to produce a novel approach to an Exp^2; somewhat as the stand-up comedian learns, with experience, to break away from memorized jokes to improvisation suited to the audience.

Besides the three sources of information about electronics just mentioned, it is helpful to have files of periodicals, The *American Journal of Physics* (and its resource letters), *The Physics Teacher, Scientific American, Science Probe,* to name a few; specialized professional journals can be sources of ideas, such as for the paint Exp^2 above. Handbooks, catalogs, encyclopedias, apparatus, and device data sheets are valuable and should be accumulated so that student and teacher can look things up. A lot of looking up goes on in Exp^2, and if you do your homework and have tried to find out on your own, experts are almost touchingly helpful in explaining aspects of their field to the serious neophyte. There is another way of looking at this question of finding Exp^2 topics. You can imagine a range of student interests: future career, sports, arts and music, hobbies. Invent Exp^2s for each category, thus:

- Lawyer—evidence, how fingerprints work, ballistics, forensic science generally.

- Accountant—a tough one. Try to relate balance sheet to properties of the product.

- Undertaker—heat energy to reduce cadaver to ash—macabre, but not more so than most murder mysteries. Think of Holmes sticking a pig carcass with a harpoon.

- Tennis—properties of ball, racket, stringing.

- Baseball—same as above, ball, bat, impact, sound, range.

- Music—How do musical instruments work? mouthpiece, air flow, aeolian tones, vibrating walls, strings, rosin, stick-slip, normal modes, spectra, Helmholtz and Sensations of Tone, etc.

Hobbies should be easy because they are full of discrimination associated with collecting or modeling; how can these judgments be quantified through measurement? Much earlier in this article we divided the discussion of Exp^2 into parts, and this long section on what teachers might do has actually defined much of the nature of Exp^2 and described how one does it. Still, there's more, and we will discuss it under the plonky title of:

Subject Matter and Equipment

Subject matter and equipment can be just about anything, but are divisible into four categories: instruments, dominated by electronics, which should include parts, power supplies, an audio or function generator, a CRO, various transducers from the world of consumer electronics, and last, lots of clip leads; materials, meaning rolls of wire, tubes and bars, wood, plastic, metal, glue, solvent and solder, and so on; tools of any and every kind; and unclassifiable "junk" adaptable by the ingenious to their ends. So much for the equipment, a somewhat disorderly but rich collection to be frowned on by the anal compulsive. But what about subject matter? That can be almost anything that leads to quantitative investigation with progress to levels of ever greater detail and sophistication, exciting to the student, his or her property, memorable for life: "I once studied the properties of paint in great detail—knew all about it, or nearly—had a ball." How to get that sort of Exp^2 going? I'll describe our way as we did it at MIT. There, most of the students signing up for 8.11, Physics Project Lab, didn't know each other, and because we wanted them to work in partnerships of two we paired them on the basis of a questionnaire about interests, goals, and hobbies. Partnerships are easier for us and often good for them: an introduction to collaboration (most of our students are academic loners—"this is my work, keep out!"), sharing, support, someone to argue with. Less satisfactory are the too frequent active–passive pairs.

We schedule interviews with the partners to choose the Exp^2 or project. Sometimes a student has a highly specific, more or less feasible idea, often the result of high school experience or a summer job. If it is at all feasible we try to start: "calibrate the photomultiplier," which sometimes takes a while and is powerfully instructive; the sort of thing taken for granted in many an account of an experiment. If the proposed experiment doesn't seem feasible, or if the students make no proposal, we ask them about their interests and try to suggest related work that they might find interesting, in the way that we described earlier. Sometimes, we say, "you could work on mechanical, electrical, acoustical or optical experiments, or on experiments with electrons, ions, and atoms in vacuum" (this last when we had access to "solder glass techniques," now lost to us). Sometimes, we have had to give three examples of each to a still-wavering, indecisive pair; examples that start simple, but can fast become very subtle. We try to avoid Exp^2s that take all term to build, leaving no time for data taking, and further cycles of improvement, and those that are intrinsically without quantitative handles. But rather than go on with generalities, I'd like to describe very briefly four actual Exp^2s from the past, which show the characteristics that we think are desirable. We conclude with a rather cryptic list of recent Exp^2s.

- A coin, spinning on its edge about a diameter goes through various characteristic motions as it slows down: precession, nutation, chattering. Various students have studied this in various ways, recording and analyzing the sound, close visual observation, high-speed photography, making larger and therefore slower models. Collectively, they're getting close.

- Fencers have a panel on their tunics with a switch that lights a light at the instant of "touché." An ardent fencer was led into a rather detailed study of switch action with all the things that happen as closing is approached: fields grow, arcs form, and electrons, ions, atoms, and light get to play.

- How is sound generated in a brass instrument? An enthusiastic player of the Sousaphone prepared an artificial mouth, which made the mouthpiece function while making it possible to measure pressures, flows, and sound spectra. We then observed the interaction of this system with both cylindrical tubes and the large brass part of the instrument. Things got too complicated for a term's work, not surprising since many have made life works of understanding the more subtle and delicate violin.

- Incandescent bulbs, represented by #47 pilot bulbs, were found to have a mean life of 30 seconds when operated at 16 volts, more than twice the rated voltage, in an Exp^2 by two future architects who were led to admit that, yes, lighting would be important in their jobs. They also studied the dependence of life time on current and modeled the results theoretically (with much help) with the idea that constant current would heat a smaller diameter region of the filament with higher resistance to a higher temperature limited by radiation, at which temperature the filament would evaporate faster, get hotter, thinner, etc. This work was done with only an adjustable power supply, meters, a stopwatch, and a $10 supply of bulbs. With more time one could use a CRO to look at the details of current and voltage variations near the instant of burn-out.

Format

This is important to the success of Exp^2. Ideally 1 day a week in the senior year should be set aside for work on Exp^2. This is not something that can be fit into free moments in a crowded schedule. It needs sustained attention. At MIT, we ask for one 5-hour afternoon a week and usually can get it; we also allow 6 hours for thinking about the work, going to the library, asking and looking around, time which is too often used on pressing and explicit tasks such as homework. But the time must be provided. Space is also needed, in that not only must there be room for instruments, stock, and junk, but also space for the students' experiments to be set up and left undisturbed from week to week. All this is a tall order to administrators who want to see efficient use of space, a sort of educational warm-bunk system.

This raises the question: Is it worthwhile? The only answer is that a generation of reasonably smart MIT students, now graduates, and their teachers think so. Answers to not-very-systematic questionnaires show that 10% of the 3,000 students who have passed through Project Lab had a terrific, memorable experience, 10% were disappointed, and the rest are in between; but it's safe to say that they all got some experience and some expertise certain to be woven into their later careers.

Table 7.1 gives a sample of Exp²s in the MIT project laboratory

TABLE 7.1
List of Recent Exp²s in the MIT Project Laboratory

The Stefan-Boltzman Law of Thermal Radiation. (How "black" is an ordinary light bulb?)

Microwaves and their applications in Radar. (Measuring velocity by Doppler Shift)

Effects of induced vorticity in a cylindrical system. (Parameters affecting flow of water out of a vessel)

The Photoacoustic Effect. (In 1881 Bell noticed that pulses of light striking a surface produced sound...)

Solar spectroscopy. (Measuring the rotational velocity of sun by Doppler-shifted Frauenhofer Lines)

Characteristics of the tones of the French horn and the Saxophone. (Harmonic content of notes, Fourrier Analysis)

Building a dye laser.

Diffraction of light by ultrasonic waves.

Transmission and reflection holography.

Oscillation of a water column in a U-shaped tube.

A look at Feynman's inverse water sprinkler.

The study of brown light.

A laser spy device. (More Doppler shift?)

Measurement of the Universal Gravitational Constant.

Diffraction patterns of waves and particles of light. (Can one make a perfect slit?)

Determination of soap film thickness by interference of light.

Speed of light. (Rotating mirror method)

Frustrated total internal reflection of electromagnetic waves. (Tunneling of light)

A study of the acoustical properties of the clarinet.

Diffraction of light by ultrasonic waves in water.

Nuclear magnetic resonance.

Optimization of an electromagnetic propulsion system.

Velocity of sound in Silicon crystal.

Laser-based eavesdropping.

Some Personal Vignettes

I grew up in various parts of the United States and Europe, often in hotels and sometimes on a farm. I collected junk. It seemed interesting, and I tried to build things, at first simulations, like a radio with strings for wires and later getting into the AC line. I eventually built a carbon arc using #6 dry cell anodes and a barrel of water as a ballast. I hooked in ahead of the meter and fuses and eventually popped the fuse in the pole pig, to everyone's delight. There were many less dangerous experiments, which included trying everything I could think of with transformers, including oil burner ignition; radio power and filament; and the famous model-T ignition coil. But I had no meters, although how I tried to get one! I even made galvanometers following nineteenth-century steel engravings in old books from the local library. They sort of worked and made me appreciate the cheap Simpson multimeter (in a red bakelite case, 1,000 ohms/volt) that I eventually bought.

Because my adult mentors were can-do mechanics, deeply nonelectrical, I did not have any guidance beyond Audel's Guides and other books also in the library. I remember spending many summer hours in a barn, wedging sticks in the pulley set-screw hole of a 1/4-horse motor nailed to a horizontal timber. Starting the motor sent the stick flying through the air, sometimes in a gratifyingly large trajectory, sometimes just hitting the ground nearby. There was a phase with explosives, and then automobiles. Finally, some discipline appeared when I came under the influence of the late Bert Little, who guided me and Fred Richards, both age 16, in building a Cavendish experiment. The major event was collecting old lead pipe and casting two 100-pound spheres in plaster-of-Paris molds formed around an 8-inch float and backed up with sand. An unwound guitar string provided an excellent cold-worked bronze torsion fiber. This should be enough to give an idea of where I'm coming from in this Exp^2 business.

8 AGENDA FOR AN UNCERTAIN FUTURE

Richard Ruopp

It is fitting that this book should conclude with as many questions as answers, because that is how good science projects always end.

In this chapter, Dick Ruopp brings together the book's three themes— the community of practice, telecomputing, and projects—in a set of action and research recommendations. His broadest and most fundamental recommendation urges teachers to take responsibility for building their own community of practice and shaping their own professional development. Further recommendations are directed at NSF, which has a critical role to play in shaping a national policy to improve science education.

NSF, he proposes, should support the development of a national science network serving Grades K–12. As a first step, NSF should, through a conference or other means, marshal the extensive knowledge of network design that is already available from numerous demonstration projects, including LabNet itself. The agency should then fund targeted experiments to fill important gaps in current knowledge.

With regard to project-enhanced science learning (PESL), he sees two missions for NSF: first, promoting PESL's use on a provisional basis, and second, funding research to evaluate its effectiveness. To encourage leadership on the part of teachers, he proposes a small grants program modeled after LabNet's highly successful Big Idea Grants. And he suggests that NSF must undertake the difficult task of finding ways for teachers and scientists to work together. To this end, he concludes with a framework for dialogue between the two groups, on what makes a project good science and good teaching.

INTRODUCTION

Will a community of practice grow and flourish among high school physics teachers, extend in time to other high school sciences, perhaps eventually reach those who teach science in elementary schools? Will networks—or better still a nationwide network like Internet—become the principal medium for teachers to talk to each other about their work, thereby supporting the growth of a national community of practice? Will student-selected and student-initiated projects spread and become the principal *leitmotif* for reshaping physics learning?

In summary, will a community of science teachers, dedicated to project-enhanced science learning (PESL), and sharing their craft via computers hooked to phone lines (telecomputing), excite more students to take physics and increase both the number of scientists and science-literate citizens? We wish we could say that the unqualified answer to each of these questions is "yes." Both by conviction and the incomplete but compelling evidence from the LabNet experience, we think that these three elements properly integrated—community of practice, telecomputing, projects—could be a powerful force for the reform of science education. But gazing into the crystal ball and predicting the direction of reform is an uncertain business at best. There is no historic precedent for a long-term, sustained, coherent, national effort to improve science (and mathematics) education.

Rather than a crystal ball, the more apt image is one of those Christmas glass balls you shake to make a blizzard. In this country the winds of educational change blow from all directions and often vision is obscured. Even when there is (at least superficial) agreement on a problem—such as falling test scores, low test scores when compared to those of other countries, fewer students taking science courses, fewer teachers preparing for science teaching—proposed solutions come from every ideological quarter, and often are diametrically opposed. Requiring more hours and days of class time, more rigorous standards, more sanctions for failure—are light-years away from attempts to engage students so that they spend more time doing school work because they want to, teaching them to tackle important questions and problems on their own initiative, helping them to see failure as an avenue to enlightenment.

This multiplicity of views of what's wrong with the schools, and competing prescriptions of how to fix them, is both the zenith and nadir of educational reform. It means continuing concern and debate. It also means endless controversy and internecine conflict. New solutions have short lives as they are displaced by contending remedies. One generation of parents may join the fray and influence new practices, but then they are gone and a new cohort has to learn the issues all over again. This is also true of school boards, teachers, and other educational professionals.

To date, no stable view of the learner and the learning process has emerged. Physics can adopt indisputably the theory of relativity. The findings of medicine coupled with techniques of Madison Avenue can decisively change smoking habits. Satellite photography can chart beyond question areas of drought and the destruction of rain forests and the traces of ancient civilizations. But what has been established about how children develop and learn is not widely understood, when known not necessarily believed, and is not now generally implemented in either public or private education (or for that matter, in the home).

And this is the nub of the issue of intentional change in education. Curriculum reform, teacher-training initiatives, reconstruction of the system to revalue the authority and role of the teacher, setting national standards, and new assessment efforts—will never be enough by themselves to fix what is wrong. For any meaningful and durable reform there must be a clearer understanding of, and more unified agreement about, who the child is and how the child learns. There must be a much better forecasting of what knowledge, skills, and attitudes the young will need to lead productive lives in their future. And there must be a much more decisive commitment to planning and action that span decades, with the concomitant allocation of necessary resources. All of these steps require wide cooperation, deep and careful thought, and a profound change in the politics of perception. Will this kind of reform happen? It is difficult to see how. But that makes it no less necessary if our children are ever to be in fact our principal national resource for the future.

Against this backdrop, what we of the LabNet staff have to say about agenda setting for the future must necessarily be modest. The LabNet project itself was a modest, although we believe seminal, effort. It was not a policy study but a demonstration—although it has policy implications. It is always tempting in the debate about improving education to be expansive. We have resisted that temptation and reduced our recommended agenda for an uncertain future to three items:

- **We think science teachers can and should take an active leadership role in building a community of practice**: They can effectively nourish both their own professional development and the growth of the community. And we believe it's critical that they do so.

- **We think the National Science Foundation has a crucial role to play with regard to telecomputing**: It should forcefully move to create a nationwide telecomputing capacity to serve teachers and students in both secondary and elementary schools. As a first step, NSF should fund an effort to collate the knowledge of system design that has already been amassed in demonstration projects. The agency should then fund "design experiments" as necessary to fill important gaps in existing knowledge.

- **We think NSF has a dual role to play with regard to project-enhanced science learning**: It should provisionally encourage implementation of the project approach. Specifically, it should launch a small grants program to enable teachers to disseminate the PESL philosophy and project ideas; and it should explore ways of bringing scientists and teachers together. And it should, at the same time, fund careful research on the immediate and long-term impact of projects on students' learning.

NOURISHING THE COMMUNITY OF PRACTICE

A community of practice is a set of concentric circles of affinity. At the center are the members most closely related in work, time, and space—for example, high school physics teachers in the same district. Let's say there are five of them. Their daily work is very similar, so they have a lot to say to each other. They can talk on the phone at essentially no cost. They can easily get together on a regular basis if they so choose. They can visit each other's classes. They can collaborate, and arrange for their students to work together. They know the local politics of education, parental expectations, resource constraints.

This is the highest level of association possible among working professionals—immediate and contextually similar. And there is no substitute for such direct work-peer contacts. Only active teachers know and understand what other teachers face each day. It is not enough to have been a teacher. It is not enough to be steeped in the literature of teaching. Teaching is a dynamic craft and art that must continually adapt to changing conditions over time. This is one of the core reasons why top-down efforts to improve education so often fail—there are rarely working teachers on both sides of the seesaw.

In the next circle are other physics teachers in the state, which is a decisive boundary in terms of curriculum used and performance measures applied. At this level, while the work is still similar, talking about it is more difficult. Phone calls now cost. Collaboration is harder to arrange, particularly among students. Local educational politics can vary a good deal from city to suburb to country. Face-to-face contact is more limited, perhaps to quarterly regional meetings and annual statewide meetings, which usually include other agendas that crosscut the boundaries of like practice.

At the regional and national level we are now quite distant from the center. Person-to-person conversation is rare, except among inveterate conference goers, and even for them the breadth of contact is perforce limited. But in this broad and encompassing domain there are vast potential riches of knowledge about substance and pedagogy that could be mined. It is in these more distant circles of affinity that network communication can be a powerful bridge to that wealth.

The Community As It Is

There is not now a national community of practice for teachers of physics, and such a community is rare at the state and local level. It is safe to say that few districts have more than one or two—certainly not five—physics teachers—there are 15,367 public school districts and only some 8,000 high school teachers of physics (in both public and private schools).[1] Simple arithmetic suggests that the documented isolation of physics teachers from colleagues who do the same work must be widespread. Permanent

---

[1] Personal communication with the Department of Education, Office of Educational Research and Improvement, Statistics Center: district data 1992; physics teachers estimated from 1987-1988 elementary and secondary surveys.

organizations like AAPT, and temporary ones like Woodrow Wilson fellows, PTRA, and LabNet, provide limited collegial opportunities for those who have learned to seize them, but this is a smallish subset of those who teach physics and physical science. The same can be said of state-level associations, and of local alliances among high school teachers of physics, biology, and chemistry (where they are not the same person), which serve some of the purposes that talking to work counterparts provide.

The Community As It Could Be

The LabNet experience has given us a glimpse of a very different possible future: A small national group of reform-minded teachers—using telecomputing as a medium for discourse, and project science as both a means and a metaphor for exploring science learning as it should be—has formed a meaningful community of practice. This statement is subject to several caveats. The LabNet participants were a self-selected vanguard. Even so, their understanding of and commitment to reform varied a good deal. Also, telecomputing is in its infancy, and though promising, is still beset with many problems ranging from cost to ease of use. And projects do motivate and inspire students, but they are more demanding of teachers (and students) and have yet to fully "prove" their worth.

Nonetheless, something important has happened. Through their interaction with each other at workshops and on the network, a significant number of LabNet teachers who did not use projects before now use them. And as the questionnaire results in chapter 3 and the teacher essays and student postscripts in chapter 6 attest, this change in practice has made a difference to students. Based on LabNet's experience, what are the key traits of the model of a community of practice we espouse?

First, it is self-generating and self-sustaining. Although the initial impetus may have come from the LabNet staff, we now see teachers supporting each other, teachers taking leadership roles. Surely these are the most important characteristics if there is to be permanent and durable change in science teaching and learning—not top-down change, but "shifting" that proceeds from the inside-out.

Second, it is a community committed to reform. This is not a necessary or universal characteristic of professional groups. Formal professional associations can be quite conservative, especially if they are self-regulating, like the American Bar Association or the AMA. And we know that high school physics teachers run the gamut of points of view about what works in education. But there are two significant differences between the science-teaching profession and other disciplines. Teaching is ultimately about learning, and learning is about change and growth. And science is ultimately about exploring the unknown. Thus, the profession has an inherent forward motion that can only be accelerated by the failure of the current textbook-lecture-lab approach.

Third, it is a community that includes educational researchers and innovators. A compelling case can be made that an outside party like TERC is necessary not only to provide the initial stimulus but also to play an ongoing role as a source of information, perhaps a gadfly to insure sufficient reflection and, most important, a pipeline to new innovations. There are important discoveries in the learning sciences on the one hand, and powerful and useful learning technologies like telecomputing and MBL on the other, that emerge in research and development settings, such as universities or specialized institutions like TERC.

Because teachers' central task is teaching, they are rarely in a position to know about these developments, nor do they have time to evaluate them independently. But through the community participation of researcher-developers, teachers can become aware of new opportunities that are directly applicable to their teaching craft.

Finally, it is a community of equals. The LabNet experience has decisively demonstrated to us the value of a collaboration in which the contributions of the partners are seen as equal. "You know about teaching physics. I know about developments that support the use of projects to enhance science learning, and about networks and MBLs as powerful tools. Let's get together and see what new syntheses we can forge that will inform both practice and further research and development. I'll respect and listen to your expertise. You do the same for mine."

It is a delicate balance: If academic and policy agencies assume, or are allowed to assume, the role of "expert" with teachers as the recipients of the "expertise," the dynamics of real reform are put in jeopardy. Teachers are on the front line, experts are not. The situation is perfectly analogous to students being passive recipients of teachers-as-authorities. They may do well on tests, but can they think and act for themselves?

In summary, the community of practice must take the responsibility to create, re-create, and sustain itself over the long run—inviting in and welcoming collaborators as they are needed. Who better to be the *agents provocateurs* of change than teachers themselves? This is a pretty heady vision: teachers reclaiming the ancient role of determining what gets taught and how it gets taught—and regaining the respect for the profession that seems to have dwindled and almost disappeared.

The Big Idea Grants (BIG) are a powerful case in point. LabNet teacher-leaders reached more new teachers in 1 year than the project staff had in the previous two. And the response to the BIG workshops, all of which featured projects as a component, was startling in the uniform enthusiasm of participants (see chapter 4). The grants were highly cost-effective in themselves and also levered a considerable amount of local resources and support.

The Need for Support

A community engaged in science-education reform, although autonomous and self-sustaining, cannot be effective without external support. Support is most important at the local level: in the school building, in the district offices and at the school board; in state education agencies and the governor's office; and most especially in the colleges and teacher-training institutions that are the seedbed for the next generation of community members. It is these local factors that set up the real dynamics of receptivity—or resistance—to change. The evidence is clear from LabNet that teachers are capable of winning support for project-enhanced science learning from recalcitrant principals, doubting parents, and dubious school-board members, and from local college and university folk.

But local support, although critical, will not be enough to address the current national crisis—a crisis that has foolishly been simplified to a matter of test-score failures at home and abroad. If it were that simple, then simple-minded remedies could be invoked. But it's not. Students who do very well on tests often don't understand the dynamics of phenomena, don't understand how to think about a problem in science, have no intuitive feel for how to search for proximate solutions (see the foreword). There is an important role to be played by the federal government in addressing this crisis. In the instance of science education, the National Science Foundation (NSF) has the responsibility for that role.

NSF's Critical Role

NSF mostly got out of the business of supporting science education for secondary and elementary education in 1975, when controversy erupted over its elementary social studies curriculum *Man: A Course of Study*. (See chapter 2, "PSSC...and its Progeny"; also Dow, 1991.) The agency has only re-entered this important sector of work since 1987. We believe that NSF is now uniquely positioned to contribute to precollege science education. Consider just one telling example:

It is a truism that science education should begin in the earliest grades; the later part of the high school years is too long to wait. Despite lip service, little has been done to implement this notion, especially in the early elementary years. This is unfortunate. Young children are particularly receptive to activities that explore the physical world. The early years are the time when an experiential foundation can be laid that would well serve later, more formal, explorations. Yet teachers of younger children typically have little or no science education in their own background, and little or no training in how to engage children in the questions of science.

But this does not mean that much can't be done, or that teachers are not willing. A quite stunning case-in-point is the National Geographic Society (NGS) Kids Network. NSF funded TERC to develop a network-based science program for Grades 4–6. NGS joined the enterprise as TERC's publishing partner. The first units were distributed in the fall of 1988. By the end of the 1991-1992 school year, on the order of 190,000 students in almost 8,000 elementary schools in all 50 states had collected and shared data via a network with 12 to 15 other schools grouped in small research clusters around the country. They worked on units like: Acid Rain, Weather in Action, What's in Our Water?, What are We Eating?, Too Much Trash? And this was a supplemental curriculum, not mandated or even listed by state departments of education. Furthermore, beyond the rapid spread in the United States, 27 other countries have participated in one or more of the units.

The dramatic success of this project demonstrates the enormous potential benefits of a carefully targeted investment in early science education. And it foreshadows one of the most important ways in which NSF can contribute to the improvement of precollege science teaching: funding the development of a national telecomputing network to serve teachers and students in Grades K–12.

NSF is the only agency capable of marshaling the resources and talent necessary to accomplish this task and provide the communications infrastructure for a community of practice. NSF is also the only agency with the intellectual authority to take the lead in promoting project-enhanced science learning, and bringing scientists and teachers together. In the next two sections, we make the case for NSF's taking on these two critical tasks.

CREATING A WORKING K–12 SCIENCE TELECOMPUTING NETWORK

In addition to NGS Kids Network, other experiments and demonstrations offer a wealth of experience on which to build; but no existing network comes close to fulfilling the requirements for a national network to serve high school science teachers.

Project-oriented telecomputing efforts like the Quill project (Bruce & Rubin, 1992), TERC's various efforts like the Star Schools project, the Kids Network, the LabNetwork, the Global Lab network—or more general networks like K-12Net, FrEdMail, PSINet—have paved the way for broader and deeper exploitation of the telecomputing medium for science teachers and their students. But efforts have been sporadic and uncoordinated.

Like the telephone system in its early days, a number of different systems exist (more than 100), both private (e.g., CompuServe, Prodigy, GEnie, America Online, AppleLink, Delphi) and public (e.g., BITNET, NSFNET, NEARnet, UUNet). Some can connect with each other, others can't. Some are sophisticated and quite easy to use, others provide only basic text transfer and are used with difficulty. Some are costly and some quite inexpensive.

Perhaps the most useful model of coordination of networks for wide-spread access is Internet (see the glossary at the end of chapter 1). It ties together more than 5,000 networks in some 107 countries primarily in the service of the university and research communities. Recently, the Virginia Public Education Network (VA.PEN) has set about making access to Internet part of a statewide educational network available to all teachers (Bull, Harris, & Cothern, 1992). A newer similar effort is taking place in Texas (Stout, 1992). These state-level efforts are demonstrations of particular importance, given the political boundaries of education.

However, except for a few experimental demonstrations like LabNet, no nationwide telecomputing network has yet been designed or redesigned with the high school or elementary school science-teaching community of practice specifically in mind. We believe such a network could contribute materially to the improvement of science learning. It is time for NSF to address this situation. And it is in the process of doing so through its participation in the development of the National Research and Education Network (NREN):

> The vision of...NREN is of an interconnection of the nation's educational infrastructure to its knowledge and information centers. In this system, elementary schools, high schools, two- and four-year colleges will be linked with research centers and laboratories... (OSTP, 1991, pp. 18-19)

Beverly Hunter (1992) of NSF described the potential of a national network to be a vehicle for education reform. The time table? "A reasonable goal is to have in place by 1995 the intellectual, technological, educational, and organizational foundation necessary for productive and efficient use of computer-communications networks for education on a nationwide scale" (p. 31). Assuming this schedule is correct, and in the usual scheme of things it's probably optimistic, there is only a short time to do a lot of important work.

The Challenge

We have asserted that telecomputing has certain characteristics that make it the communications medium of choice for supporting the high school (and elementary) science-teaching community (and also students engaged in projects—although we see this as a secondary, though not unimportant, priority at this time). To reiterate the key points, telecomputing:

- **Is fast**—but unlike the telephone, more like the mail, permits a delayed response. This is obviously of great importance to teachers with demanding schedules.

- **Is inclusive**—whereas the mail function tends to be person-to-person, a forum can include many voices and a wide range of points of view.

- **Is self-recording and reusable**—unlike a phone call or a fax or a piece of mail—an electronic message can be saved, edited, and re-used as needed. A project suggested today can be distributed to a class tomorrow.

- **Is ubiquitous**—wherever there's a computer hooked to a modem, immediate contact can take place: the school office, the classroom, the teacher's (or student's) home.

- **Is neutral**—the medium is not the message. In the telecomputing piazza, discussion can be about anything. The content comes from the user.

- **Is self-regulating**—leaving aside bad taste and criminal activities, telecomputing is self-regulating. Poor questions or trivial answers on a forum will be ignored (or chastised in the privacy of personal mail).

- **Is egalitarian**—unless a hierarchy is set up, the structure on a net-work is horizontal. Users react more to the content of a message than the status or location of the sender.

There are three kinds of issues that must be addressed if a *working* national network in support of science education is to be achieved. The first two deal fundamentally with ease of use and access: The telecomputing technology needs to be improved and the cost to the local school has to come down, or be borne by the public (as in Virginia and Texas). For example, the TERC Alice project is creating both user and host software that will make possible easy transmission of text, data, and graphics from different computers over virtually any network that makes use of it (Parker, 1992). Costs will come down as demand rises and the public benefit is established.

The third issue is much more substantive: What message on this medium will make a difference to working teachers? Solving the problems of ease of use and cost by themselves won't guarantee that the community of practice will be strengthened or that science learning will be improved. Having the ability to easily transmit and receive information won't ensure its utility. Reduced costs may not correlate with increased value. It is precisely the intellectual content on a network and its utility for the daily needs of the working teacher that is at issue. Being able to tap the information sources of the nation is meaningless unless that information is in a form that can be used. We know something about what's important to teachers of physics from LabNet, and a bit more from the literature detailing other projects. We need to know much more if we are to specify accurately the human dimensions of a working K–12 science-telecomputing network.

It is very important not to let technological capacity determine the future of telecomputing in schools. Telecomputing is a tool, nothing more.

There now has been enough experience to derive a good deal of knowledge to inform both practice and further action research. It is appropriate for NSF to act in two areas.

Collating What We Know

It would be timely to assemble a compendium of what has been learned about the human factors operative in telecomputing. There is now a fair amount of literature on the subject that could be organized and plumbed both for meta-insights and yet-to-be-answered questions. Perhaps a conference on "Assessing the State of the Art of Telecomputing" could be used as a mechanism for rapidly drawing together needed information. What in fact inhibits or ensures the success of a network? What are the clues that could keep an expanding national science network from becoming a modern-day Tower of Babel? Do we already know how to organize a network in support of science improvement so that it doesn't fall prey to a new kind of education bureaucracy? These and other pertinent questions should organize our way of looking at what we know in the service of improving practice.

Implementing Design Experiments

There are things we may not know yet from the literature. For example, if we want to build and test an on-line database of project ideas, how can it be done most effectively? What taxonomy should be employed? How can users contribute a running commentary of their experience? How much management is required? Can it be done by volunteers? The assumption is universally held that access to information will lead to good things. This assumption needs to be tested.

There are many design experiments of this kind that could profitably be carried out. What kind of "training" best prepares teachers for telecomputing? How can teacher-training institutions be made active collaborators in building a national network? The Virginia PEN is organized regionally—is this an advantageous arrangement? Is it transportable? Does giving teachers access to telecomputing from their homes fuel more rapid development of the community of practice? What are the best ways of incorporating working scientists and others from allied professions on a network? (TERC's experience in this matter is far from clear.) As an alternative or addition, could college science students be effectively utilized as "telecomputing aides"? How do you effectively organize a network with thousands of users to serve local needs? What is the best way of keeping alive and making easily accessible many topic threads on a forum? How can students doing projects be integrated on a network without adding heavy administrative layers or excessive "volunteer" teacher time?

Again, a design conference to lay out an action research agenda, tied to developments like NREN, could be a powerful way to narrow attention to the most crucial questions.

PESL: NSF Support, Research and Collaboration

Supporting PESL

It can be fairly said that NSF has a long history of supporting both proto-project and project enhancement of science learning. Certainly the PSSC curriculum dating from the late 1950s would fall in the former category. TERC efforts like the NGS Kids Network, LabNet, and Global Lab would fall in the latter. Although more research needs to be done to establish the value of project-enhanced science learning (discussed later), there is enough compelling anecdotal data (Kids Network, LabNet) and some analytic evidence (Shymansky, Hedges, & Woodworth, 1990), and no serious contraindication, to suggest that NSF should stay the course of actively supporting PESL-centered projects and activities. Among the many efforts that could expand the use of PESL, there are five we think could successfully promote project use and at the same time be design experiments in their own right:

1. One LabNet activity stands out as being particularly effective and at the same time quite low in overhead costs, because most of the administration was done on the LabNetwork. The teacher-to-teacher Big Idea small-grant program was a resounding success in reaching new teachers and introducing them to PESL (and, in many cases, to telecomputing and MBLs). Participants uniformly liked what they experienced, and many planned to use in their classroom what they learned about PESL. It would be unwieldy for NSF to administer directly a small-grants program of this size ($6,000–$37,000 with a $17,000 average in the case of LabNet).

   NSF should expand this kind of small-grant teacher-enhancement program, using colleges, universities, and nonprofit institutions like TERC as grantors and grant administrators.

2. The LabNetwork took on a PESL focus, not by mandate but through inclination and usage. As a result, Forum messages focused more and more on teaching, and at the center were projects. A network that takes a substantive tack like this offers an opportunity to look at a particular reform "close up."

   NSF should encourage the use of the PESL approach on networks it supports for K-12 teachers.

3. Teacher-training programs tend to lag in introducing future teachers to the latest in reform efforts and new technologies. We think PESL could be particularly useful to potential teachers of science and mathematics. Project activities engage adult students as much as younger ones, and raise both substantive and pedagogical issues. If telecomputing were added to the mix, it could be a formative force.

   NSF should encourage the exploration by teacher-training programs of PESL linked with telecomputing.

4. More detailed information is needed about teacher-supported student-to-student collaboration in projects across the distances that telecomputing can span. The experience of the TERC-NGS Kids Network suggests that a project orientation coupled with network communication can energize students and raise significant questions of science (see Candace Julyan's essay in chapter 7). This occurred even though the Kids Network is a quite highly structured environment, and broad-ranging experiments are not part of its program. In LabNet, students used the network with their teachers primarily to carry out class-level data sharing (the heating day project), or to ask for information about a particular project. The network could support other PESL activities as well (e.g., students in different schools could jointly develop projects that had features of longer term data collection, exchange, and analysis).

NSF should encourage demonstration projects that involve high school students in multischool projects that use telecomputing as the medium for information exchange.

5. The use of projects to enhance science learning is particularly applicable to the elementary years. The foundation for "science readiness" can not be laid too early. The Kids Network has demonstrated both high motivation of participants and their engagement with serious science questions. But much more needs to be known about the intersection of project content and developmental readiness—especially in the younger years.

NSF should solicit a wide range of grants that address the use of the PESL approach in the elementary years.

A Research Agenda: Does PESL Work?

A second area in which NSF can play a key role is funding research on the effectiveness of project-enhanced science learning.

We take a "parallel-processing" approach to PESL. We have urged that NSF promote PESL because we believe the project approach makes sense; that is, it has face validity, and its effectiveness is supported in a preliminary way by all the data available. We are convinced that doing what scientists do—pursuing questions about the physical world that take you into uncharted waters (for you), cause you to think and rethink your approach, make you struggle to understand the data you collect, force you to travel down unanticipated paths, perhaps lead you into a cul-de-sac that makes you abandon your tack and start over—has to be a powerful way to learn about real science. Yet at the same time we acknowledge the need for formal studies of the impact of PESL on students' measured skills, their selection of careers, their general literacy in matters of science and technology.

This need gives rise to two related questions: What measures should be used to assess the success of PESL? And how should evaluation studies be designed?

Assessment Measures

As we argued in chapter 3, virtually all existing standardized tests are geared to the textbook-lecture-lab approach and are inappropriate for gauging the effectiveness of PESL. The former regime is built on the assumption that worthwhile knowledge of physics can be distilled and codified, and that students who feed back a sufficient amount of that knowledge in the same form in which it was given "know" physics, but this knowledge certainly isn't of the "how to do science" kind.

Projects, on the other hand, have to do with doing—with knowing how to frame a question, assemble tools, apply them to the unknown, and make sense of what you find. The textbook-lecture-lab modality requires students to have highly developed information retention and retrieval skills. The project approach requires "clinical" skills. No common assessment system can possibly measure both skill-sets. An analog is learning to fly. There is book learning about weather, communications, flight rules, and so on, and these "facts" are tested in an ordinary paper-and-pencil way. But when it comes to flying itself, you go up in a plane with an examiner and demonstrate that you actually can fly. Different measures are applied to different knowledge domains.

New assessment systems need to be developed for projects to take their place alongside the existing ones. This happened with the PSSC curriculum in the late 1950s. The College Entrance Examination Board created a whole new set of tests geared to what PSSC was trying to teach (Finlay, 1966). Measures appropriate for PESL might be based on students' abilities to identify a scientifically interesting problem, formulate specific research questions, design and conduct experiments, or apply scientific concepts in unfamiliar contexts, to cite just a few examples. (Such measures might also be a direct contribution to practice, giving teachers an alternative basis for grading.)

However, it should be stressed that the issue is not a contest between textbook-lecture-labs and projects. Both approaches to teaching and learning have their place. What textbooks teach about physics (not necessarily how they teach it) may be important to know when you're doing a project. And doing a project may well inform reading or listening to a lecture. The activities are not mutually exclusive. This is one reason we chose the word "enhanced" to attach to projects. Textbooks will not disappear overnight even if projects prove to be the powerful learning device they already seem to be. So standard measures will continue to be used for the one and should be created for the other.

Evaluation Design

How can we find out if projects work, short of a major longitudinal study? There are at least three promising avenues for natural studies. First, we could study high school students at work, focusing on the inquiry skills previously mentioned. Second, we could ask how project-experienced students do in college and beyond. Such studies could be either retrospective, focusing on students already in college or graduate school, or prospective, focusing on students just entering college. A third possibility is to look closely at the biographies of a number of successful scientists and pinpoint what was formative in their careers. Possible evaluation designs, like possible assessment measures, are limited only by the ingenuity of the researcher.

In summary, we advocate the use of projects on the basis of available evidence, while agreeing that more systematic studies would be of value. What value? Stimulating discussion, formulating policy, convincing the unconvinced, finding areas of ignorance. In the context of developing a consensus about children's learning, it makes sense that our theory will need deepening and revision. But that's like bringing a microscope into focus. If the image is blurry, you don't throw out the microscope, you improve the focus.

Working Teachers and Working Scientists

Working teachers and working scientists would seem to be natural collaborators in project-enhanced science learning . The concatenation of these two allied but very different pursuits seems to us critical. It is reasonable to suggest that physics teachers can draw sustenance from the full-time scientist, just as it is important that scientists take a hand in the education of those from whom their replacements will be drawn.

But in fact teachers and scientists do radically different work and assumptions about productive relationships between these professions need to be carefully explored. NSF can take the lead in fostering this exploration in several ways: careful inclusion of scientists on PESL-oriented networks; increased attempts to join scientists and teachers at the local and regional level; and finally, small working meetings of teachers and scientists around the task of reviewing critical questions about projects, especially their scientific worth. This particular dialogue we see as potentially most fruitful. It is the subject of the last major section of this chapter.

CRITICAL DIMENSIONS IN PESL: A FRAMEWORK FOR DIALOGUE

Projects were at the heart of LabNet—both our metaphor and means for valuing the interaction of student with the stuff of science. Reflection about one's work is an imperative skill if change is to have meaning and direction. We end this book with a series of questions about projects meant primarily for the working teacher but also of value to the working scientist interested in science education.

Teachers need a way to evaluate projects, both at the idea stage and upon completion. They need to be able to help students select the topics and methods of investigation that are most likely to prove productive, and they need a basis for assessing the outcomes of the project experience. Obviously, scientists have much to contribute to the evaluation of projects—knowledge of subject matter, experimental design, apparatus, and so on, and, crucially, of the skills that will best serve future scientists. Perhaps less obviously, the scientific community also has a real stake in the quality of student projects, because the work that students do today has a direct bearing on the caliber of tomorrow's scientists.

In short, evaluating projects is an area in which scientists and teachers have a compelling common interest and complementary expertise. Yet the territory remains almost unexplored because teachers and scientists operate in two separate worlds. In the hope of stimulating this very necessary dialogue, we have identified five issue domains—scientific, pedagogical, practical, curricular, political—that we think provide a useful framework for looking at and testing the project approach.

The Scientific Quality of a Project

Surely whether a project is good science must be one, perhaps the most, critical dimension—projects range in their scientific quality from the trivial to the profound (as distinct from the simple to the complex). One would want students to experience the profound end of the array, but how can one tell? What makes a project good science?

The main goal of PESL is that students learn science by having opportunities to examine scientific problems critically, and to experience scientific practice in the quest of solutions.

In this context, there are four questions to ask about a science project:

- *Is it a scientific problem worth investigating?* Student and teacher need to be able to argue convincingly that there is a scientific value in investigating a particular phenomenon in a particular way, that there is a valid question or inquiry into the matter.

- *Does working on the subject represent a scientific process in terms of tools and mode of investigation?* Are the instruments used, and the kind of research done, appropriate for learning about the phenomenon?

- *How well can the targeted topic be researched and identified as the phenomenon under study (scientific rigor)?* With what certainty will we be able to construct the phenomenon and how will we be able to know when we can't?

- *Can the project help the student develop a critical view of both the subject matter and the research methods (critical awareness)?* How well does the project allow a balanced insight into both content and process in the investigation?

We have teased out the science from the pedagogy, but we are aware that the selection of a project is influenced by the learning environment and educational goals: If a student is truly engaged, won't he or she learn something important even from a "simple" oft-researched project of modest scientific merit? (We take up the pedagogical issues in the next section.)

There is a tangled knot of issues in the domain of scientific quality: Does a project have to be original to be good science? (We would not expect high schoolers to invent new basic principles, but LabNet students came up with applications of existing principles that, so far as we at TERC know, were new.) What weight should be given to originality in relation to scientific rigor? Or the scope of a project? Or its theoretical implications? In the domain of scientific quality, teachers often find themselves in a characteristic dilemma: "Should I let a student re-invent the wheel?"

Experiencing and Learning From Projects

Different kinds of projects must provide different kinds of learning outcomes. Is there any way for teachers and students to assess the pedagogical value of any project? We need to be able to judge the effectiveness of carrying out projects.

We look at this dimension from three perspectives, which interact to form the learning environment:

- *Student readiness*—When are students ready for what kinds of projects? How does a teacher determine readiness? Can students learn how to make self-determinations about their readiness? Can students learn to assess the potential risks and rewards of a particular project, so they can make more informed choices? When do students know enough about science to generate an inquiry that would be useful to them? (See chapter 2 for a short discussion of student readiness).

- *Teacher readiness*—When is a teacher ready to plunge into a project? What kinds of teaching experience, leadership, pedagogical knowledge, and scientific experience and knowledge are needed? Should the teacher have had a good deal of direct project experience?

- *Classroom readiness*—How does a teacher determine readiness of his or her students to carry out projects? What is necessary to prepare the student for the project approach? Are there any precursor activities necessary—that is, how does a teacher best prepare inexperienced students for project activities? Is it best if they begin with some kind of pre-project activity that prepares them, or should they just "sink or swim"? How much teacher intervention, of what kind, enhances or compromises student learning at what stage?

A common teaching dilemma in this domain is the continuation of re-inventing the wheel: "If I criticize you for re-inventing the wheel, then I am more interested in wheels than inventing."

The Project-Enhanced Classroom: Dealing With What There Is

Teachers face many classroom administrative, and management tasks every day. Space arrangement, noise control, group organization, time scheduling, grading schemes, different activities going on at the same time, travel arrangements, equipment needs. How do projects affect these management activities? What approaches are most effective in handling projects?

We mention three components of classroom setting:

- *Social organization of the class*—Projects seem to demand a different classroom setting from regular science classes. How should students be grouped to do projects, and who should group them? What kinds of relationships should students have with other members of the research community (such as mentors), and how should they work with the teacher?

- *Tools and materials for projects*—What tools and materials best support project efforts? Especially, how do computer-based tools like MBLs enhance projects? What about simple materials? What is a realistic approach to the use of tools like computers, given budget and other constraints?

- *Assessing/grading*—This is a painful matter. What's the best way to deal with required material: textbooks, state-mandated testing, AP exams? How can projects "cover" this material? Can they? What are ways to evaluate students' projects? Should they be evaluated based on their efforts? On the results? Should they be active participants in the evaluation process? In what ways?

A shift to projects seem to demand a critical view of this matter. Teachers find themselves asking, how do you assess a student on the invention of a new wheel or re-invention of an old one...?

The Project-Centered Classroom and the Science Curriculum

The task of trying to fit projects into the existing curriculum is complex. What's the best way for students to learn science (and teachers to teach it)? Is it possible, and desirable, that physical science should be learned solely by the project approach? What would this look like? How would it work? Two elements are highlighted in particular:

- *Balancing out projects with other classroom activities*—The search is for a sound approach to learning science. Projects, we believe, have a critical role, but other learning techniques also can complement science learning or teaching. How can students benefit from multiple methods, such as traditional labs, demonstrations, lectures, films, new interactive multimedia experiences? What is lost in the process of doing projects? What is gained from other techniques? What's the optimal mix?

- *Curricular demands*—Many teachers don't have the option of an all-project approach, even if they think it would be a good idea. They are still required to use textbooks, they may enjoy giving an occasional lecture, there are state exams and SATs on which their students expect to do well. How best can these competing demands be balanced?

Learning about science most likely calls for various learning situations. Do they all occur in the context of doing projects? When should inventiveness be stressed (new wheels) and when should basic scientific knowledge be encouraged (old wheels)?

Projects and the Politics of the Educational Community

Gaining support for project science is undoubtedly a political process in many schools. What are ways and modes of persuasions to engage principals, parents, some students, perhaps even school boards in promoting change in science learning?

Many teachers would like to gain support from and form a partnership with the various members of the educational community:

- *Persuasion*—How is the task of persuasion best done? What evidence can be brought to bear of the effectiveness of project-enhanced science learning? What arguments are most persuasive? How can one argue the cost-effectiveness of the project approach?

- *Involvement*—How can local industries and individual science-trained adults be persuaded to become contributing members to science teaching of students? What kinds of opportunities for involvement can be provided to them, such as mentoring, actively making equipment, lending technical and technological resources, offering their professional skill, perhaps even money, on a continuing basis?

Such support can be vitally important in extending the teacher's reach, by adding more shoulders "put to the wheel."

FROM CURRENT PRACTICE
TO PROJECT-ENHANCED SCIENCE LEARNING:
A FINAL WORD

What are we finally to conclude about projects and their place in the curriculum? Persuaded as we are, we still have only limited anecdotal and analytic evidence of the power of projects. In addition, history hasn't durably established the worth of learning-centered education. On the other hand, the textbook-lecture-lab regimen clearly isn't a proven remedy for the declining science test scores (which are themselves questionable as the most appropriate measures). We suspect that a mix of methods, as always, will prove better than an all-project classroom. However, projects do promise to be the yeast in the mix. That is why we selected the term *project-enhanced* science learning (not teaching).

Projects are real to students. They excite attention, lend themselves to cooperation and the possibility over time of true collaboration. They do tap those distinctive American virtues of inventiveness, self-reliance, gumption, stick-to-it-iveness, common sense, and the like. They seem to work with a broader range of students than more traditional methods, among them those students called "underserved." They lead to learning, often in surprising ways.

It is true that projects can create problems. They don't fit school schedules well; they take more teacher thought, time, and energy than more traditional methods; they spill over into evenings and weekends; they can cost money; they can be noisy and untidy.

Nonetheless, there is an appeal to PESL that has caught the attention and dedication of several hundreds of LabNet participants. It has enlivened their teaching lives, and energized their professional community. Still, we can't end with a definite prescription. We don't yet know enough to convince policy makers that projects are cost-effective. Besides, we very much like the way things have grown, without much fanfare, with teachers teaching teachers as the principal means of getting the word and the practice of projects out. That is what this book has been about.

Appendix A: The LabNet Teacher Community

LabNet teachers are listed alphabetically, with their school and the year they joined the project. The list does not include the 393 teachers who were part of the Big Idea Grant workshops in 1991-1992:

Robert **Adams**, Caesar Rodney High School, Camden, DE, 1989
Millicent **Anderson**, Venice High School, Los Angeles, CA, 1989
Norman **Anderson**, Cedar Falls High School, Cedar Falls, IA, 1989
Kenneth **Appel**, Yorktown High School, Yorktown Heights, NY, 1989
Jeffrey **Applegate**, Fairfield High School, Fairfield, OH, 1990
Hilda **Bachrach**, Dana Hall School, Wellesley, MA, 1989
Earl **Barrett**, Dobson High School, Mesa, AZ, 1989
Cherie Ann **Behn**, Bishop Dwenger High School, Ft Wayne, IN, 1989
Curt **Bixel**, Whiteman School, Steamboat Springs, CO, 1990
J. Timothy **Black**, La Cueva High School, Albuquerque, NM, 1990
Robert **Blakely**, Martin Luther King Jr. High School, Detroit, MI, 1989
John **Blythe**, Kenowa Hills High School, Grand Rapids, MI, 1989
Jerry **Bodily**, Fowler High School, Fowler, CA, 1990
S. Thomas **Bond**, Bridgeport High School, Bridgeport, WV, 1990
David **Braunschweig**, Madison West High School, Madison, WI, 1989
Derek **Brown**, Red Bank High School, Chattanooga, TN, 1989
Gerald **Buck**, The Prairie School, Racine, WI, 1989
Daniel **Buckley**, Medford High School, Medford, MA, 1990
Peter **Burkholder**, St. Andrew's Episcopal School, Bethesda, MD, 1989
Harry **Burridge**, Crescent Valley High School, Corvallis, OR, 1989
Gregory **Bush**, Antilles High School, Fort Buchanan, PR, 1989
Dave **Button**, Osbourn Park High School, Manassas, VA, 1989
Jack **Cadigan**, Centralized Correspondence Study School, Juneau, AK, 1990
Robert **Capen**, Canyon Del Oro High School, Tucson, AZ, 1990
Veanna **Carpenter**, Alamo Heights High School, San Antonio, TX, 1990
Gregory **Cauller**, Northeastern High School, Manchester, PA, 1989
Elizabeth **Chesick**, The Baldwin School, Bryn Mawr, PA, 1990
Ted **Cizadlo**, City High School, Iowa City, IA, 1989
John **Clarke**, Tewksbury Memorial High School, Tewksbury, MA, 1990
Quinton **Cole**, St. Paul's School, Clearwater, FL, 1989
Catharine **Colwell**, Mainland Senior High School, Daytona Beach, FL, 1990
Jean **Condrey**, St. Gertrude High School, Richmond, VA, 1990
William **Cox**, Dowling High School, W Des Moines, IA, 1989
Mary Elizabeth **Culbreth**, Texas Learning Technology Group, Austin, TX, 1989
Robert **Cutter** Lynnfield High School, Lynnfield, MA, 1989
Judy **Dadah**, Grafton Memorial Senior High School, Grafton, MA, 1990
Robert **Dean**, Livonia Stevenson School, Livonia, MI, 1989
John **Despres**, Brunswick High School, Brunswick, ME, 1989

David **Drummer**, Kutztown High School, Kutztown, PA, 1989
Gene **Easter**, Streetsboro High School, Streetsboro, OH, 1990
Adam **Edmondson**, Hazleton Senior High, Hazleton, PA, 1990
Andria **Erzberger**, Palo Alto High School, Palo Alto, CA, 1990
Carole **Escobar**, Bellport High School, Brookhaven, NY, 1990
Ronald **Esman**, Abilene High School, Abilene, TX, 1990
Steve **Ethen**, Burnsville High School, Burnsville, MN, 1990
Merrill **Falk**, Milan High School, Milan, MI, 1990
Linda **Frederick**, Freedom High School, Bethlehem, PA, 1989
Diane **Friedel**, St. John's College High School, Washington, DC, 1990
Merlin **Fritzen**, Forest Hills Public Schools, Grand Rapids, MI, 1989
John **Garrett**, Sheldon High School, Eugene, OR, 1989
David **Gewanter**, Simsbury High School, Simsbury, CT, 1990
George **Gittens**, Sheldon High School, Eugene, OR, 1989
Gita **Hakerem**, Framingham North High School, Framingham, MA, 1989
James **Harpel**, Horton Watkins High School, Ladue, MO, 1989
Curtis **Hendricks**, Richmond Heights High School, Richmond Heights, OH, 1990
Edward **Henke**, George Westinghouse High School, Pittsburgh, PA, 1990
Lowell **Herr**, The Catlin Gabel School, Portland, OR, 1989
T. Gayle **Hodges**, Winter Park High School, Winter Park, FL, 1989
Elizabeth **Holsenbeck**, Jefferson Davis High School, Montgomery, AL, 1989
Carey **Inouye**, Iolani School, Honolulu, HI, 1990
Michael **Jablin**, Senior High School, Billings, MT, 1990
Bruce **Jones**, Kentucky Country Day School, Louisville, KY, 1990
Paul **Jones**, Montezuma Community School, Montezuma, IA, 1990
Bruce **Keyzer**, Guilford High School, Rockford, IL, 1989
Guy **Konkle**, North Central High School, Indianapolis, IN, 1989
Eugene **Kowalski**, North Denver High School, Denver, CO, 1990
Roland **Lackey**, Cuba Independent Schools, Cuba, NM, 1989
John **Laffan**, Clinton Central High School, Clinton, NY, 1989
Joanne **Langabee**, Papillion La Bista High School, Papillion, NE, 1990
Roger **Larson**, Boulder High School, Boulder, CO, 1989
William **Lash**, Westwood High School, Austin, TX, 1989
William **Leader**, Loara High School, Anaheim, CA, 1990
Franceline **Leary**, Troy High School, Troy, NY, 1990
Harold, **Lefcourt**, Morris Knolls High School, Rockaway, NJ, 1989
Robert **Lehman**, Howard County Public Schools, Ellicott City, MD, 1990
Greg **Lockett**, West Valley High School, Cottonwood, CA, 1989
Loren **Lund**, Eisenhower High School, Yakima, WA, 1990
Richard **Lyon**, Nooksack Valley Junior-Senior High School, Nooksack, WA, 1989
Mike **MacMahon**, Huffman Magnet High School, Birmingham, AL, 1990
Steven **Matusow**, Blackford High School, San Jose, CA, 1989
Edward **McDonnell**, Brooklyn High School, Brooklyn, OH, 1989

James **McGahan**, Northwest High School, Grand Island, NE, 1990
Curtis **Miller**, Wheatridge High School, Wheatridge, CO, 1989
John **Mirabella**, Downey High School, Modesto, CA, 1989
Nancy **Moreau**, Ketcham Senior High School, Wappingers Falls, NY, 1990
Nina **Morley**, Orange High School, Hillsborough, NC, 1989
Thomas **Mulholland**, Staten Island Technical High Schl., Staten Island, NY, 1989
Mary **Nickles**, Rochester Institute of Technology, Rochester, NY, 1989
Ira **Nirenberg**, Ben Franklin High School, New Orleans, LA, 1989
Martin **O'Toole**, St. Xavier High School, Louisville, KY, 1990
Thomas **Odden**, St. Andrew's School, Middletown, DE, 1989
Wilfred **Oswald**, Napa High School, Napa, CA, 1990
Albert **Palumbo**, Wellesley Senior High School, Wellesley, MA, 1989
Margaret **Park**, Illinois Math and Science Academy, Aurora, IL, 1989
Pete **Parlett**, McKean High School, Wilmington, DE, 1989
Sister Mary Ethel **Parrott**, Notre Dame Academy, Covington, KY, 1990
Ross **Partington**, Monroe County AVTS, Bartonsville, PA, 1989
Helen **Perry**, Mississippi School for Math and Science, Columbus, MS, 1989
David **Pinkerton**, Smoky Hill High School, Aurora, CO, 1989
Marek **Plucinski**, Great Bridge High School, Chesapeake, VA, 1989
John **Potts**, Custer County District High School, Miles City, MT, 1989
Nevin **Ranck**, Northern Lehigh High School, Slatington, PA, 1989
Sister Marion **Rappl**, Our Lady of Mercy High School, Rochester, NY, 1989
Charles **Rasweiler**, Uniondale High School, Uniondale, NY, 1990
Andree **Reed**, Chaparral High School, Las Vegas, NV, 1989
Dave **Reid**, Green Mountain High School, Lakewood, CO, 1989
Daniel **Replogle**, Central Noble High School, Albion, IN, 1989
Sandra **Rhoades**, North Cobb High School, Kennesaw, GA, 1990
Jane **Rich**, Shawnee High School, Shawnee, OK, 1989
Emmett **Riordan**, Battelle Youth Science Program, Columbus, OH, 1989
Robert **Roe**, Jr, Highland Park High School, Dallas, TX, 1989
Patricia **Rourke**, St. Stephen's and St. Agnes School, Alexandria, VA, 1989
Luis **Santana**, Papa Juan XXIII, Bayamon, PR, 1989
William **Satterthwaite**, Milton Academy, Milton, MA, 1990
Robert **Seal**, Cathedral High School, Indianapolis, IN, 1989
Paul **Serri**, Churchill High School, Livonia, MI, 1989
Robert **Shaner**, University of Wisconsin at Madison, Madison, WI, 1990
Namie **Smith**, Ridgewood High School, Ridgewood, NJ, 1989
Sheron **Snyder**, Mason High School, Mason, MI, 1990
Gary **Sokolis**, Amador High School, Sutter Creek, CA, 1989
Anthony **Soldano**, New Rochelle High School, New Rochelle, NY, 1989
David **Sonday**, Corning East High School, Corning, NY, 1989
Richard **Sorensen**, Sherwood High School, Sherwood, OR, 1989
Danielle **Spaete**, Pleasant Valley High School, Pleasant Valley, IA, 1989

Douglas **Squire**, Union High School, Union, OR, 1990
Robert **Stefonowicz**, Dickinson High School, Dickinson, ND, 1989
Lorenz **Steinbrecher**, Mira Mesa High School, San Diego, CA, 1990
Virginia **Taylor**, Franklin-Simpson High School, Franklin, KY, 1989
Pete **Test**, Western Hills High School, Fort Worth, TX, 1989
John **Thomas**, Fagaitua High School, Pago Pago, American Samoa, 1990
Steven **Thomas**, Gravenhurst High School, Gravenhurst, Ontario, 1990
Albert **Thompson**, Ponderosa High School, Parker, CO, 1989
Tom **Thompson**, Sheridan High School, Sheridan, OR, 1990
Rajee **Thyagarajan**, Health Careers High School, San Antonio, TX, 1989
Bob **Tinnell**, South Salem High School, Salem, OR, 1989
David **Trapp**, Sequim High School, Sequim, WA, 1989
Therese **Tremmel**, East Central High School, Miles, IA, 1989
Louis **Turner**, Western Reserve Academy, Hudson, OH, 1989
Thomas **Vining**, Saguaro High School, Scottsdale, AZ, 1989
Geriann **Walker**, Elmira High School, Elmira, OR, 1989
Richard **Warner**, El Dorado High School, Placerville, CA, 1990
Tom **Warnock**, Craftsbury Academy, Craftsbury, VT, 1990
Kelly **Wedding**, Santa Fe High School, Santa Fe, NM, 1989
James **Weidner**, Stevens Point Area Senior High, Stevens Point, WI, 1989
Michael **Weiss**, Hialeah Senior High School, Hialeah, FL, 1989
John **Wheaton**, St. Francis High School, Louisville, KY, 1989
Robert **Wilber**, John F Kennedy High School, Denver, CO, 1989
Dave **Willig**, Northridge High School, Middlebury, IN, 1989
Maxine **Willis**, Gettysburg Area Senior High School, Gettysburg, PA, 1989
Thomas **Wolters**, Central High, Red Wing, MN, 1989
Brother William **Wright**, Bishop Kearney High School, Rochester, NY, 1989
Ernest **Young**, Floresville High School, Floresville, TX, 1989
Jay **Zimmerman**, Brookfield Central High School, Brookfield, WI, 1990

APPENDIX B: CREATING PERMEABLE BOUNDARIES FOR REFLECTIVE EXPERTISE: COLLABORATIVE EVALUATION ON A NETWORK

Sister Mary Ethel Parrott, Shahaf Gal, and Greg Lockett

The work on the teacher questionnaire used throughout the book was carried out by two teachers and an educational researcher. This is an unusual collaboration—generally teachers and educational researchers keep their distance.

In this section, we reflect on our personal experiences of the process. We expand ideas about the capacity of telecommunication networks to be used for sharing expertise, and for collaborative professional encounters such as the one we had. Mary Ethel Parrott focuses on the progress of our work and vividly describes the difficulties of becoming a telecommunication team member and working with people who have different thinking styles. Shahaf Gal highlights some of the problems involved in sharing knowledge among teachers and researchers. In his section, Greg Lockett reflects on our internal discourse and raises the ever-important questions about the relevancy of our work to our audience and also the toughest question: "what difference does all this make to science education?"

"REFLECTION" ON THE PROCESS

Sister Mary Ethel Parrott

On the Myers-Briggs test, I am an introvert, an intuiter, a thinker, and a perceiver. I like to deal with ideas, and especially with the overall picture. Given these traits, it sometimes surprises me that I am also rather good at editing and attending to details. When a message appeared on the LabNet Forum asking for volunteers to help with the teacher questionnaire report, I applied for one of the positions. In general, I enjoy both writing and the analyzing of data, and one of the many things I like about working with students on projects is the opportunity that it gives me to help them develop these tools.

I have always found that in writing for others, I also write for myself. Working on the report would make me take the time to think more clearly about the significance of my LabNet experience. That would be worthwhile in and of itself, apart from whatever use would be made of the document.

I had a special interest in the LabNet project because of its breadth. Forum entries that I had followed throughout the 1990-1991 year had served as some indication of the telecommunication involvement of participants. I was curious about participation in other areas of the project. Also, apart

315

from a generally positive feeling, it was not totally clear to me what I thought about the LabNet project. Science projects, the aspect that I thought would be the most useful when I had applied for the program, have not yet come to be in any significant way. Yet, I was very enthusiastic about other things— especially telecommunication, which was relatively new to me when I entered on the Michigan LabNet workshop experience in the summer of 1990.

Originally, I understood that the bulk of the report work would be completed over a period of a few days during the summer. This proved to be far from the case! Both technical difficulties and the nature of the on-line discourse that ensued dictated a much more extensive time frame. This time was further dilated when Greg and I had to continue within the constraints of full-time teaching: something that requires actual contact and preparation time, affects one's energy level, and sometimes seems even to usurp one's ability to think!

Greg and Shahaf introduced themselves to me over the LabNetwork. After I had also introduced myself, Greg and I found that we had met one another at a previous physics program—but did not know one another well enough for me to recognize his last name. We have learned much more about one another from our networking during the process of developing this report. I have not yet met Shahaf in person.

From the beginning, it was evident that I was entering into communication with a pair who had already initiated a significant philosophical discourse via the LabNetwork. I had engaged in many philosophical discourses, but it had never occurred to me to use the network to that end. I was one who enjoyed the first couple days of "philosophy sessions" at the summer training, but thereafter would have much preferred to devote my time to more pragmatic concerns. Philosophizing about projects was impeding my progress on my summer project! Nonetheless, I was very intrigued by Greg and Shahaf's philosophizing about the accomplishment of change in teaching. It was obvious that this process was going to involve a lot more than the rather dry interpretation of data that I had originally envisioned.

There were some technical difficulties from the start. Because I was working on a Macintosh platform, as were Shahaf and a research assistant, Greg Geboski, at TERC, my problems were at the level of mild frustration rather than a major obstacle. Greg Lockett was trying to use an Apple II with considerably more difficulty. The data analysis Hypercard program that worked fine at TERC would not quite work on my machines. I could read the data, but could not easily manipulate it to see relationships. The database information sent would have been fine, except that my only database program was Microsoft Works, and it would not accept the number of fields needed. As luck would have it, the fields that I needed for the part of the report for which I would be the primary writer were mostly beyond the MS Works limit. Greg Geboski and I tried to patch things up over the network with little success. I had a good understanding of where the problem was but did not know enough to fix it. I thought I was communicating the problem to TERC with perfect clarity. When I would read the response, I would immediately know that the solution was to a problem that I did not have! Then I was sent another version of the Hypercard stack; yet, somehow, it managed to be the same defective version I had been struggling with for weeks. In the end, Greg Geboski and I were able to make a voice telephone connection. Within a few minutes we had the difficulty resolved and I could proceed.

I liked the on-line process of discussing ideas and sharing the composition of the report. Ordinarily, I absolutely refuse to be part of any writing project that has to be done in committee. I prefer to write on my own. Hence, sharing the composition responsibilities without what I consider the handicaps of physically getting together to discuss at every stage was somewhat ideal for me. As an introvert, I take in things quite readily, but do better to process them in peace without having to provide immediate feedback. Greg and Shahaf often formulated their thoughts more quickly than I did, but I was comfortable with that. I found the on-line aspect very suitable for a person of my bent. The writing went faster than in committee, and the feedback was a little slower. But the exchange could still be quite frequent. At the busiest times, it was not unusual for me to be on-line several times a day. The system was not perfect, and we experienced its limitations. Not being able to preserve formatting when transmitting ideas and not being able to send graphs and tables in final form was inconvenient. Exchanging information via the Mail feature required executing frequent carriage returns when transmitting long sections. But overall, I found the process effective.

As far as I could judge from the network communication, all of us were open to having our ideas critiqued by the others. We wanted to get at what the data meant. We did not always have exactly the same opinion, but neither were we ever poles apart. My tendency would ordinarily be to qualify things a bit more, whereas Greg and Shahaf have a greater tendency to make their points by contrast. Hence, they outline the extreme cases, indicating that they know that they may not actually exist in this extreme form. I accept this as a valid approach so long as they make clear what they are doing—and they are very intellectually honest about it. I can say in all sincerity that I have come to regard them as my respected colleagues, and I think anyone would be fortunate to have the opportunity to bounce ideas off them.

As we came closer to the final stages of the "product," the limitations of the telecommunication network became more evident. At a certain stage in writing and editing, being able to preserve formatting becomes essential. Except for general comments, telecommunication was not particularly useful. It made clear to me how important it is to develop some kind of system that allows for easy, formatted transmission across different computer platforms. The postal and overnight services became much more important at the final stages.

In summary, my experience with telecommunication was a good one. It did have limitations. I do not know the extent to which the information in this report will be disseminated or heeded in the design of future projects. I think we have made some important points. Hopefully, these have been stated with a clarity that allows others to evaluate them and take their own position with regard to them. I personally think there are many acceptable ways of doing most things, but think it is wise to give a hearing to alternate proposals. At any rate, thinking about the LabNet experience has been valuable to me in its own right. I have also had a valuable association with two colleagues whom I now consider friends, and hope to network with them in the future.

COLLABORATION: A WORD WITH A NICE RING AND TOUGH REALITIES

Shahaf Gal

Collaboration among educators—find a person who would disagree that this is a needed condition for effective learning, teaching, and gaining knowledge. There is a nice ring to the word. But in reality it is tough to create situations that enable professionals, especially across disciplines, to work together. In fact, both implicitly and explicitly, professional life discourages collaborative sharing of knowledge.

My intention here is not to elaborate on the conditions related to these statements. However, I do see them as part of the initial boundaries we had to cross in order to collaborate. Mary Ethel and Greg are teachers, and I am a researcher. TERC, an educational research organization, is my workplace. Theirs are two different schools: Greg works at a public school, and Mary Ethel at a private academy. By the espoused criteria of our life situations: I "think about education" and Mary Ethel and Greg "educate"; I think about "aggregates of data," and they work in a particular setting, their classrooms; I look for "educational trends," and they "practice." In the system's organizational hierarchy, doing and working on a local scale is considered "low," and thinking on a large scale is "high." Mary Ethel and Greg are employed by educational systems. My project, by the nature of its funding, empowers me to voice my opinions and perceptions about how to improve the educational practice of which Greg and Mary Ethel are unique contributors as teachers. I believe we had to overcome these boundaries so that they would not interfere with our joint work.

It is one thing to be aware that these boundaries are present, and it is another experience to cross them. Fear and anxiety are associated with the actual move in this direction. Let me describe mine. Should I expose my knowledge and put it to the test with teachers? Could I risk hearing from them that my expert opinion fails, is inaccurate, needs to be fixed, or does not specifically apply to them? And then there was another layer. Would Greg and Mary Ethel feel safe to criticize my work? Would they feel comfortable sharing their perceptions with me? Would they feel that their opinions were as valid as mine? And could our joint effort gain recognition by members of both communities of teachers and of educational researchers?

The geographic distance placed an additional twist to the collaborative effort. We live far from one another. Could we bridge the distance, geographic and situational, by the use of telecommunication?

I think that the task of making sense of data that is relevant and intriguing to all of us has been the important common denominator for our particular situation. We joined efforts. This became so because Mary Ethel, Greg and myself were part of the same project. We brought to the task multiple perspectives as result of our different roles in the project. Being engaged in an interpretive process helped glue us together. What added to the process, I believe, was that we constructed the task so that each of us had room for his or her voice, as well as a place for joint work.

Voices. In the academic community and among teachers, personal voices tend to be muffled. In the academic community personal voices are usually muffled or get transmitted through "objective" tools in order to support the claim of impartiality. Among science teachers the common perception is that, as teachers, they are merely conduits of existing knowledge; therefore, they too tend to muffle their voices.

The maintenance of objectively perceived voices is often strengthened in both social arenas by the tendency to avoid conflict. People strive for consensus. Societal mufflers tend either to sound essentially the same or to stifle differences. We agreed to first make our voices clear and opinionated, and second to seek common ground. What we gained was an understanding about personal ownership of and commitment to our own voices. Our voice as a team evolved in the process and has been made transparent to outsiders by the fact that we kept clear the authorship our individual pieces.

Transparency. What images do we have of one another? I had met Greg once, in the midst of a migraine headache that made him leave the meeting we both attended, and another time in a project advisory meeting. He was then in my environment, which is far from his own. I have never met Sister Mary Ethel, and have heard her voice only once over the telephone. Telecommunication helped me form an image of a person. Greg and Mary Ethel became transparent to me in a particular light, as thinkers who "textualize" their thoughts and feelings. Their transparency is conveyed in their writing. In this way, each of our voices is transparent to readers of this report.

People skills. Why do we always end up saying that "people skills," those hard-to-describe, unpredictable, unstable, and fuzzy human communication skills, make the difference, beyond technology and organizational barriers? And why do we tend to leave them to last place, as if they are the exception to the rule and not the rule that largely accounts for why a social system either works or fumbles? I think that our experiment is not an exception to the rule in that it will probably be repeated by others who share the perspective that people are at the heart of our educational adventures. People need to communicate, and how they communicate is what comprises the educational enterprise. To be serious about it in a context of research about people, I believe that we need to avoid offering a prescription about how to make things work. Rather, I see the value of our work in making our experiences and our learning available to all so that they can raise *their* voices, critique our work, and see the benefits of a collaborative approach of this kind.

My personal learning involved:

- seeing the limitations of being confined to one voice that my professional community wants to hear and considers valid.
- gaining multiple perspectives on the LabNet project, which alone I could not have access to.
- more than before, I have had to come to terms with the limits of social science research and with the process of "extracting" data out of context, and of trying to make it "objective."
- feeling the limits of social research in its stubbornness to avoid making the issue of the social value of knowledge and its social utilization part of its agenda.

It makes sense for me to continue to seek opportunities to create collaborative learning environments that are more accessible to researchers, staff, and teachers. Much work is left to be done. We need to improve the technology to support such processes. There is also a need to design such experiences much earlier in a project's life. For example, early in the project, a joint research team of teachers-researchers could be formed. It could decide on the research questions, design the tools for data collection, collect the data, and interpret it. Through the use of telecommunication the team could make all the data available for all teachers in the project, and engage them in making sense of the information. Making a communal interpretation of findings could generate a highly valued and valid voice of a community of practitioners.

AN INTROSPECTIVE RETROSPECTIVE
Greg Lockett

Several factors motivated my participation in this project. First, the TERC coordinator was Shahaf Gal. Shahaf and I had been discussing, on the LabNetwork, science education for many months prior to TERC's advertisement for teachers interested in analyzing participant responses to a LabNet questionnaire. Our dialogue had introduced a component of intellectual challenge and stimulation that had been missing in my life since my return to high school teaching. I was very interested in continuing this exchange of observations and ideas. Second, I had been very critical of TERC's handling of the "project" component of LabNet. I was interested in studying the experiences of other teachers and seeing if my criticisms had been valid. Finally, there was a modest salary for the work that would cover the cost of a new modem. Although the pay was really incidental to my involvement, it was an additional incentive.

When I keep a narrow focus and compare the results with my initial goals, I am quite satisfied. During the summer and beyond, my computer conversations continued to be the most stimulating aspect of my professional life. On a personal level, I began to understand why practitioners and advocates of project-enhanced learning are exiled to the fringes of professional respectability. I also feel that this dialogue brought me closer to understanding 10 years of largely ineffectual efforts to reform science education in this country. Some of those understandings are reflected in my contributions to this report.

I learned a great deal more about the project component of LabNet as experienced by others. I now recognize that my earlier critique of TERC was flawed, but I was open to that possibility. I recognize that being honest is not equivalent to being right. I won't elaborate on my changed views; however, I will say that being confronted with your errors is always tough and humbling, but quite valuable in other ways.

My personal and professional relationship with Shahaf continued to flourish as the project progressed. Among the many relationships in my 44-year life, ours has been unique. We were born and raised in different cultures. We have only met briefly and only in professional settings. In spite of this, I feel a real bond of personal friendship and intellectual affinity with this man. In California, "distance learning" is on the current hit parade of buzz words. As such, I grate at the concept. However, my computer conversations with Shahaf have opened a deeper appreciation of the possibilities of "distance learning." Our interaction has gradually transformed my perception of evaluation. In broad metaphorical terms, I am changing from a structural engineer to a gardener. This has been a very positive change. I also want to recognize Shahaf's pivotal role in this project. All along, he claimed that Mary and I had the hard parts. I disagree. Shahaf was responsible for writing our collective conclusions. He deftly wove ideas from each author into a fabric that all of us admired. This was the hard part.

Getting re-acquainted with Mary Parrott was an unexpected, but delightful, bonus. I had been one of her students at a PTRA training institute conducted many years before at Bozeman, Montana. I still use materials and ideas that she presented at that time. We both quickly made the connection with that past encounter. During our work on the questionnaire, I renewed my appreciation of her thoughtful intellect and genuinely enjoyed reading her contributions to the report and her analysis of our work. In the future, I hope that we will be able to build more telecommunication bridges that will lead to exciting, meaningful experiences for our students.

My satisfaction with the experience does not mean that it was without problems. If this process is valuable and to be repeated, several issues need to be addressed. The time commitment required to create a document of this type must be realistically assessed. Originally, it was estimated that 3 days in July would be sufficient. It is now November, and I am still writing. In part, this reflects the temperament and high standards of the authors. In part, it reflects various technical problems encountered along the way. Most of these problems were related to mastering new software tools and the incompatibility of files exchanged by the authors. In addition to technical difficulties, time was required to evolve a working relationship that was new to each of us. Cooperative writing between geographically distant authors linked by telecommunication requires new skills and strategies unique to this process. None of these factors was fatal to the project. However, they can and should be addressed prior to any future endeavor of this sort. I should add that with all of these problems eliminated, I still believe that completion of a document of this type requires much more than 72 person-hours.

Any consideration of future improvements and adjustments to the process inevitably leads to a deeper and more fundamental issue. Is this report worth the time and energy that we invested in it? Specifically, is this report going to have any effect on the course of science education in this country? More generally, can collaborative evaluation efforts between researchers and high school teachers effectively analyze current projects and enhance the success of future projects? I believe that cross-disciplinary groups of this sort can offer unique and valuable perspectives on programs at all levels. I am much less optimistic about the ability of such reports to influence current science education practice.

Reflecting on this report has reminded me of an earlier time in my life when I was a researcher at Lawrence-Berkeley Laboratory and helped to produce reports at the end of each grant cycle. Sitting over one of those reports in 1972, I realized that although the research was excellent and personally engaging, it was not going to change or improve the world in any measure. It was an obscure piece of specialized environmental research that would only be of interest to a handful of other specialists working in the same area. This event ultimately lead me back to high school teaching. I wanted to make a difference. When I teach, I know that I am making a difference in the lives of my students. It is enough to get me up in the morning and to keep me going through the years. When I read our report, I remember that other report read many years ago and wonder, "Is this really going to influence science education in this country?"

In spite of my pessimism, the honest answer is that I don't know. I see our work as an experiment with two parts. The first part, the writing of this report, is near completion. I believe that this part was successful. At the very least, it was an engaging experience that helped me to grow in understanding and brought a real measure of personal satisfaction. Now the second part begins. This document will be offered to a wider audience of individuals concerned with education and specifically, science education. Personally, this part is scarier. In part, it must be what politicians feel on election night. Having done their best, the matter is now out of their hands. They can only wait for the judgment of others. Unlike politicians, however, I won't have the answer in the morning.

APPENDIX C: SPRING 1991 TEACHER QUESTIONNAIRE WITH DATA

Labnet Project : Teachers Questionnaire (Spring 1991)

We are sending this questionnaire to all participants to assess the effectiveness and range of participation in the LabNet project. Your experiences will give us valuable information about the program. Your name or other identifying information will not be used in any reports. Please return the questionnaire to **TERC** by **July 15, 1991**. A self-addressed stamped envelope is enclosed. We appreciate your cooperation.

Shahaf Gal, TERC LabNet Program Evaluator

RESPONDENTS 1990: 78 (100%)

1. Sex M: 59 (76%); F: 19 (24%)   2. States: 33 (of 50)

3. School location (Check **one**): Urban 25 (32%); Suburban 37 (47%); Rural 16 (21%)

4. Number of years teaching physics: Avg. 16.5

5. Number of years teaching science: Avg. 20.6

6. Number of science courses you teach: Physics Avg. 3.0; General Science Avg. 0.7; Chemistry Avg. 0.7; Biology Avg 0.1

For all your science classes, give the approximate number of students in each of the following categories:

7. Male Avg. 50.2; Female Avg. 41.8; African-American Avg. 4.9; Latina/Latino Avg. 9.1; White Avg. 70.6; Asian/Pacific Islander Avg. 6.5; Native American Avg. 0.5; Other Avg. 1.

9. Number of computers available for science courses that you teach (April 1991): Avg. 7.9

10. Are you connected to a telecommunication network? Yes 63 (83%); No 13 (17%);

General Experience with LabNet

11. Please respond to the following questions about your expectations of LabNet. Use the following scales:

	Expectations:	Whether they were met:
	3 = High expectations	3 = Fully met
	2 = Moderate expectations	2 = Partially met
	1 = No expectation	1 = Not met
	When I first joined LabNet, I **expected**	Were your expectations met?
To learn to use new technologies (MBL, telecommunication) for physics teaching	3: 57 (73%) 2: 21 (27%) 1: 0 (0%)	3: 48(62%) 2: 28 (36%) 1: 2 (3%)
To learn about and to develop ideas for projects to use in my classroom	3: 43 (55%) 2: 29 (37%) 1: 6 (8%)	3: 37 (47%) 2: 36 (46%) 1: 5 (6%)
To collaborate with other physics teachers about science teaching	3:49 (64%) 2:26 (34%) 1:2 (3%)	3:29 (37%) 2:47 (60%) 1:2 (3%)

The following refer to your experiences with LabNet for June 1989–April 1991

Classroom Activity

12. Are you currently active on the LabNet network or involved in LabNet?
    No 20 (26%); Yes 58 (74%).

    If you decided **not** to be active or involved in LabNet, describe the reasons. -
    20 responses

13. To what extent do you use microcomputer-based laboratories (MBL) in your classroom? (Check **one**.)
    Use extensively   19 (24%); Use moderately   47 (60%); Do not use at all   12 (15%)

14. Did LabNet influence what students do in your classroom? Use the scale below:
    3 = Do more   2 = No change   1 = Do less

    3: 54 (70%), 2: 23 (30%), 1: 0 (0%)   Students carrying out projects

    3: 46 (60%), 2: 31 (40%), 1: 0 (0%)   Students collaborating on class activities

    3: 3 (4%), 2: 55 (72%), 1: 18 (24%)   Students using textbooks

    3: 60 (79%), 2: 16 (21%), 1: 0 (0%)   Students using computers

    3: 2 (3%), 2: 60 (80%), 1: 13 (17%)   Students preparing for standardized tests

    3: 41 (55%), 2: 33 (45%), 1: 0 (0%)   Students raising questions about science concepts or
    issues that were not included in the regular curriculum

    If LabNet influenced activities in your classroom, please provide the most notable example.
    54 responses

Students' Projects

15. To what extent are projects used in your science teaching? (Check **one**.)
    Used extensively   8 (10%); Used moderately   62 (79%); Not used at all   8 (10%)

    > If you checked **Not used at all,** go to **Question #21**.
    > Otherwise, continue with this section.

16. Briefly explain your method of introducing and carrying out projects. (Include how projects are selected, how students are grouped, and how you coach students while they are doing their project.)
    65 responses

17. Do your students use MBL while doing their projects?
    No 34 (49%); Yes 35 (51%)

    If Yes, please provide an example of the use of MBL in student projects.
    32 responses

18. How many different projects will a student typically be involved in over the academic year? Avg. 4.1

19. About how many days will the average project(s) take to complete? Avg. 14.2

20. How do you evaluate what students learn from doing projects?

    I **do not** evaluate projects   5 (7%); I **do** evaluate student projects   63 (93%)

    Projects are roughly 16.8% of a student's final grade in a grading period.

    I evaluate projects on the basis of: (Check **all** that apply.)

    34 (52%)   Group skills (for example, collaboration, discussion)

    32 (49%)   Observation of students' technique (for example, taking a reading on an instrument)

    20 (31%)   Student notebooks

    47 (72%)   Student presentations

    45 (69%)   Written final reports

    7 (11%)   Quizzes/Tests

    26 (40%)   Other:

Support For Classroom Activities

21. Did you need support in implementing the LabNet activities? (Check **one**.)

    11 (14%)   A great deal of support

    48 (63%)   Moderate support

    17 (22%)   No support

22. When you needed support, from which of the following did you look for it? (Check **all** that apply.)

    16 (26%)   Teacher Liaison Consultants (TLC)

    21 (34%)   Teachers in your school

    18 (30%)   School administrators

    36 (59%)   Teachers on the network

    27 (44%)   TERC staff

    9 (15%)   Other:

23. To what extent do you use the LabNetwork? (Check **one**.)

    12 (16%)   Use extensively

    49 (64%)   Use moderately

    16 (21%)   Do not use at all

    If you do **not** use the network, please indicate the main reason why not. (Check **one**.)

    3 (19%)   Technical problems

    5 (31%)   Lack of equipment

    1 (6%)   Lack of experience

    2 (12%)   Saw no use for the network

    5 (31%)   Other:

    If you checked **Do not use at all** on Question #23, go to **Question #28**.

24. How often, on the average, do you use the network? (Check **one.**)

    6 (10%)   Less than once each month
    21 (34%)   Once or twice each month
    29 (48%)   Once or twice a week
    5 (8%)   Three or more times a week

25. Below is the screen view of the LabNetwork main menu. Check **all** features that you have used at least once.

    *** Network Info ***

    Mail 61 (98%)   Using LabNet 39 (63%)
    Forum (Messages) 61 (98%)   Entry Log 20 (32%)
    Databases 9 (15%)   Member Directory 40 (65%)
    Exit (Log-off)   Workspace 11 (18%)
                                      Help 41 (66%)

26. To your best approximation, give the number of messages you've sent via Mail since 9/1/90: Avg. 33.5

27. What were the major benefits of the network for you? Use the scale below:

    3 = Very beneficial
    2 = Moderately beneficial
    1 = Not beneficial at all

    3: 26 (45%), 2: 26 (45%), 1: 6 (10%) Exchanging ideas about specific projects with students and teachers

    3: 10 (20%), 2: 29 (57%), 1: 12 (24%) Discussing general teaching approaches

    3: 19 (34%), 2: 34 (61%), 1: 3 (5%) Conversing with network colleagues (social exchanges)

    3: 25 (45%), 2: 25 (45%), 1: 6 (11%) Requesting/giving technical support

    3: 4 (8%), 2: 22 (42%), 1: 27 (51%) Exchanging and analyzing student-collected data

    3: 6 (67%), 2: 3 (33%), 1: 0 (0%)   Other:

    Give a specific example of how the network proved useful for your science teaching.
        49 responses

'Big Idea' Collaborative Outreach Grants

28.   Did you apply for a 'Big Idea' Collaborative Outreach Grant?
    No   53 (69%); Yes   24 (31%)

    If you answered **No**, please check the **one** main reason you did not pursue this opportunity.

        23 (51%) Didn't have time/had other commitments

        4 (9%)   Needed more skills to prepare a grant proposal

        6 (13%)   Did not feel prepared enough to consider disseminating LabNet ideas

        2 (4%)   Expected administrative difficulties at my school

        10 (22%) Other:

Additional Remarks (Feel free to use extra paper.)

        43 responses

Thank you!

Appendix D: The Big Idea Grants—Summaries

This list, alphabetized by the name of the grant project director, was current as of March 1992, when most of the Big Idea Grants had been fully implemented.

Norman Anderson

Type:	High school teacher workshop
	MBL and telecommunication
Grantee:	Cedar Falls Community School District
State:	Iowa
Teachers:	19
Schedule:	July 1991
Grant:	$15,200
In-kind:	$4,000

Norman Anderson conducted a 5-day workshop in July 1991 at the University of Northern Iowa. Using IBM computers equipped with PSL units, he helped participants create their own MBL projects. ULI and MPLI interfacing units for Macintosh and Apple II series computers were also available for participant use. In addition, several project activities were introduced, including bottle rockets, resolution experiments (with the help of the Iowa Laser located in Cedar Falls), holography, and other laser projects.

In recruiting participants, Norm sent out information on the workshop via PSINet, spoke with state science supervisors and announced the workshop at the physics update conference at UNI. Members of his physics alliance group were invited, as well as teachers with little or no experience using telecommunication or MBLs.

Jack Cadigan

Type:	High school teacher workshop
	Telecommunication and project-enhanced science
Grantee:	Jack Cadigan
State:	Alaska
Teachers:	7
Schedule:	September 1991, plus ongoing telecommunication
	contact throughout the academic year
Grant:	$20,068
In-kind:	$4,183

The primary focus of this project has been to encourage female and minority students (Indian, Aleut, and Eskimo) to consider careers in science through both exposure to positive role models and experience with a project-enhanced approach to science.

A 3-day workshop was conducted in Anchorage for seven teachers from rural high schools. (Jack later worked individually with two teachers who could not attend the original workshop session.) One day was devoted to telecommunication, and 2 days were devoted to project-enhanced science. During this time, both students and teachers had the opportunity to interact with science and engineering professionals and to explore new project ideas.

Over the course of the academic year, three mentors have continued to work with teacher participants and their students on a collaborative project initiated at the workshop. The goal of the project has been to build a submersible robotic, similar to "Jason," with each site to build a portion of the robot. Sites coordinate their efforts via telecommunication. When completed, the robot should be able to drop through two meters of water in the dark, take a picture of the "ocean floor," and pick up a sample or object from the pool bottom. Testing is slated to take place in the spring of 1992.

Additional funding for this project was provided by the Christa McAuliffe foundation.

ROBERT CAPEN

Type:	High school teacher workshop
	MBL, telecommunication, and project-enhanced science
Grantee:	Robert Capen
Affiliate:	Canyon del Oro High School
State:	Arizona
Teachers:	16
Schedule:	July 1991
Grant:	$11,192
In-kind:	$9,730

Bob Capen held a 5-day workshop for 16 teachers of mathematics, science, and technology from the Tucson area at Canyon del Oro High School. The workshop built on and modified the *Principles of Technology* curriculum produced by Arizona's Center for Occupational Research and Development, which integrates project design and construction from the industrial arts field with project testing and experimentation from the physical sciences.

Bob aimed to help participating teachers integrate microcomputer-based laboratories and hands-on projects into their classrooms. Approximately equal numbers of "science-trained" and "industrial arts-trained" participants attended, fostering collaborative and cooperative learning among the participants. In two-person teams, teachers designed, constructed, and tested a small car to meet defined specifications. MBL, spreadsheets, and word processors were all components of their workshop experience.

GENE EASTER

Type: High school teacher training
project-enhanced science, MBL
Grantee: Streetsboro City School
State: Ohio
Teachers: 20
Schedule: 10 workshop meetings between March 1991 and March
1992; 8 conference presentations between June 1991 and
June 1992.
Grant: $21,400
In-kind: $3,300

This project aimed to disseminate information on project-enhanced science and to create new projects for the classroom. A staff comprised of university professors and teachers from neighboring county schools met regularly to evaluate the teacher sessions. These meetings were used to guide the development of projects in participants' classrooms.

A core group of 20 teachers attended 10 workshop meetings during the school year from March 1991 to June 1992. During these meetings, the group developed project activities for their students. The teachers then organized themselves into teams of three or four, based on a specific topic or MBL probe. The 20 teachers met at a different host school each month, where teams demonstrated the projects on which they had been working. As a complement to the teacher-oriented work, one or more students from the host school also presented their project work at each meeting.

A further goal of this grant is to produce a project-enhanced MBL lab book, to be uploaded to the LabNetwork forum and also produced in hard copy. The first 100 copies are to be given out free; additional copies will be available at cost. The core group have been and will continue to disseminate the results of this project through presentations at professional conferences and, when possible, through publications.

RON ESMAN

Type: Network among science classrooms within a school
district
Grantee: Ron Esman
Affiliate: Abilene High School
State: Texas
Teachers: 7
Grant: $4,600
In-kind: $5000

This project has developed a packet radio network among science classrooms within the Abilene school district that allows students and teachers to work together sharing ideas and projects. Two high schools and five middle schools have participated in the network. Through the summer and fall of 1991, teachers received training in the use of packet radio equipment toward the procurement of their amateur and technician HAM Radio licenses. The network has been used for a number of student projects, including contact with NASA, an animal nutrition study, and a student olympiad. In conjunction with the computer network, a newsletter has been distributed to teachers and students as a way to stimulate interest in and enhance the reach of the network.

EUGENE KOWALSKI

Type:	Curriculum reform, integrating science with other subjects
Grantee:	North High School
State:	Colorado
Teachers:	10
Schedule:	May 1991 through June 1992
Grant:	$22,246 (Operations: $22,246)
In-kind:	$9,432

The goals of this project have been (a) to develop curriculum that integrates science education with other academic and vocational disciplines within the high school; and (b) to improve computer and MBL literacy and project-enhanced approaches to learning among the students in the high school.

Ten teachers from North High School worked together to develop and write curriculum for MBL and project-enhanced learning. In addition, through this project, a network has been established between the Macintosh computer lab in the science department and the English Macintosh laboratory. Participants have worked to develop project-enhanced methods of science instruction, to provide the science department with increased experiential learning opportunities, and to develop intra- and interdepartmental instruction for academic and vocational education.

FRANCELINE LEARY

Type:	High school teacher workshop MBL and project-enhanced science
Grantee:	Franceline Leary
Affiliate:	Rensselaer Polytechnic Institute
State:	New York
Teachers:	14
Schedule:	June 1991 workshop, plus follow-up sessions in October 1991 and March 1992

Grant: $16,853
In-kind: $7,392

The 5-day workshop in June was held at Rensselaer Polytechnic Institute with computers borrowed from Troy High School, and MBL interfaces for the Macintosh loaned by David Vernier. Its focus was on expanding the use of projects in the classroom, gaining experience using different types of interfaces, and discussing misconceptions of physics learners. Participants also spent a short time exploring the LabNetwork.

During the 1-day weekend follow-up sessions, participants have addressed problems associated with the use of the Sonic Range Finder, solid state physics, the misconceptions related to electricity and magnetism and other issues that concern the misconceptions of physics principles, and the use of telecommunication.

HAROLD LEFCOURT

Type: High school teacher workshops
MBL and project-enhanced science
Grantee: Rutgers University
State: New Jersey
Teachers: 24
Schedule: November 1991 through March 1992
Grant: $9,130
In-kind: $3,340

The goal of this workshop has been to expand upon the already established regional sharing sessions of the New Jersey section of the American Association of Physics Teachers.

Facilitators have led a 1-day workshop to promote project-enhanced learning, attended by 24 teachers. So that participants may better implement project activities in their own classrooms, they have worked with microcomputer-based laboratory equipment, shared ideas on how to use "high" and "low" technologies in the execution of project activities, and experienced the construction of a computer interfacing device that has direct applicability to the curriculum materials they are using.

Two half-day follow-up sessions provided participants with an opportunity to discuss questions and to promote further inquiry about projects. Part of the sessions were devoted to telecommunication so that the participating teachers could learn how to utilize the existing statewide network to share ideas and to communicate with teachers not able to attend the sharing sessions.

MIKE MACMAHON

Type: High school teacher workshop
MBL and project-enhanced science
Grantee: Birmingham Southern College
State: Alabama
Teachers: 10
Schedule: October 1991 through April 1992
Grant: $15,570
In-kind: $575

The project consisted of a series of five Saturday workshops for 10 high school physics teachers from central Alabama. The workshops were conducted at Birmingham Southern College and introduced participants to computer interfacing and the future of physics teaching.

The first workshop introduced spreadsheet functions and Macintosh software. Participants investigated motion and acceleration. Successive workshops addressed, among other topics, the force probe and applications of Newton's second law; the principles of heat and temperature; calorimetry, electricity, and Ohm's law. During the fifth workshop, participants demonstrated applications that they had discovered or experiments with ULI equipment that they had modified for classroom use.

Each participant received a ULI and set of probes upon completion of the final workshop session.

NANCY MOREAU

Type: High school teacher workshop
telecommunication and project-enhanced science
Grantee: Nancy Moreau
Affiliate: Oneonta State University of New York
State: New York
Teachers: 12
Schedule: August 1991
Grant: $9,740
In-kind: $3,735

This 1-week workshop conducted by New York State physics mentors and teachers investigated the use of computers for statewide communication and project development. The workshop was held at Oneonta State University using IBM, Zenith, and Macintosh computers.

Participants focused on problem-solving activities, closely following the New York State Regents physics syllabus, and on how to incorporate hands-on activities into their classrooms. They spent the week writing up physics activities, exploring telecommunication, and developing a regional student activity to collect and share data on ultraviolet radiation. The final outcome of the project has been a newsletter for physics teachers, distributed throughout New York state and posted on two telecommunication networks.

A follow-up session was conducted at the state science conference so that participants could re-acquaint themselves with one another and discuss their experiences.

TOM ODDEN

Type:	High school teacher workshop
	MBL, telecommunication, and project-enhanced science
Grantee:	Tom Odden
Affiliate:	Clarion University
State:	Pennsylvania
Teachers:	26
Schedule:	August 1991 workshop;
	follow-up sessions in November 1991 and June 1992
Grant:	$29,680
In-kind:	$27,325

This 1-week workshop involved 30 teachers, including 5 staff members. All teachers participated on the telecommunication networks and completed projects. The initial, week-long workshop was held at Clarion University.

The workshop borrowed from PRISMS Physics, the Physics Teach to Learn (PTTL) program used to test and clarify misconceptions about physics, and Neal Beard's workshops. Participants were introduced to both the LabNetwork and the Penn State network. Activities included applications of digital timer in the laboratory, the egg drop activity, and toothpick bridge activity.

In follow-up sessions, participants shared their experiences with telecommunication, presented completed student projects, and discussed new ways to experiment with the digital timer.

The Pennsylvania STEP Program provided additional support for this project.

DAVE REID

Type:	High school teacher workshop
	MBL, telecommunication, and project-enhanced science
Grantee:	Colorado School of Mines
State:	Colorado
Teachers:	25
Schedule:	June 1991 workshop;
	three follow-up sessions from August 1991 through April 1992

Grant: $34,420
In-kind: $2,000

The Colorado School of Mines hosted this workshop, which was organized into three instructional blocks: (a) microcomputer-based laboratories, (b) project-enhanced learning, and (c) telecommunication. The workshop focused on how to integrate project-enhanced learning with telecommunication.

Participants were secondary teachers of physical science, mathematics, biology, and earth science. Financial assistance was available to rural and inner-city teachers who were either minority teachers or who instructed in schools with significant minority populations.

The participants sampled an instructional cycle used at LabNet summer workshops during the summers of 1989 and 1990. The project-enhanced learning component had two parts. First, the participants constructed a radon counter to be used in conjunction with photographic film. Second, groups of three participants designed their own independent studies using MBL probes.

The Saturday meetings were spent in discussion, working on individual problems, and compiling radon data into a master report. Between follow-up sessions, participants kept in touch via the LabNetwork. The radon report will be made available for TERC, local school boards, Colorado Department of Education, county and state health departments, state legislators, and the news media.

SANDRA RHOADES

Type: Middle school teacher workshop
MBL and project-enhanced science
Grantee: Sandra Rhoades
Affiliate: RESA Educational Services Center
State: Georgia
Teachers: 24
Schedule: August 1991, plus a December 1991 follow-up meeting
Grant: $27,638
In-kind: $19,750

The primary objectives of this 7-day workshop were to improve the physical science skills and qualifications of middle school teachers, to improve the attitude of middle school teachers toward the physical sciences, and to provide training for these teachers in process-oriented skills so that they could bring these skills into their classrooms.

The participant population was from the Southeast RESA, representing nine counties that are entirely rural, heavily minority, and deemed most underserved in Georgia. To ensure that participants received adequate administrative support, each had to provide in advance of the workshop a written endorsement from a principal or designated associate. The workshop provided five Georgia Department of Education staff development credits or five graduate credits from Georgia Southern College for participants. In order to receive credit, participants had to conduct a mini-workshop of their own.

The middle school teachers expanded their understanding of Georgia's Quality Core Curriculum, as well as the use of hands-on activities, MBL, and project-enhanced learning to make science more exciting and appealing for pre-high school students. The participants did holography projects; used PRISMS materials for creating hands-on motivational learning opportunities with instruction from an authorized PRISMS project workshop presenter; and constructed a computer interfacing device for motion and temperature measurements and graphing studies that they took back to their classrooms. In addition, each teacher received a take-home "Science Suitcase" of science materials and a handbook.

A 1-day follow-up workshop was held in December to update participants and address issues surrounding the implementation of workshop materials and ideas in the classroom.

ROBERT ROE

Type:	Developing a network of high school science and mathematics teachers and students
	High school teacher workshops
Grantee:	The O'Donnell Foundation
State:	Texas
Teachers:	25
Schedule:	Four workshop meetings between September 1991 and March 1992
Grant:	$6,150
In-kind:	$3,000

This grant developed a network that connected four public school districts. The network has been used as a forum to expand the exchange of ideas and information on how to integrate computer-based learning activities into the classroom. Fax machines and modems have been used to transmit text and graphics. Two of the high schools were connected to the Dialog Service; one continued as a member of LabNet and was connected to additional electronic services.

In addition to the exchange of ideas, teachers involved in this project organized and attend four half-day workshop sessions during the school year. Each school hosted one workshop. At these workshops, teachers demonstrated the use of computer software, computer control of laser disk players, laboratory interfaces, and shared reports on mutually interesting topics.

TONY SOLDANO

Type: Upper elementary school workshops (teachers, students, and parents)
MBL and project-enhanced science
Grantee: City School District of New Rochelle
State: New York
Teachers: 24
Schedule: Six workshops for teachers between September 1991 and May 1992;
Six "family science nights" for students and parents
Grant: $16,362
In-kind: $1,920

The objective of this grant has been to prepare fourth- and fifth-grade students to take physics when they are in high school by reaching out to teachers, students and parents when the students, are still young.

The six workshops for fourth- and fifth-grade teachers were held during school hours as part of staff development. The workshops provided physical models of systems (e.g., pendulums, spring clocks, spring firing mechanisms, circuit boards, and the Joule water paddle). In addition, participants worked with MBL probes to explore characteristics of these systems.

There were also active student follow-up sessions. Fourth- and fifth-grade teacher workshops were followed by afternoon and evening activities for students and their parents, called "family science nights." At the end of the year, the students participated in a science fair.

LORENZ STEINBRECHER

Type: High school teacher workshop
project-enhanced science, telecommunication and MBL
Grantee: Mira Mesa High School
State: California
Teachers: 10
Schedule: July 1991, plus a follow-up session in March 1992
Grant: $6,770
In-kind: $1,372

Larry Steinbrecher's objective was to stimulate better science teaching through new colleagues, new ideas, and new projects. He designed his workshop for teachers of physics and physical science at the secondary level.

Three staff members helped teacher participants explore ways of integrating project-enhanced instruction into their practice. Initially, electricity and magnetism were emphasized. A number of electronic circuits were assembled; as participants gained confidence and expertise, they moved on to complete several of the "Vernier" type kits. (Because many of these kits have been designed to interface with a computer, they lend themselves to project extensions.) One activity centered around the dedication of a single computer to a classroom task. Participants also worked on a collaborative project assembling two Maglev Race tracks. They studied magnetic levitation, aerodynamics, and propulsion systems as they designed cars to race on the tracks. And, finally, teachers were instructed in the use of the network

To support the "human network" during the 1991-1992 academic year, a Saturday session was held that focused on sharing classroom experiences and on introducing others to the network.

TOM THOMPSON

Type:	Developing a local network for high school teachers
	Telecommunication workshops
	MBL and project-enhanced science
Grantee:	Yamhill County Education Service District
State:	Oregon
Teachers:	15
Schedule:	October 1991 through December 1991, plus ongoing
	telecommunication contact
Grant:	$16,044
In-kind:	$5,000

This project had two principal objectives: to improve communication among science teachers, and to provide them with greater access to MBL and interfacing units for exploratory activities.

Because there has been a serious need in the Polk, Marion, and Yamhill county districts to improve communication among science teachers, the first component expanded the telecommunication system that connects these three districts. This project chose to use PSINet for its network because the Oregon server was already located in Portland and because, although it is currently dedicated to physics, it has the capacity to be used for more than just physics. To encourage involvement in telecommunication, this project funded in-service training for teachers and small matching grants for the purchase of telecommunication equipment. In addition, districts committed additional release time for continued training sessions.

For the second component, interfacing units were purchased for an interface "loan library." Many teachers have been interested in using MBL materials but have been unable to afford a classroom set or else could not yet justify the purchase. The MBL materials will become a permanent resource in the interfacing lending library located in the Yamhill ESD. Borrowers must have attended training sessions before using the materials.

Materials are shipped to the schools through the current courier service that links the three counties.

GERIANN WALKER

> **Type:** Curriculum development and telecommunication
> **Grantee:** Geriann Walker
> **State:** Oregon
> **Teachers:** 2
> **Schedule:** August 1991 development; September 1991 through May 1992 implementation
> **Grant:** $4,195
> **In-kind:** $810

This grant developed two project-enhanced curriculum guides, with telecommunication activities to accompany each. Geriann Walker has shared the curriculum generated by this proposal over the LabNetwork. The two curriculum pieces focus on acid rain and biome activities.

In the acid rain unit, students use the process of data collection and analysis to sample and compare water from their area. Background information and basic chemistry is covered in introductory activities; then a general guide for telecommunication activities and divergent, student-initiated projects is provided.

The biome unit involves collecting and compiling ecological data locally and regionally. For example, the High Desert or Great Basin region is a rich resource for student exploration and investigation; data collected there has been useful to the Forest Service and to other organizations such as the Oregon Desert Association.

MAXINE WILLIS

> **Type:** High school teacher workshop
> MBL, telecommunication, and project-enhanced science
> **Grantee:** Gettysburg Area Senior High School
> **State:** Pennsylvania
> **Teachers:** 18
> **Schedule:** July 1991, plus November 1991 follow-up session and ongoing telecommunication support
> **Grant:** $37,481
> **In-kind:** $1,531

During the initial week-long workshop, six instructors focused on the comprehensive use of computer tools, spreadsheet and graphical analysis, MBL, and telecommunication. Teacher participants were introduced to new teaching methods such as experiential learning cycles, guided inquiry techniques, how to create a cooperative learning environment in the classroom, and how to reduce student misconceptions in physics. Participants spent an entire day working on ways to implement a project in their classrooms. Teachers were also introduced to the LabNet telecommunication system.

A 1-day follow-up session was held late in the fall, in which participants got together to discuss implementation issues and to review telecommunication procedures. Four instructors have maintained ongoing contact with participants through the school year, largely via telecommunication.

Jay Zimmerman

Type:	High school teacher workshop
	MBL, telecommunication, and project-enhanced science
Grantee:	Wisconsin High School Physics Projects
State:	Wisconsin
Teachers:	63
Schedule:	Four separate workshops from October 1991 through April 1992
Grant:	$19,645
In-kind:	$11,750

The Wisconsin Physics Projects (WPP) group has worked with 63 teachers over the course of several half-day workshops, each focusing on the use of interfacing hardware and software.

In addition, the WPP group has been working on a computer lab manual with sections specific to IBM, Mac, and Apple II series computers. The manual provides a flow chart for simplified set-up, offers suggestions on experiments to perform, presents guidelines for "projects" or project extensions, and includes an appendix of technical explanations and suggestions about where to purchase workshop equipment.

By offering these workshops on MBL and project-enhanced science, presenting papers describing the workshops to local, regional, and national meetings of physics teachers, attending national meetings of physics teachers to keep members up-to-date, and by interacting with other LabNet teachers and staff, the WPP intends to become self-supporting and to expand the core curriculum of these workshops throughout Wisconsin and, eventually, the country.

REFERENCES

Alberty, H. B. (1927). *A study of the project method in education.* Columbus, OH: Ohio State University Press.

Apelman, M., Hawkins, D., & Morrison, P. (1985). *Critical barriers phenomena in elementary science.* Grand Forks, ND: North Dakota Study Group on Evaluation, Center for Teaching and Learning, University of North Dakota.

Argyris, C., Putnam, R. W., & McLain, D. (1985). *Action science.* San Francisco CA: Jossey-Bass.

Argyris, C., & Schon, D. A. (1974). *Theory in practice: Increasing professional effectiveness.* San Francisco, CA: Jossey-Bass.

Bamberger, J. (1991). *The mind behind the musical ear: How children develop musical intelligence.* Cambridge, MA: Harvard University Press.

Bamberger, J., Duckworth, E., Gray, J., & Lampert, M. (1982). *Analysis of data from an experiment in teacher development.* Cambridge, MA: MIT University (NIE Grant #G-78-0219).

Bamberger, J., Duckworth, E., & Lampert, M. (1981). *Final report: An experiment in teacher development.* Cambridge, MA: MIT University (NIE Grant #G-78-0219).

Bamberger, J., & Schon, D. A. (1977, February). *The figural formal transaction: A parable of generative metaphor* (Working paper). Cambridge, MA: MIT University.

Bamberger, J., & Schon, D. A. (1983, March). Learning as reflective conversation with materials: Notes from Work in Progress. *Art Education, 36*(2), 68-73.

Barker, R. (1968). *Ecological psychology: Concepts and methods for studying the environment of human behavior.* Palo Alto, CA: Stanford University Press.

Bartlett, A. A. (1992). The Feynman effect and the boon docs. *Physics Today, 45*(1), 67.

Beals, D. E. (1991, April). Computer-mediated communications among beginning teachers. *T.H.E. Journal,* 74-77.

Berman, P., Greenwood, P. W., McLaughlin, M. W., & Pincus, J. (1975). *Federal programs supporting educational change.* Santa Monica, CA: Rand.

Black, S., Levin, J. A., Mehan, H., & Quinn, C. (1983). Real and non-real time interaction: Unraveling multiple threads of discourse. *Discourse Processes, 6,* 59-75.

Bourdieu, P. (1990). *The logic of practice.* Stanford, CA: Stanford University Press.

Bourdieu, P. (1991). *Language and symbolic power.* Cambridge, MA: Harvard University Press.

Bronfenbrenner, U. (1979). *The ecology of human development: experiments by nature and design.* Cambridge, MA: Harvard University Press.

Brousseau, G. (1986). Basic theory and methods in the didactics of mathematics. In P. F .L. Verstapen (Ed.), *Second conference on systematic co-operation between theory and practice in mathematics education* (pp. 109-161). Enschede: Institut voor Leerplanonwikkeling.

Bruce, C., & Rubin, A. (1992). *Electronic quills: A situated evaluation of using computers for writing in classrooms.* Hillsdale, NJ: Lawrence Erlbaum Associates.

Bull, G. L., Harris, C. M., & Cothern, H. (1992). Considerations underlying the architecture of a state public school telecomputing network. In R. F. Tinker & P. M. Kapisovsky (Eds.), *Prospects for educational telecomputing: Selected readings* (pp. 121-134). Cambridge, MA: TERC.

Clifford, J. (1988). *The predicament of culture: Twentieth-century ethnography, literature, and art.* Cambridge, MA: Harvard University Press.

Cohen, D., & Garet, M. S. (1983). Reforming educational policy with applied social research. In P. Hauser-Cram & M. F. Carrozza (Eds.), *Essays on educational research: Methodology, testing, and application.* Cambridge, MA: Harvard Educational Review, Reprint series, 16.

Cohen, S. A. (1974). Finding a Ph.D. thesis topic. *American Journal of Physics, 42,* 12-14.

Corwin, R., & Friel, S. (1990). *Statistics: Prediction and sampling (Used numbers* series). Palo Alto, CA: Dale Seymour.

Cremin, L. A. (1961). *The transformation of the school: Progressivism in American education, 1876-1857.* New York: Alfred A. Knopf.

Cuban, L. (1986). *Teachers and machines: The classroom use of technology since 1920.* New York: Teachers College, Columbia University.

Czujko, R., & Bernstein, D. (1989). *Who takes science? A report on student coursework in high school science and mathematics.* New York: American Institute of Physics.

Delpit, L. (1986). Skills and dilemmas of a progressive Black educator. *Harvard Educational Review, 56,* 379-385.

Dewey, J. (1897). My pedagogic creed. *The School Journal, 54*(3), 77-80.

Dewey, J. (1916). *Democracy and education: An introduction to the philosophy of education.* New York: Macmillan.

Dewey, J. (1929). *The quest for certainty: A study of the relation of knowledge and action.* New York: Minton, Balch.

Dewey, J. (1933). *How we think, a restatement of the relation of reflective thinking to the educative process.* Boston: Heath.

Dewey, J. (1938). *Experience and education.* New York: Macmillan.

Dewey, J. (1939). *Intelligence in the modern world: John Dewey's philosophy.* New York: Modern Library.

Dewey, J. (1956). *The child and the curriculum* and *The school and society.* Chicago: University of Chicago Press.

Dewey, J. (1964). *John Dewey on education: Selected writings.* New York: Modern Library.

Dewey, J., & Dewey, E. (1962). *Schools of tomorrow.* New York: Dutton

Dow, P. B. (1991). *Schoolhouse politics: Lessons from the Sputnik era.* Cambridge, MA: Harvard University Press.

Duckworth, E. (1987). *The having of wonderful ideas and other essays on teaching and learning.* New York: Teachers College Press.

Duckworth, E., Easley, J., Hawkins, D., & Henriques, A. (1990). *Science education: A minds-on approach to the elementary years.* Hillsdale, NJ: Lawrence Erlbaum Associates.

Erickson, F. (1986). Qualitative methods in research on teaching. In M. C. Wittrock (Ed.), *Handbook of research on teaching* (3rd ed., pp. 119-161). New York: Macmillan.

Finlay, G. C. (1966). Physics in the high school: The Physical Science Study Committee. In W. T. Martin & D. C. Pinck (Eds.), *Curriculum improvement and innovations: A partnership of students, school teachers and research scholars* (pp. 67-108). Cambridge, MA: Robert Bentley.

Forman, G. (1988). Making intuitive knowledge explicit. In G. Forman & P. B. Pufall (Eds.), *Constructivisim in the computer age* (pp. 83-104). Hillsdale, NJ: Lawrence Erlbaum Associates.

Gal, S. (1990a). *LabNet 1990: Participants background and expectations.* Unpublished manuscript, TERC, Cambridge, MA.

Gal, S. (1990b). *Network report: September 1–November 21, 1990.* Cambridge, MA: TERC.

Gal, S. (1990c). *TERC LabNet teachers survey: Fall 1990.* Cambridge, MA: TERC.

Gal, S. (1991, May). *Collaborative telelearning of physics: Expanding the teaching experiences of physics teachers.* Paper presented at ECOO/ICTE conference, Toronto, Canada.

Gal, S., Lockett, G., & Parrott, M. E. (1991). *LabNet teacher questionnaire report.* Cambridge, MA: TERC.

Gardner, H. (1983). *Frames of mind: The theory of multiple intelligences.* New York: Basic Books, Inc.

Gardner, H. (in preparation). *The creators of the modern era.*

Geertz, C. (1973). *The interpretation of cultures.* New York: Basic Books.

Geertz, C. (1983). *Local knowledge: Further essays in interpretive anthropology.* New York: Basic Books, Inc.

Guba, E. G. (1985). The context of emergent paradigm research. In Y. S. Lincoln (Ed.), *Organizational theory and inquiry: The paradigm revolution* (pp. 79-103). Beverly Hills, CA: Sage.

Hall, G. E., & Hord, S. M. (1987). *Change in schools: Facilitating the process.* Albany, NY: State University of New York Press.

Halloun, I. A., & Hestenes, D. (1985). The initial state of college physics students. *American Journal of Physics, 53*(11), 1043-1055.

Hancock, C. M., Kaput, J. J., & Goldsmith, L. T. (in press). Authentic inquiry with data: Critical barriers to classroom implementation. *Educational Psychologis t 27*(3).

Hord, S. M. (1987). *Evaluating educational innovation.* New York: Croom Helm in association with Methuen.

Hunter, B. (1992). Linking for learning: Computer-and communications network support for nationwide innovation in education. *Journal of Science and Technology, 1*(1), 22-34.

Julyan, C. L. (1989a). Messing about in science: Participation not memorization. In W. Rosen (Ed.), *High school biology: Today and tomorrow* (pp. 184-193). Washington, DC: National Academy Press.

Julyan, C. L. (1989b). Real science in elementary classrooms. *Classroom Computer Learning, 10*(2), 30-41.

Julyan, C. L. (1992). A developer's perspective on telecomputing. In R. F. Tinker & P.M. Kapisovsky (Eds.), *Prospects for educational telecomputing: Selected readings* (pp. 33-38). Cambridge, MA: TERC.

Katz, M., McSwiney, M. E., & Stroud, K. (1987). *Facilitating collegial exchange among science teachers: An experiment in computer-based conferencing.* Cambridge, MA: Educational Technology Center, Harvard Graduate School of Education.

Knorr-Cetina, K. D. (1981). *The manufacture of knowledge: An essay on the constructivist and contextual nature of science.* Elmsford, NY: Pergamon Press.

Krapfel, P. (1989). *Shifting.* Cottonwood, CA: Author.

Latour, B. (1987). *Science in action: How to follow scientists and engineers through society.* Cambridge, MA: Harvard University Press.

Latour, B., & Woolgar, S. (1979). *Laboratory life: The social construction of scientific facts.* Beverly Hills, CA: Sage.

Lave, J. (1986). The values of quantification. In J. Law (Ed.), *Power, action and belief: A new sociology of knowledge* (pp. 88-111). Boston, MA: Routledge & Kegan Paul.

Lave, J. (1988). *Cognition in practice: Mind, mathematics, and culture in everyday life.* Cambridge, UK: Cambridge University Press.

Lave, J., & Wenger, E. (1991). *Situated learning: Legitimate peripheral participation.* Cambridge, UK: Cambridge University Press.

Laws, K. (1984). *The physics of dance.* New York: Schirmer Books.

Laws, K., & Lee, K. (1989). The *grand jeté:* A physical analysis. *Kinesiology for Dance, II* (4).

Levin, J. A., Riel, M., Miyake, N., & Cohen, M. (1987). Education on the electronic frontier: Teleapprentices in globally distributed educational contexts. *Contemporary Educational Psychology, 12,* 254-260.

Lewin, K. (1946). Action research and minority problems. *Journal of Social Issues, 2*(4), 34-46.

Lewin, K. (1947a). Frontiers in group dynamics: I. Concept, method, and reality in social science; social equilibria and social change. *Human Relations, 1*(1), 5-40.

Lewin, K. (1947b). Frontiers in group dynamics: II. Channels of group life: Social planning and action research. *Human Relations, 1*(2), 143-150.

Lewin, K. (1948). *Resolving social conflicts: Selected papers on group dynamics.* New York: Harper.

Lightfoot, S. L. (1983). *The good high school: Portraits of character and culture.* New York: Basic Books.

Mason, R., & K aye, T. (1990). Toward a new paradigm for distance education. In L. Harasim (Ed.). *Online education: Perspectives on a new environment* (pp. 15-38). New York: Praeger.

Mestre, J. P. (1991, September). Learning and instruction in pre-college physical science. *Physics Today, 44*(9), 56-62.

Mokros, J., & Russell, S. J. (1992). *Children's concepts of average and representatives* (TERC Working Paper 4-92). Cambridge, MA: TERC.

Morrison, P. (1963). Less may be more. *American Journal of Physics, 31,* 441-457.

National Center for Educational Statistics. (1980). *High school and beyond study.* Washington, DC: The Statistics Center for the Office of Education Research (formerly NCES).

Neuschatz, M., & Covalt, M. (1988). *Physics in high schools: Findings from the 1986-7 Nationwide Survey of Secondary School Teachers of Physics.* New York: American Institute of Physics.

OSTP—Office of Science and Technology Policy, Federal Coordinating Council for Science, Engineering, and Technology. (1991). *Grand challenges: High performance computing and communications* (FY 1992 U.S. Research and Development Program). Washington, DC: Committee on Physical, Mathematical and Engineering Sciences, c/o the National Science Foundation.

Papert, S. (1980). *Mindstorms: Children, computers, and powerful ideas.* New York: Basic Books

Parker, P. (1992). Alice: Telecommunications for education. In R. F. Tinker & P. M. Kapisovsky (Eds.), *Prospects for educational telecomputing: Selected readings* (pp. 111-120). Cambridge, MA: TERC.

Pea, R. D., & Gomez, L. M. (in press). Distributed multimedia learning environments: Why and how? *Interactive Learning Environments.*

Polanyi, M. (1964). *Personal knowledge: Towards a post-critical philosophy.* New York: Harper & Row.

Popkewitz, T. (1984). *Paradigm and ideology in educational research: The social functions of the intellectual.* New York: Falmer Press.

Popkewitz, T. (Ed.). (1987). *Critical studies in teacher education: Its folklore, theory and practice.* New York: Falmer Press.

Popkewitz, T. (1991). *A political sociology of educational reform: Power/ knowledge in teaching, teacher education, and research.* New York: Teachers College Press.

Putnam, R. W. (1991). *Putting concepts to use: Re-educating professionals for organizational learning.* Unpublished doctoral dissertation, Harvard Graduate School of Education, Cambridge, MA.

Resnick, L. B., Levine, J. M., & Teasley, S. D. (1991). *Perspectives on socially shared cognition.* Washington, DC: American Psychological Association.

Rhoades, S., & Franklin, C. (1989). The art of physics. *The Science Teacher, 56*(3), 64-66.

Riel, M. (1987). The intercultural learning network. *The Computing Teacher, 14,* 27-30.

Riel, M. (1990). Cooperative learning across classrooms, *Instructional Science, 19,* 445-466.

Riel, M., & Levin, J. (1990). Building electronic communities: Success and failure in computer networking. *Instructional Science, 19,* 145-169.

Roberts, N., Blakeslee, G., Brown, M., & Lenk, C. (1990). *Integrating telecommunications into education.* Englewood Cliffs, NJ: Prentice-Hall.

Rogers, C. R. (1951). *Client-centered therapy.* Boston, MA: Houghton Mifflin.

Rogers, C. R. (1969). *Freedom to learn.* Columbus, OH: Charles E. Merrill Publishing.

Rogoff, B. (1990). *Apprenticeship in thinking: Cognitive development in social context.* New York: Oxford University Press.

Rousseau, J. J. (1957). *Émile.* London, England: J. M. Dent & Sons Ltd.

Sarason, S. B. (1982). *The culture of the school and the problem of change* (2nd ed.). Boston, MA: Allyn & Bacon.

Sarason, S. B. (1990). *The predictable failure of educational reform: Can we change course before it's too late?* San Francisco, CA: Jossey-Bass.

Schifter, D., & Simon, M. (1991). *Assessing teachers' development of a constructivist view of mathematics learning.* Paper presented at the annual meeting of the National Council of Teachers of Mathematics conference.

Schon, D. A. (1983). *The reflective practitioner.* New York: Basic Books.

Schon, D. A. (1987). Educating the reflective practitioner. San Francisco, CA: Jossey-Bass.

Shymansky, J. A., Hedges, L. V., & Woodworth, G. (1990). A reassessment of the effects of inquiry-based science curricula of the 60's on student performance. *Journal of Research in Science Teaching, 27*(2), 127-144.

Skrtic, T. M. (1985). Doing naturalistic research into educational organizations. In Y. S. Lincoln (Ed.), *Organizational theory and inquiry: The paradigm revolution* (pp. 185-220). Beverly Hills, CA: Sage.

Star, S. L. (1991). Power, technology and the phenomenology of conventions: On being allergic to onions. In J. Law (Ed.), *A sociology of monsters? Power, technology and the modern world* (pp. 27-57). Oxford, UK: Basil Blackwell.

Star, S. L., & Griesemer, J. R. (1989). Institutional ecology, 'translations' and boundary objects: Amateurs and professionals in Berkeley's Museum of Vertebrate Zoology, 1907-39. *Social Studies of Science, 19*, 387-420.

Stormzand, M. (1924). *Progressive methods in teaching.* Boston: Houghton Mifflin.

Stout, C. (1992). TENET: Texas education network. In R. F. Tinker & P. M. Kapisovsky (Eds.), *Prospects for educational telecomputing: Selected readings* (pp. 135-140). Cambridge, MA: TERC.

Swartz, C. (1991). The physicists intervene. *Physics Today, 44*(9), 22-28.

Tinker, R. F. (1991). Thinking about science. Unpublished manuscript, TERC, Cambridge, MA.

Tinker, R. F., & Kapisovsky, P. M. (Eds.). (1992a). *Consortium for educational telecomputing: Conference proceedings April 18-19, 1991.* Cambridge, MA: TERC.

Tinker, R. F., & Kapisovsky, P. M. (Eds.). (1992b). *Prospects for educational telecomputing: Selected readings.* Cambridge, MA: TERC.

Traweek, S. (1988). Discovering machines: Nature in the age of its mechanical reproduction. In F. A. Dubinskas (Ed.), *Making time: Ethnographies of high-technologies organizations* (pp. 39-91). Philadelphia, PA: Temple University Press.

Vermillion, R. E. (1991). *Projects and investigations: The practice of physics.* New York: Macmillan.

Warren, B., Rosebery, A. S., & Conant, F. R. (1989). *Cheche konnen: Learning science by doing science in language minority classrooms.* Paper presented at the First Innovative Approaches Research Project Symposium, Washington, DC.

Weir, S. (1992). Electronic communities of learners: Fact or fiction? In R.F. Tinker & P. M. Kapisovsky (Eds.), *Prospects for educational telecomputing: Selected readings* (pp. 87-110). Cambridge, MA: TERC.

Weir, S., Krensky, L., & Gal, S. (1990). *Final Report of the TERC Star Schools Project.* Cambridge, MA: TERC.

Wenger, E. (1990). *Toward a theory of cultural transparency: elements of a social discourse of the visible and the invisible.* Unpublished doctoral dissertation, Department of Information and Computer Science, University of California, Irvine.

West, M. M., & McSwiney, M. E. (1989). *Computer networking for collegial exchange among teachers: A summary of findings and recommendations* (Tech. Rep. # TR89-1). Cambridge, MA: ETC, Harvard Graduate School of Education.

West, M. M., Inghilleri, M., McSwiney, E. , Sayers, D. , & Stroud, K. (1989). *Talking about teaching, by writing: The use of computer-based conferencing for collegial exchange among teachers* (Tech. Rep. # TR89-12). Cambridge, MA: ETC, Harvard Graduate School of Education.

Wittgenstein, L. (1958) *Philosophical investigations.* New York : Macmillan.

Author Index

Subject Index